Effective
School
Leaders

SCHOOL LEADERSHIP AND MANAGEMENT SERIES

Series Editors: Brent Davies and John West-Burnham

Effective School Leaders

How to evaluate and improve your leadership potential

JOHN MACBEATH AND KATE MYERS

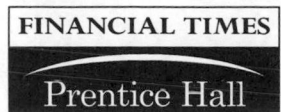

An imprint of PEARSON EDUCATION

Harlow, England · London · New York · Reading, Massachusetts · San Francisco · Toronto · Don Mills, Ontario · Sydney · Tokyo · Singapore · Hong Kong · Seoul · Taipei · Cape Town · Madrid · Mexico City · Amsterdam · Munich · Paris · Milan

PEARSON EDUCATION LIMITED

Head Office:
Edinburgh Gate
Harlow CM20 2JE
Tel: +44 (0)1279 623623
Fax: +44 (0)1279 431059

London Office:
128 Long Acre, London WC2E 9AN
Tel: +44 (0)207 447 2000
Fax: +44 (0)207 240 5771
Website: www.business.minds.com

First published in Great Britain 1999

The right of John MacBeath and Kate Myers to be identified as authors
of this work has been asserted by them in accordance
with the Copyright, Designs, and Patents Act, 1988.

ISBN 0 273 63958 7

British Library Cataloguing in Publication Data
A CIP catalogue record for this book can be obtained from the British Library.

10 9 8 7 6 5 4 3 2 1

Typeset by Pantek Arts, Maidstone, Kent.
Printed and bound in Great Britain.

The Publishers' policy is to use paper manufactured from sustainable forests.

Contents

■ ■ ■

Dedicated to
Johnny Thomassen and Dorothy Myers

Acknowledgements

■ ■ ■

We would like to thank those who contributed to this book. There are many people, too numerous to mention, whose research and writing about leadership have influenced our thinking, and many who provided us with their personal accounts of the triumphs and dilemmas of school leadership. Thanks to Sue Adler and Diana Leonard who read and commented helpfully on Chapter 6, and to Sandra MacBeath, Evelyn Gittoes and Elaine Kirkland who contributed to drafts at various stages of gestation.

1

■ ■ ■

Competences, Competencies and Context

Leadership. It is vital for teams, for organisations, for countries and even, if we are to believe the popular press, for the world itself. 'The world cries out for firm leadership', said the *Daily Mail* of 31 August 1998, citing the simultaneous crises of Russian and American presidencies. It is at times of crisis – the collapse of the economy, the risk of instability, the threat of war – that people look to leaders to sort things out, to rescue us, to make things right. In a historical study of 35 dictatorships (Hertzler, 1940) it was found that all of them had emerged during times of social distress. Commenting on this need for authority figures, Ronald Heifetz (1994) says that it is when people are 'unhinged from their habits' that they look with the greatest intensity to authority figures for remedies.

Much has been written about 'world leaders', heroic individuals who have shaped the flow of human affairs and left their imprint on the course of history. Their achievements and leadership styles are researched with the purpose of learning lessons which can be applied in other contexts, in personal relationships, in business, in schools. One of the earliest of this genre of researchers was Napoleon Hill, the young journalist commissioned by Carnegie in 1928 to go out and interview 500 notable leaders and to return in 20 years with the completed book. Among the outstanding leaders he wrote about were Woodrow Wilson, Howard Taft, Alexander Graham Bell, Theodore Roosevelt, Thomas Edison and Henry Ford. Many of these were distinguished as much by their idiosyncrasies as by the convergent strands which thread through their differing accounts. But running through all their stories Hill found a core of common characteristics and leading principles.

More recently Howard Gardner (1997) wrote about 'leading minds' of our time and, from biographies as diverse as Mohandas Gandhi, Pope John Paul XXIII, Martin Luther King and Eleanor Roosevelt, sought to draw out the traits which distinguish exemplary leaders. In the language of the management text-book these would be described as 'competen*cies*', that is, qualities that people bring to their task and infuse the job they do with new meaning and direction. These are different and distinct from 'competen*ces*' – the prescriptive reper-toire of skills that a job requires.

Competencies and competences

The conceptual difference underlying this technical distinction between 'com-petences' and 'competencies ' is a fundamental one in the study of leadership. Some people are attracted and others repelled by the terminology. None the less it is crucial to our understanding to separate the analysis that starts with jobs and roles and the analysis that starts with people. Napoleon Hill and Howard Gardner favour this second approach. It looks for people who have distinguished themselves in some significant way as leaders. Having chosen those people and been explicit about criteria for their selection, they then try to identify and understand what took them into positions of leadership, their driving motives, their strengths and frailties.

The competences approach, by contrast, takes as its point of departure the nature of the job to be done, the vacancy to be filled. The competences are, therefore, not free-floating but located in an organisational context with a set of preconditions. Recruitment and selection for headship quite typically exem-plifies this. Heads, irrespective of who they are, require subject degree qualifications, teaching certificates, experience of classroom teaching, expert-ise in managing people, organisational and communications skills and so on. As we move down the competences route these pre-specifications become tighter, more detailed and more objectified.

Much of this is sensible, but we must also recognise that the more pinned down the competences and the more scripted the role, the more we risk pre-cluding the X factor – the surprise, the chemistry, the shift in perspective that may be brought by a candidate who does not fit the arithmetic but may, none the less, bring a magical quality to the leadership task. Despite their failure to meet required competences, they can still bring a freshness of thinking, a per-sonal vision or challenge to the preconceptions of the framemakers.

'Headhunting', another practice imported into education from the business world, may lay emphasis on the competence or the competency model. People may be sought for their special personal qualities or because they appear to meet the competences specification of the job. Most recruitment practice, however, approaches from both directions, attempting to find a closeness of fit between personal competencies, on the one hand, and job competences on the other.

Context

A third dimension, or a third way of looking at leadership in practice, is to move beyond the person and beyond organisational role and status to examine the context in which leadership is exercised. When leadership is viewed in this way, our focus of attention is on the hinterland rather than the foreground. In the process the figure in the foreground may become less distinct, of less immediate interest than the context in which he or she is located. The focus on context has been described in the past as 'situational leadership', based on the view that leaders tend to be creatures and products of their time. So a given set of circumstances coalesces to allow a Gandhi, a Churchill, or a Kennedy to seize the day. On the less dramatic stage of school leadership it is also evident that headteachers, too, are often creatures of time and place.

In order to come to the fullest understanding of school leadership, therefore, we need to examine the range of school and community contexts in which heads are required to lead, and where sometimes they are required to follow. From this perspective we may discover that leadership has many facets and many faces. There is no simple linear relationship between leading and following, between hierarchy and authority, between formal status and personal influence. A Keele University study (Barber and Brighouse, 1992) reported that teachers found the implicit notion of their role as followers inadequate:

> *they are, after all, professionals making decisions in every lesson in ways which they know affect the real business of the school, the learning and development of pupils. Teachers know they make the vital decisions. In a sense they know they are the people who are really leading by example . . . (p. 51)*
>
> *(Brighouse and Woods, 1999)*

The three approaches – competences, competencies and context – may be characterised as the who, what and where – 'Who make good leaders?' 'What kind of leaders do we want?' and 'Where can leadership be found?' We examine each of these in turn.

Who make good leaders?

Among the qualities found in exemplary leaders (seven men, three women) identified by Howard Gardner were:

- a readiness to confront authority
- risk-taking
- resilience in the face of failure

- confidence in one's own instinct and intuition
- the ability to see and keep in mind the big picture
- being driven by a moral commitment
- a sense of timing, allowing one to stand back, reflect and learn from experience.

Gardner (1997) writes:

> *The capacity to take risks speaks to a confidence that one will at least sometimes attain success; implacability in the face of opposition likewise reflects a willingness to rely on oneself and not to succumb to others' strictures and reservations. (p. 33)*

These larger-than-life leaders were marked out by their ability to strike out in new directions, with enough self-confidence to ignore the forces of inertia and conservatism pushing them back to shallower waters. They also had the inner resilience to confront the possibility of failure and recrimination. These are not the kind of competences that are easy to define or prescribe. They are qualities that reside deeply within individual experience and express themselves most cogently at times of critical decision-making. The competencies approach owes much to the American group known as McBer. They studied leaders in a range of different occupational contexts (Spencer and Spencer, 1993) including medicine, the military, social services and education. The 360 distinctive items of personal behaviour which they identified were conflated to produce 20 competencies (Figure 1.1). These were described by McBer as 'generic compe-

Achievement and action	Helping and human service
<ul><li>achievement orientation</li><li>concern for order</li><li>information seeking</li><li>initiative</li></ul>	<ul><li>interpersonal understanding</li><li>customer service orientation</li></ul>
Managerial	Cognitive
<ul><li>developing others</li><li>directiveness</li><li>teamwork and co-operation</li></ul>	<ul><li>analytical thinking</li><li>team leadership</li><li>conceptual thinking</li><li>technical/professional expertise</li></ul>
Impact and influence	Personal effectiveness
<ul><li>influence</li><li>organisational awareness</li><li>relationship building</li></ul>	<ul><li>self-control</li><li>self-confidence</li><li>flexibility</li><li>organisational commitment</li></ul>

Figure 1.1: McBer's generic competencies
(*Source*: Spencer and Spencer, 1993)

tencies' because, it was claimed, they apply across the whole range of contexts in which leadership is exercised.

One of the distinguishing qualities of leaders which emerged from one of the early McBer studies (Spencer, 1978) was 'rule-breaking'. Even within the rigid structures of the military, rule-breaking appeared to be the key to success. It might even be argued that the more authoritarian or the more bureaucratic the structure, the greater the premium on rule-breaking. There is an echo of this in Gardner's research and an interesting parallel in Boylett and Finlay's (1996) survey of 1000 headteachers. They identified one of the most important characteristics of the successful headteacher to be 'a healthy disrespect of authority'. To describe disrespect for authority as 'healthy' is provocative but a reminder of the unhealthy respect which has historically led people down a perilous path.

The deviousness needed to circumvent authority and constraining formal systems of control brings into sharp focus the difference between competencies and competences. No set of job descriptors would be likely to identify disrespect for authority, rule-breaking and deviousness as desirable competences, since they are by definition antithetical to the requirements of any rule-bound organisation. At least on the surface. Yet when we turn to the educational leaders who left a mark on history it is often by virtue of those very subversive qualities.

The upsetting of conventional wisdom was the hallmark of educational heretics such as Sanderson of Oundle, Arnold of Rugby and Neill of Summerhill, all of whom shook the conventions and foundations of schooling in their respective eras. There are many accounts of larger-than-life headteachers and smaller-than-life schools which failed to accommodate to one another. A famous Scottish dominie and contemporary of Neill, R.F. Mackenzie, published prolifically in the 1960s under such titles as *Escape from the Classroom* and *The Unbowed Head*, yet like others before and after him, he came famously unstuck within the state sector. Without the freedom of reign enjoyed by Arnold, Neill and Sanderson in the independent sector, Mackenzie found it impossible to follow his principles through at Aberdeen's (ironically named) Summerhill Academy. His attempts to abolish corporal punishment were a rule-break too far, given the deeply institutionalised approach to chastisement in the Scottish culture at that time.

A close parallel in yet another 'hill site' – Risinghill in Islington – was the high-profile demise of Michael Duane who, like Mackenzie, put principles before pragmatics. In retrospect we might describe Mackenzie and Duane as having the competencies of potentially great leaders, but out of their time – visionaries without the competences of compromise.

David Winkley (1989) says in relation to Michael Duane:

> *It is not good enough for the leader merely to fashion enlightened ideas. There were forty-nine teachers pro-Duane, and twenty-nine against; the opposition was too great for progress by imposition. What Duane needed was not ideas, but strategies. (p. 23)*

Without strategy, vision has no momentum. Without vision, strategy leads to a mundane place. David Winkley goes on to say about democratic leadership:

> *The argument here is that democracy, with the careful understanding of its meaning in the context of the school, is something a leader needs to work towards if he wishes the school and the staff to grow and develop their full potential. There must, however, be two essential qualifications. First that the head can never absolve himself at any stage in his leadership from the responsibility of leadership. Secondly, that democracy has to be understood in relation to accountability; that is to say, the 'democracy' of the staff decision making process needs to be seen in relation to wider questions of democracy for parents, children, and the community at large. (p. 23)*

In Chapter 3 we look in more detail at a group of 27 headteachers and attempt to plot some of the common attributes they brought to their jobs. The differences among them are in some respects as strong as the similarities which unite them. They have in common a desire to be democratic and collaborative, but recognise that this is relative to the expectations which others hold, the stage of growth of the school as an organisation and the stage in their own personal and professional development. They are aware of the fluidity of competencies and their juxtaposition, often in delicate balance. As one of these secondary heads says:

> *Knowing when to push and when to back off, when to give strong lead and when to support. Different situations and different times need different approaches.*

Another head describes personal qualities which might be hard to encapsulate in competences language – 'a sensitive heart but the skin of a rhinoceros'.

Schools that have involved children in the interviewing of candidates for headship have found that pupils' spontaneous untutored questions go naturally beyond the obvious job competences and beyond the formal role to the personal and human issues. Children ask candidates about themselves and about their lives outside school. What, for example, did they like doing when they were not being a teacher? What were their hobbies? Did they have pets or pet hates? While none of these qualify easily as competences, they are, from a child's eye view, revealing. What these children were looking for was, as one pupil put it, 'the inside person'. A Scottish primary school which involved children in the selection of teachers reported that the pupils' selection was made primarily on the basis of the candidate who took the greatest interest in them and their work and used their first names when talking to them.

What kind of leaders do we want?

In common practice the kind of leaders we look for tend to be viewed from the perspective of the job they are required to do, and our expectations of them are shaped by our past experience of those who previously occupied the role. When we elect prime ministers and presidents we fit them into the mould of successful prior incumbents. American presidents, for example, have, with only one or two exceptions, been white Protestant men over six feet tall. There is an in-built phenotype, a conservative inertia which defines the parameters of the role, provides the frame for what we see and furnishes the terminology of our thinking.

This conservatism operates powerfully in relation to school leadership. We look for certain job qualities that have proved themselves in the past. These tend to be similar, whatever perspective they are viewed from – national policy-makers, local authorities, governors, parents, teachers or students. Perhaps, as Gerald Grace (1995) argued, this is because a deeply ingrained public school imagery of headship has shaped our conceptions of the role:

> *although formed in the exclusive context of upper-class education in England, it can be seen to have had significant cultural and pedagogic mediations in other sectors of English schooling. Its construct of school leadership and its culture of headship as personal, powerful, controlling, moralising and patriarchal has become an important constituent in the subsequent discourse and practice of school headship. (p. 11)*

Competences from a pupil perspective

However much they look for the 'inside person' in their selection of a new head, children are also inherently conservative in their descriptions of competences. Their view of headship is determined almost exclusively by what they see and know from direct first-hand experience. This can be illustrated from the Effective Leadership study (MacBeath, 1998) in which we asked six- and seven-year-olds to draw and write about their headteachers. Many portrayed their heads as sitting in their office, thinking, reading or on the telephone. An equally large number portrayed their headteachers leading the singing or playing the piano. These were illuminating sources of evidence, illustrating the contexts in which children met and 'framed' their heads, in assemblies or behind the office door marked 'headteacher'.

Some of the children depicted heads visiting classes, often to say 'well done' or to hand out sweets. Young children accepted these roles at face value while their teachers read into these a deeper, and sometimes more sinister, intent.

Danish teachers were the most antagonistic to surprise visits, seeing them as 'spying on colleagues'. Yet pupils in those same Danish schools placed a positive value on this and wrote statements such as 'The job of good heads is to ensure that teachers are teaching well.' This illustrates the usefulness of alternative viewpoints on the headteacher role and the value of the 'worms-eye view' in challenging more conservative and egocentric perspectives.

Despite their inherent conservatism as 'insiders' of the system, children and young people provide another lens from which to view leadership. If children were more likely than their teachers to emphasise the overseeing role of the head, this could be explained by their more varied and multi-faceted experience of school. In secondaries in particular they had a broader intuitive understanding of the variabilities and vagaries of the many teachers they met on a day-to-day basis. Students, as we have found in many studies, are much more keenly attuned to issues of fairness and equality than their teachers, and for them this arbitration in the life of the school community by a headteacher was most highly valued. A Scottish nine-year-old wrote:

> She should treat all pupils fairly and make sure that teachers act fairly as well. It is her job to make sure teachers act correctly because they are not all fair.

Among the list of qualities, or 'competences', for heads mentioned by primary pupils were:

- accepts complaints
- pays attention to unhappy kids
- doesn't use the rod
- talks about the good news
- cheers you up
- protects education
- keeps the playground tidy
- has music/sporting skills
- is good with bad children, for example, keeping them in at playtime
- posting letters to parents of very bad children.

Older primary children, with a greater breadth of experience and often keen perceptiveness, wrote about their heads in these terms:

> A headteacher has to make learning as fun as possible so children will want to learn. She has to make sure we have all the resources we need to do our work.

> A headteacher is the foundation of the school. Without a headteacher there would be caous.

He/she will make sure the school is a nice place for the children and the people who work there. They help the school have a good reputation.

Secondary students tended to lay greater emphasis on the human side of leadership. The largest cluster of 'competences' identified by secondary age students were:

- listens
- talks with pupils
- is nice/kind to pupils
- takes care of pupils
- understands pupils
- someone you can trust
- establishes good relationships
- has a sense of humour
- is accessible/approachable
- doesn't shout at you
- is loyal to pupils/staff.

Taken together, these may be categorised as 'establishing positive relationships,' which for older students is manifestly the most important criterion of good headship. There is an interesting juxtaposition of this with 'strictness', a quality frequently mentioned by English and Scottish students but not once among the 146 statements made by the Danes. For the UK students there were no apparent contradictions in this but there is a caveat, expressed in these terms by a Scottish student: 'A good head is someone who is strict when he needs to be but righteous in his judicial decisions.' Indeed, as with the primary pupils, the second largest cluster of qualities of good heads had to do with fairness, justice and equality.

Other aspects of the role, such as being 'financially knowledgeable' or 'good with money', only figure occasionally in students' lists of competences. Given that there is a greater degree of financial local management of schools in England, it is perhaps surprising that secondary students in English schools failed to mention this aspect of the head's role at all. For them the emphasis was almost entirely on the nature of relationships and personal qualities that a good head should exemplify. Analysis of pupils' writing and incidence of key phrases was recorded and ranked by the research team. From a total of over 50 phrases from each country, a top ten was compiled. These are shown in Figures 1.2 and 1.3.

	Denmark	No. of phrases	England	No. of phrases	Scotland	No. of phrases
1	Kind	29	Tells children off if they're naughty	45	Is nice/kind	59
2	Sympathetic	7	Good organiser	42	Ensures there is no bullying	43
3	Keeps school orderly	7	Helps teacher/ children	25	Sense of humour/good fun	37
4	Tells children off if they're naughty	7	Buys things for the school	25	Strict/good discipline	36
5	Solves problems	6	Runs the school properly	22	Understanding	32
6	Arranges good outings	6	Sorts out arguments/ problems	21	Helpful	29
7	Happy	6	Friendly to parents	15	Happy/cheerful	24
8	Good to kids	4	Teaches classes	15	Treats children fairly	23
9	Walks the school	4	Praises children	11	Likes children	22
10	Keeps the school clean	2	Makes sure children are OK/safe	11	Listens to what we have to say	21

Figure 1.2: Primary pupils' responses to questions regarding what a head does and what a good head is like

	Denmark	No. of phrases	England	No. of phrases	Scotland	No. of phrases
1	Listens	37	Fair	16	Listens	67
2	Talks with pupils	36	Good relationships with pupils/ teachers	9	Is understanding	55
3	Kind	30	Accessible/ approachable	7	Treats children fairly	46
4	Nice to pupils	29	Caring	7	Strict/good discipline	45
5	Treats pupils equally	24	Understands pupils	7	Someone to talk to/talks to us	45
6	Keeps school nice, clean/ orderly	23	Takes account of pupils' opinions	6	Good relationships with pupils	44
7	Takes care of pupils	19	Good listener	6	Sense of humour/good fun	35
8	Manages the school	16	Responsible	5	Looks after/ capable of running school	27
9	Respectable	15	Treats people equally	5	Is nice/kind	24
10	Understands pupils	14	Maintains discipline	4	Not too strict	21

Figure 1.3: Older students' responses to the question 'What is a good headteacher?'

A parental view of competences

As with pupils, parents' views might be expected to reflect what they were familiar with from their own experience. But, like students, they emphasise above all else the human qualities, the interpersonal skills such as communication, empathy, accessibility, and the ability to motivate and inspire young people. In common with their children, they wanted headteachers to be accessible, approachable and open. They wanted discipline too and, while less liable to mention fairness and equality, they did make the link between discipline and morality, stressing the moral authority of the headteacher and her adjudicator role. The head was often seen by parents as the final arbiter among different stakeholders, understanding and even-handed, representing and responding fairly to differing interests. The emphasis on consistency and fairness was perhaps an indication of the importance attached to the adjudicator role.

The supervision and professional development of staff was a related issue and also came high on the list of parental priorities:

> *The head has to know what's going on and I would want him to make sure he passes that on. Like professional development – it's to the advantage of the pupils that the teachers know about new methods and the head needs to ensure they're up-to-date. He needs to ensure information is coming in from the outside and the place isn't stagnating.*

Of all groups it was the Danish parents who were most likely to mention the role of the headteacher as professional developer. They did not want their heads to be in the front line, teaching classes; but behind the teachers, motivating and encouraging them to keep their knowledge and expertise up to date. As with students, money and resource management took a back seat. Although parents were more likely to mention it and see its importance, they also saw it as much less significant than personal relationships and people management:

> *For a headteacher this [managing the budget] should come quite low down; children and people should come before money. I'd rather a school had poor resources but a good atmosphere than good resources and a poor atmosphere.*

Competences from the teacher's perspective

Being a good communicator was the quality identified as most important from the teacher's point of view. This did not, however, refer to the competences of the headteacher as a persuasive speaker, an effective memo writer or manager of communication systems. What teachers placed most value on was the ability of the head to listen to others:

The previous head knew what he wanted and made a bee line straight for it. He was not deterred by what we thought or anyone thought, for that matter. He was the world's worst listener. When we were looking for a new head I said to our teacher rep on the School Board, 'I don't care whether he or she wears purple tights and has three heads . . . all I want is a good listener'.

The importance of accurate, or empathic, listening is not easy to dissect in terms of specific competences. The constituent parts do not come together to make a whole, yet there is evidence to suggest that effective listeners do a number of identifiable things. They are able to achieve an accurate grasp of the content, the meaning and the feeling. In behavioural terms they:

- can repeat accurately what was said;
- identify correctly the feelings lying behind the words;
- identify correctly the meaning that the word and feelings have for the person concerned.

There is an interesting gender dimension to this set of skills which we deal with in more depth in Chapter 6, but attempts to pin down some of these competences simply underline the significance of their less tangible and elusive qualities. This theme is taken up by the researchers Cave and Wilkinson (1997) who tried to find a way of describing some of the more subjective competences of leadership. They identified four 'higher order' skills which they described as 'reading the situation', 'intuition', 'balanced judgement' and 'political acumen'. 'Reading the situation' they described as 'keeping antennae out' and 'picking up vibes', not very precise in terms of behavioural competences and clearly difficult to train for, but cerebral activities that neurology is helping us to identify with greater precision. Thanks to thermal imaging technology, these once elusive skills can be revealed as having an identifiable locus in the emotional centres of the brain.

David Hargreaves (1997), writing about 'social intelligence', says:

social intelligence, the ability and sensitivity to understand and predict other people's mind and intentions, and behave skillfully in social relationships – has always been highly esteemed by employers. It is now seen by some evolutionary biologists and social scientists as the root of all intellectual development. (p. 3)

In his book *What's Worth Fighting for in the Principalship?* Michael Fullan (1997a) offers four apparently simple precepts – maintaining focus, making your position clear to those above you, managing time accordingly, and saying no. None of these is possible to prescribe in any set of competences because they rely so heavily on social intelligence. They rely not only on reading the situation correctly, but then acting on that reading in a way sensitive enough to convey authority while supporting the authority of the other(s) in the relationship.

One of the headteachers in the Effective Leadership study (MacBeath, 1998) described a simple precept given to him by a predecessor – 'Don't ask about the parrot'. As illustrated in Figure 1.4, however conspicuous the parrot, only by ignoring it will you prevent it from being transferred to your own shoulder. While admitting the wisdom of the counsel, this headteacher had found that it was not after all a simple precept, but one that called not for a blind eye, but a very far-seeing one.

These 'soft skill competencies', as McBer describes them, contrast sharply with some of the hard-edged competences of the management literature and with some of the tenets and assumptions of 'new public management'. They do not sit comfortably with the emphasis on 'strong' leadership, in which strength appears to be equated with single-mindedness, intransigence and 'managing' people so as to align them with the mission or vision of the organisation. Some of the headteachers whose accounts are given in Chapter 3 spoke of the necessity for strong leadership yet, while valuing listening as an important leadership skill, seemed compelled to add a disclaimer to the effect that this should not be seen as 'soft' or 'wimpish'.

Figure 1.4: The parrot

In the United Kingdom people are increasingly being appointed to head-teacher roles by virtue of their perceived capacities for 'turning the school round'. This evokes an image of a ship steaming off in the wrong direction and requiring to be set on a totally new course, presupposing someone with the requisite strength, authority and singleness of purpose to achieve this. For the Danes in the Effective Leadership study this was a disquieting image. The continual reference to 'strong' leadership struck an alien and disturbing note with them. It was particularly disliked when used to refer to a conferred position within the school hierarchy. Titles such as 'Head of', 'Senior' and 'Manager' were notably missing from the Danish vocabulary, with preference for terms such as 'Chair' or 'Co-ordinator', terms indicative of a more collaborative form of organisation. They laid much greater emphasis on school leaders maintaining and preserving the school culture through collaborative effort within the traditionally Danish, flat structure and through a culture of collegiality which has deep historic and cultural roots. For the researchers it was much harder to see any personification of leadership among the headteachers of the Danish Folkskole, but by virtue of this there were greater opportunities for what we might call 'contextual leadership'.

Contextual leadership

The focus in the literature, in research and in policy-making on the person of the head reveals a lot about how we frame our view of leadership. Much of management training takes as its central focal point the person, the role and their interrelationship. While both competence and competency approaches have validity and utility, there is always the danger of missing the woods for the trees. Studying the ecology of the woodland will often tell a far more compelling story.

One way of looking at leadership is through real situations which call for someone to take a lead, to show initiative, to mobilise others. Some examples are:

- A group of people stand on the bank of the river watching someone drowning.
- A fire has broken out and people are rushing around helpless and confused.
- A group of young people sit around aimlessly, arguing about what to do, where to go.
- Someone has been knocked down in the street. Everyone is trying to help but has anyone called an ambulance? Does anyone know first aid?
- A hill-walking party is hopelessly lost and none more so than the guide.
- On a school trip some of the boys are using racist language. The teacher in charge appears oblivious.

Assuming leadership in these situations will mean taking the initiative, organising other people, bringing order out of chaos, finding a structure amidst the confusion. It may, in some of the instances suggested above, mean usurping the authority or control of people with more formal leadership status. The imperative of action is the impetus to leadership.

In these situations leadership is spontaneous. Permission is not sought but is implicitly granted by those who failed to exercise it. The status of leader is self-conferred among a group of equals – *primus inter pares*. Or, as in some of the examples above, formal authority is ignored and informal leadership is taken, perhaps implicitly granted by others or explicitly resisted by them. Where people follow, it is often gratefully, because they have been relieved of the responsibility of deciding for themselves, because they themselves lacked the knowledge or skill, or perhaps because they didn't have a clear vision of the likely outcome.

This informal character of leadership is important to keep in mind when it comes to examining an organisation such as the school. Schools are not simply planned and ordered places in which the pyramidal hierarchy of power has a one-to-one relationship with the exercise of leadership on a day-to-day basis. In schools accidents happen, fires break out, people go on field trips and get lost and they sometimes drown. Newspapers carry stories of heroic leadership from unexpected quarters or dereliction of leadership by 'people who should have known better'. And on a much more mundane level, acquiescence to, or struggles for, leadership are played out in classrooms, playgrounds, lunch halls, toilets and staff rooms.

It is deceptively easy to start and to end the discussion of leadership by reference solely to this formal organisational context. Much of what we read about school leadership does, in fact, refer to the functioning at a given locus within the organisation, whether in a school or business enterprise. The hierarchy of position and status tends to be taken as a given, and the point of entry for the study of leadership is with the person or persons occupying the highest formal position. Leadership is seen as located at the top and passed down through each successive layer, while those at the bottom of the hierarchy have assumed the role of followers.

This is a form of conditioning which undermines people's own personal authority and capacity for leadership. Ronald Heifetz (1994) suggests that:

> *Many of us have been so conditioned to defer to authority that we do not realise the extent to which we are the source of the authority's power. We forget that we are the principals. (p. 58)*

He adds:

> *Habitually seeking solutions from people in authority is maladaptive. Indeed it is perhaps the essence of maladaptive behaviour. The flight to authority is particularly dangerous . . . because it disables some of our most important personal and collective resources for accomplishing adaptive work. (p. 73)*

Conceptions of leadership which refer to hierarchical authority need to be constantly challenged. Thanks to an evolving literature and the practice of exemplary schools, we are offered new lenses through which to test our own preconceptions. This is what is meant by the term 'reframing', a new perspective brought about by virtue of how the borders and setting of the picture allow us to see its contents quite differently.

Bolman and Deal (1991) in their book *Reframing Organisations,* suggest that we have tended to concentrate too much on the actors and not enough on the stage where the action takes place. They propose that instead of thinking in terms of 'leaders make things happen' we should consider the corollary – 'things make leaders happen'. When we take this perspective we come to realise that leaders are not necessarily prime movers. The story doesn't always start with them. Rather, they enter the stage at some point in the action and are as much shaped by the unfolding drama as shaping it.

Brighouse and Woods (1999) describe teachers as 'the real leaders in the everyday business of schooling'. These exemplary leaders are not *created* by their headteachers, but discovered. Brighouse and Woods quote a study in which they asked pupils to nominate teachers who exercised classroom leadership and received 450 nominations for one teacher. The primary quality of this teacher was 'as developers of other people's skills, actions and beliefs' (p. 49). As in a sequence of Chinese boxes, headteachers and senior management nurture the conditions in which teachers can be leaders while teachers in turn exercise stewardship so that their students can take up the running.

In the Effective Leadership study, Australian secondary students wrote about leadership in quite different terms from their European counterparts. For them the sharing of school leadership was a dominant theme. Neil Dempster and Lloyd Logan (1998), who conducted the Australian part of the study, commented:

> *Students perceived a lack of leadership opportunities for members of the school community other than the principal. Students thought that the responsibility of leadership should be extended to include staff, parents and, more often, students. Indeed, most student responses advocated participation of students in school leadership irrespective of age. Their tone ranges from rational suggestion to direct demand. Three examples illustrate the point.*

> *Quite often the leadership of schools is determined by teachers, with minimum input from students. This needs to be changed so that the students have a lot more say.*

> *I think that a strong leadership team consists of student leaders, teachers, Deputy Principal and parents.*

> *Generally I think that leadership in schools is concentrated too highly in the people high in the hierarchy of schools. I think that leadership opportunities should exist in the staff and with all students in all year levels. (p. 84)*

There is an apocryphal anecdote about the inspector who, in his final report, comments that 'in this school the teachers are doing all the work while their pupils do none'. It is probably a quite common observation because it is so endemic to the structure of schools as we know them. Brighouse and Woods, (1999) conclude, with reference to teacher and student involvement:

> *The work, like the responsibility, has to be shared. Unless the responsibility is shared, however, the bank account of credit in work will soon run dry. They haven't got a stake in where the school is going. (p. 50)*

The bank account metaphor is an apt one. Steven Covey (1989) writes about the 'emotional bank account' that is the investment we have in relationships and teamwork. This is where the motivation, generosity and goodwill lie. This is where the investment in shared leadership pays off. Within hierarchical structures there is a tension between the leadership conferred by the organisation and that which is exercised in spite of the hierarchy. Fluid contextual leadership means being alive to, and embracing, opportunities for people at every level to take the initiative and for headteachers to lead as and when and where appropriate.

This daring, risk-taking notion of shared leadership has too often been sacrificed at the altar of systems management. While there are those who see the distinction between management and leadership as a spurious one, the current of events and their impact has served to sharpen our awareness of the distinctions and their vital importance. Management and leadership may indeed, as critics argue, be integrally and inseparably related but there exist not only two separate words in our vocabulary but two underpinning conceptual worlds and two distinctively real worlds in practice.

The literature is replete with tables distinguishing management from leadership. They sometimes risk presenting cliched and facile dichotomies but it is, none the less, worth looking at these distinctions with a critical eye to see whether or not they stand up to scrutiny. John Kotter (1996, p. 11) proposes the distinction shown in Figure 1.5.

This is not a definitive list but one way of conceptualising the differences, and may be used as a starting-point for a school to evaluate its own approach to management and leadership. (See Figure 1.6.)

Management	Leadership
• planning and budgeting • controlling and problem-solving • organising and staffing	• establishing direction • aligning people • motivating and inspiring

Figure 1.5: The management/leadership distinction

Leadership	Management
•	•
•	•
•	•
•	•
•	•

Figure 1.6: What are the key differences in your school?

Steven Covey (Covey and Merrill, 1994, p. 36) depicts leadership and management, in a sense, as left and right hands – 'leadership decides what "first things" are, it is management that puts them first – day by day: moment by moment'. In this model leadership is the sifting through and prioritisation among values and competing priorities, thereafter passing the job over to the order-loving systematic manager-within-the-leader. In our experience the relationship is rarely that neat. In the Effective Leadership study there were inspirational leaders who were relatively bad managers and effective managers who relied on others for leadership. There were also successful teams who shared the responsibility of management and leadership, complementing one another.

It is vital to recognise that management is, by definition, expected to produce a degree of predictability and order, to meet the short-term expectations of stakeholder groups, to plan and to work to a more or less rational model. Leadership is more at home in the world of the unpredictable, the spontaneous and creative. The popularity of management and the predominant focus on managerialism in the literature is, Kotter (1996) argues, because management is easier to teach than leadership. Information systems, time management, finance and planning can be taught. Heightened efficiency can be measured and shown to work. People can save time and energy through efficient management. It is therefore not too surprising that management training has developed into such a major industry. Leadership, on the other hand, which is more about people, relationships, intuition, values and moral judgement, is hard to teach because these things are in themselves not easy to identify and difficult to dissect. The attendant danger is that the energy invested in efficient management may be purchased at the expense of leadership.

The now dated managerial literature holds that effective organisations demand systematic supervision and monitoring. Indeed, this was the underpinning philosophy of inspectorial systems from time immemorial and is seen in its most contemporary guise in OFSTED. The term 'supervision', says Sergiovanni (1998, p. 42) 'has a negative tinge that conjures up factory images of "snoopervising" foremen checking up on workers'. It is not surprising, therefore, if teachers, who regard themselves as professionals, resent what they see as an intrusive and controlling practice. However, Sergiovanni does go on to discuss the original meaning of 'supervision', which has more of a flavour of stewardship. Exercised well, it means creating opportunities for pupils, teachers and parents to face their problems and take the initiative in solving them. Sergiovanni uses the term 'empowerment' to describe this form of stewardship. Yet it is a word that has become overused and devalued, as well as misused. Two American authors, Binney and Williams (1997) argue that you cannot 'empower' people but you can disempower them very easily by the normal everyday workings of the organisation. They go on:

> *You will really begin to change, take initiative, take risks, provide real feedback, when people have opportunities to learn from mistakes and accept responsibility for what they are doing, when they feel sufficiently confident to do so and are provided with a clear framework . . . Achieving this type of relationship is not easy. It requires much effort, openness and willingness to learn – and some humility. It feels uncomfortable, particularly for leaders in organisations where this style is not the norm. It requires a high degree of self-belief and a willingness to try. (p. 69)*

Lao Tzu, the Chinese sage, put it most eloquently. Perhaps he was thinking of schools when he wrote those often-quoted words:

> *Go to the people*
> *Live among them*
> *Start with what they know*
> *And when the deed is done*
> *The mission accomplished*
> *Of the best leaders*
> *The people will say*
> *We did it*
> *Ourselves.*

Appendix 1.1
Common points of agreement on the good headteacher

In the Effective Leadership study (MacBeath, 1998) there was, across all stakeholder groups and across all four countries consensus that:

- The headteachers' first and foremost commitment should be to their school. That meant being in and around the school, monitoring its everyday life. Their role in the community or on the larger national stage was given low priority.

- School leaders should have a vision for their school. What 'vision' meant was, however, not exactly the same for different countries. While English and Scottish parents wanted a strong hands-on leader who would lead from the front, the Danes and Australians wanted their leaders to be more collaborative. Danish teachers understood 'vision' to mean an ongoing dialogue between the headteacher and staff, as well as other involved groups, about the future direction of the school, building a vision in concert with teachers. This was consistent with descriptions of the head's desirable characteristics – 'loyal', 'humane', 'engaged' and 'co-operative'. The image of leader as manager was generally unpopular, but most unpopular of all with the Danes.

- School leaders should be approachable and have good communication skills. Communications skills were, however, much less frequently mentioned by the Danes, perhaps because leadership operates within flatter structures in which the head's communication skills are less evident and less important.

- While less of a priority with students, teachers, governors and parents were agreed that the head should encourage and motivate staff to keep up to date professionally.

- In all countries students gave high priority to headteachers treating them fairly and equally and ensuring a climate of equal treatment. Instilling a sense of order and discipline was given much greater emphasis by the English and Scots than by the Australians and Danes.

Appendix 1.2
Headteacher competencies – a view from the Industrial Society

The Industrial Society produced its own list of headteacher competencies. They tend to fall into clusters. Five are specifically concerned with 'the human side', recognising the importance of support and encouragement and minimising anxiety:

- supporting other people
- recognising individual effort
- promoting other people's self-esteem
- developing other people
- minimising anxiety.

Three, closely linked to the above, have to do with the leader as reflective and empathic listener:

- seeking to understand before making judgements
- listening to individual ideas and problems
- actively encouraging feedback.

One, which might be seen as a consequence or overarching principle for all of the foregoing, is about empowerment:

- giving those doing the work the power to make decisions.

Three of the 20 refer to personal modelling of behaviour:

- demonstrating personal integrity
- practising what they preach
- showing enthusiasm.

Four fall more into the directive category, in which the leader takes a pro-active role in decision-making and target-setting:

- providing direction
- taking decisions
- agreeing targets
- promoting understanding of the key issues.

Three are about managing change:

- looking at possible future challenges
- encouraging new ways of doing things
- treating mistakes as learning opportunities.

One is explicitly about teamworking:

- encouraging teamwork.

2

■ ■ ■

Putting Organisations to Work

It was the best of times, it was the worst of times. It was the age of wisdom, it was the age of foolishness. It was the epoch of belief, it was the epoch of incredulity. It was the season of light, it was the season of darkness. It was the spring of hope, it was the winter of despair. We had all before us, we had nothing before us.

(Dickens, A Tale of Two Cities)

It is as true of the new millennium years as it was of Charles Dickens's mid-eighteenth century. We are living in an age of two paradigms. One is pushing us back towards a mythical past; the other towards a wholly unforeseeable future. It is 'back' to basics, as if in some distant golden age we were all taught to be numerate and literate. Whole-class teaching, setting and selection are promoted as if they had somehow proved themselves in the past. Toughening up and tightening up, more supervision and control are advocated alongside exhortations to produce self-driven lifelong learners, professional teachers, self-improving, 'full-service', 'fresh start' and 'new community' schools. We read about change management, about future-oriented, flexible and creative leadership, but the political context for these seems to leave less and less room for flexibility, spontaneity and originality.

If Dickens had been more fluent in the language of modern management he might have described these opposing currents as a 'force field'. Plagiarised by management theorists from physics, the force field can be illustrated with a simple graphic. To one side of the school are forces helping to push it forward towards its goals, on the other side are the counteracting and constraining forces pushing it back (see Figure 2.1).

Figure 2.1: The force field acting on the school

This device is used in management training to help people to clarify what they see as the brakes and accelerators acting on their organisation. Figure 2.2 is an example of how one headteacher depicted his situation.

Figure 2.2: One headteacher's brakes and accelerators

The three 'brakes' identified by this headteacher may be seen as operating at three levels: (1) at the level of the structures and hierarchies of the schools as we know them; (2) the community level with its socio-economic capital as a given; (3) the school itself, with its financial parameters and performance targets. On the positive side, the three sets of accelerators refer primarily to people – staff , students and parents – who represent the major resource for change and improvement – the intellectual, emotional and energy capital of the school.

Examining each of these brakes and accelerators in turn may help us to see how an organisation can be put to work more effectively.

The brake of structure and hierarchy

Schools have for decades successfully resisted attempts to change their structure. There is a voluminous critique of the compartmentalised 'egg crate' school and there have been many bold attempts to break up the egg crates and to create more democratic learner-friendly organisations. When this movement of ideas crossed one bridge too far, into deschooling society (Illich, 1971), there was a rapid return of the pendulum, swinging back to the tried, trusted and instantly recognisable models of school. The 'progressive', 'child-centred' schools of the sixties and seventies were deemed to have been a failure, and the open-plan integrated-day primary schools of Oxfordshire and Berkshire ceased to attract the American teachers who had visited them in droves in the early seventies. In Leicestershire the radical innovations of community colleges retreated to a safer, more familiar, set of structures. Reschooling, as it was known, was a systematic concerted retreat to the safer ground of 'real schools'.

The defining landmark in the move backwards to the safety of structure and hierarchy was the Rutter Report, *Fifteen Thousand Hours* (1979). It defined, as two decades of effectiveness studies were to do thereafter, the essential structural features of effective schools – orderly climate, high expectations, achievement-oriented policy, co-operative atmosphere, time on task, and reinforcement and streaming. With the benefit of two decades of hindsight these features appear bland, vague and contestable by turn. Yet their impact has been incredibly far-reaching. Michael Rutter and his team could not have foreseen where this seminal study was to lead, and some members of that team have since been publicly highly critical of the cherry-picking, selective use made of it by politicians and policy-makers. None the less, Rutter's and other school effectiveness studies offered to policy-makers irresistibly neat blueprints for the monitoring and evaluation of schools. These included indicators and performance criteria by which schools could be held to account. The studies appeared to satisfy the need for some clear and simple answers, and showed that research does not always have to be tentative, equivocal, ambiguous and impenetrable. Following on from Rutter, school effectiveness studies consistently singled out 'strong leadership' as a key constituent and reaffirmed the place of the headteacher in the structural hierarchy.

The hierarchical nature of school, as in many other types of organisation, not only frames our view of leadership but, by its very nature, contributes to what Peter Senge (1992) has called 'organisational learning disabilities'. These are a consequence of a mind-set and the accompanying processes which, Senge argues, conspire to defraud the business enterprise, the public agency or the school, of its own innate potential and latent capacity for shared leadership.

How organisations become disabled

Learning disabilities are often a function of hierarchies, even in organisations which appear to require such structure. The most unadulterated form of this can be seen in the military hierarchy, as portrayed by Hollywood in films such as *Full Metal Jacket*, *The Hill*, *An Officer and a Gentleman*. These films depict new recruits being systematically stripped of initiative, individuality and independence of thought and action. This takes place first and foremost through training to conform and obey, but it is also seen as the first step in preparation for leadership which comes in time to those who have learned the lessons of reflex obedience and unquestioning followership.

While reflex obedience may be seen as an asset, and a dream scenario for the beleaguered teacher, it both models and reproduces a particular view of what leadership is. It sees leadership and followership in unambiguous inter-relationship to one another. Followership, in this simple-minded model, is bought at the price of sacrificing the individual to a greater good, while the 'natural leaders' emerge because they are the resilient survivors. The model carries within it the unintended consequence of disabling the organisation as a whole. This happens because the process, by design or default, diminishes both individual and organisational intelligence, as demonstrated in the words 'Who asked you to think, Private? Thinking is injurious to your health.' This has the effect, in a very literal sense, of shutting down the neurological circuitry in the brain. Multiplied from recruit to recruit, it not only reduces their collective intelligence, but systematically reduces the IQ of the organisation as a whole. 'Well *don't* think, then!', is a line that has, unfortunately, been uttered by many teachers over the decades.

This belief in the value of reflex followership, of systemic built-in learning disabilities, has brought in its wake a harrowing history of human misery and disaster. Paschendale is simply one episode in a shameful catalogue of military incompetence – hundreds of thousands of allied soldiers sent to their deaths by generals poring over maps, far removed from the front line.

In her best-selling book *Longitude* Dava Sobel (1997) tells the story of the ship *The Association*, which foundered on the pinnacle rocks around the Scilly Isles because the captain, outraged by the intelligence of a junior seaman who warned of the imminent danger, had him immediately hanged from the yardarm. Two other ships, *The Eagle* and *The Romney*, followed *The Association* to their own destruction. As Dava Sobel tells it:

> *Such subversive navigation by an inferior was forbidden in the Royal Navy, as the unnamed seaman well knew. However, the danger seemed so enormous by his calculation, that he risked his neck to make his concerns known to the officers. Admiral Shovell had the man hanged for mutiny on the spot. (p. 9)*

This story, told before the discovery of longitude, has a frightening contemporary parallel. The modern version is the *Challenger*. The launch of the *Challenger* spacecraft was on an unusually cold day for Florida. Two technicians were concerned that the unexpected cold might have a deleterious effect on the rubber seals of the spacecraft, and tried to voice their concern to a management that was unable to listen or learn from members so low in the hierarchy. The first and only teacher in space was to be a victim of NASA's learning disability.

A similar frightening tale is told by Daniel Goleman (1996) in his book *Emotional Intelligence*. It recounts the story of McBroom, the airline pilot who exerted such a fearful authority that his co-pilots were too scared to tell him that he was on course for disaster. The result was that the plane crashed, killing ten people because, in Goleman's words, 'his crew co-pilots were so fearful of McBroom's wrath that they said nothing, even as disaster loomed' (p. 148).

These dramatic episodes are examples of failure in true leadership. They may seem, on the face of it, to have little application in the context of schools, but on a more modest scale schools also repeat and relive their mistakes from generation to generation. Schools too may be guilty of failing to learn from their most junior members, from young teachers, from pupils, from support staff, parents or even casual visitors.

In Peter Senge's (1992) list of organisational learning disabilities the first is this – 'I am my position.' In other words, 'The value and weight of what I say is commensurate with my organisational status.' 'I am the headteacher', 'I am the school-keeper' or 'I am chair of the board of governors.' It impels us to ask in our own context – 'To what extent in our school do we filter our corporate "intelligence" through the prism of status?' What does the head say and how is it said? How does management see it? What is the authority's stance? What is the departmental view? The potential disabling lies in testing the value of an idea or practice by the institutional level at which it is endorsed. There is an important discovery to be made – that when people are freed from those hierarchical constraints and enabled to leave position behind them, new possibilities and insights open up and leadership is allowed to emerge in the most unexpected of places.

'Nothing fails like success' is another in Senge's canon of disabilities. In the hierarchical organisation in which status is all, junior staff must, like that all-too-prescient seaman of *The Association*, learn quickly and not be too conspicuously successful because it will be seen as undermining authority. It may risk tarnishing the gloss of those who have a need to occupy centre stage.

This is in the very nature of hierarchy. It is, of course, not always that brutal, cynical or self-serving. It can be benevolent. It can be comfortable and reassuring, but only through the most scrupulous of efforts can it avoid the divisiveness and disabling of its members. That has been the goal pursued by the most visionary heads and reformers who have battled for decades to liberate staff and students through learning-focused leadership. The onus is directly on those who, by virtue of policy and history, are pushed to occupy centre stage, to expose the disabilities of the organisation and help staff, students and parents to recognise and confront them too. A key feature of participative leadership is the capacity to be surprised. As Hampden-Turner and Trompenaars (1993) put it:

> *participation is not a technique designed to get workers to do what their managers wanted in the first place, but a willingness to be surprised by an unforeseen initiative or suggestion. (p. 28)*

The brake of local management

Schools in this brave new world must hereafter manage themselves. The logic of the move to site-based management, as the Americans call it, comes from the international quest for improved quality and competitiveness in world markets. It is driven by economic crises and a culture of accountability and VFM – value for money. Decentralisation and autonomy are government's gift to schools, depicted as thwarted over the years by controlling local bureaucracies. In exchange for this liberation, government's gifts to itself are closer monitoring, evaluation and intervention mechanisms. If schools, along with other public bodies, are to be held to account for their new-found autonomy, it means improved knowledge of performance – of pupils, of teachers and of schools as a whole.

School leaders, located by government policy, at the apex of the organisational pyramid, are expected therefore to be visionary driving forces. This role is graphically depicted in one headteacher's 'self-portrait' as at the wheel of 'the internal combustion engine' impelled by forces largely out of his control (see Figure 2.3). The paradox within the picture is the 'internal' nature of the combustion because, with responsibility devolved to the school, it is the constrictions of its new-found freedoms that fuel the inertia. The devolution of financial accountability to individual school level requires more energy to be invested in the driving, keeping at least one eye on steering the course, leaving less scope for side excursions, interesting detours or exploration of the terrain. There is less opportunity to lead in new directions and more time must be invested in administration. More time must be given to financial management and the political negotiation that comes with the territory.

There is less energy left for cultivating the leadership of others. As Julia Evetts (1994) has argued in her study of secondary heads, when decisions were reached together with the authority, those decisions were based on an accepted consensus of educational needs and priorities. Following devolution

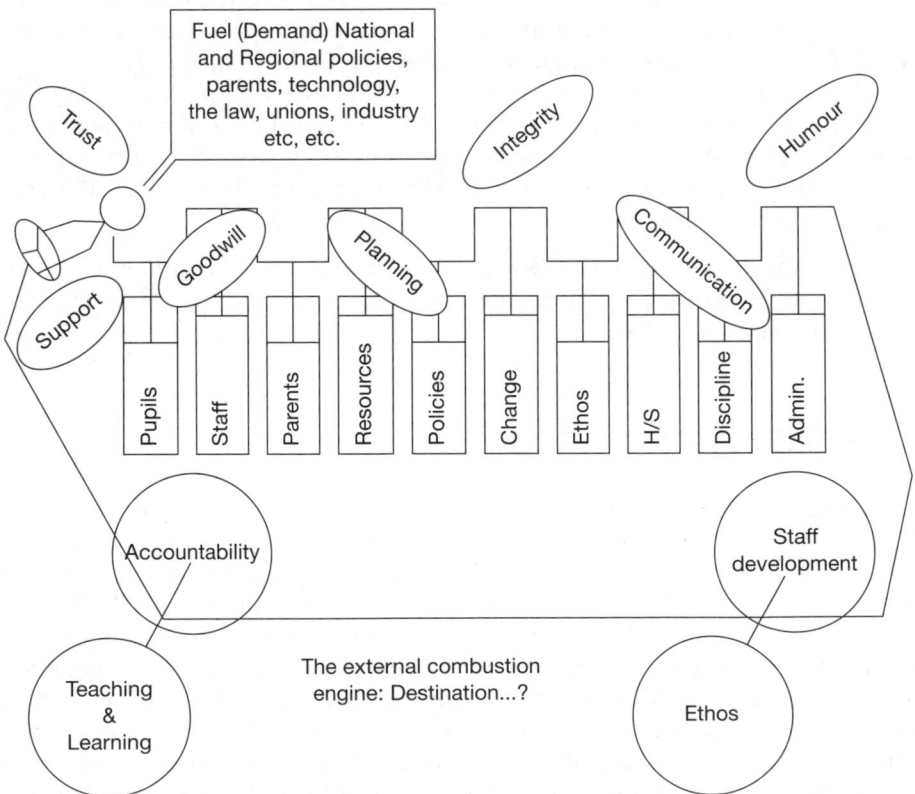

Figure 2.3: The internal combustion engine

to individual schools, however, decisions have tended to be taken more and more on financial and pragmatic grounds and, where once the headteacher negotiated with the authority, the focus of financial bargaining has now turned inwards to the micropolitics of the school.

With local management of schools (LMS) headteachers found that they became involved, and sometimes even obsessed, with things such as furniture and furnishing, heating and lighting, maintenance and repairs, telephone, fax and communication systems, ordering and bookkeeping. For some this proved to be a welcome distraction. For many it was one of the great liberating features of LMS – no more waiting a year for the appropriate authority department to get round to repairs. They were able to circumvent the long delays. Heads could find good deals on the open market, effect instant repairs at minimal cost, install up-to-the-minute communication systems and take advantage of special offers.

However, as the headteachers in Evetts's study discovered, this financial latitude had its downside. Their new-found freedom and flexibility brought with it a tricky juggling of options and priorities. It was no longer a straightforward matter to simply appoint the best person for the job, especially when the school already had a preponderance of staff at the top of the scale. Local management brought with it, too, an increased need to meet with governing bodies. In Evetts's schools, instead of meetings once every six weeks, meetings or sub-committee meetings in some schools became a weekly institution and there was now an increasing pressure on the head and other members of the senior management team to provide information, guidance and direction. Ordering and repairs might have been speeded up but, as the heads in Evetts's study reported, there was an extra burden of bureaucracy and a 'slowing down the whole process of running a school' (Evetts, 1994, p. 112).

There are close echoes of this in a study of Chicago school principals (Bennet et al., 1992). It compared what school principals actually did subsequent to site-based leadership (SBL) and what they believed they should have been doing (illustrated in Figure 2.4).

Site-based leadership had increased the principals' workload and expanded the repertoire of skills they were required to utilise. They were working harder, 60 hours a week or more, but with the feeling that there was never enough time, never enough resources to become effective leaders. Asked to identify roadblocks to exercising the kind of leadership they had envisioned when entering the job, they cited those listed in Figure 2.5.

While some of these are perennial issues of school management, many are either new or come with a new edge and urgency to them. They have close parallels in the United Kingdom. The four roadblocks expressed most often and most strongly by English heads in the Effective Leadership study were very close to those cited by their Chicago counterparts. They had to do with time, funding, professional development and how to deal with inadequate teachers.

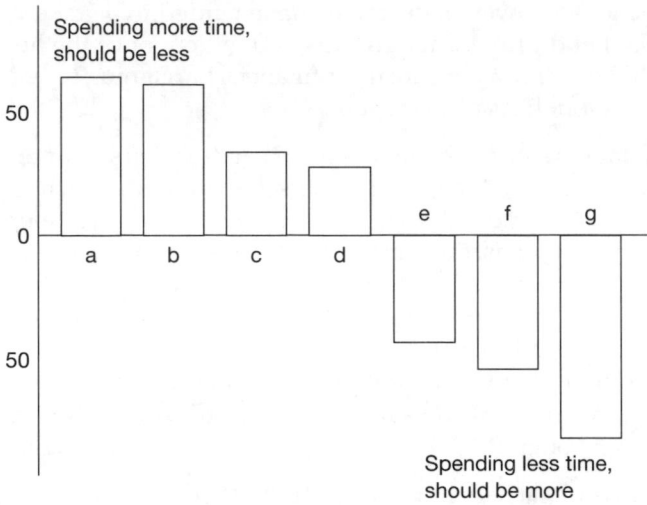

Key   a School management   b Central office
           c Discipline   d Parents and community
           e Student activities   f Instructional leadership
           g Professional development

Figure 2.4: The effect of site-based leadership
(*Source*: Bennet *et al.* (1992), p. 25.)

Roadblocks	% saying 'serious'
Lack of time for professional development	66
Difficulty of removing poor teachers	65
Time taken for administrative detail at the expense of more important matters	55
Inability to obtain funding	58
Parents apathetic or irresponsible about their children	53
Collective bargaining agreements	54
State or federal mandates	39
Problem students	35
Poor communication from central office	37
Resistance to change from staff	23
Standardised testing practices	26
Lack of recognition/reward for principals	27
Lack of flexibility within the school district	18

Figure 2.5: Roadblocks to leadership
(*Source*: Bennet *et al.* (1992), p. 25.)

Although LMS has been broadly welcomed by headteachers it had, in Evetts's view, changed the nature and orientation of their work. It has had the effect of:

- opening the distance between 'management' and staff;
- increasing the isolation of the head;
- reducing contact with pupils;
- increasing competition;
- requiring greater computer literacy and use of information management systems;
- requiring new skills and frustrating the use of pedagogic skills.

Not all of these are necessarily 'bad' or unwelcome from a head's point of view. Some have enjoyed the reduction of contact with pupils and for some, distance has enhanced their personal status; some thrive on competition. Yet, the effects of this significant change in the context of schools and school leadership have to be clearly understood.

The brake of community capital

'We are being held accountable for the educational capital of the communities in which our schools are located,' said a headteacher whose school was 50th out of 52 in his authority's ranking. He claimed there was a virtually day-to-day pressure on him from the press, a few of the governors, and a handful of parents, to raise standards. He was committed to doing so and had been successful in pushing his school from 52nd to 50th in a year. It was a modest advance but in a context where his competitors were engaged in the same zero-sum game. One of the brakes on his improvement of aggregated attainment data was his special unit for emotionally and behaviourally disturbed children. In addition, there were more than a dozen refugee families newly arrived in the area: some were passing through briefly; others were still to come. The community profile included large numbers of elderly people at one end of the spectrum and a large number of young-parent families at the other. The high rate of pupil absenteeism was, to some degree, explained by responsibilities to the extended family, children looking after sick parents and grandparents or younger siblings. Less than 2 per cent of the adult population in his community had a further, or degree, qualification.

State schools in areas such as his do not have the luxury of choosing their clientele. They must work with those who choose them or increasingly come to them by default, because those parents are less able to exercise choice and their very inability to do so is a salient aspect of the educational capital they bring with them. The rhetoric of choice has to be set against a background of increasing relative poverty and growing disparity in life chances.

Despite a general improvement in living standards, the number of people living in poverty in the UK has increased threefold since 1979 (Mortimore and Whitty, 1999). The proportion of children living in poor households is now 32 per cent compared to the European Union average of 20 per cent. The distance between rich and poor, privileged and underprivileged, has grown progressively during the Thatcher and post-Thatcher years. Mortimore and Whitty conclude:

> *Our country has been exceptional in that the difference between the 'haves' and 'have nots' seems to have resulted from official policies designed to lift the constraints affecting the rich. These policies have sought to penalise the poor in the interest of freeing them from the so-called 'dependency culture'. Britain stands out internationally in having experienced the largest percentage increase in income inequality between 1967 and 1992. (p. 2)*

'It is unethical', says the Canadian researcher Ken Leithwood (1999), 'to hold schools and teachers accountable for things beyond their control.' Raising expectations and standards of achievement is, of course, in part within the compass and power of teachers, and a sharpened sense of accountability is an antidote to unacceptably low expectations and self-fulfiling prophecies. But the famous words of Basil Bernstein (1970) are as relevant now as they were in the 1960s: 'School cannot compensate for society.'

A Spanish observer of the English scene (Tiana *et al.*, forthcoming 1999) commented with some degree of astonishment on the assumption that parental choice of school should, or could, be guided by comparisons of test and examination scores:

> *the only thing taken into consideration are pupils' results in almost exclusively cognitive tests or examinations. The school and even the school management itself run the risk of becoming solely guided with this objective in mind, without really taking into account the complexity and necessary subtlety of implementing change and learning strategies which do not neglect the more formal, personal aspects of the act of learning . . . In view of the fact that, generally speaking, teachers cannot involve themselves to any large extent in systematic curriculum improvements at the national level, the end result is that through intermediate outside institutions the State regains power of control over teachers' instructional activity and in general, over the management and everyday life of schools.*

The double jeopardy is that while diverting teachers from their essential tasks, it is obvious to even the least sophisticated of critics that there are more accurate measures of a community's educational capital than the quality of the school. It is not surprising, then, that of all the brakes on the optimism of leaders for school improvement, it is community capital that is the most challenging, as Micheal Fullan (1997b) explains:

*It is easy to be pessimistic about educational reform . . . there have are many legiti-
mate reasons to be discouraged . . . In the same way that crash diets don't work, we
must abandon the search for the quick fix. There is a consistent message in the new
books on change: have good ideas, but listen with empathy; create time and mechanisms for personal and group reflection; allow intuition and emotion a respected
role, work on improving relationships, realise that hope, especially in the face of
frustrations, is the last healthy virtue. (p. 14)*

It is hope in the face of frustrations that harnesses the energy of the other side
of the force field – the accelerators.

The accelerators

Concealed within the negative forces which push against school improvement
are the latent positives. Leadership means making the organisation work for
you rather than against you, harnessing the negative energy and changing its
polarity. It means finding ways of living within the imposed structures, working along the grain in the short term and seeking to break through and
transform inhibiting structures in the longer term. The single most powerful
asset in this is the school's staff and, however much they may constitute a
minority, the committed staff. It is their synergy which can, over time, change
the culture.

The accelerator of commitment

The commitment of teachers in the face of adversity is a constant mystery and
source of inspiration. How, in the direst of circumstances, in the most heart-
breaking of communities and damaged children, do teachers find the energy
and good will to persist? Margaret Wheatley (1994) found an answer to this
question in demoralised organisations where there 'ought not to have been'
commitment or energy, but despite their surroundings people were optimistic
and motivated. The secret ingredient was that these people made meaning for
themselves:

*They were staying creative, making sense out of nonsense, because they'd taken the
time to create a meaning for their work – one that transcended present organisational circumstances. They wanted to hold on to motivation and direction in the
midst of turbulence, and the only way they could do this was by investing the current situation with meaning. (p. 72).*

This is echoed in the findings of two researchers, Hackman and Oldham (1976,
p. 157), who identified three conditions which kept people going. They called
these:

- 'experienced meaningfulness' – the extent to which a person perceives work as being worthwhile or important, given his or her system of values;
- 'experienced responsibility' – the extent to which a person believes that she or he is personally responsible or accountable for the outcomes of efforts; and
- 'knowledge of results' – the extent to which a person is able to determine on a regular basis whether or not the outcomes of her or his efforts are satisfactory.

The essentially emotional nature of these three conditions is amplified in Andy Hargreaves's (1995) description of what motive power drives good teaching. He says:

> Good teaching is not just a matter of being efficient, developing competence, mastering technique and possessing the right kind of knowledge. Good teaching also involves emotional work. It is infused with desire, pleasure, mission, creativity, challenge and joy. Good teaching is a profoundly emotional activity. (p. 52).

Tapping into that reserve of emotional energy is what the prescient leader does as a matter of high priority. She understands that a staff's commitment is enhanced by a sense of professional autonomy and collaboration. Being in control is a basic human need. In his book *The Sickening Mind* Paul Martin (1997) cites biological evidence on the significance of personal control and concludes:

> It is hardly surprising that our minds – and those of other species – should be so attuned to a sense of personal control, since control over the immediate environment is vital for most organisms' survival. Control signifies autonomy, mastery and empowerment. (p. 145).

Lack of control induces panic, anxiety, disequilibrium. It is not only those at the apex of the pyramid who need to feel they are in charge. It runs through the whole school from top to bottom. It includes middle management, support staff and teachers. As Willard Waller (1932) wrote more than 60 years ago, the fear of losing control runs like a thread through the whole of a teacher's professional life.

Martin cites evidence to show that:

- control or lack of it is closely related to mental and physical well-being;
- people with less power and control in organisations are more prone to heart disease than people with greater power and control;
- a sense of being in control helps to deal with and lessen stress;
- social support and networking lessens stress and risks of illness.

He goes on to suggest a matrix with two key dimensions – demand and control – see Figure 2.6.

Figure 2.6: Demand and control matrix
(*Source*: Martin (1997))

He demonstrates that the worst situation to be in is high demand/low control. When there is pressure from above, it diminishes performance, exacerbates stress and reduces resistance and immunity, making people more susceptible to illness and disease. On the other hand, as Csikszentmihalyi (1990) has shown in his work on 'flow' – the psychology of optimal experience – a high level of control but little demand leads to apathy and boredom, providing no incentive for improvement.

The paradox for leadership is that, alongside the personal need to be in charge of events, a sense of control is just as vital for the most junior members of the organisation. In some sense, indeed, they need it most. Paradoxically, the headteacher can most easily relinquish control because she will reap the benefits when control is exercised at the lower levels of the organisation. Raising standards and improving schools then come not through 'levering up' or from downward pressure, but from an intrinsically satisfying challenge which engages and enhances the professional skills of the teacher.

This is what Thomas Sergiovanni (1992) describes as 'pedagogical leadership'. He provides a helpful distinction among four aspects of leadership which he terms 'bureaucratic', 'visionary', 'entrepreneurial' and 'pedagogical'. Bureaucratic leadership, he suggests, is characterised by systems which emphasise supervision, evaluation and incentives. Visionary leadership relies on inspiration and 'a powerfully spoken sense of what must be done'. Entrepreneurial leadership, applying market principles, encourages competition, incentives and sanctions for winners and losers. Pedagogical leadership invests in and builds capital. The capital which it builds is the professional and intellectual capacity of teachers. With this a school is in a position to enhance the social and academic capital of its students.

In its popular connotation, 'strong' leadership is unlikely to equate with pedagogical leadership as described by Sergiovanni, yet 'strong' may indeed be the most apt term for it because, among the four types, pedagogical leadership is the one that requires the greatest inner strength and moral integrity. It is not 'strong' as in the exercise of personal or institutional power, but strong in inner conviction that goals will be achieved through strengthening the status and commitment of others, even at the cost of diminishing self.

This is not the image of 'strong' leadership in the popular and political idiom. Its vocabulary is of a quite different register. It does not use the vocabulary of 'driving up' and 'levering up' standards, of the 'push' and 'pressure' and the rationale that where this fails it is due to 'resistance' by teachers and 'obstacles' in the path of government's 'drive'. The lexicon underpinning this model of strong directive leadership is so deeply ingrained and is lent such reinforcement from national policy and popular press that it is hard to resist. 'Pedagogical leadership is a nice idea', said a headteacher in our research study, 'but how can it work in the real and pressured world of schools?' As Simkins *et al.* (1992) points out, in the nineties world of schools, the world of corporate management, control lies firmly at the top:

> *The shift from the sixties/seventies to the eighties/nineties has been away from people-centredness and consensus to competition, personal assertiveness, firm leadership, strong control – the characteristics of corporate managerialism. (p. 120)*

Pedagogical leadership is a riskier business. One headteacher spoke about risk-taking in these terms:

> *It was a gamble I suppose, but I wanted to test the waters, to break the mould of Buggin's turn and the time-server's charter. I appointed an NQT [newly qualified teacher] to chair a working party, in it some senior members of staff and a few old hands – very old hands. But I thought we would all learn something. Even if it seemed like a disaster. I reckoned we had the reserve capacity to cope and to move forward.*

The headteacher who gave responsibility to the youngest teacher in the school to chair a working party knew she was taking a risk, had weighed up the consequences of possible disaster but had carried it through none the less because she saw in it an opportunity for everyone to learn, including herself. It was an opportunity to loosen the grip on the reins of control and allow it to be enjoyed and exercised by others. It was an opportunity to be surprised by what commitment can bring.

Commitment multiplied may be described as 'synergy', the collective force that is greater than the sum of its parts. Warren Bennis (1997), who has examined what he called 'great groups', found that 'people in great groups seem to become better than themselves. They are able to see more, achieve more and have a far better time doing it than they can working alone' (p. 196).

Although the ability to work together towards a shared goal was a prerequisite for membership of a great group, being amiable, or even pleasant, wasn't. Bennis says:

> *Great groups are probably more tolerant of personal idiosyncrasies than ordinary ones, if only because the members are so intensely focused on the work itself. Their all-important task acts as a social lubricant, minimising frictions. Sharing information and advancing the work are the only real social obligations. (p. 203)*

While Bennis is referring here to high-powered groups such as those engaged in the Manhattan Project, it is a thought-provoking conclusion when applied in an educational context. Probably everyone can remember, from their own school experience, teachers who were idiosyncratic to the point of eccentricity and neither 'pleasant' nor 'amiable' in any conventional sense, but who had a passion for their subject and for their pupils. Contemporary schools appear much less diverse and tolerant of idiosyncrasy and senior management teams tend increasingly towards the managerialist executive image.

People who are engaged in ground-breaking collaborations, concludes Bennis, 'have high regard for people who challenge and test their ideas' (p. 203). While great groups have their own individual leaders, these leaders are *primus inter pares*. The emergent leader in a great group is described by Bennis as a 'curator'. Their job is not to make, but to choose. They have insights into where to go to find answers and who to choose for a job. Like conductors, they may not be able to play the instrument, but they have an understanding of the qualities that it should produce. James Dyson, whose name has been lent to a household product just as Hoover's was before him, argues that advances in engineering are not always made by engineers and that inventions are frequently the product of people working outside that particular field. They dare to ask the naïve questions which no one has asked before, and in so doing shake and change the very foundations of the enterprise.

Commitment is an accelerator and increases velocity to the extent that opportunities are created for people to form coalitions, to lead and to challenge, to exceed their own boundaries and expectations. A strategic procedure for a school's management team is what one research team has called 'appreciative inquiry' (Cooperrider and Srivasta, 1999). It builds on and multiplies energy and proceeds in four stages:

1 appreciate the best of what is
2 ask what it could be like if you could only have more of the good things identified
3 encourage discourse in order to find out what it should be like
4 decide what it will be like.

The accelerator of professional learning

Commitment to the school, to the job, to colleagues and to pupils generally carries with it a commitment to professional development. In turn this implies confronting the disabilities of the organisation and identifying what we might call the learning *ability* of the school. This is a form of appreciative inquiry. In order to do this we need to apply what we know about how individuals learn and how they overcome blocks and barriers to learning. There are some things we can say with confidence about this process, based on the best evidence from psychology, neuroscience and educational research. People learn when there is:

- a reason or a stimulus to learn
- a climate which encourages exploration and risk-taking
- models to observe and learn from
- opportunities to test out what is being learned
- the possibility of success
- opportunities to learn from mistakes
- support and encouragement
- feedback about success and progress
- self-belief
- an audience to share in the benefits of learning.

Applying these as a set of criteria by which to examine the school as an organisation suggests that some criteria are easier to meet than others. We might test these as seen through the eyes of the newly qualified teacher who comes with fresh insights and is keen to know what kind of school this is. She may ask: 'Is it one that will recognise the knowledge and expertise that I already possess? Will it value the peculiar assets and talents I bring with me? Will it appreciate the optimism and expectation that has brought me to make this commitment? Will it make allowances for my self-doubt and allow me to take risks and to fail sometimes, as well as providing the best conditions for success? Will it offer me the opportunity to share openly with others what I have done well and feel free to admit to private disasters? Will I have the occasion to learn from others and will others be "big" enough to learn from me? Is this a school in which people talk about learning and on a daily basis ask of themselves as well as of their pupils, "What did you learn in school today?".'

There are many countries in which most of these criteria could not be met. Teachers have their own classrooms and their own classes, and they teach unobserved by other adults, sometimes for the length of their professional career. As 'qualified' teachers, well versed in their subject, there is no impetus to learn more, no corporate ethos to encourage it, no feedback, and no wider audience than the cohorts of pupils who pass through from year to year. This was the character of many schools in Britain within the recent past, and many schools still retain some of those characteristics.

In a world that is changing so rapidly, however, the nature of professional knowledge is being challenged and needs to be continuously recreated. The teacher of French language may have comparatively little still to learn about her discipline, but will forever have to wrestle with the problem of how to share her knowledge with all her pupils. The older she gets the more distanced she will become from the life experiences of those she teaches and, without strenuous and sensitive effort, less able to tune into and empathise with their situation. She may have a high level of expertise in the methodology of teaching French to children, but find it difficult to help a newly qualified teacher do what she does so effortlessly. She may do many things well but lack the vocabulary and conceptual insight to explain it to others, to her colleagues, to parents. She may have little idea of how to advise a parent on how to support their child through difficulties and low self-confidence. She may see no reason to share her knowledge with the teacher of Physics, to observe a lesson in Home Economics or to learn from the teacher of Mathematics.

Argyris and Schön (1978) write about 'self-sealing' systems. These are organisations that do not know how to progress and improve. They have no mechanisms or tools to confront their own practices and to create their own intelligence.

Salomon and Perkins (1998) describe 'self-sealing systems' in a school context where school leaders and teachers 'pursue agendas while concealing them', and in which 'individuals aim unilaterally to protect both themselves and others against the stress of negative feedback'. Breaking the seal means engaging in 'double-loop learning'. The first stage is 'single-loop learning', providing feedback so that people can become aware of, and change, their behaviour. The second stage, the second loop, is where people reflect on that single-loop process and share it with others. In Salomon and Perkins's words:

> *This involves helping individuals to air and test their tacit assumptions publicly, avoid unilateral protection of themselves or others, and come together in collective problem-solving process that deals with large-scale tacit issues, not just surface technical issues. (p. 15)*

Making knowledge for yourself, as a group of staff, is the most exhilarating impetus that a school can enjoy. This happens, says David Hargreaves (1999), when school leaders work forward 'with the grain' of teachers' experience and motivation. He uses a horticultural metaphor ('beloved of educationists since Plato') to describe the process through which teachers create knowledge for themselves. The five stages are sowing, germinating, thinning, shaping and pruning, and showing and exchanging. This casts the headteacher in the role of estate manager, whose primary task is to maintain the climate for growth and tend to the process of cross-pollination.

The first stage is the sowing of ideas. Teachers possess an immense repertoire of tacit knowledge which is expressed in what they do spontaneously, naturally, intuitively, but is inaccessible to others until it can be transformed into explicit knowledge. The 'seeding' is the collegial dialogue and networking, but in order for germination to take place incipient growth needs to be guarded and protected. Good ideas – especially when they come from new or more junior colleagues – are fragile and may well need protection by the most experienced teachers from colleagues inclined to intellectual infanticide. 'Cynics kill knowledge creation', says Hargreaves. Thinning means ensuring that growth is not choked by so wild a proliferation of ideas that the good and the best are not given the space to flourish. Shaping and pruning is the stage of validation of new knowledge, testing its resilience and its capacity as a new and viable strain. The self-conscious attempt to validate practice requires opportunities for teachers to both watch one another at work and develop a conceptual frame for talking principles-in-practice. The 'third eye' of critical friend or inspector may well be necessary to add the critical edge to what is seen and how it is judged. So, the final stage in the horticultural sequence, 'showing', takes place with a high degree of confidence that the practice is open to scrutiny and amenable to wider distribution.

Hargreaves's extended metaphor does, however, lack one essential ingredient, that is, 'grafting'. It is through grafting that new strains are created, frequently with unexpected consequences. Ultimately it is probably grafting that will allow the kind of divergent growth that underwrites the school's future.

In the Hargreaves model the role of the leadership is more implicit than explicit but it presupposes a high level of gardening skills – a deep knowledge, a light touch, a passion for growth. Such passion in the horticultural model is about tending to the growth of others. To do this successfully, as the gardening metaphor suggests, means being one step ahead in anticipation and planning, but constantly open to surprise and new insights.

The accelerator of parental partnership

A school may see its primary task as reaching out to its community to play a part in enriching its educational life and working with other agencies towards a more civilised future for its children. In our experience, young teachers often find teaching most challenging and rewarding in areas of economic disadvantage because they can see that they make a difference. The most rewarding aspect of a teacher's job is to see evidence of children and young people's growth as individuals, as social and emotional beings infused with self-belief and with a commitment to learning.

In challenging areas good teachers find it profoundly satisfying to work with the community, helping to rebuild a trust in the world and shoring up fragile self-esteem. When required to sacrifice this often slow and long-term goal for pragmatic, short-term, and competitive gains, however, they become rapidly disillusioned. In a recent survey for the National Union of Teachers, Galton and Fogelman (1997) found that there had been, in recent years, a narrowing and limiting of opportunities for 'spontaneous encounters' and loss of those 'magic moments' which made teaching enjoyable and rewarding. They concluded, 'Such encounters help forge the excellent teacher–pupil relationships on which effective learning must be based.' They might have added to that the equally significant home–school relationship within which effective learning is seeded and nurtured.

The Canadian researcher Peter Coleman (1998) describes this fertile ground-bed of learning as 'the power of three'. Figure 2.7 illustrates a number of different versions of this triadic relationship. The first, represented diagrammatically by three pluses, is the relationship most likely to produce high achievement. As we have learned from Reuven Feuerstein *et al.*'s (1980) work, the difference between success and failure is less explained by what happens in schools and classrooms than by what happens beyond the school gates. Nor, as Feuerstein *et al.* demonstrate, is the determining factor poverty, parental education or income. The key issue is how learning is mediated by adults or older siblings.

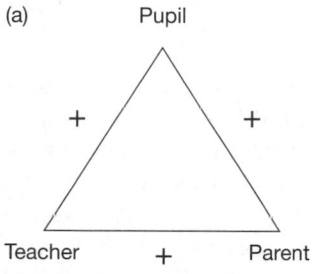

The ideal, where learning is built on educative relationships among parents, teachers and pupils working to common goals.

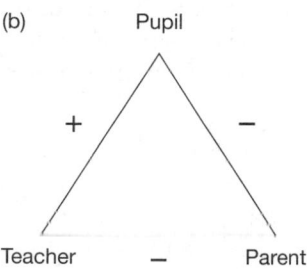

There is a positive learning–teaching relationship in the classroom but this cannot compensate for the lack of educative relationship in the home or between teacher and parent.

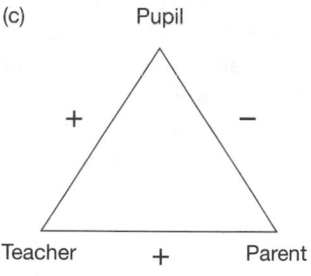

There is a strong teaching–learning relationship in the classroom and a supportive parent relationship. The parent needs support and help to deal with the negative relationship with the pupil.

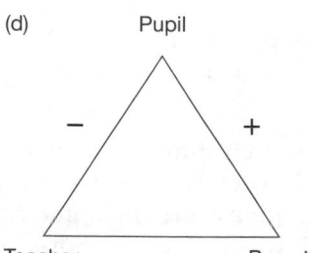

The positive relationship between parent and child and between parent and teacher cannot compensate for the negative teacher–pupil relationship. There is enough positive energy to find a solution, but the onus is primarily on the school to find that solution.

Figure 2.7: Versions of the triadic relationship

Parents or other adults help to structure meaning for children in the critical years when they are building their neural networks and developing theories about themselves and about the nature of the world. Emotionally secure, self-confident adults can give that quality of support to their offspring and shepherd them through the challenges of childhood, encouraging them to face and overcome those challenges for themselves, knowing there is a secure supporting hand behind them. Where this occurs it is a priceless gift for the teacher, who can not only build on these well-laid foundations, but knows that she can go on building successfully in concert with a concerned parent.

In the second example (Figure 2.7 (b)) the teacher–pupil relationship is the only strength (one plus as against two minuses). Where this is the case there is a constant uphill struggle, one that is highly inimical to success unless strategies can be found to work with the other two sides of the relationship. Family-centred learning and projects which bring parent, teacher and child together, either in a school or home setting, are examples of how this can be tackled. These strategies may also be used where school and home (or teacher and parent) forge a positive relationship but the parent–child relationship is problematic (Figure 2.7 (c)). Inter-agency work, or parental workshops that help parents rebuild their relationships with their children are ways in which this has been tackled.

The fourth example (Figure 2.7 (d)), where the teacher–pupil relationship is weak but the other relationships are strong, is the one in which both the problem and the solution rest more with the school and school leadership than in the home or in the home–school interface. In this area the school's, and the leadership's, accountability is most clear-cut. Reorganising classes and timetabling may be one solution; team teaching and changing of roles another. Changing the context of the relationship through extra-curricular activities, residential experience or after-school study support have been shown, in many instances, to effect a significant change in the relationship. Very often it is not the pupil who has to do the adjustment but the teacher, who not only begins to see the pupil in a new light but come to a new understanding of learning and the learning relationship. Parent involvement in study support is a plus, but more valuable in some cases than others.

In all of these initiatives schools have a role to play. In addressing this sensitive but immensely significant issue it is helpful to be reminded of the very different contexts in which children and young people are required to pursue their learning. Peter Hannon (1993) makes the distinctions between school and home learning shown in Figure 2.8.

The *Home from School* (MacBeath *et al.*, 1986) research study found that schools could often provide a richness, flexibility and closeness of relationships and conversation not to be found in the home. In some cases the home environment, or even the child's own private world, was fuller and more complex than the threadbare learning offered in their classrooms. In other cases still

School learning	Home learning
• shaped by curriculum	• shaped by interest
• bounded by sanctions	• spontaneous
• timetabled	• flexible
• contrived problems	• natural problems
• restricted language	• everyday language
• limited conversations	• extended conversations
• special resources – limited access	• 'natural' resources – unlimited access
• recognition of achievement in approved areas	• recognition of achievement in many areas
• horizontal age group	• vertical age group
• distant relationship with adults	• close relationship with adults
• pupil role	• multiple roles
• accounts for little variation in academic achievement	• accounts for much variation in academic achievement

Figure 2.8: Distinctions between school and home learning

there was a similar depth, or shallowness, of experience in both school and out-of-school contexts. In relation to the experience of young children, Peter Hannon (1993) has argued that parents can be, in some important respects, more effective teachers of reading than school teachers. He concluded from his own research that:

- pre-school teachers seriously underestimated the value of parental support for children's reading;

- the quality of children's experiences in reading to their parents was in some respects superior to what happened in school;

- home readings were longer and had fewer interruptions than reading sessions in the classroom;

- parents' relationship with children allowed them to relate what they were reading to children's experience;

- teachers used praise more, but it was often a mechanism of control and a reflection of their more distant relationship with the child.

In the *Home from School* study it was the first-hand experience of extended conversations with children and their parents in their own natural surroundings that emphasised to the researchers the differential quality of classroom and home, and the immense complexity of the interrelationship of these two sites for learning and socialisation. Schools that asked young people at different stages to keep a detailed log for one week, documenting what they did, who with, and how long they spent on it, were surprised and at first disbelieving about what young people did in trying to manage learning for themselves away from the pressures of the classroom. There were some who had private tutors in a range of school subjects and, at the other extreme, young people who, left entirely to their own devices, invested huge amounts of time on ineffective, unfocused copying or reading, struggling to make their own sense of the printed page or giving up at the first hurdle. Some had the physical and psychological space, encouragement and support from parents or peers who knew little about the subject-matter but had a lot of good sense about timing and pacing and strategies for finding out. Some lived in conditions which crowded out all possibilities for school-related learning.

Teachers involved in that study confessed to knowing very little about the context for children's learning out of school and gained a great deal from the log-keeping exercise. Very often the pupil logs and follow-up exploration of these individually and in groups revealed an underlying failure on the part of the school to think through the relationship of in-school to out-of-school learning. While learning *in* school had in some primary schools become more varied, more differentiated and more imaginative, learning *out* of school seemed to be stuck in a time warp. Classroom learning was often stimulating and inventive; pupils worked in pairs and groups and discussed and shared what they were doing. In the evening, work at home was, as one boy put it, 'a lonely and tedious activity'. Homework tasks were not given the same thought as to the needs of the learner, nor to the coherence and progression of learning.

Advice to young people and their parents often betrayed a lack of understanding of the character of children's learning out of school, for example advocating a quiet place to work, a desk and a desk light, an upright chair, a place free from interruptions. Young people were encouraged to plan their time over the week, by means of a timetable for a routine of work in the early evening or after school. These failed to reflect the reality of young people's lives. Like adults, they worked in a variety of ways and places and at times which suited their domestic routines or personal biorhythms, or fitted the ecology and social composition of the home.

Children and young people need a high level of support to move between these two contexts, and few schools are really good at building effective bridges between home learning and school learning. But it is a growing priority and with it there is growing a body of good practice. Wilhite and Basnet (1999) conclude:

> *Making learning that happens outside the classroom more intentional doesn't really require great changes in the way we teach. It requires only a change in the way we think about teaching and learning and about who is responsible for it. (p. 2)*

The most challenging question for leadership – individual and collective – is 'Who is responsible for learning in the school?'

In conclusion

Good leadership means putting the organisation to work. The first step is to be aware of the nature of the organisation that, as a headteacher, one is required to lead. The second step is to share that awareness among all stake-holders. They need to see and understand how organisations can inhibit the wider development of initiative and shared leadership and how schools can so easily become disabled by their very own structures. Identifying the brakes and accelerators is one practical way forward. Through appreciative inquiry the school can engage in the progressive removal of barriers to a wider and more profound meaning of leadership.

Appendix 2.1
Seven steps to the learning school

The following may be seen as stages, pursued in sequence, or as key con-stituent parts which come together over time to form a coherent whole.

1 **Promote a learning climate**: The school leadership models learning in action. Instead of MBWA (management by walking about) they exem-plify LBWA (learning by walking about), using opportunities to tune into what Jennifer Nias (1989) calls 'the secret harmonics' of the school. Talking and reading about learning is encouraged. Seminal education research publications are available and referred to.

2 **Identify the green shoots of growth**: Where in the school are the exem-plary learners – not necessarily the very best teachers but those who are most open and keen to learn and to share? Who are the best listeners? Who encourage feedback from their pupils? Who talk about learning in the staffroom? Who seek out alliances with other teachers across dis-ciplines? Which members of staff use positive language? Who are the energy creators? 'Appreciative inquiry' is the name given to this process.

3 **Identify the barriers:** Improvement is less likely to be helped by innova-tion than by removing the blocks and barriers to learning. Where is the energy and intelligence of the school being drained off? What and who are the high energy consumers? Where does the cynicism creep in? What practices and protocols have never been challenged?

4 **Share pedagogical leadership:** Provide opportunities for exemplary learners to exercise leadership. Offer opportunities for newly qualified teachers to lead groups and build teams. Involve pupils in feedback and decisions about learning and teaching, and give them a role in consulta-tive and policy-making groups.

▶

5   **Create intelligence from within:** Make learning the central focus and business of the school. Encourage the belief that knowledge can be found as much within the school as from external sources. Build alliances and networks of learners. Provide time and support for the networkers. Challenge people to move beyond their comfort zone.

6   **Use critical friends:** Engage one or more outside 'experts' to work with staff as a friend of the schools but ensure that they are people with not only the skills to listen sensitively and support good practice but the skills and courage to challenge and to draw theory out of tacit knowledge. Consider other critical friends internal to the school who might also play that role for their colleagues.

7   **Build resilient networks:** Seek out allies from whom you can learn and who are equally open to learning from you. They may be local or they may be in another country. Internet and European projects have made inter-country exchanges (of personnel, ideas, good practice) more feasible. Practices do not always transplant easily into new soil, but if the underpinning principles are sound they can be adapted and grafted to thrive in another climate.

3
■ ■ ■

Talking Heads

How and why do teachers become headteachers? What motivates and inspires them? What are their primary sources of satisfaction in the job and what do they find the least satisfying aspects? What competencies do they bring and what competences are expected of them from those they are expected to serve? And why did they come to enter teaching in the first place?

These were some of the questions addressed to headteachers in a series of interviews published in the *Times Educational Supplement* under the generic title 'Talking Heads' (Myers, 1995–1998). It involved 27 teachers from nursery, primary, special and secondary schools, 20 of them from British schools, 2 from Canada, 2 from the USA and 1 each from New Zealand, Australia and South Africa. This was not a 'scientific' selection of heads. What they had in common was that somebody, somewhere, had recommended them as a 'good' head and as someone who would be interesting to interview. In this chapter we try to draw together some of the common and disparate strands from those interviews. They illustrate the importance of context, of leadership style, of stages in career progression, and highlight some of the differences between experiences of a first and a second headship.

Why did they enter teaching in the first place?

When asked why they had become teachers the heads divided themselves into three distinct groups:

- The Drifters
- The Late Starters
- The Determined.

Of those 27 heads interviewed, eight had not consciously chosen teaching as a career but had entered the profession through sheer accident and/or serendipitous events. For The Drifters, teaching had not been part of any original game plan. They came into teaching due to lack of career advice; unwillingness to go straight to work after graduating; lack of any clear alternative options; or because their university subject led them nowhere else but into teaching. Some had enjoyed the experience of temporary teaching jobs and then decided to go to college or university to qualify as teachers.

> *After I'd graduated from high school, I travelled through South America and went to visit my sister in Ecuador. She was teaching and I applied for a temporary job in the same school. I thought they'd give me a crash course in teaching but I just got a set of books and was left to swim or sink. I liked it so much that I decided to come home and get a degree in elementary education at the university of New Mexico.*
>
> *(Male primary head, USA)*

Some of the heads interviewed started out in other careers but found the work environment of the bank, the treasury department or the office uncongenial and discovered what they had been looking for in teaching.

> *I left school at 16 and worked in a bank for two years but did not really like the office environment. I went to speak to one of my old teachers, a nun, who advised me that teaching might be what I was looking for. (Female primary head, England)*

Being 'surprised', 'enthused' or 'inspired' by their first experience of teaching had, for some, kindled the 'flame' which had been burning below the level of consciousness:

> *When I left school I worked for a year as a technical surveyor and became interested in photogrammetry. However, because of apartheid I was told that there was no future in that field for me and so I had to rethink my life. I spoke with an English woman who had been my biology teacher and she suggested teaching. She kindled a flame that had probably been burning all the time. (Male primary head, South Africa)*

The phenomena of drifting into the profession has been noted elsewhere, for example in Julia Evetts's work. It has significant implications for recruitment and teacher supply, making prediction difficult and undermining rational planning. It is difficult to influence and control the flow when, for a significant number, deciding to become a teacher has more to do with chance and circumstance than any overt rational career plan.

The next group, The Late Starters, consisted mainly but not entirely of women, at least two of whom started teaching because of a connection with the school that their own children attended. It was the example of individual teachers that had enthused them and, as one of the interviewees said, it was the way in which primary teachers seemed to be 'thinking about the nature of learning' that had ignited her interest.

> *I had three babies close together so took up part-time work in FE. As my own children started school I started to realise how important primary education is and I was very impressed by the way primary teachers seemed to be thinking about the*

nature of learning. One day when I took my youngest child to school, I was asked if I was a teacher and if I'd be interested in applying for a part-time remedial reading job. I did, got the job, gradually increased my time until I was a class teacher and then a language post holder. I learned on the job like an apprentice, watching what other people were doing. (Female primary head, England)

The final group, The Determined, had known from a very young age exactly what they wanted to do. They had not so much 'drifted' into teaching as moved almost seamlessly into the profession because their parents were teachers; because they had 'played school' when they were young; because the profession was a respectable one to enter; or because they been brought up in an environment which made them inclined to see teaching as a natural progression.

I always wanted to be a teacher. When I was young, being a teacher was very respectable here in my community and I grew up playing school. (Female secondary head, USA)

I always wanted to be a teacher partly because my mother was one. (Female primary head, England)

Some heads spoke about specific events, 'moments of truth' that set them on a course into teaching. The unique and idiosyncratic nature of these key moments is illustrated in the following description from a Scottish primary head teacher:

I wanted to be a teacher from the time in primary school that I sprained my wrist, and because I couldn't write the teacher allowed me to read for three days which were the most wonderful three days of my life I decided I wanted to teach so that everyone could read. I then remember going to see Mrs McOuat, the head, to ask her something and found her sitting in front of the fire in her office reading the paper. Although she spent a long time trying to convince me that she'd been in school since very early that morning and that this was the first time she had sat down, I still thought that this must be a wonderful way to spend your time. (Male primary head, Scotland)

Satisfaction in teaching was not felt because it was seen as an easier, more comfortable life, but, for several of the heads, because it was challenging.

I started teaching ROSLA (Raising of the School Leaving Age) . . . in a school that was under siege. The staffroom was regularly boarded up after thefts. There were about twenty probationary teachers and we gave each other a great deal of support. After three years I became a year tutor and did that for five years, then moved on to a larger school as head of year. I loved it and stayed for six years before becoming pastoral deputy and then curriculum deputy at another . . . school. (Female secondary head, England)

I worked with juvenile delinquents, including murderers and rapists and was at the same school for 14 years – probably too long. ... It was a great place to work. (Male secondary head, Canada)

For people outside the profession it might seem a surprising conclusion that such a school could be 'a great place to work', but the challenge, collegial support, the knowledge that the work was valued and the recognition that this was something that you could do well, had been a major factor in these people staying in teaching and moving on eventually to become headteachers.

Many of the heads interviewed recognised from an early point in their teaching careers that they were good at what they did:

> *I was a successful teacher and loved children. (Male primary head, USA)*

Not all were quite so confident. One Asian primary head described her own uncertainty:

> *I was very happy at the school, I loved teaching and stayed for ten years . . . The [next] school was involved in an HMI exercise and I was observed teaching by four different inspectors at the same time. I was sure that I must be doing something terribly wrong and that I was going to get into trouble but it turned out that they were very impressed with what they saw. (Female primary head, England)*

Becoming a head

The interviewees' answers to why they had become heads divided them into four different groups:

- The Inadvertent
- The Premeditated
- The Strategists
- The Civic Servants.

Very few of the heads had thought about headship at the beginning of their careers and had described themselves as having 'no clear ambition'; they did not see themselves as heads even 'in their imagination'. They seemed to get there *inadvertently*.

> *I did not map it out when I started. I've always done the next job that presents itself. (Female primary head, England)*

> *It was accidental . . . I tend to jump and see what it's like when I get there. (Male primary head, England)*

> *I never set out to be principal. (Female secondary head, Australia)*

> *The only active career move I made was moving from being a pastoral head to becoming a deputy. (Female secondary head, England)*

Many of them just climbed the next step up the promotion ladder without any particular career plan and only knew they wanted to become heads when they had reached the level of deputy. It was not before this stage that the possibility of headship emerged. This is not surprising for those for whom there had been no role model to follow.

> *I had no clear ambition to be a head. When I started teaching I had no role models; the concept of a female headteacher in mixed secondary schools did not exist. (Female secondary head, Scotland)*

The next group knew as soon as they started teaching that they wanted to become heads. For The Premeditated there were no doubts about this career objective.

> *Once I became a teacher I knew I wanted to be a head. (Female primary head, Scotland)*

> *I did not always want to be a teacher, but once I became one I always wanted to become a head. (Male secondary head, Wales)*

> *Once I started teaching, I wanted to become a head because of the inspirational heads I worked with. (Male primary head, Scotland)*

The third group, The Strategists, decided they wanted to be heads when they realised that this was the only way to get things done.

> *When I started I knew I wanted to influence what happened which meant becoming a head. (Male primary head, England)*

Impatience to 'make things happen' had motivated some to move from the classroom to the larger stage of school management. They wanted to 'influence what happened', which meant having the power and authority to effect it. There was a tension here, though, for those who got a lot of satisfaction from the classroom.

> *I wanted to stay in the classroom but I also wanted to make things happen. (Female primary head, England)*

The members of the final group, The Civic Servants, were both from the USA. These two very different heads (one Hispanic male primary, from Albuquerque; the other black American, female secondary from Memphis) both described their desire to make things happen in terms of civic responsibility, of 'giving something back'.

> *This is the community I grew up in and it has now become virtually abandoned leaving the poorest of poor families. I thought it was time to give something back. (Female secondary head, USA)*

> *I believe that good people have a civic responsibility to step forward and apply for leadership positions, whatever arena it is. (Male primary head, USA)*

These American heads spoke without reservation or embarrassment about 'service' and, although they may well have felt a similar mission, none of the British headteachers spoke in this way. This might be explained by a culture which discourages such overt discussion of community service, or perhaps it can ascribed to the Thatcherite and post-Thatcherite ethos of self-interest, managerialism and 'me firstism'. It may also be due to a perception of teachers and heads that their value has been diminished and their work undermined by successive governments and popular media. In this context the feeling of belonging to a 'noble profession' perhaps seemed less appropriate, while the notion of contributing to the 'public good' did not sit easily with the current recruitment crisis and performance-related pay.

Living up to expectations

Becoming a head involved not only a shift in role, but also a change in status and relationships. The biggest surprise for many of these heads was the way in which they were now perceived by others. While they saw themselves as 'the same person with the same feelings and emotions; others responded to them with a new deference and distance, investing them with authority and omniscience – as one primary head put it, 'thinking you can resolve the problems of the universe':

> I could not believe the deference and how important people thought you were just because you were principal. It astounded me . . . as a principal you must never underestimate the impact you have. (Male secondary head, Canada)

> what I hadn't fully appreciated was the business of being perceived as an all-powerful figurehead. Wherever you are in the school people are checking you out and your words have a significance – if you don't smile people wonder if there's a reason. I've stopped making throw-away jokes because all sorts of things get read into them. People treat you differently even from when you're a deputy. (Female secondary head, England)

As one primary head said, it was a surprise not to be treated any longer as a colleague but suddenly 'to be taken so seriously'. In the words of a secondary head, 'People put great store by what you say'.

The next big surprise for heads was the reality of being 'in charge' and 'in control'. The 'buck stopping here' came as a shock to some of them, who described this aspect as 'intimidating' and 'daunting'.

> I was very daunted initially though they probably did not realise it. At first I also found it difficult to cope with the fact that there was no one after me – I was in charge. (Female primary head, England)

> Everything [was different than expected]. There was no one to ask what to do or to turn to when I had a problem. Everyone expected me to be in control all the time. It is having to manage everyone else and no one to manage you but yourself. (Female primary head, England)

> *I'd had experience of being an acting head but even so the most shocking thing when I first came here was that people expected me to know things. (Male secondary head, England)*

Trying to live up to the expectations of a range of different audiences, and trying to 'please everyone by being nice' were unexpected traps. Some heads were unprepared for the number of hats they were required to wear, 'from social worker to financial whiz kid', and the multiple sources of pressure from staff, students, parents, the education authority, DfEE, OFSTED, the public generally and local and national politicians. One head commented that managing adults was more difficult and complicated than managing children.

Several were surprised at how long real, embedded change took.

> *Understanding that change cannot happen overnight; it is a longer, slower and ongoing process. The realisation of the constraints that heads work under and the various audiences that have to be addressed and whose interests need to be managed. You cannot go on a training course for that, the skill has to evolve and develop – be honed on the job. Although I have been a head for eleven years, I'm still learning. When I stop is the day to pack it up. (Female secondary head, Scotland)*

'To build up a good school takes a long time', said one primary head; the amount to learn was greater and 'the picture was much bigger' than anything that had gone before.

> *At first there were lots of headaches and heartaches. I was not au fait with the system things like legal every day requirements, staffing, ratios, funding. I was so green. It was a crash course in learning! (Female head all-age school, New Zealand)*

Some of the interviewees had underestimated the resistance to change and others' belief that staff would want to play a larger role in decision-making had met with the disappointing realisation that democracy takes longer. There was a somewhat poignant comment from the South African head:

> *I thought that teachers would welcome playing a role in running their school. I think I underestimated the legacy of apartheid that enslaved so many of us. I thought that with democracy everything would become much easier but it will take time – for example for teachers to become affirmed in meetings. (Male primary head, South Africa)*

The second-timers

Three of the heads interviewed were on their second headship and had all noted differences between their first and second experiences of headship.

> *The main difference is that the second time you know what you want and are far more confident about it. In your first headship you grow into the job and become a head. In your second headship you arrive as a head. (Male secondary head, Wales)*

There are strong parallels with the Effective Leadership study in which head teachers reported being 'different people' in their second headship. As reported in Reeves and Dempster (1998), who you are, who you become, and how you change are all deeply affected by the context in which you work and the expectations that people hold of you.

> Contextual factors meant that transfer of learning from one situation to another was not necessarily straightforward or helpful. They felt very strongly that the way in which a school leader operated had to be understood in this light. Context was highly significant and the same person, they argued, placed in different contexts acts differently because of different opportunities and constraints. (p. 155)

Although the second-timers are, in a sense, still growing into and learning on the job, the second time around they are doing so with more confidence and clarity.

> When you arrive at your second school you have to be careful not to assume things you put in place in your last school are in place here – it's a new school. The context has changed. In my first headship I had to create the agenda, but now you have to be ready to respond more sharply. The pressure is on as you walk through the door. Even though I knew a lot more when I started this job, I never stop learning. (Female secondary head, England)

The second-timers were all convinced that what works in one school will not necessarily work in another.

> It's different in this school from my last one. In my last headship I was more directive. That style was not appropriate here. (Male primary head, England)

Leadership styles

The issue of leadership style was a predominant theme in the interviews with the 27 heads. They were asked how they would describe their own leadership style and how they thought others would describe them. Their responses can be categorised under three headings:

- Collaborative and collegiate
- Flexible and mixed
- Strong and up-front.

Collaborative and collegiate

While collaborative leadership was a common theme, there were different emphases, to some extent dependent on the size of the school, sector and culture. A headteacher of a New Zealand school referred to 'whanau', a Maori term for the extended family, very important in the Maori culture, to underline the importance of consensus in decision-making: 'We don't make decisions until everyone is in agreement', adding 'our collective vision is far greater than individual personalities'.

A nursery head expressed the view that in a small school there was no option.

In a little school it has to be co-operative and based on consensus. (Female nursery head, England)

Other heads spoke about participative management and shared leadership. Participative management was described in these terms by one primary head:

I feel very strongly about the importance of participative management and creating a culture that involves all staff and children which empowers them to grow personally. Everyone is a manager. I'm obsessively committed to trying to create positive attitudes. I think it is very important as a head to create a space for other people to talk about what's going on. (Male primary head, England)

A secondary head used the term 'multiple leadership' to describe his attempts to let different people in the school take the lead. Another secondary head, while advocating shared leadership, adds the following caveat:

I'm willing to listen but I am no wimp. (Female secondary head, USA)

Some heads recognised that a collaborative or democratic style was desirable but were not convinced that all their colleagues wanted to participate in decision-making.

I hope it's [leadership style] not autocratic though it's not totally democratic either. I am aspiring towards a corporate style of management. I give people the opportunity to give suggestions and share ideas. Some do it willingly and openly though some are just not ready to be equal parts of the team. I want us all to work together effectively to manage the change which is constantly coming our way. (Female primary head, England)

Others spoke of the difficulty of going against the grain of people's expectations. For teachers who had been used to a more authoritarian style of leadership, dependency could be more comfortable and more difficult to break out of. Again this was particularly pertinent for the head from South Africa.

I would like to think that I have a democratic approach to leadership, though this approach is not easy. It's difficult for teachers who have been used to an old-style authoritarianism. It's easy to criticise but a bit more difficult when you have to live with the decisions you make. The threat of accountability is very real when you cannot just blame others. Also democratic decision-making takes a lot of time. It particularly takes time to try and reach a consensus rather than just go for a majority decision.

Teachers have a very heavy workload and so more and more meetings after school are not always popular and the ethos of meetings has not previously been cultivated. Some staff are not familiar with meeting procedures and sometimes they suggest I make the decisions myself. In the old days when one person made the deci- sions you knew where to go to lobby if you did not agree with it. But once decisions are made by the whole staff they cannot be revoked by one person. Far more is expected of teachers now and some of them don't like that. (Male primary head, South Africa)

Flexible and mixed

Some of the heads suggested that they had a flexible approach to leadership and adopted a range of styles depending on the context. They believed that 'situational leadership' was the appropriate mode of leadership for heads – that is, adopting the style which is most fitting and most pragmatic for the job in hand:

My perspective relates to the job I've had to do. In a different kind of school the answer might be different. There are different styles of running schools and you have to be true to yourself, which is not always easy when some styles are in fash- ion. (Female secondary head, England)

'Situational leadership' is a term that has been used to describe the variation in styles of leadership to meet different demands and different contexts. Five of the women headteachers interviewed spoke about having a mix of styles and were aware that they did use different styles for different purposes. They could be consultative, autocratic, or *laissez-faire,* depending on the situation. Moving in and out of roles according to demand is described by one head in the following terms:

There are times when I need to be compassionate, gentle and thoughtful and other times when I need to be strategic, innovative and astute. I move in and out of roles according to what is demanded. (Female secondary head, Australia)

Different situations and different times need different approaches, said one secondary head. The challenge was 'knowing when to push and when to back off, when to give a strong lead and when to support'. A nursery head spoke about the need to be clear about what is and is not negotiable:

I have a framework of negotiables and non-negotiables so, for example, having respect for the children and their parents and believing that all our children are capable of wonderful things is not negotiable. The way we achieve this is. (Female nursery head, England)

Strong and up-front

A few of the heads did not believe that you could operate without a very up- front leadership style. As one headteacher put it, taking the money and doing the job you are required to do necessarily implied 'strong leadership'. Another outwardly rejected the notion of decision-making by consensus, adding:

> *I do not believe in decision-making by consensus but I do believe in listening and I can be influenced. I don't think you can have collective responsibility in a school. It's a bit like a ship's captain in a storm – you can't go into discussions in this situation: you need a strong helmsman. (Male primary head, England)*

There is, in this account, a clear recognition of the 'I' who listens, makes the decisions and takes responsibility. The head whose deputy described her as a 'devious autocrat' is unashamed about making clear who is the boss and where responsibility for final decision-making lies:

> *I lead from the front but my deputy says I am a devious autocrat. When people apply to work in the school I am very clear about my style of leadership. I am the kind of person that, when the director of education says 'jump', I say 'how high?' I respect authority and have the same expectations of everyone else. Staff know exactly what I expect and why I expect what I expect. I do not ask them to do anything I would not do myself. I like to make sure that the staff are with me so I gather their opinions before I make a final decision. Some of our most successful initiatives have come from discussions at staff meetings. At first as a head you are unsure about your strengths – now I know what they are and I have learned to handle them better. (Female primary head, England)*

Leading from the front meant being clear about the model of leadership you were offering, setting high expectations of yourself in order for others to follow. Some recognised this as a potential weakness:

> *I probably work too hard and I know I have appointed other people who work too hard – we know that's a danger. I have very high expectations of myself and other people. (Female primary head, England)*

> *I have high expectations of myself and the staff. People probably think of me as a workaholic. (Male secondary head, England)*

Common to all of these accounts is the recognition that the demands of leadership require flexibility of response. The responses required range from a recognition of push and pull, and an acknowledgement of the need to be clear about what is and is not up for negotiation. They also thought it was important for their colleagues to know where the leader stands and what the leader stands for.

Learning from and becoming models

Several of the heads spoke about the importance of modelling – how their behaviour gave important signals and clues to the adults and children they worked with.

The similarity in the following three quotes from men and women heads in different contexts illustrates a very similar way of thinking about the importance and functioning of modelling.

I think it's important to lead by example. The way you speak to people is very important. I try to treat everyone with respect, teaching and support staff, children and parents, and hope that they then do the same. (Female primary head, England)

I think 'modelling' in relationship to the children and the curriculum is vitally important. I try to work closely with teachers to show what is possible and what our children are capable of. (Male primary head, England)

He or she [the head] is also an important role model. For example how I relate to students is how I expect staff to relate to students. (Male special school head, England)

Modelling assumed particular significance for one of the black primary head-teachers who saw herself as a role model for her pupils to aspire to. Her comment that her own role model had been her mother illustrates why modelling assumes such significance and how it is passed on from generation to generation.

My mother . . . was the first black headteacher in Wales. In spite of being told by her own teachers that she could never be a teacher because of her colour, she has been very successful. She has always felt strongly about the importance of education. (Female primary head, England)

As Peter and Jo Mortimore point out, the experience of being managed by others and observing those heads at work informs the way teachers attempt to behave when they assume that role. The irony is that it is often the negative role model that has the most potent influence.

Some poor role models taught me how not to do things. More positive models are Charles Handy who taught me at the business school has a great ability to write enlightening common sense. I take bits from all sorts of places from the Leadership Secrets of Attila the Hun and Peter Drucker to educational thinkers and academics including Peter Mortimore and David Reynolds. Also I believe that aspects of the way you seek to work are profoundly part of who you are and what you are, which is why leadership style is so different with different people and can be equally successful. (Female secondary head, England)

Stages in leadership

When you are a new head you can never imagine being an experienced one. (Female secondary head, England)

One of the primary heads interviewed had previously written about the stages of leadership, describing three stages which he called the autocratic, democratic and withdrawal stages. As a new head autocracy comes naturally and it is understandable and even perhaps necessary to assert the centrality of the head's position.

It has distinct virtues. It brings the staff together so that as a group, it identifies the position of the leader clearly, it creates security; psychologically, it is not far removed from the approach a new headteacher might take to a new class – the early days required a firm statement of the teacher's expectations. (Winkley, 1989, p. 17)

This does not, of course, give the head permission to 'plough furrows through the feelings of staff' and over time the head has to resist 'a dangerous totalitarian temptation to remain the boss' and, argues Winkley, it is dangerous for the school to remain fixated round this centrifugal point. So the leader has to work towards careful understanding of the meaning and context of the school if she wishes the school and staff to grow.

The third stage strengthens the autonomy of the group and the leader is able to withdraw, changing her role to allow staff to take the initiative, providing opportunities for leadership to be exercised by other members of staff. The role of the head becomes more of an advisory, evaluative one in which she can take part as an equal member of the group. Teamwork is a characteristic of this third mature phase.

Teamwork

The importance of working with teams was mentioned by several of the interviewees. The collective ownership of ideas is contained in the following account from a secondary head:

I hate the phrase 'my school' – I really do believe in teams. I can honestly say that I often do not know which ideas have come from me and which from the rest of the senior management team. (Male secondary head, England)

Others spoke about the importance to them personally of being part of a team, recognising their own weaknesses and relying on the team to add their strengths and synergy. Synergy and shared responsibility are illustrated in the following example from an American headteacher who described the creation of independent teams:

There is no way I can do all the things that need to be done without the help of staff. Everyone on my staff belongs to a design team (working party) which is independent of me. We have design teams for curriculum development, curriculum adoption, student success, teachers' well-being, community liaison, correspondence [communications], pupil support, resources and PTA. This leads to more synergy and shared responsibility. (Male primary head, USA)

Doing it 'with' rather than 'through' staff was how one secondary head described it, while another saw himself as 'the new Captain Kirk':

I try to work in teams. I see myself in the new rather than the old Star Trek style. The original Captain Kirk stayed on the bridge making decisions; the new one calls meetings. (Male secondary head, Wales)

Three of the explicit purposes of teamwork were to utilise the different talents available, get things done more effectively; and enhance professional development:

> *I like being part of a team and I'm a good starter, full of enthusiasm, but not so good at finishing, which is where the team is so important. (Female primary head, England)*

> *I believe in empowering other staff to take opportunities – for their own personal development but most importantly because this is the way to get things done effectively. You can't have an ego trip and believe that heads are the sole font of wisdom or the only ones that can do anything well. An effective school has a team approach. (Female secondary head, Scotland)*

> *It is important to be able to recognise and build leadership in others. For me it's building a community of learners and utilising the strengths of those around me. (Male primary head, USA)*

It was, in the view of some heads, a source of job satisfaction to see the growth, moving on and promotion of their colleagues. Three of the women heads spoke about the importance of, and enjoyment in, seeing others develop and creating the opportunities for them to do so:

> *I do genuinely enjoy seeing other people develop. (Female primary head, England)*

> *I believe in creating an environment where there are opportunities for other people to grow. It is very rewarding when people you work with get promotion and move on. (Female secondary head, England)*

> *I always encourage staff to develop themselves, professionally and personally. At the moment, two of us, out of a staff of nine, are doing masters courses. (Female primary head, England)*

The significance of the school itself as the prime site for learning is also a common theme. One primary head who described himself as 'a facilitator of learning' sees this as being achieved through a clear message to staff that they are valued and that where mutual trust and a learning climate exist, effectiveness can follow:

> *School must be a place where they [staff] are seriously valued. I don't expect to create personal friendships among the staff but do want to create relationships that allow us to trust and respect each other so that we can take the risks necessary to be more effective. We are all learners and my role is to facilitate the learning. (Male primary head, Canada)*

What is the most important aspect of the job?

There was a remarkable level of agreement among heads about the most important aspects of their jobs, regardless of their sex, country, or phase of school. There were three predominant themes:

- managing and motivating others
- creating an environment, or ethos, for people to grow and function more effectively
- establishing a direction and creating a vision.

'Leading', 'motivating', 'inspiring, and 'encouraging' were words used in describing the relationship with staff. However collegial those relationships, heads clearly saw a distinctive leadership role.

> *To make sure it is possible for teachers to do their job and that they do it. (Male primary head, Scotland)*

Another primary headteacher recognised the delicate balance between leadership directed at children and leadership which is motivational for staff.

> *To lead and motive others [is the most important aspect of my job]. After I had been here for a short time one of the teachers told me that I cared about children more than the staff. It made me rethink what I was doing and I realised that an important part of my job is to manage people. Adults need your care as well. (Female primary head, Scotland)*

A secondary head was convinced that his energies had to be devoted to staff:

> *No question. Working with staff. In the end the quality of education to kids is delivered in the classroom. The head has to make life more bearable for staff by making the working conditions better, creating resources, and supporting policies that set perimeters. It all depends upon what people are doing in the classroom. (Male secondary head, England)*

Further light is thrown on this delicate balance by a secondary headteacher who emphasised that 'getting the best out of people' means not only support but confronting and raising expectations.

> *Getting the best out of people you work with: staff, children and parents. Some children come here from extraordinary circumstances. They need to feel secure and supported but not patronised. We expect the same standards from them as anyone else and the idea of low expectations because of disadvantage is anathema. (Male secondary head, England)*

Getting the best out of people was seen by a number of heads as a process which comes through an ethos of opportunity, creating resources, 'conditions', 'environment', 'context' which enable people to work effectively and well.

> *To provide the context and opportunities for staff to make an effective contribution to the running of the school and to curriculum development. (Female secondary head, Scotland)*

> *A good head creates the environment to allow other people to do their job to the best of their ability. (Male special school head, England)*

*Creating a school culture where the weakest member at any given time is being sup-
ported in their growth in the recognition that all of us including the principal, are
the weakest member at some point in time. (Male primary head, Canada)*

Three male primary heads spoke about the importance of establishing and
maintaining a vision.

*Clarity of vision, knowing what a school could be like and being able in whatever
way to communicate that. (Male primary head, England)*

*To establish the direction and vision, ensure that there is a shared vision and a clar-
ity of purpose which is to serve this community and help the children and their
parents in every way we can. (Male primary head, Scotland)*

*Leadership and vision. I've been in schools where everyone is doing their own thing
and in schools where everyone is moving in the same direction. Both are hard. But
by far, doing your own thing in isolation is much harder. (Male primary head, USA)*

What is the most enjoyable aspect of the job?

What is important and what is enjoyable may often coincide. Most of the
heads spoke about loving the job, the satisfaction, the challenge and excitement which one head described as a 'privilege'. It was, according to a primary
head, 'the best job in the world'. Asked what they enjoyed most about their job
it was the 'people things' that came immediately to the fore – 'working with
people', 'interaction', 'engagement' and 'sharing'. Regardless of the age group
they were responsible for, most of the heads spoke about the pupils as the
main source of their enjoyment:

*I enjoy the interaction with kids and the variety. Every day is different . . . It's a
good feeling helping kids and knowing that school is the only safe haven for some of
them. (Male secondary head, Canada)*

Rather than seeing children as a drain on energy, they could be the *source* of
energy, as one American head describes it.

*I love being around young children and find that some of their energy transfers to me.
When I'm stressed I head straight for the kindergarten. (Male primary head, Canada)*

Although the exhilaration of being with children was a predominant theme
among primary heads, secondary heads also found it a source of personal and
professional satisfaction to see children grow, through the teenage years and
into adulthood.

*Seeing children achieve and develop into confident young adults who feel at ease
with themselves and the community they live in. (Male secondary head, England)*

*I love teenagers; their excitement of life. They are fresh and honest with their feed-
back. They are at a stage in their lives when they are learning about themselves.
(Female secondary head, Australia)*

Working with young people. There is a constant source of reward watching them develop and sharing their pleasure in the things they've achieved. Only in secondary schools do you get real engagement with young adults. They make extraordinary progress between the ages of eleven to eighteen. (Female secondary head, England)

Meeting ex-pupils was also an important source of satisfaction for two of the primary heads. Being remembered, getting 'a pat on the back' was a tangible token that, however little feedback there may be during the school years, the long-term investment in young people's learning is eventually recognised and pays off:

In the summer I went to the retirement function of the head of my previous school. I met some of my ex-pupils who are now adults, had been to university and done really well. They remembered me as a good teacher. (Female primary head, England)

My greatest enjoyment is when pupils from high schools come back and pat us on our backs. When they come back and ask us for advice it shows they still have confidence in us as teachers, even though they left us four or five years ago. (Male primary head, South Africa)

The challenge, the opportunities, the variety, and the constantly evolving nature of the job prevented boredom and apathy. 'No two days are the same', 'no one day is the same as the next' were persistent themes, and although the job is demanding and stressful, as a headteacher you could 'make things happen'.

[I enjoy] Most of it! It's never boring, you deal with a huge variety of issues – a distressed child one moment and writing a policy the next. The job is fantastically varied – very demanding and very interesting. It's a privilege to see children developing with you. When you're a head you can make things happen for staff or for children. It's great! (Female secondary head, England)

What is the most difficult and least enjoyable?

The most difficult aspects of the job turned out to be the least enjoyable too. There was considerable agreement about what this was:

- criticising staff
- dealing with redundancy
- selection and retention
- low status of teachers
- misinformation about state education
- administration
- pace of change
- lack of time.

Almost all the heads, regardless of their sex or phase, found criticising staff the most difficult thing they had to undertake as part of their job:

having to confront staff when things are not going according to plan. I want to be encouraging, praising and accentuating the positive, but sometimes there comes a time when you have to point out that someone's practice is not in line with our policies. It's difficult to balance my high expectations that everything will be perfect at all times, with the reality of school life which is tiring and challenging. (Female nursery head, England)

It makes me sad when I have to criticise adults about something. I know I have to do it sometimes but I do not like hurting people and inside I am thinking this is really hard. (Female primary head, England)

It's very rare but occasionally I've had to talk to a teacher about something that I do not like happening in a classroom which is against the ethos and beliefs of the school. (Female primary head, England)

Having to confront other people with things that aren't going right and trying to do it in a way that helps people accept it and be able to grow through it. (Female secondary head, England)

Dealing with disciplinary issues involving staff or students – making judgements about people that are so significant and important. (Male secondary head, England)

The next most difficult and least enjoyable thing they had to face was making staff redundant.

In my first term of headship I had to make four staff redundant. If I had known that was going to happen I would not have applied for the job. For a long time after, understandably, staff were mistrustful of management and I had to work hard to change that. (Female nursery head, England)

A few cited staffing selection and retention issues as the most difficult thing they did.

Not being able to keep young, eager, good teachers because of staffing constraints. Selecting for posts when there is more than one good candidate. (Female secondary head, Scotland)

I find the process of selecting staff difficult too. We do it scrupulously but I don't relish the process of selection because it means rejection and that sometimes includes good people because there are not enough vacancies. (Male secondary head, England)

I find staff selection very hard, probably because I'm aware how important it is. (Male special school, England)

The heads, particularly the men, were very unhappy about the status of teachers in society and the amount of misinformation about state schools that was current.

The status of teachers, which has been undermined and can only make the job more difficult. I think raising the status of teachers is even more important than an increase in salaries. (Male secondary head, England)

We are suffering from chronic centralisation of the intellectual agenda. There's a sense in which we're under siege from people who don't teach and who treat teachers with subliminal contempt. I worry about the nature of power of men in these centralist positions – most of them are men and most people in teaching are women. Teachers have been disenfranchised from the debate. They are like the First World War troops in the trenches. I'm not complacent about schools; we've hardly tapped into what children can do, but this is not the way forward and not the way to encourage young people into the profession. (Male primary head, England)

The frustration of having the wrong story told about education. Having to spend huge amounts of time dispelling untruths and fighting against the consequences of the disparagement of the British system. I often wonder why the brightest and best young people would ever want to come into teaching given what they hear about it although it is in reality one of the most wonderful jobs. (Male secondary head, England)

This view was not restricted to the UK contingent. It was echoed by a Canadian head too.

The amount of criticism and misinformation that is around about education. Schools are blamed for every ill of society. Plus [I do not enjoy] the paperwork, lack of funding and political interference. (Male secondary head, Canada)

Most of the primary heads mentioned administration as one of their main dislikes.

I think I'm a teacher rather than a head so I find the administration difficult. I've discovered that if you leave it for a long time a lot of it becomes out of date. (Female nursery head, England)

Paperwork. Sometimes I come in and want to burn it all. (Female primary head, England)

The pace of change and the lack of time to do the job were mentioned frequently as pet hates.

Not having enough time to engage in the remarkable number of things teachers have to deal with. Some changes have been needed but the pace of change and the lack of resources to support change have not been helpful. (Male secondary head, England)

Lack of time to do things and so not being able to achieve all you want to. (Female secondary head, England)

A few heads did not enjoy having so little time for themselves and complained about finding it difficult to find time for thinking. Again, this was not just the English:

Staying on top of everything and taking time for myself. (Male secondary head, Canada)

And one experienced head (who has since left headship) was worried about how long you can sustain the role:

> *keeping going. The pure remorselessness of the job can be demanding and worrying. (Male primary head, England)*

Managing the budget was an additional cause of concern for one secondary and two primary heads.

One of the heads interviewed after the first round of OFSTED inspections was clear that she had not enjoyed the experience of being inspected.

> *Although we got an excellent report, I did not enjoy the pressure that the OFSTED inspection put us under. I could not believe how much it affected me and the staff. Once it was over I thought it was wrong and felt abused by the process even though some good things came out of it. We stood still for a year. We did not develop, we just polished things that were already excellent. During that time we did not grow as a school. We are now growing again. (Female primary head, England)*

Given another chance . . .

The heads were asked if they would have done anything differently, knowing what they know now. Almost all of them mentioned pacing themselves differently, not being so impatient, doing some things a little slower and others a little quicker.

> *Be more focused and more realistic. Not to expect changes to happen immediately. (Female primary head, England)*

> *As a new head you try too hard – you can kill yourself or burn yourself out. I worked very hard and got very tired. (Female primary head, England)*

> *Pace myself a bit better, the first few years were very draining and demanding. I would learn not to be frustrated that you cannot do everything at once. (Female secondary head, Scotland)*

> *Be a bit less conscientious. When I came to the school it had to be changed; it was 'do or die' and extraordinarily hard work. A lot of fun though! I'm not sure I could do it differently. (Female secondary head, Scotland)*

> *Loads of things. Particularly space things out better, be a bit less urgent and obsessional and not allow myself to get so over-tired. (Female primary secondary head, England)*

And finally, one of the interviewees summed up what he thought were the essential attributes of a successful head.

> *I try and have a sensitive heart but the skin of a rhinoceros. (Male primary head, England)*

4

■ ■ ■

The Dilemmas of Leadership

With the arrival of a new headteacher, schools can 'turn around' and move from disaster to triumph. Losses are turned into gains. Low achievement becomes high achievement. The new head knows what to do to put things right because there is an unwritten rulebook of good, and even 'best', practice.

Viewed from a distance this seems to describe what actually happens, and the gloss in the literature and the rhetoric of the politician endorses that neat and tidy state of the art. Headteachers who have had an impact on schools, however, tell a different story. The Effective Leadership study (MacBeath, 1998) which included 40 heads from four countries, explored the anxiety, the stress, the dilemmas, the human side of leadership. It failed to find a golden rulebook or recipe for effective leadership but did identify ways of increasing our understanding of, and response to, dilemmas.

A common response among headteachers, no matter their country of origin, was to assume a mask of efficiency and confidence. Their dilemmas were dealt with behind their office door, often a very lonely place. Angus Macdonald, a Scottish headteacher who was a participant in that study, described how you can fool most of the people most of the time. Whether as a conscious strategy or simply by virtue of status and position, staff, parents and pupils assume that a head knows what he or she is doing. He or she is seen as operating in a rational and strategic manner, weighing the evidence, considering alternatives, drawing on considered knowledge of the school and its community, behaving rationally and with forethought. The reality, says Angus Macdonald, is nothing like this. Drawing on his own experience as a headteacher, he proposes the matrix shown in Figure 4.1.

Leaders, he suggests (Macdonald, 1998), quite often make decisions and judgements in the condition of surprise. This is an ability admired and valued by others. But he writes:

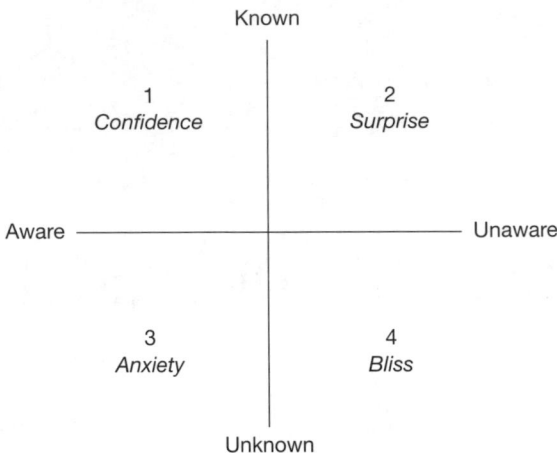

Figure 4.1: Macdonald's matrix
(*Source*: Macdonald (1998))

> *In this condition, the leaders surprise themselves. It occurs where a new situation has arisen and the leader is surprised to find himself or herself reacting with a sense of sureness of touch, of knowing just what to do and then doing it. It is as though the leader was unaware of what he or she knew until the situation itself demanded the response and he found it already formed. It may be to do with unarticulated knowledge, or it may be to do with the ability to see through the detail of the situation to the fundamental issues, and then to apply the relevant principles to produce a resolution. Whatever, it is much prized by others because it conveys a sense of ability to 'think on one's feet', or of a very profound depth of experience. It inspires confidence and trust. For this reason, the wise leader will keep his or her sense of surprise well hidden and will look exactly as they would have, had they been aware of this all along. (p. 167)*

In terms of how it looks from the outside, this (quadrant 2 of Figure 4.1) is virtually indistinguishable from quadrant 1. Perhaps, suggests Macdonald, this is why it is so seldom acknowledged. It is in quadrant 3, anxiety, that, he claims, most decisions and judgements are made. Many situations do not allow a headteacher time to research all the things she should do and should know about, but shrewd leadership means minimising the uncertainty as far possible, consolidating, developing fall-back positions, 'staging' any commitment to the decision, to allow flexibility of response as more information emerges. None the less, Macdonald continues:

> *the degree of uncertainty creates anxiety and the more the leader is aware of what he or she does not know, the greater the anxiety will be. This condition also can lead to the paralysis of leadership, because it can of course affect the individual to a major degree; this is why leadership requires real courage. One of the most difficult tasks a leader has is to sustain both flexibility of response and the belief in the outcome that*

inspired the decision in the first place, during the gap between the commitment to the decision and the realisation of the outcome itself. Anything that goes wrong within this time gap, however unconnected it may seem to be, tends to be linked to the original decision, especially if it was contentious. The leader must uphold and defend the decision while bearing in mind the possibility that the connection might, in truth, be there. (p. 168)

There is a close parallel with David Hargreaves's matrix (Figure 4.2). Hargreaves (1998) distinguishes 'recognised knowledge', 'recognised ignorance', 'unrecognised knowledge' and 'unrecognised ignorance'. The last of these is Macdonald's state of 'bliss' (quadrant 4 in Figure 4.1). But as Macdonald says, it is also the *terra incognita*, the rock on which leadership may perish.

If this were a Mediaeval Management Matrix, this quadrant would be clearly marked 'Terra Incognita' and 'Here be Monsters' for this is truly unknown territory and monsters do lurk here – the monstrously unlucky, the monstrously unlikely and the monstrously unfair – and they can take any form. Every leader carries this 'Terra Incognita' into every situation, however familiar, or new, it may appear; this condition is so all-pervading and permanent that we cease to recognise it and we operate in practice often as though it does not exist. Perhaps this is necessary or else leadership would really be paralysed; except that good leadership allows for it and takes action. (p. 168)

In the blissful state *terra incognita* is devoid of dilemma. The dilemmas occur very explicitly in quadrant 2 – when we become aware of our own ignorance. But they also occur in quadrant 1 – becoming fully aware of what we know but then paralysed by that very knowledge. It has been said that to know all is to forgive all, and that is a far more problematic state psychologically than the bliss of quadrant 4.

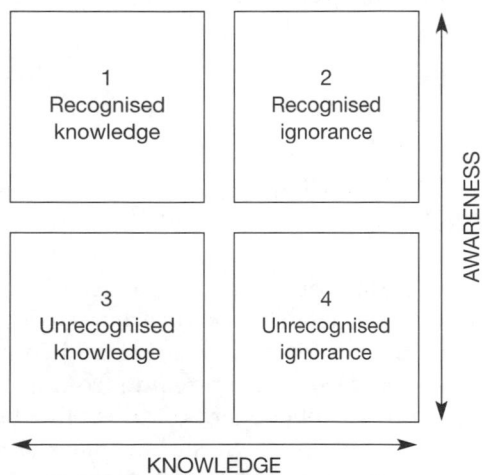

Figure 4.2: Hargreaves's matrix
(*Source*: Hargreaves (1998))

In the study that Angus Macdonald describes, headteachers did not find it easy to explore in depth with one another their most acute ethical dilemmas. Perhaps they did not know each other well enough to dig too deeply into those private struggles. Perhaps the issues raised were too painful and personal to revisit in depth. Interviews with the research team did, however, offer a more confidential and safe context, and exploration of diaries and spontaneous informal discussions revealed many of the anxieties that headteachers face. As researchers, we were sometimes admitted into that lonely place where dilemmas are resolved and decisions made, sometimes agonisingly.

At these moments of weighing the balance, often intuitively rather than with an array of considered alternatives, headteachers had recourse to their fundamental values in guiding their actions. Where there was a conscious counterbalancing of options, the dilemmas were framed in terms of competing principles:

- children's entitlement or good financial housekeeping?
- targeting children who might improve the school's position in the league tables or attending to those with the greatest learning difficulties?
- the good of the school as a whole or one's own personal kudos?

This wrestling with the complexities of ethical decision-making is an important, enduring and increasing feature of professional life. That is the conclusion of researchers who have explored beneath the surface of headteacher behaviour. A recent study by Clive Dimock (1996) in Australia concluded that situations were more likely to be perceived as dilemmas when four conflicting conditions were present:

- there was an expectation of, or perceived need for, a successful resolution;
- the leader would personally have to shoulder the responsibility for the outcome;
- there was a commensurate lack of control or influence over the outcome;
- there was a high degree of incompatibility between resolving the issue and attainment of other desired goals.

In other words, there was, inherent in the situation, a counterpoint of conflicting expectations, 'not only from the outside but from the inside too', as one headteacher put it. From the outside, parents, teachers, students and governing bodies looked to certain outcomes, to assured leadership, but also to a listening and receptive ear. There was a desire to be consulted and involved and at the same time a wish for authoritative and conviction-led decision-making. Conflicting sets of expectations came from the inside too, from 'the internalised others', from the inner board of directors who could at times push and pull in different directions. The author Jack Black (1994) describes the tensions from his own personal inner board which, he says, includes Richard Branson, Billy Connolly and Jesus Christ.

Clive Dimock classified dilemmas in two ways. There are those that revolve around tensions of personal role, status and position. Then there are those that are concerned with the purposes and functions of schooling, its structures and processes, its curriculum, the nature of teaching and learning, and the flow of resources. The second set of dilemmas has greatly increased as a consequence of educational restructuring, but they bring in their wake a sharpening of the first set of dilemmas too.

Examples of dilemmas to do with role and status include the following:

- To what extent am I personally accountable for the short-term attainment outcomes of my pupils? How do I reconcile this with my own priorities to help staff focus on lifelong learning?

- To what extent am I the director of a self-managing school and to what extent an agent of external bodies (the local authority, the Department, the Government)?

- Is my first duty to the internal community of the school, to the external community, or to parents?

- To what extent should I maintain and preserve the *status quo,* and to what extent should I be the initiator of change?

- Should I emphasise school evaluation for development and improvement purposes or for accountability?

Dilemmas to do with restructuring include:

- How do I maintain the traditional structures but introduce new ways of working?

- How do I preserve status and position while challenging hierarchy and rigid adherence to authority?

- How can staff morale be maintained in the face of limited opportunities to offer incentives and rewards?

- How do I empower parents and students without disempowering or threatening teachers?

- How do I find the balance between academic/cognitive and personal/ social development?

- How do I encourage a more effective use of time and resources when both are in increasingly short supply?

Dimock's separation of these two sets of dilemmas is in some senses an arbitrary one since both rest on basic values, on such questions as 'what is the moral purpose of education?' and 'what scope and responsibility do I carry for realising that moral purpose?'

Those moral purposes are, perhaps, best understood in terms of stability and change, the tension between stable moral values and unstable social norms. The impulse which took someone into teaching, and ultimately into a position of leadership, may sit uncomfortably with how that role is being redefined in a changing national and international context. The roots of the dilemma have their origins in those first uncomplicated days and weeks in the learning classroom.

The origins of ethical dilemmas – the classroom teacher

When considerations of security, salary and career are set to one side, the common driving motivation to be a teacher is to bring about a change in the lives of children and young people. As in medicine, counselling, social and community work, there is one underpinning value position – to bring about changes that are in the client's own best interests. As Neil Dempster (1998) describes it, the surgeon alters the physical status of patients by operating on their bodies in order to improve their health; the psychologist aims to bring about improvements in a client's mental health by means of specialised conversations; and the teacher provides experiences that will help children to make the transition to more informed and effective adults. The headteacher orchestrates relationships and environment so as to allow teachers and pupils to learn and grow together.

It is when these deep moral purposes seem to be compromised by pragmatic and political considerations that dilemmas begin to surface. The young teacher with her first class may experience an initial exhilaration: 'This is what I came into teaching for.' Learning and teaching is all that exists in her world, and there is a pristine simplicity in the blossoming relationship of teacher and learners. With time, however, things change. Other considerations begin to loom larger. There are demands from outside – demands on monitoring attendance, formal assessment, tracking progress, marking and returning homework, chasing the miscreants, threatening and employing sanctions, having recourse to higher authorities to intervene, keeping up with the imperatives of a changing curriculum. There is a shifting perception of role from 'me in my classroom' to 'us in the school'. You are no longer a teacher in a classroom with your door closed, but a member of a corporate enterprise in which teaching is not your own and in which even you are not your own.

The internal honeymoon relationship within the classroom undergoes a change too, sometimes sooner rather than later. The term lengthens, the nights become longer, the weather worsens. There are shifts in relationships within the classroom. It becomes a more complex place. The lives of children begin to unfold in greater complexity. There is neither the time nor the permission to get to 'know' the 30 children let alone the 150 or 200 that a secondary teacher may see in the course of a week. Keeping distance is the first rule and one that, when breached, leads to a tortured place.

The moral dilemmas of the classroom have been portrayed vividly in first-hand accounts of teachers. The imperative of distance is vividly described by

Gary Cornog (1970) in the collection of essays entitled *Don't Smile Until Christmas*.

> *It seemed to me that I became more effective as I became less genuine as an individual. When I had periodic lapses into my actual personality I felt these were invariably detrimental in my attempt to teach. They hurt me because they made me vulnerable to attempts by the students to fraternise. Fraternisation made objectivity difficult for me and totally destroyed my credibility as an enforcer of discipline in the class. (p. 15)*

In his book *The Way it Spozed to be* James Herndon (1968) describes the massive inertia he faced in trying to move beyond the conservative expectations of his pupils. 'That's not the way it spozed to be, Mr Herndon', was their reflex response to any attempt to innovate, to challenge, to bend the expectations of a class of black children in a Harlem junior high school.

The tension between inspirational teaching and way it 'spozed' to be continues as a common strand as classroom teachers move on to become departmental heads, deputy heads and headteachers. While they may not always want to, they experience a strong need to move up the ladder and to move progressively away from the prime motive which brought them into the profession. While a few may be relieved to escape from the classroom, leaders tend to be chosen from those who made a success of classroom teaching. As heads, they want to keep their connections with teaching and learning, with children and young people. Most of the English and Scottish heads in our study wanted to spend time with children. They were interested in learning. This was particularly true of primary heads. Most didn't want to be managers or chief executives. They didn't want to spend their time on paperwork, policy and politics. Yet they found they had to give priority to external relationships, to manoeuvring and negotiation, to compromise and ingratiation.

In Chapter 2 we described the dilemma of the Chicago principals. These American heads had grown away from their roots. They were gradually losing touch with the motivations that had brought them into the profession. The balance of work has shifted, highlighting deep-seated tensions between maintenance and development, between managing and leading schools. As reported by studies of leadership in other countries, principalship find the job a lonely one.

Thomas Sergiovanni (1992) writes:

> *The most dramatic change in moving from your staff position into a leadership role is the loss of peers . . . promotion also diminishes support. You will not always have to respond entirely alone but you will usually have to respond first and orchestrate the response of others who will take their cue from you and most key leadership decisions, especially sensitive ones, are made in relative isolation. (p. 151)*

The dilemma of the headteacher is decision-taking in isolation and with a keen eye to the 'way it spozed to be'. So, like new teachers, new heads may try not to move too fast but experience the forces of inertia pushing them to conserve while innovating, stabilise while changing, bend while remaining unbending. The world-wide trend to devolve responsibility to the individual school and thence to the person of the head – where the buck stops – simply intensifies the dilemma.

Managing devolution

The American terminology of 'site management' puts the nature of the dilemma in stark terms. The 'site' is a large complex physical space demanding constant vigilance and maintenance. It is occupied by adults and children representing most of the age spectrum, a cross-cut of the socio-economic population, bringing with them day on day the full gamut of social problems into this compact arena. Security from the world outside, policing of the world inside, managing personnel, ensuring financial viability and long-term sustainability are the bottom-line preoccupations from which many headteachers and principals never manage to escape.

The devolution of authority to the school site is perhaps the most acute source of the ambivalence in leadership. It goes variously by the name of LMS – local management of schools, DSM – devolved school management, SBM – site-based management or SBL – site-based leadership. In the measure that it has brought increased latitude and powers to school senior management, it has commensurately increased accountability. And dilemma.

In the Effective Leadership study heads were asked to identify their dilemmas, to describe them, and then to join with others in finding ways of addressing them. This helped them to recognise that their dilemmas were not free-standing roadblocks but were closely interconnected. This information helped the heads deal with the dilemmas that had to be dealt with in the knowledge and understanding of their contextual interrelationship.

The following identifies the four main dilemmas.

Dilemma 1

In all countries school leaders faced the issue of what to do with underperforming or 'incompetent' staff. In England the difficulties have been exacerbated by the high political profile given to the issue in recent years under both Conservative and New Labour governments. It has become increasingly acceptable to use the language of 'incompetence' to refer to teachers, and taking a tough line on individual teachers is seen as equally justifiable as in any business context where poor performance is intolerable.

For some headteachers this eased rather than heightened the dilemma because it recognised and endorsed the validity of their problem. It gave them hope that someone or somebody might come along like a *deus ex machina* and painlessly extract the troublesome member. This was seen by some as a benefit of OFSTED and if OFSTED's interventions were viewed more positively by heads than by teachers, it was because of this mandate from an external authority against poor teaching.

However, OFSTED's interventions did not necessarily address the ethical dilemma for heads who were conscious of their own complicity or collusion. One problem for heads is that they have also been teachers and can identify with the dilemmas that teachers face at classroom level. They have been there themselves.

Empathy is an important attribute of good leaders but its strong moral content only exacerbates the dilemma, and leaders have to remind themselves from time to time of the first rule of teaching – measured distance. One head expressed the view that it was a no-win situation because to identify, to empathise, meant losing the critical distance, but to distance oneself too much risked compromising the human supportive quality of the relationship. Michael Fullan (1997b, p. 7) says about teachers, 'the more that they become emotionally detached the poorer the decisions they make'. This may also hold true for headteachers.

Dilemma 2

The issue of how to deal with 'incompetent' teachers is related to the second dilemma, expressed as frequently in the Effective Leadership study as among a study of Chicago principals. It has to do with what is described in the USA as 'outcome-based education'. In many countries during the late 1980s and early 1990s governments shifted the educational policy focus from concern for inputs to concern for outcomes. Measures of student achievement became critical yardsticks of how parents and members of the public were enjoined to make judgements about a school's performance. One English headteacher in the study expressed it in this way:

> *We know that we lose quite a number of good local students to other schools in the city because their parents see our results in the League Table – results which, because of our student base, place us in the bottom third of the list. The Council wants to set aside some money from this year's budget to offer ten students from our local primary schools a substantial bursary to attend this school. This money would be taken from the little we have at our discretion and I am troubled by the 'gung-ho' manner in which Council members are discussing a decision which they say will lift our standards. (English headteacher)*

The 'student base' which this head refers to is the social and educational capital of the students refined through aggregated measures of ability of the whole student body. A 'poorly performing school' is one in which those aggregated measures compare unfavourably with other schools. In their book *Good School, Bad School* John Gray and Brian Wilcox (1995) argue that 'raw' exam or test results 'run the distinct risk of rewarding schools for the "quality" of the intakes they can attract rather than what they actually do for pupils'. Quality is treated as synonymous with measured attainment and human beings are treated as some kind of inferior commodity. When figures are then presented to parents as a yardstick by which they can choose schools, it sets in train a downward spiral, a self-fulfilling prophecy, in which poorly performing schools become further impoverished. The nature of the self-fulfilling prophecy has been well documented by school effectiveness researchers for more than a decade. It has been described as the 'compositional effect', which shows that the more a school is drained of its motivated and high-achieving pupils, the greater the downward drag on those who remain. This point is illustrated in MacBeath (1999):

> the point at which individual achievement falls or rises depending on who your peers are and how many of them are high or low achievers. As Douglas Willms showed in the Scottish context, when high achieving pupils leave, some of the school's positive energy source is drained off. Further, when high achieving pupils leave to go to a 'better' school, they may also take with them their more assertive parents and further drain the school of a potential energy or irritant source. (p. 13)

Whether or not school leaders are conversant with the research or the technical concepts, they recognise intuitively and through experience the reality of the importance of intake and the danger of the self-fulfilling prophecy. It is the very awareness of the multi-dimensional nature of the issue that lies at the heart of the dilemma.

Dilemma 3

While much has been made of the isolation of the headteacher, decision-making is not always his or her province. While accountability for outcomes may rest with them, the control over decisions is not necessarily theirs. English headteachers have governing bodies, some of whom are all too willing to defer to the head's judgement but sometimes are also ready to challenge judgements in a way that is not only time-consuming but also contentious. The following dilemma, from a report by the National Association of Head Teachers (NAHT), England and Wales (Rafferty, 1995), illustrates this issue:

> The growth in the number of disputes with governing bodies is causing alarm, with the union reporting an increase in the number of heads under suspension . . . heads were being suspended because they did not see eye-to-eye with their governing bodies and because inspections were creating a 'football-manager syndrome', where the head has to carry the can for poor reports and low league-table placings. (p. 1)

In one school in the Effective Leadership study, a governing body had made a decision in the head's absence. The head, seeing this as running counter to his values and his goals for the school, presented a paper to the governing body. It expresses the frustration that Csikszentmihalyi (1990, p. 7) says is 'deeply woven into the fabric of life'. This was the head's paper:

Head's Expectations of the Governing Body

(1) To be always aware that they are partners, with staff, parents and the community, through the local authority, in providing the best education possible for the children who attend the school they govern.

(2) To recognise that although they have been given the ultimate responsibility and authority for the management of the school, the fundamental responsibility in practice rests with the headteacher and the staff.

(3) To recognise that their value to the partnership is directly proportional to:

a) their knowledge and understanding of the process of education
b) their awareness of current issues that relate to the education system
c) their knowledge and experience of how the school is managed and how the children are educated
d) their relationships with all the other partners
e) their knowledge and understanding of the children's needs.

(4) To recognise that a) to e) demand a commitment of time and energy that has to be prioritised so that they are able to offer what most benefits the education of children.

The report from the NAHT has its own evidence of governors 'stepping over the mark', at least as seen from a headteacher perspective:

we do not find it acceptable for a head to return to the office to find governors who have gone through files and then make comments about the headteacher's efficiency . . . governors should leave the day-to-day running of schools to the head, but those who are happy to take the lead from the head when things are going well should not then dissociate themselves when things go wrong. Delegates complained that some governors liked the power, but walked away from responsibility. (Rafferty, 1995, p. 2).

From the governors' side, however, comes the counter-argument:

Governors are not just heads' supporters clubs. In many cases they do not do all their tasks and the head moves into the vacuum. But where they do take on their full role, they find the head does not like it. (National Association of Governors)

From the head's viewpoint, the dilemma is created by a failure to grasp the differences between strategic and operational issues, those things that are the province of governors and those things that belong in the province of the head. Drawing a clear line in the sand between these two proves, however, not to be a simple matter. Neat distinctions may lie in the domain of logic but, like all dilemmas, the solution also lies in the emotional and moral arena.

Dilemma 4

'Problem students' was one of the roadblocks identified by Chicago principals. Others might have expressed the same issue somewhat differently. They might have talked about 'students with problems' or 'problems created socially' or even by the school itself. All of these have a perennial quality but they have taken a more acute form in the 1990s. The pervasiveness and perniciousness of the 'drug culture' is a new phenomenon and the dilemmas created by it have also to be seen in the context of the three issues discussed above.

Drug abuse among young people is viewed with horror by most parents, and schools tread a wary line, anticipating the exposé by a sensationalist press. The following dilemma, articulated by an English headteacher in the study, illustrates the tension between the marketplace of public relations and the need to address an important educational issue:

> *I dare not admit publicly that we've got a drugs problem in the school in case it damages our reputation. This would mean that we would lose pupils and therefore funding. Yet, if I don't admit it we can't undertake a concerted effort with the parents and support services to tackle it properly. Neither do I want to permanently exclude the offending students as other schools have done even though I know that would improve our reputation. (English headteacher)*

Seeking solutions

How, then, are dilemmas resolved? They tend to be resolved pragmatically, 'on the hoof', often with retrospective *Angst* – Was it the right decision? What could have been done differently? Critical incident analysis is one useful tool in helping to take a more objective and systematic view so that it is possible to learn from mistakes as well as successes. Understanding critical incident analysis helps people to stand back from the event and unpack it in detailed sequence. This can identify where the key points of decision-making lie, and raise issues about influences on decision-making. With the wisdom of hindsight it is possible to ask – 'What could have been done differently?', 'Who was best placed to do that?', 'What would I/we do differently next time?'

Another useful strategy is 'reframing'. Like critical incident analysis, this can be used in hindsight to revisit a situation and see it in a different light. Better still, it can be used prospectively at the point of decision-making. The metaphor of the 'frame' is a useful one. The theory is that in any situation we enter we put a frame around it. Like a photograph it is 'snapped' from a chosen angle, mentally cropped beforehand (and perhaps physically cropped afterwards) to tell a story, convey an image, contained and bounded on four sides. This focuses our attention on key features. The frame defines what we see and, both helpfully and unhelpfully, limits what we see. Without the frame it is difficult to interpret events, but with the frame in place it can be understood more easily in terms of past events or with reference to other similar scenes from our recorded experience. The kind of frame we choose for any given situation will, however, vary according to all kinds of historical and psychological factors. It may or may not be the appropriate frame for that particular situation, and when we don't frame it appropriately we may be led towards the wrong conclusions.

Bolman and Deal (1991) have written extensively on the subject of reframing, applying the principle to organisations, roles and goals, motives and motivation. They identify four kinds of frame:

- the structural frame
- the human resource frame
- the political frame
- the symbolic frame.

The first kind, the structural frame, views the organisation in terms of goals and roles. It is concerned with strategic management issues, the vertical command structure and the lateral informal structures. A headteacher walking through the entrance hall and witnessing a scene of disorder might interpret what she sees in terms of 'Who is in charge here?' 'What rules are being broken?'

The human resource frame sees things more in terms of needs and motives. It perceives an environment in which people's behaviour is shaped by their expectations, satisfactions and priorities. Coming upon disorder from this point of view, the headteacher may immediately wonder what sets of environmental conditions or interactions have provoked this and can explain it. How might the environment be changed to redress the situation?

The political frame focuses on authority, resources, struggles for influence and power, bargaining, trade-off and compromise. If the disorderly conduct is viewed from this political frame, the headteacher may instinctively think in terms of win–lose or win–win, preserving her own authority, while also saving face for others.

The fourth and final frame, the symbolic frame, looks for meaning and symbols. It sees in metaphors, ritual and ceremony. It tries to understand situations with terms of deeper values such as trust, hope, commitment and faith. The head with this mind-set may feel deeply disappointed that her trust appears to have been betrayed and may feel that disorder is simply pointing towards some deeper unfulfilled human need to be addressed rather than dealing only with its surface manifestations.

Framing is both an instinctive and a learned response. The instinctive response to a meeting with a gorilla is to frame it as a flight, or fight, situation. The Jane Goodalls of the world, who have lived with gorillas, have acquired a quite different framing response. Their way of seeing has been learned and then internalised as a habit of insight. So reframing in school leadership can also become habitual, a way of responding instinctively and intuitively in that moment when a decision has to be made. The school leader who has acquired the ability to view things through many frames is in possession of the tool of 'multi-framing'. Her advantage is in seeing the situation simultaneously through a number of different lenses.

Reframing offers new insights. That is an intrinsically valuable asset for school leaders. But it need not stop there because reframing almost always requires that action follows. In common with other leadership gurus, Steven Covey (1989) advocates the logical extension of this as going for the 'win–win'. Indeed, Covey describes the 'win–win' as 'a frame of mind'. It is one that

> *constantly seeks mutual benefit in all human interactions. Win–win means that agreements or solutions are mutually beneficial, mutually satisfying. With a win–win solution, all parties feel good about the decision and feel committed to the action plan. A person with a win–win attitude sees life as a co-operative not a competitive arena. (p. 207)*

We might test the tools of reframing and the 'win–win' by applying them to the dilemmas above. How might we see the incompetence issue (dilemma 1) differently? Figure 4.3 illustrates a tool that has been used in a management context to categorise staff. It has an immediate appeal to management because it is easy to begin to slot people into their niche. We might even say it 'frames' them beautifully. The act of doing so, however, is likely to freeze them more permanently into that posture. Reframing would take them out of the frame and offer them four possible choices of frame, dependent on time of day, week, year, or dependent on mood, context, events, relationships. Aren't we all dead-beats at some time or other? Aren't we all go-getters in some aspects of our personal and professional lives? Haven't we all got subversive and political tendencies when it seems appropriate?

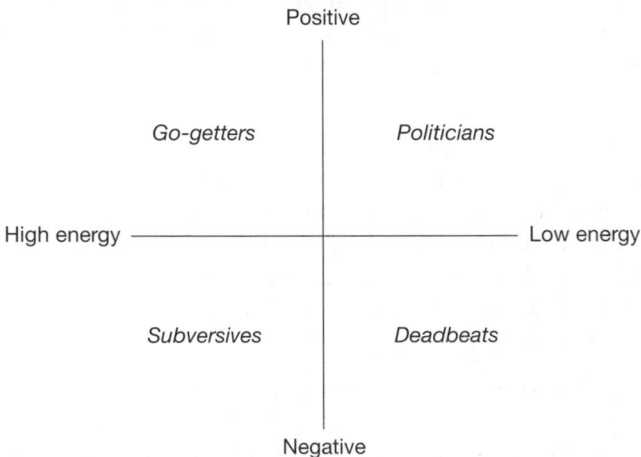

Figure 4.3: The framing grid

Rather than looking at the qualities of the individual as if they were inherent, the reframing (Figure 4.4) looks at the situation which constrains people to act in certain ways. It moves from Bolman and Deal's structural frame to the human resource frame. Reframing the issue of incompetence involves a shift of focus away from the portrait to the landscape, removing the individual as the central figure and focusing instead on the wider scene.

Ted Wragg (1998) warns against too easy an acceptance of the kind of labelling that comes easily to the lips of politicians and journalists. In an attempt to redress the lack of research evidence on the subject, he is concluding a two-year study, the Teaching Competence project, which is amassing evidence from 1800 interviews and 650 case studies. He finds evidence that so-called 'incompetent teachers' may be viewed as 'competent' in another school context. He warns of the danger of ascribing the perceived competence or incompetence to the inherent qualities of the individual rather than to the context in which they find themselves, or to the interaction between the individual and their behaviour setting.

This is not to deny that there are, by virtually all measures, teachers who should not be in schools. There are those who have given up or become disillusioned, their ingrained cynicism and antipathy to their own learning and professional development having managed to survive the decades. There are teachers who, by their own admission, cannot exercise their own will over thirty young people, yet cling on through suffering for want of other alterna-

1　Individually write the name of a place, a time of day/week/year, an activity or event which makes you feel positive/high energy, negative/low energy and so on.

2　Come together as a group to discuss what you have written. Identify three things that might be done to shift negatives to positives.

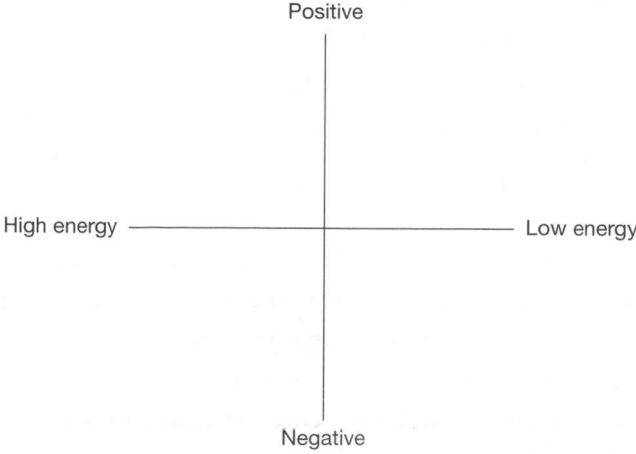

Figure 4.4: A staff exercise in reframing

tives. This does not invalidate the attempt to seek a 'win–win'. Some of these teachers might be excellent in different roles or within different kinds of structures and in different kinds of relationship, perhaps in individual tutoring, mentoring or study support. A key point in relation to seeking the win–win is, in Covey's terms, some investment in the emotional bank account. When that is not present it is probably a futile waste of energy to try for the win–win, and the win–lose may be in the interests of all but the immediate loser.

For example, the drug issue (dilemma 4) could be reframed in this way:

Old frame

- What is the problem? – Drugs
- Who are the problem? – Students who use drugs, students who sell drugs, the media, parents
- What is my problem? – The reputation of the school, what people will think
- What are my feelings about it? – Apprehensive, angry at market forces
- How am I behaving? – Reactive, dishonest
- What is my strategy? – Deny? Conceal? Gloss?

New frame

Reframing and looking for the win–win (Figure 4.5) might lead the head to turn the situation round by being proactive, enlisting the help of students and parents, contacting the media and having a story to tell:

The school that turned its back on drugs

Britain's first drug-free school?

Young people declare war on drugs

Parents and pupils unite against drugs

Raising the standard – Healthy Living Centres

- Who are the allies? – Students who don't use drugs, students who do use drugs, parents of students who don't use drugs, parents of students who do use drugs, the LEA, the health authority, the government, business, funding charities
- What is the opportunity? – To use this as a stimulus for everyone to learn
- What are my feelings about it? – Apprehensive, excited at the possibilities
- How am I behaving? – Proactively, honestly, politically
- Who are the potential winners? – Everyone
- What is my strategy? – Engaging people with the issues, forming alliances to confront the issues honestly and openly.

1 Identify the dilemma
2 Reframe
3 Consider:
- What would win–lose look like?
- What would a lose–win look like?
- What would a lose–lose look like?
- What would a win–win look like?
- How to get there

Figure 4.5: Going for the win–win

In conclusion

There are no simple one-fits-all solutions to the dilemmas which heads experience. The shifting sands on which their schools are founded, the capricious social norms and the changing expectations around them require ways of seeing and thinking rather than ready recipes. Reframing and thinking win–win are examples of how dilemmas may begin to point to their own solutions and can at least help heads to glimpse a way through.

Appendix 4.1
Frames of reference for dealing with an ineffective teacher

	Neither ethical nor practical	Practical but unethical	Unethical but practical	Both ethical and practical
Encourage personal and professional target-setting				
Assign targets				
Provide incentives and rewards				
Employ escalating sanctions				
Pair the teacher with another effective colleague				
As a head, teach co-operatively with the teacher in question				
Encourage and support self-evaluation				
Send on relevant courses				
Invite external review				
Engage an external critical friend				
Appoint internal advisers/'fellows'				
Use support materials/packages				
Assign to 'easier' classes				
Reduce class size				
Reassign to learning support				
Reassign to administrative duties				
Give other duties				
Monitor closely and regularly				
Provide support in seeking other employment				
Make life difficult, increase pressure				

Appendix 4.2
Dealing with distance

Michael Schratz (Schratz and Steiner-Löffler, 1998) uses this activity to differentiate a range of attitudes among a school staff. He suggests a normal distribution with the following divisions.

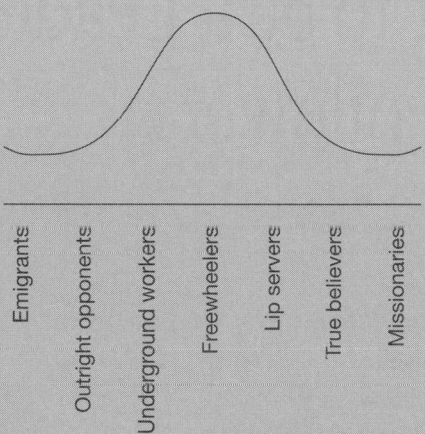

This is a practical activity that can be undertaken as a staff development exercise, during a workshop, conference or INSET.

Volunteers are asked to take up roles, for example the true believers and outright opponents. They stand about fifteen feet apart, facing one another. Their task is to convince the other person of their case (for example, the need for change in methods of teaching, the value of students evaluating teaching).

The true believer makes a statement. The outright opponent is asked to step forward if in agreement, backward if in disagreement. The size of the backward or forward step is left to the individual's strength of feeling. Remaining in place is also an option.

The outright opponent then makes a statement, perhaps a reply to the previous statement. The true believer then responds by a forward or backward step.

This may continue for five minutes or so. The audience can then be brought into the analysis of how people reach agreement or move further apart.

5

■ ■ ■

Learning to be a Leader by Being a Follower

Good leaders are excellent learners. They know how to follow and to give others their place.

> *In a learning organisation leaders may start by pursuing their own vision, but as they listen carefully to others' visions they begin to see that their own personal vision is part of something larger. This does not diminish any leader's sense of responsibility for the vision – if anything it deepens it. (Senge, 1992, p. 352)*

As we know from a substantial body of research, from our own direct experience and from the accounts of school leaders in Chapter 3, this is easier to write about than to achieve in practice. The conventional structures and life histories of schools militate against their becoming learning organisations.

All too often the place called the school is seen by headteachers as 'theirs', and it bears their imprint. It is commonplace for heads to refer to 'my school' and 'my staff' and although in some cases this may be no more than a conventional shorthand, for others it is a literal expression of how they see themselves in relation to the school. It is a tradition of long standing in British education for the headteacher to be seen as synonymous with the school and for everyone else but the head to remain anonymous. It is a powerfully entrenched tradition and has been given further impetus by the new Labour government. A DfEE press release on 3 December 1998 carried these words from the Secretary of State:

> *Good heads are the key to success. We need to develop strong leaders, reward them well and give them freedom to manage.*

> *Successful heads who have turned around the most challenging schools could earn up to £70,000 a year, with strengthened appraisal and the option of fixed-term contracts.*

We will also set up a National College for School Leadership to strengthen headship training and give it a new more dynamic focus drawing on the best that education and business can offer.

As the person at the apex of the organisational pyramid, the head can be credited with, or held to blame for, the effectiveness and standards of the school.

The nature of the high stakes involved is reflected in media coverage of schools and their heads. Shortly preceding the Secretary of State's announcement, in November 1998, the *Birmingham Evening Mail* ran a banner headline 'School head not a failure'. It was a journalistic counterblast to the school being labelled as 'failing its pupils' by OFSTED inspectors. The paper reported that the headteacher, a 'good' and 'very experienced' head, had suffered a breakdown as a direct consequence of the report. However, his identification with the school as failing has made him a 'failing head' not only in his own eyes but also in the eyes of teachers, parents, policy-makers and the wider community.

There is both a plus and a minus to this sense of ownership. The strong identification with the school and its success is a personal driving force and powerful asset to the school. Its very power is, however, also the source of its potential weakness. When impetus is driven from above and commitment is sustained by that individual drive, the school itself may become disempowered.

Leadership is a relational concept. In other words, it carries within it an implicit notion of followers, leading logically and directly to the conclusion that the main function of leaders is to create followers. The compelling logic of the language, as Henry Mintzberg (1994) argues, may lead us straight to an erroneous conclusion – and to a practice that is inimical to personal and organisational learning.

What ought to be a matter for debate becomes instead structured into language with the danger that we become so enamoured of this cult of heroic leadership that we fail to see its obvious contradictions. For example, in the name of empowering the workers, we actually reinforce hierarchy. So-called empowerment becomes the empty gift of the bosses, who remain firmly in charge. (p. 80)

Henry Mintzberg is not alone in his criticism of this model of heroic leadership, a critique now widely rejected by most management experts yet a persistent and pervasive way of seeing leadership in the British school context. In the Effective Leadership study it was the English heads who felt they were expected to be more like the heroic leader than their counterparts in other countries, in which there was a much greater emphasis on the sharing of influence and power amongst all stakeholders. In another study (Brighouse and Woods, 1999) some heads were described as 'casting such a big shadow' that it crowded out the rest of the staff.

In his research into the experience of newly appointed heads Geoff Southworth (1995) found that the experience of headship is a bit like a *déjà vu* experience, a revisiting of the initial experiences of teaching. The sense of isolation and uncertainty impels many new heads to establish themselves as strong, independent and dominant. Like the new classroom teacher, she follows the counsel to start tough and relax later because it is almost impossible to make it work the other way round. To expose yourself immediately as having a lot to learn is as risky a business for an untried head as it is for a novice class teacher. New heads and new teachers recognise that they are on trial and they know that a successful trial is one in which you convince the jury on their grounds, meeting their expectations and playing skilfully to their prejudices.

There is time later to become a learner and follower, once the terrain has been surveyed and the groundwork laid. Every new headteacher has an idea, possibly a vision, of what kind of a school she would like it to be, even if simply to maintain the *status quo*. How, over time, can that vision be realised? By maintaining a strong assertive leadership, setting out the stall from day one, leading from the front? Or can it better be achieved in the longer term by encouraging and following the leadership of others?

The answer to these questions may well depend on the stage of a school leader's career. Research by Rosenblum and colleagues (1994) in the USA found significant differences between experienced and new school principals. In the early stages the principal was often referred to as a 'visionary', an 'inspiration' and a 'change agent'. However, at a later stage, as they relaxed and matured into their job, they were more likely to be referred to as 'facilitator', 'mentor' or 'standard-bearer'. As Rosenblum concluded, this was because they were able to let go, release ownership and cede control to others. These insights find a close echo in the accounts of the 'talking heads' in Chapter 3.

While different stages place different demands on school leaders and what is effective at one stage of development may be less appropriate later on, there are, as Thomas Sergiovanni (1992) describes it, different underpinning theologies of leadership. He suggests five different ways in which headteachers may derive their authority:

- bureaucratic
- psychological
- technical–rational
- professional
- moral.

Bureaucratic authority is hierarchical, and in bureaucracies hierarchy equals perceived expertise. Those at the top know more than those at the bottom. They set standards which teachers have to reach. They enforce these through the 'expect and inspect' strategy. In-service training is provided when teachers fall short, and accountability is from bottom to top.

Psychological authority is the appliance of management wisdom. It is underpinned by working at human relations, by congeniality, by recognising people's needs and encouraging and rewarding them. The strategy is 'expect and reward'. The reward culture is an implicit statement of accountability from bottom to top.

Technical–rational authority is grounded in research, in evidence, in science. Knowing the research, being aware of good and best practice and being able to defend the position allow the head and senior management to provide the right kind of in-service support. This gives teachers the skills that have been identified by experts. Accountability is implicitly and explicitly from the bottom to those at the top.

Professional authority is where there are collective and agreed norms which are translated by teachers into professional standards. Professional knowledge is created in use, by teachers working together and sharing knowledge. Teachers recognise their mutual responsibilities to one another and hold one another accountable. They require little monitoring from the top.

Sergiovanni's final category – moral authority – derives from the explicit shared values of a community. These are not necessarily 'professional' values but those that hold a community together and of themselves guide actions and accountability. What people do is driven not by what is rewarded, or by what works, nor by self-interest. It is led by what is right and in the interests of the whole school.

Whether or not these can ever be neat discrete types, and whether or not we accept Sergiovanni's typologies, there are valuable insights to be gained from thinking about the culture of the school in relation to these five models. Perhaps the most valuable insight of all is that authority need not be located in the person of the leader but can be 'out there', in between and among people. If this can be achieved, its force is much stronger. It is mutually reinforcing. Where that shared authority is absent, psychological tricks of management come into their own and 'management' is precisely what is required to sustain the motivation. Reinforcing through reward comes into its own too where such psychological mechanisms fail, with the ultimate fall-back position being a reversion to a simple command structure.

Emile Dürkheim, the German sociologist, famously said that 'where mores are sufficient law is unnecessary, where mores are insufficient law is unenforcable'. It is a fundamental law of teaching that to lead by command is inimical to effective long-term learning. It is short-term, pragmatic at best, and carries with it a singular and indelible message about personal and institutional authority. The 'Mafia Manager' (Figure 5.1) illustrates a set of principles which directly counter those of Dürkheim, and which by virtue of their organisational origins confirm the theory that enforceable laws are likely to be short-lived.

For the teacher who has succeeded in establishing a shared set of mores, the test is to leave the classroom in the expectation that at whatever time she returns the class will be on task, working co-operatively or individually. The equivalent test of effective leadership is what happens when the headteacher or the whole senior management team are out of the school.

Where there is professional and moral authority in a school, the headteacher is freed to be a follower and a learner. Where there is professional and moral authority, it is much easier to accept disagreement and conflict. Indeed, disagreement and conflict become part of healthy organisation because people can only disagree usefully when there is an already-established ground for agreement. The improving school is one in which differences are not simply respected but engaged with, and there is a common search for meaning. David Bohm (1983), the physicist, makes the distinction between discussion (the Latin *discutio* – to tear to pieces) and the Greek *dialogos* (literally meaning flowing through it).

If you think and act solely for your own benefit you will reach the top.

'A man who wishes to make a profession of goodness in every thing must inevitably come to grief among men who are not so good. Therefore, it is necessary to learn how not to be good, and know how to use this knowledge and not use it according to the necessity of the case.' (Machiavelli, *The Prince*)

Live with wolves and you will learn how to howl.

Beginner's rules are simple:
Keep your mouth shut, your eyes open and your fly zipped, and do what you are told. Naturally, as in any business, beginners are required to kiss ass – that is, as someone once observed in another connection – you must have the morals of a whore and the manners of a dancing master – but as time goes by and you advance, these imperatives will become fewer, until finally you have become the guy presenting his cheek to be bussed.

The prudent manager will concentrate on keeping his people happily well bribed, keeping them in line, keeping them loyal and keeping the deaf, dumb and blind – in a manner of speaking of course.

When you make an example of someone make sure that everyone knows what the lesson is. Punish one, teach a hundred.

It is proper to delude others but never yourself. That is, as you work your manipulations, never become so caught up in them that you lie to yourself.

If you allow your enemies – or your friends – to think they are your equals they will immediately think they are your superiors.

If you want to be loved buy a beagle.

Most people see kindness as a weakness; because of this they welcome being told what to do in forceful terms.

Treat soldiers roughly and they will follow your orders willingly.

Be consistent, except occasionally – your inconsistency can then be used as a tactic to shake your staff out of complacency.

If you are going to walk on water you have to know where the rocks are.

Every rule is only an arbitrary border, waiting to be crossed by adventurous people. Those who would break rules may prove to be your best people.

You must set the organisation's objectives, establish a chain of command, set policies, establish controls, appraise performance, adjust and act again. In short you must manage.

In struggles for power your judgements should be based entirely on self-interest and finding as direct a route to your goal as possible.

People respond from greed; people respond out of fear. That's human nature.

Figure 5.1: Excerpts from *The Mafia Manager* by 'V' (1996)

Understanding comes first

'Seek first to understand before seeking to be understood.' This is Covey's fifth of seven hallmarks of highly effective people (Convey, 1989). He describes it in this way:

> 'Seek first to understand' involves a very deep shift in paradigm. We typically seek first to be understood. Most people do not listen with the intent to understand; they listen with the intent to reply. They're either speaking or preparing to speak. They're filtering everything through their own paradigm, reading their autobiography into other people's lives. If they have a problem with someone – a son, a spouse, an employee – their attitude is 'That person just doesn't understand'. (p. 63)

It is a sweeping claim that 'most people do not listen with the intent to understand', but a small sample of conversation overheard on trains, in bus queues, restaurants, common rooms and staffrooms would quickly prove the statistical validity of Covey's claim. In a context where there is pressure to act and executive decisions to be made, it is doubly difficult for school leadership to listen with careful intent. Yet a genuine attempt to understand is, as Covey argues, an extremely powerful process. It is disarming both to the speaker and to the listener. It effects a paradigm shift. It can, of course, be used as a powerful technique in one's repertoire of psychological tricks. It can be employed as yet another useful management technique. In these cases it may well work in a pragmatic sense and even in a professional sense, but it will ultimately fail in a moral sense if it is not 'congruent', that is, aligned with a genuine desire to learn and to grow as a person and as a leader. Richard Paul (1996) describes the true learner as possessing these characteristics:

> a passionate drive for clarity, fair-mindedness, a fervour for getting to the bottom of things, for listening sympathetically to opposing points of view, a compelling drive to seek out evidence, a devotion to truth as against self-interest. (p. 13)

When we are truly learning, a fundamental change takes place, physiologically, cerebrally and emotionally. When we are *listening to learn*, we are alert, working hard, exercising the neural networks which send messages in complex patterns around the brain. This engages the logical, intuitive, emotional and memory centres which form and change our understanding. The activity, however much located inside our head, is essentially social. It is 'out there', a product of the people with whom we interact. Teachers do not 'teach' their leaders in any recognised sense of that limiting term, but they help to mediate and magnify what leaders can learn when the intellectual window of opportunity is open.

Three types of non-learning

Peter Jarvis (1997) describes different forms of confronting new knowledge, some of which he describes as non-learning. He distinguishes three types of non-learning that are as applicable to leadership as to the pupil in the classroom.

The first type of non-learning Jarvis calls 'presumption'. It may be summarised as 'I trust the world as it is known to me and I wish to maintain its fundamental validity'. To disturb the current stock of knowledge and previous learning experiences may be destabilising. It may undermine one's ability to do the job effectively on one's own terms within one's own comfort zone. This first type is 'non-learning' because it precludes change. The following statement from a deputy headteacher captures its essence:

> *She was an exciting speaker. She got everyone going and there was some heated argument among the staff following her presentation. I was unhappy she had been invited because her ideas were frankly quite seductive, if you allowed yourself to get carried away with them. I worried that it undermined the confidence of some of my colleagues in what we had committed ourselves to do as a school.*

A second type of non-learning is 'non-consideration'. This differs from the first by being an unconscious bypassing of the opportunity to learn. There's too much to do, too little time, and either learning is not seen as a priority or the potential of learning from the situation is recognised but the leader does not know how to take advantage of it. It was expressed in these terms by one departmental head:

> *In our last departmental meeting this young teacher, James, came up with this wonderful idea. To be honest I can't even now remember what it was, but I had to make a decision at the time – there is potentially something important in this for all of us. But then I lost the moment. We moved on to other business and I have just not had the time or energy to pick the idea up with James.*

A third kind of non-learning is 'rejection'. Rejection is a conscious decision not to learn because it may be seen as too difficult, too complex, too time-consuming, or too far removed from present needs to be applicable or valid. It is captured in these words from a team leader:

> *I was urged to read Perkins's book* Smart Schools. *I was finally given it as a present to make me read it. I started it and it was interesting enough but I couldn't really engage with it. I couldn't really see how it was going to help me in any practical way in managing my team.*

Jarvis then goes on to describe three types of reflective learning which he calls contemplation; reflective skills; and experimental learning.

Contemplation is thinking deeply, with the only source of reference oneself. In Jarvis's terminology this is 'pure thought'. In a leadership context this type might be captured by the following anecdote from a headteacher:

I often wake at about five. I sometimes find myself thinking about a situation even before I am awake. It is very relaxing to lie there and rehearse it carefully in my head, picturing it, seeing the detail of it again, seeing what I did, what I might have done, teasing out the principle, coming to understand it better. Then I get up and write it down, and find that a whole hour has passed.

The second category, reflective skills, describes a form of learning on your feet rather than in your bed. In their day-to-day work, leaders meet many situations in which they have to make rapid decisions and develop skills to meet them, sometimes in Macdonald's condition of surprise (Figure 4.1). It is important that the value of these reflective skills is recognised and added consciously and systematically to the leadership repertoire. Macdonald (1998) uses the term 'metacognition' to describe this quality of reflectiveness in action:

It would be an unremarkable statement to say that leaders in schools, as in other situations and organisations, rely upon their knowledge in making judgements and decisions. The difference between good and successful leaders and those who are less so may depend in part at least upon their awareness of the state of their knowledge. (p. 166)

Experimental learning, the third type of reflective learning, takes place when something is consciously and deliberately tried out. In a leadership context it may be a form of risk-taking in the hope that something might be learned from it, either through success or failure. The three examples that follow all stemmed from a conscious and proactive decision to follow where others might lead you.

In the first example, from a Clydebank primary school outside Glasgow, the headteacher joined in the after-school study club with the primary six and seven pupils. She said:

I achieved something I had missed for a long time as a head and something I regained by my decision to let my guard down at the after-school study club. I have been a head now for twelve years but this was the first time I had a real open adult-to-adult discussion with eleven and twelve year olds and I learned so much in the process. The relaxed environment of study club, the easy-going relationships let me drop my guard, be myself and listen to what they had to say about their lives, in the community, in the school. I think that was the first time I really began to understand, I mean really understand, what it was like to grow up in Clydebank and come to this school. And how I must appear to them normally with my guard up, and what school must be like from where they stand, or sit.

The use of the phrase 'adult-to-adult' is a provocative one. Eleven- and twelve-year-olds are not adults, yet, as the work of transactional analysts has illustrated, we all (adults and children) have three inner components to our thinking and behaving. These three components are the child, the parent and the adult. As adults, we often allow the child within us free reign. We can regress emotionally or behaviourally to a ten-year-old or five-year-old level with a little provocation, usually when someone else (an official or bureaucrat or partner) addresses us from their parent mode. Children are, in a sense, no different. They are frequently compelled to play the child role in response to the teacher or headteacher as 'parent'. However, when they play at pretend school they know how to adopt the parent role very effectively, and when treated as mature thinking beings by an 'adult-in-the-adult', they respond with the 'adult-in-the-child'.

The adult-to-adult transaction is sometimes difficult to find in the day-to-day transactions of school life. It is in the quality 'time out' which suspends the norms and releases people from their roles that this kind of adult interchange can most easily take place. It allows the headteacher to see herself in a different light, through a different lens.

The second example, from a headteacher in a secondary school, illustrates the adult–adult relationship in another 'out-of-hours' context.

> *Three lads came to see me wanting to start a guitar club. They wanted space to do it and support. They wanted to advertise it and run it themselves with a teacher to supervise. It was a spur of the moment thing but I suppose I intuitively recognised the opportunity it offered me. I volunteered to be the supervising teacher because I play the guitar myself. Badly I have to say. As the supervising teacher I had nothing to do except keep on eye on things, watch and listen. I became a regular member. They were a million miles ahead of me in guitar technique. They recognised that pretty quickly too and helped me along from where I was, not from their pinnacle of expertise. Gently but challengingly too. They were excellent teachers. They taught me so much. I think I learned a bit too about organisation and teamwork and something about pedagogy as well.*

This example illustrates something about adult learning. Its character is closer to tutoring or coaching than to teaching. In this relationship there is a greater fluidity and interchangeability of teacher and learner roles. It is a microcosm of what a school might be like if it could exceed its conventional parameters and open itself up to the possibilities of collaborative learning.

The third example is also drawn from an out-of-school context which permitted deeper learning for all. The deputy head who accompanied a Year 10–11 class on a trip to Paris said:

> *I anticipated some of the issues that would arise, issues around smoking, drinking, drugs, late nights, the temptations of Pigalle and the red light districts, red-blooded fifteen and sixteen year olds, adults or on the verge of it. I knew how futile it was to lay down the rules. I spent a lot of time before, on the journey there, over meals, in the evenings together with them exploring the issues and trying to reach an honourable and honest set of ground rules for us all. It took us into some pretty deep territory. How much I had to learn about young people's real lives. How much did I want to know? How much should I know? I worried that in some ways it would make my job harder next term back at school because we established such a close relationship on that trip. I was the man who knew too much. A strange concept. We*

knew more about one another than perhaps would be good for discipline, respect, drawing lines and all that. What I found when I was back at school was an immense support and no one ever crossed the formal lines that school required. They understood as well as I, if not better, how formal and informal organisations work.

It is significant, perhaps, that in all three cases it was outside the formal school day that these opportunities arose. In the adult–adult relationship pupils learned more than might have been good for discipline and distance back in the school setting. But in all three situations described there were lessons to be carried back into the mainstream of school life. Because they had been allowed to exercise their adult component, students were much more aware and more mature in their understanding of the constraints and formalities of organisational life back at school.

In all cases the experience had helped young people to recognise that head-teachers are not all-knowing while pupils know nothing. These young people had learned something about the nature of learning, the nature of institutions and the character of leadership. By modelling reflective learning and follower-ship, school leaders were able to model the quality of learning which they expected of their pupils.

In Fulfen Primary School in England there is a poster on the wall of every classroom, in the corridors and lunch room. It says 'What did you learn in school today?' The poster is aimed at pupils, asking them to reflect every day on things they have learned. Like everything else in the school environment, the poster may become all too familiar and invisible unless it is kept conspicuous and to the fore. Teachers and management need to keep the issue 'live' – by sharing with the class what *they* have learned today.

What do teachers learn in their own classrooms? Possibly very little about the subject they are teaching. The lessons they learn which stay with them for a lifetime and spill uncontrollably into their own leisure time are about human relationships, about authority, and about knowledge – its transmission and creation, and the diverse and perplexing paths it takes on the way to its destination. For good teachers – that is, reflective, critical, inquiring teachers – this is a lifelong journey and a continuously compelling one.

What does the student learn in the classroom? Something, it is hoped, about the subject they are there to study. What stays with them for a lifetime is essentially the same as for the teacher. Deeper and deeper embedded, hour by hour, day by day, week by week, is the lesson of *how* we learn individually and socially. The structure, context and tools of the classroom 'teach' where knowledge comes from, how it is made, what it is worth and how it can be used. This is more typically an unconscious than a conscious activity but, like the good teacher, the good student is able to reflect on learning itself and in so doing give shape and momentum to her thinking.

This principle must hold true for the effective headteacher. The learning opportunities are wider, more complex, and less distilled or formally mediated by another party. The sources are all around. For the headteacher who really wants to learn, the best source is perhaps the least obvious. We have a tendency to want to look elsewhere, to other schools, to other countries, to the authoritative literature, to the definitive research, to in-service courses and conferences. Yet a school and its community present immediate and abundant opportunities. These may be informal or formal, planned or unplanned. Informal ways of learning are gained through being around, by walking about, by being attuned to the spontaneous moment.

Learning by walking about is different from MBWA (management by walking about). The management walk is essentially a monitoring walk. Part of its purpose is to demonstrate the visibility of the head, a reminder of her presence, perhaps a pre-emptive strike against slackness. Its focus tends to be on predetermined things. It is a quality assurance or quality reassurance walk. The learning walk, on the other hand, anticipates surprises. It is open to seeing things differently. It is ready to spark ideas.

The difference may be highlighted by two events in two schools serving the same neighbourhood.

In school A the head is an ubiquitous presence in the school, in the corridors, in the lunch rooms, at the buses. He exchanges banter with the students and sometimes joins their table at lunchtime to talk about how they are getting on, the netball, the football team, how they are faring with their studies and with school generally. Deciding that the head might actually have wanted to hear the truth, a senior student volunteered that he found the school atmosphere 'tense' and 'oppressive'. The head turned to the three others in the group: 'That's an odd description of St J's. I'm not sure everyone would agree with you. What do you three think?' The three shrugged, laughed it off but said nothing.

In school B the head was also a constant presence around the school. He took lunch with different groups and decided to use such opportunities for a more open discussion about the school. The head sat down with a group of students, simply engaging in their conversation, disclosing a little about his job, answering a few of their questions about what other schools he had worked in and how it compared with this one. He put the question back to them. How did they think this school compared? The immediate reply was that they liked it. It was a good school. And if there was one thing you would like to change? he asked. After starting nervously with criticisms of the lunches and the attitudes of the dinner ladies the students began gradually to get the confidence, and sense the trust, to open up. The head listened quietly, nodding not necessarily in agreement but to show he had heard. Much of it he already knew. Some of it surprised him. Some of it he realised he hadn't wanted to hear. He thanked them for their honesty and said he would give it a lot of thought. He explained that some of what they said would be difficult to act on and that he didn't want to raise their expectations too high for immediate resolution, but he promised to return to them with some ideas and further questions at a later date.

Hall and Hord (1987) use the term 'one-legged conferencing' to describe this informal process through which intelligence is gathered and alliances built. The term is used to represent graphically the position adopted informally in a hallway or doorway, with knee bent and one foot resting against the wall behind. Joseph Macdonald (1989) writes about his own use of this informal learning by walking about in his role as an external critical friend to the school. His conclusions may be equally applicable to the role of the internal critical friend or school leader.

> *Those inclined to regard serious work inside the schools as a matter of achieving and applying power are unlikely to believe this. They will believe that one-legged conferencing is a weak strategy, much inferior to such strategies as formal class-room observation and critique, curriculum invention or the design of a new policy. I would argue, however, that strategies based on power relations . . . are more likely to engender destructive resistance than constructive change. The studied casual-ness of one-legged conferencing, on the other hand, leaves room for the perspectives of both insiders and outsiders to emerge in ways that facilitate constructive collabo-ration over time. (p. 209)*

The combined insights of outsiders and insiders is vital for the learning school. For school leadership the daily life of the school presents an abundance of opportunities to listen and to learn. It is salutary for anyone in a leadership position to consider how, when, where and from whom they can learn. What opportunities are there to learn:

- from teachers?
- from students?
- from parents?
- from support staff?
- from governors?

Learning leaders, says Warren Bennis (1997), 'are confident enough to recruit people better than themselves because they revel in the talents of others'. It requires a high degree of self-confidence not to be threatened by people per-ceived as 'better' than you, but the strength to acknowledge it is the very quality that enhances leadership in the eyes of others. People cannot fail to perceive such a strength of character, however subliminally it enters their con-sciousness. Leaders who see opportunities to learn from others 'walk the talk' with a very different demeanour from the monitoring supervisory walkabout.

Some heads have found the grid shown in Figure 5.2 a useful method of evaluating their learning.

Describe a recent occasion when you learned something.

From:	About the school	About learning	About leadership
A student or students			
A teacher or teachers			
A parent or parents			
A governor or governors			
Others			

Figure 5.2: A learning grid for heads

Learning leaders need friends

Heads may find it difficult to learn in their own school without the support of someone from outside. A critical friend with the requisite expertise and experience can be an invaluable asset, but finding the person with the right repertoire of skills is crucial. This person, or people, may be from the local authority, a university, another school, a local business person – indeed anyone who brings the insight and skills to both support and challenge effectively.

In the European Project Evaluating Quality in School Education (MacBeath *et al.*, 1999) the 101 schools were assigned, or chose, a critical friend. At the end of the project their assessment of that friend's impact was analysed and summarised in the project final report. The following were some conclusions:

- The greater the clarity and boundaries of the critical friend's role, the better the quality of collaboration.
- The facilitative role was more likely to help the school become self-directed than the more directive steering role.
- The work of the critical friend is likely to be easier and more effective where a culture of reflection and critique already exists in the school.

In the Scottish Improving School Effectiveness project (MacBeath and Mortimore, 1994) schools worked together with a critical friend whose role it was to listen carefully, to tune in to the secret harmonies of the school and to be alive to its discordances as well. Critical friends often found themselves engaging in one-legged conferencing, reaching parts it was difficult for insiders to reach. They also found themselves faced with tricky decisions about how to feed back sensitive and confidential information both to the headteacher or senior management team when such information was vital to the future welfare of the school and to them personally and professionally.

One example comes from a school in a middle-class area in the suburbs of a large British city. The school fares well in performance tables but not, in the view of the head, as well as it could, given the background of the students. The critical friend was invited in to help analyse where the school's strengths and weaknesses lay. She was given *carte blanche* to talk to staff, to students, to wander around the school, and to sit in classes for as many days as it took. At the end of day two, the critical friend had a pretty good idea of where the problems lay. She met with the headteacher at the end of the second day and reported that staff morale was low. Staff were acutely aware of divisions within the senior management team. They were less and less inclined to put in time in the school. When they talked informally the topic of conversation generally turned to the 'mismanagement team', as they were commonly referred to.

After some discussion, some denial, and an eventual concession from the head that he might be part of the problem, it was agreed to have an away-day session with the management team. The critical friend started the session by giving each member a large sheet of poster paper and asking them to draw the senior management team as they saw it. One drew the team in classic systemic analysis style, arrows back and forward describing shared jobs, communication flows, roles, responsibilities. Another member of the team drew the five members standing in a circle, each facing forward around the circle. Each held a knife buried deep into the back of the one in front – a perfect suicidal circle, as he later described it. It provoked considerable laughter but the joke had a serious purpose. The ensuing discussion helped to unearth some of the deep-lying resentments over promotions and non-promotions, credit and blame, exclusions and inclusions. There were also some deep personal hostilities and histories.

While recognising that some of the mutual dislike and resentment would remain, the team were able to see more clearly where the professional accountabilities lay and with some deep and painful learning, knew for the future how better to spot and bypass the hidden agendas and games-playing. Handling of sessions such as this requires an outsider but makes high demands on her skills and insights.

Another example from the Improving School Effectiveness study (MacBeath and Mortimore, 1995) provides some insights into the systems aspects of management and the people aspects of leadership. In that study teachers, middle managers (heads of departments) and senior managers (headteachers, deputies and assistant heads) all filled in a questionnaire with a range of common items. Data were then fed back to the schools by the critical friends, working with the staff, and sometimes parents and pupils, in sifting and interpreting the data. One of the 54 items in the questionnaire was particularly challenging for senior management in most of the schools in which it was used, carrying with it some sharp lessons for the leadership team as learners in their own school. This particular item was greeted with dismay by the head and the senior management team in one particular school. It suggested a very different set of views as to the efficacy of communication in the school (see Figure 5.3).

Percentage saying agree/strongly agree n = 65	Teachers	Middle management	Senior management
There is effective communication between the senior management team and teachers	28	43	89

Figure 5.3: Response to questionnaire item by one school

The data showed a significant mismatch between the perceptions of those at the bottom, those in the middle and those at the top of the hierarchy. How could such data be explained? They could be dismissed as erroneous or irrelevant. They could be blamed on the wording and ambiguous nature of the question. They could be explained by the timing of the survey. They could, on the other hand, be seen as a vital sign, an opportunity to learn something important about communication, about the nature of the organisation, about management, about leadership and followership. In the event, senior management responded in this way:

> This is so unfair. We have taken communication systems very seriously. We have done everything we could to put procedures in place. We circulate everything. We follow up with reminders. We raise issues at staff meetings. We ask for feedback. We check. We have a daily newsheet and a termly newsletter. I would say we are actually very good at communication.

Why then did staff have such a pessimistic view of communication? The following comment from a teacher was also a fairly typical response and helped to explain the less sanguine view from the bottom up:

> The management team sit at one end of the school in the management wing as it is called. Memos flow out in a pretty steady stream. There is lots of paper. Some of it I read, some of it frankly I don't. I would say they are pretty efficient but to say there is 'good' communication is another story. Good communication is not about what you say but how you say it and how you mean it. It is about the relationships in which you hear or speak.

There is some degree of comfort for this senior management team when data from the other 35 schools in the project were listed alongside the school's own data (see Figure 5.4).

Percentage saying agree/strongly agree n = 2,605	Teachers	Middle management	Senior management
There is effective communication between the senior management team and teachers	46	48	87

Figure 5.4: Response to questionnaire item by rest of schools

These national data from the 36 participating schools suggest that there might be something generic and endemic rather than specific to this one school. Indeed, the differential nature of the data appears to be a function of hierarchy and distance, often expressed symbolically in the administrative geography of the school (as in the school described above), and in the official nature of communication. The few exceptional schools that did not fit the general pattern, however, proved the rule in the most challenging of ways.

Commenting on similar exercises across a range of organisations, Margaret Wheatley (1994) comments that perceived lack of communication is a characteristic and endemic feature but not an inevitable one. It depends on how the organisation, school or otherwise, understands and responds to new insights and knowledge. Each new piece of information enters the system as 'a small fluctuation'. The leadership may choose to ignore these fluctuations, but ignoring them does not make them go away. They create a disturbance which can be allowed to take its own course or can be directed into positive energy. Wheatley (1994) concludes:

> However long we may drag our feet, we will be forced to accept that information, freely generated and freely exchanged, is our only hope for organisations. If we fail to recognise its generative properties, we will be unable to manage in this new world. (p. 65)

The word 'information' to which Wheatley draws our attention, is a potent reminder of the nature and structure of communication in a school where leaders are truly learners and know how to follow. The weight of evidence suggests that the support and challenge of an informed, sensitive and skilled critical friend is of immense value to a school when it comes to sifting through the difficult issues that affect the flow of its social and educational life.

This book started with examining competencies, distilled from studies of exemplary leaders. Bennis and Nanus (1985), two of the leading authors in this field, identified one competency and essential competence above all else:

> Learning is the essential fuel for the leader, the source of high-octane energy that keeps up the energy by continually sparking new understanding, new ideas, and new challenges. It is absolutely indispensable under today's conditions of rapid change and complexity. Very simply, those who do not learn do not long survive as leaders. (p. 188)

6

■ ■ ■

Sex, Sexism, Sexuality and Sexual Harassment

all educational leaders should be good stewards of gender and should be committed to creating positive school environments that are gender-inclusive, not simply gender-neutral. New conceptualisations of educational leadership, therefore, should embody the recognition that effective leaders are activists about gender. (Riehl and Lee, 1995, pp. 911–12)

Being an activist on matters of gender may not figure in a list of competences but is a growing imperative of leadership. The more we learn about how organisations work, and the more knowledgeable we become about the human side of management, the greater the need to take an informed pro-active stance on sex and gender.

Among school staff sex and sexuality are often treated as invisible factors or are referred to in a self-conscious way, often through jokes and innuendo. In such a climate sexual harassment can take subtle and insidious forms. It isn't always crude and overt. It is often seen (mainly by men) as just part of the give and take of relationships. Neither denial nor ritual political correctness are helpful in a context where teachers need to model an informed approach to the issues with their pupils.

For the majority of human beings sex is a given. It is decided on the basis of the reproduction functions which, for most species, are different for males and females. Gender, on the other hand, is the social ascription of sex which by definition is not given. Gender-assigned roles can differ among cultures and can change over time. Gender is not neutral but, when treated as such, can blind people to significant features of the social landscape. When this occurs in a research context it can result in misleading findings, treated as having 'scientific' validity, but resting on the assumption that gender could be treated as an insignificant variable. For example, Piaget's work on child development and Kohlberg's work on moral development were both based on research with boys. In these studies boys were seen as the norm and the findings were immediately generalised to include girls but with no evidential base for this. Gilligan (1982) subsequently demonstrated that when girls are included in such work the findings can be very different.

In organisational research and theory-building, which had also typically treated women as invisible, new insights emerged and old assumptions were challenged when experiences of women were taken into account:

> almost inevitably, by making the invisible category of women explicit, this work has focused attention on the invisible – because – ubiquitous category of men. Thus, out of feminist or women-centred research had grown a more expansive category of gender research, which encompasses masculinity in organisational life as also problematic. (Riehl and Lee, 1995, p. 878)

Gender, like ethnicity and class, is such a fundamental part of every individual's identity that it cannot be ignored as a factor in organisational life. The school is an arena in which children's sense of self is progressively shaped over the years, placing on teachers and headteachers a professional responsibility to be informed and to behave intelligently when it comes to matters of sex and gender.

Sex and gender

There is an ever-expanding body of literature and research on sex and gender, much of it still contested, that has contributed to demythologising and questioning of easy assumptions about innate differences. Building on the biological fact that males and females are, in some respects, essentially distinct, claims have been made about intelligence, attitudes and aptitudes for leadership. Neuroscience and evolutionary biologists make new claims on a virtually daily basis about what men and women are 'hard-wired' to do and not do, and the debate has to remain open to emerging evidence and its implications. Steven Pinker (1998), who has written extensively on the genetics of sex difference, nevertheless sees the detail of the debate as distracting from the real issues and agrees with Gloria Steinem that 'there are really not many jobs that actually require a penis or a vagina, and that all the other occupations should be open to everyone' (p. 50).

Whatever physiological, biological and genetic differences there are, they are inevitably interlinked and interwoven with the socialisation process. When specific traits are assumed by and ascribed to each sex they give that sex permission to exhibit, practise and develop them. So, for example, it may well be that because they have less testosterone than men, women are likely to be less aggressive, but it is also true that women have fewer opportunities to practise aggressive behaviour and have such conduct reinforced. On the other hand, Adler *et al.* (1993) suggest that women have more behavioural options open to them than men. They can outdo men on their own territory by being more stereotypically male than most men would wish to be and still be admired for this behaviour (a prime example of this is Margaret Thatcher), or they can be warm and approachable without being seen as violating their gender stereotype. It is much more difficult for men to imitate stereotypically female behaviour without at the same time losing status and standing. Another problem for boys and young men is that the socialisation process they are subjected to frequently denies them the opportunity to practise and develop their emotional intelligence.

Whatever innate differences are found, in most aspects of human activity there is likely to be a wider range *within* each sex than between them. For example, although the average man is taller than the average woman, the range between the tallest man and the smallest man is far greater than that between the average man and woman. Whatever generalisations are made, therefore, there will be large numbers of men and women to whom this does not apply.

Nevertheless, it is still valid to assume that, regardless of innate differences between males and females, men and women who have reached headship in the UK by the early part of the twenty-first century have on the whole been reared differently and exposed to different experiences. They also have to interact with a range of people (professionally and personally), many of whom will have different expectations of them, dependent on their gender.

These expectations can be *culture*-specific or *role*-specific.

Culture-specific expectations

> *Men may cook or weave or dress dolls or hunt hummingbirds, but if such activities are appropriate occupations of men then the whole society, men and women alike, votes them as important. When the same occupations are performed by women they are regarded as less important. (Mead, 1949)*

Cultural expectations are often based on tradition. Almost inevitably this is linked to the status of the task being considered and, of course, the reward. Throughout the world, if the task is performed by men it is likely to be seen as high status and comparatively well remunerated. The fact that there are more female doctors in the old USSR compared with the USA, for example, had more to do with status and salary (much lower in the USSR) than physiological differences between men and women.

Examples of gender-based cultural expectations are plentiful in the UK and overseas. For instance, responsibility for the market in Castries, St Lucia is solely a female province whereas in Marrakesh, Morocco the privilege belongs to the men. These expectations are not always national and can be regionally based. For example, although the number of women heads of mixed secondary schools has increased in England, there are still parts of the country where there are very few – we know of at least one northern LEA where, at the time of writing, all the secondary heads are white males.

Sometimes cultural expectations are mis-assigned to a group by outsiders based on stereotype rather than factual information. One example is provided by two schools no more than three miles apart, serving similar intakes. In one of the schools it was widely believed that there was no point in bothering too much about the education of Asian girls as they were all going to be forced into arranged marriages before school leaving age. At the other school the concern was about the over-ambition of the Asian girls who apparently all wanted to be doctors or pharmacists.

Role-specific expectations

The fact that embroidery is generally considered a female skill whereas the sewing needed for suits (tailors) and bodies (surgeons) is male has more to do with role expectations than dexterity. Lifting heavy weights is usually seen as a man's job but nursing, traditionally seen as a female occupation, is one where a capacity to lift heavy weights is important. Nurses are taught how to do this and their female 'frailties' do not seem to be problematic when they are in that role. Maintaining discipline is often believed to be better done by male teachers. Looking for a 'strong man' is not confined to the lonely hearts personal ads. It is not unknown for governing bodies to fall back on similar stereotypes when trying to fill a vacant deputy or head position.

Time and expectations

We get used to seeing men and women/girls and boys performing different tasks, but expectations can change over time. Not so long ago, indeed when Margaret Thatcher was a young MP, the idea of a woman prime minister was almost inconceivable, as was the idea that women could be directors of education (there were only two in the country) or even television newsreaders. The famous historical example cited by Franks (1999) is that of office workers who in the mid-nineteenth century were mainly male and had a relatively high status. As this changed to office workers being 98 per cent female, so did their status and remuneration. There is an interesting conundrum here, as it is not always clear whether the job in question has lower status because it is primarily associated with women or whether, because the job is of comparatively low status, women are allowed in. So were women encouraged into office work as its status changed or was it because the status changed that women started to be employed in this area? The answer of course does not have to be either/or, and almost certainly there is a feedback loop making both statements true. The important point here is that if much of what is accepted as 'the norm' is different in different parts of the world and can change over time, our stereotypes are more likely to be due to socially ascribed rather than innate differences.

Women and headship

Many writers are now suggesting that contemporary education leaders are likely to be more effective if they are less hierarchical, good at dealing with conflict, good at listening, concerned about the social and emotional development of pupils, and supportive of their staff. According to stereotypes, women should be good at these tasks. However, in 1997, women accounted for 67.3 per cent of the teaching profession but only 49.5 per cent of headships. The breakdown of women within each phase of education was as shown in Figure 6.1.

Women constitute the vast majority of the profession but they are not proportionally represented at managerial level. With regard to women aspiring to become headteachers, the picture is slightly more optimistic if registration for the (soon to be mandatory) National Professional Qualifications for Headteachers (NPQH) is anything to go by. Although still not in proportion to their numbers in the profession, more women are taking the qualification. Figure 6.2 gives details of one of the cohorts.

There are various explanations as to why we have more male than female heads. For example, men and women may have a different rationale for entering the profession in the first place.

> *Whatever the reasons, a number of studies support the notion that the motivation for entering teaching differs for men and women. Most women enter teaching to teach but most men enter teaching to administer. (Shakeshaft, 1989, p. 87)*

	Proportion of teachers (%)	Nos	Proportion of heads (%)	Nos
Primary	82.9	150 600	55.1	11 400
Special	67.2	9 800	41.2	500
Secondary	53.7	99 000	24.9	1 100

Figure 6.1: Women within education

(*Source*: Statistics of Education: Teachers: England and Wales 1998, DfEE.)

Note: Unfortunately statistics showing the numbers of black and ethnic minority teachers and heads have not been collected, though the TTA is now trying to rectify this.

	% of women candidates, cohort 5	Proportion of women teachers in the profession
Primary	72.2	82.9
Special	61.5	67.2
Secondary	43.6	53.7

Figure 6.2: Women taking NPQH
(*Source:* TTA unpublished data.)

Once in the profession, women may be less likely than men to:

- have relevant role models;
- have a career plan;
- be given appropriate experiences/opportunities in school;
- be sent on relevant inset courses, e.g. financial management/timetabling;
- have had the time to do a higher degree;
- believe they are capable of being a head (or just as important, be encouraged by someone else to believe so);
- want to move into 'management' and leave the classroom;
- be mobile;
- be willing or be able to commit the necessary time to the job.

It is of course also plausible that some appointing committees prefer to appoint men.

These are just a few possible explanations and they apply to some men too – but as can be seen from the statistics, not nearly so many. The explanations will have different weighting in the different phases. So, for example, women in primary education are more likely to have interacted with female role models than those in the special or secondary sector. Some of these explanations can be described as covert (and usually unintentional) sexual discrimination. But many women also face overt and intentional discrimination. Black women often find this compounded by racism (both covert and overt). Because there are so few of them, black and ethnic minority teachers are less likely to have had role models and may have found it harder to get the relevant whole-school experience necessary to go for promotion. This is particularly true for those who have spent large proportions of their careers involved in Section 11 work (Home Office Grant for children of new Commonwealth origins.)

Much of the list is easily rectifiable by male and female managers who can help women aspirants overcome these obstacles. So, for example, if it is true, as suggested by one of the women heads in Chapter 3, that men apply for posts when they think they can do 20 per cent of the new job, whereas women apply when the proportion is nearer 80 per cent, managers could do something about it. As well as providing opportunities and encouraging women teachers to undertake a range of experiences, they could facilitate confidence-building activities such as one-to-one coaching or mentoring from experienced female heads or inspectors they know. Several of the women interviewed in the previous chapter spoke about the support and encouragement they had received during their career from their male and female managers (heads, deputies and heads of department) and from inspectors.

Age of headship

Women tend to be appointed to their first headship later than men. In England, 37 per cent of the women heads who registered for Headlamp training (available on taking up first headship) were between the ages of 45 and 49 (compared with men, who were more likely to be between 40 and 44). A significant number of women were over 50 (18.2 per cent compared with 8.1 per cent of the men who registered). The reverse was also true, with a significant number of the men coming from a younger age group (18 per cent were aged 35–39 compared with 11.2 per cent of the women). (*Source*: unpublished TTA figures.)

Women with children may have taken career breaks and they may have waited until their children reached a certain maturity before applying for promotion. Also, many women will have taken a less direct career path than men, as illustrated in Chapter 3 (for example, trained later; moved around because of their spouse rather than for promotion purposes; or were unable to move around for promotion purposes). But applying later for headship could have as much to do with confidence and believing themselves capable of the job as anything else. It may also have some connection with all the other things they have to do outside their paid work.

Domestic responsibilities

How many men do what I do? I leave the school at the back of five, do the shopping make the tea, listen to the tales of woe from the kids, help the youngest with her homework then spend anything up to an hour with my older daughter who's struggling with her GCSEs. Only after that, often after nine o'clock at night I sit down to the management task I have for the following day. (Female secondary head in conversation)

Women are more likely than men to have the sole or major responsibility for domestic life. By the time they have reached headship it is not unlikely that they will have responsibility for teenage children and an ageing parent/parent-in-law or relative. Of course some men have these responsibilities too, but what is commonplace for women is idiosyncratic for men.

Increasingly *both* men and women resent the long hours needed to cope with professional middle-class jobs:

> *it is the professional middle classes in particular who have become the modern 'work-rich, time-poor'. Headteachers, doctors, lawyers, bankers, consultants are all affected by a long-hours culture, and all worry about the social cost. (Franks, 1999, p. 70)*

Women with childcare and/or elderly-relative-care responsibilities may not have the luxury of choice in this matter.

Being a woman head

As well as addressing these issues as a manager, some female heads still have to cope with overt and covert sexism directed at them – it does not simply stop when headship is reached. Some women find they are responsible for people (teachers and support staff) who do not want, nor in some cases believe they should, be managed by women. The resentment is not always far below the surface. Riehl and Lee (1995), for example, found that in schools with women heads, male teachers tended to rate their head less positively than did their female colleagues.

A women heads' group was formed in one London borough after a small group of newly appointed heads got so fed up with the way they were treated (chairs of governors being patronising, school keepers being rude and aggressive, delivery people assuming they were the secretary – this was particularly true for the black headteachers). The group, which started as a support group, soon expanded into training and development. For some years, with the help of the local inspectorate, they ran successful, and oversubscribed, women-only courses for heads and aspiring heads. But not all women believe they need support from other women. Some who have found promotion easy and have not faced personal discrimination may find it difficult to empathise with women who have had a less fortunate experience.

Managing women

While these issues are of daily concern to many female headteachers, they are also the concern of male and female heads who manage women staff. How rife is sexism in the school? Is racism tolerated? Are these issues addressed through the curriculum and in school policies? Are there clear guidelines about what happens if a member of staff or a pupil is subjected to a sexist or racist incident? What sort of role-models are available for the pupils to learn from?

How 'family-friendly' is the school? What happens when staff want to take time off to see one of their children in a school concert or have to take time off because one of their children is ill? What happens when childcare arrangements break down and a teacher finds it difficult to stay for a meeting after school? What happens when women returning from maternity leave say they would prefer, for a temporary period, to become part-time but not lose their allowance? How are part-time staff (predominantly women) treated? For example, are they encouraged (and, where appropriate, paid) to attend meetings and INSET?

The head's main responsibility is, of course, to the pupils in her school, and any teacher absence is going to have an effect on children. But staff can be absent for a range of reasons and the kinds of reasons cited above tend only to apply to a minority. Moreover, in terms of a whole career, child-rearing years are a relatively short period. A staff who believe they are well and fairly treated are also likely to have a positive effect on children – both in and out of the classroom.

Gender differences are not just concerned with child-bearing and child-rearing responsibilities. If heads are to attempt to create and sustain a motivated workforce, it is important to be aware of the different factors that motivate women and men and to understand possible explanations for this.

In one study (Varlaam *et al.*, 1992) of over three thousand teachers (including heads and deputies) extensive differences were found between men and women teachers. Women and men rated different issues as more important for them.

> *Particularly notable differences between the sexes were noted in the proportions of men and women [with far more women suggesting] that it was very important to be kept informed about what was going on in the school, to be valued by colleagues and by management and to have a manageable level of paper work/record keeping. (p. 8)*

When asked which factors they considered unsatisfactory, men and women revealed sizeable differences. Women were more often dissatisfied with the availability of part-time work, the amount of non-contact time and the size of classes. Interestingly, in light of proposals to link performance with pay, women were not as dissatisfied with pay as men. Performance-related pay may consequently prove to be even less of an incentive for them.

Sexuality

Sexuality is a neglected aspect of organisational life, yet it is present as a constant undercurrent, part of the social processes that are linked to and underpin management/workforce relations. (Ozga and Walker, 1999)

There is a range of incidents that heads have to deal with or choose to ignore. In most schools consensual intimate relations between unmarried staff are usually not an issue these days (though in recent memory this was not the case). But heads may take a different view if the relations are adulterous and involve, for example, relationships between a member of staff and a parent. Heads have to decide if and when they have a proper concern and then what they should/can do in the circumstances. In sixth forms, 'consensual' relations can take place between a member of staff and a student, and here the waters can get very murky. The nature of 'consent' in the asymmetrical relationship of teacher and student is problematic given the power of the teacher and the 'added value' that organisational status confers. New legislation which makes this a crime punishable by a prison sentence may act as a powerful deterrent for staff, but for heads it presents a 'high-stakes' set of dilemmas.

Heads have to contend with the implications of their own sexuality as well as those of the people they manage and of the pupils in their care. Lesbian and gay heads have particular issues to face, for example, whether or not to be open about their sexuality. Many of those who make the decision to keep their personal lives private live in fear that someone will attempt to 'out' them. Uninformed (and wrong) confusions linking homosexuals to paedophiles are a particular threat for gay primary heads and teachers. Even when 'out', gay and lesbian heads know that at any time the media can zoom in on their sexuality rather than (or as well as) whatever school issue has come to their notice. The pervading homophobia of the tabloids was well illustrated by the treatment meted out to Jane Brown, a primary head in Hackney, when she came into the public eye after turning down tickets for *Romeo and Juliet*. Whatever the rights or wrongs of the issue, it was her sexuality that seemed to be of interest to the press.

While she was strongly supported by parents and local activists, exonerated by a local committee of inquiry and praised by an Office for Standards in Education (Ofsted) inspecting team, she was forced to make a humiliating public apology before national TV cameras, was attacked repeatedly in the press over a prolonged period, her privacy was invaded, she received hate mail, death threats, was physically assaulted and forced into hiding, her partner outed, her partner's children and ex-partner harassed and her work and career deeply affected. (Epstein and Johnson, 1998, p. 90)

The ethos which a head seeks to create will be all-important here. The way in which he or she behaves towards gay and lesbian teachers will be noted and discussed. Theories will be constructed on the evidence of how they respond to teachers who are 'outed', how they deal with homophobic parents or governors, or whether 'queer' is an acceptable form of pupil-to-pupil abuse in the school. Too frequently gay and lesbian adults talk about the homophobic treatment they received at school which was either not taken seriously or ignored by staff. It is very salutary that so many of them felt isolated and thought there was no teacher they could confide in (Epstein, 1994). In one study of lesbian and gay teenagers, 19 per cent had contemplated suicide (Trenchard and Warren, 1984, p. 145).

Policies that deal with these issues can be helpful, especially if they have been produced by a large group of stakeholders. But just as critical is the example set by the head. The significance of signals picked up from observing others was mentioned by several of the heads interviewed in Chapter 3 who emphasised the importance of 'modelling'. Key messages are picked up in this way.

Sexual harassment

Sexual harassment is unwanted, unwelcome and unsolicited behaviour, usually of a sexual nature or with sexual overtones, towards people in less powerful positions or circumstances (adapted from Herbert, 1992, pp. 2–3). In schools it can take place between adults; between adults and children; and between children. It is about the power of one person over another. Power in this sense does not necessarily mean formal status, so it is possible for a teacher to sexually harass his head of department and for students to harass their teacher. Sexual harassment is about trying to put someone else down – making them feel small, intimidated and power*less*. Though men and women can both be guilty of harassment, the vast majority of reported cases are males to females. This is not surprising when, in the rest of society, power is generally seen to rest with men. In schools it is not unknown for women teachers to be subjected to sexual harassment from male pupils. As both Walkerdine (1987) and Reay (1993) have demonstrated, young children can be very sexually aware, and harassment is not confined to secondary schools. Describing boys' resistance in a nursery school, Walkerdine transcribes two four-year-old boys talking to their teacher.

> *Various people on reading this transcript have commented that they are surprised and shocked to find such young children not only making explicit sexual references, but having so much power over the teacher. (p. 167)*

Reay, a former infant school teacher, described her experience as follows:

I have frequently felt oppressed by the boys in my charge, I have been verbally abused and, on a number of occasions, physically assaulted. At the time I rationalised that I was not a 'good enough' teacher. Since then I have seen women teachers in similar situations, challenged and upset by the aggression of a few boys in their class, and realised the problem is not of individual ineptitude, but of sexism. (p. 16)

This type of behaviour is likely to be even more overt with older children, and can be manifested through jokey innuendoes, pointed comments about clothes and appearance (size of breasts etc.) and questions about the teacher's sex life. 'Touching up' women teachers by male pupils is also not unknown – in the classroom and in packed corridors. Needless to say, if the ethos of the school allows this sort of behaviour towards teachers to go unchecked, it is likely that female pupils will suffer more and worse. Lesbian and gay teachers and pupils are particularly vulnerable in these situations and can be at the receiving end of appaling behaviour (see for example an anonymous account in De Lyon and Migniuolo, 1989 and various accounts in Epstein, 1994).

Sexual harassment (like racial harassment) is learned behaviour and, as such, can be 'unlearned'. How the head deals with these issues is again all-important. If the head makes it clear that sexual harassment will not be tolerated in any form, adults and children are less likely to condone it and more likely to report it if it occurs. Again, his/her own behaviour towards pupils, colleagues and other adults will be noted and taken as a model.

Conclusion

In this chapter we have tried to demonstrate that sex, sexism, sexuality and sexual harassment are issues that concern schools. Ignoring them will not make them go away. Both the intended and unintended behaviour of heads with regards to these issues can have an enormous impact on the ethos of the school and the individual lives of all those connected with it.

7
■ ■ ■

Evaluating Leadership – from the Outside

You get the credit for everything that's right, for example a good concert, when really the teachers involved should get the credit and for everything that goes wrong, for example lost PE shorts. (Female secondary head)

Being a head has always been seen as an important job, but recently it has become high-profile and high-stakes too. In England, there are now qualifications for aspiring heads (NPQH); financial support for in-service training for newly appointed heads (Headlamp) and courses for experienced heads (Serving Heads programme). The role of the head is seen as pivotal to the success of the school, and there are many success stories which confirm the power of the head to revitalise a school. They can no longer work behind closed doors, and it is not unusual for heads to be removed and replaced if their school receives a bad inspection report. This can mean being publicly pilloried or quietly shuffled off stage. The analogy with the company CEO or football manager is becoming less and less far-fetched as the pressure for results intensifies. The tenure of heads in English schools is more and more likely to rest on the evaluation of OFSTED inspectors.

Whereas the criteria for effective headship have in the past been largely implicit and intuitive, these are now more explicitly spelt out and judgements are made and published on the basis of those criteria. The job is increasingly open to public scrutiny, and heads have to be demonstrably and measurably effective. Getting an accurate diagnosis of the effectiveness of the leadership of a school is not, however, a simple exercise, and a range of issues have to be addressed. For a start, there has to be a dialogue about who constitutes 'the leadership' and what is meant by 'effective'. Is this different in different schools? Do staff, students, parents, LEA officials, governors, central government, have similar or different views? Whose views are important? Who needs to know?

It is important to be aware of the political context which frames the discussion and to recognise the 'philosophy', 'ideology' or set of assumptions that underpin what is often referred to as 'new public management'. Managing schools cannot be analysed and prescribed as if it occurs in a neutral, apolitical context; nor can it be evaluated in some objective, dispassionate way. More than twenty years ago Ernest House (1973) challenged the notion of objectivity in evaluation and reminded us of its inherent political purposes:

> *Contrary to common belief, evaluation is not the ultimate arbiter, delivered from our objectivity and accepted as the final judgement. Evaluation is always derived from biased origins. When someone wants to defend something or to attack something, he often evaluates it. Evaluation is a motivated behaviour. Likewise, the way in which the results of an evaluation are accepted depends on whether they help or hinder the person receiving them. Evaluation is an integral part of the political processes of our society. (p. 60)*

More recently there has been a growing critique of the common-sense claims of policy-makers who appear to believe that the process of evaluation can be somehow neutral, apolitical or objective (Gray and Wilcox, 1995; Wilcox and Gray, 1996; Ouston *et al.*, 1998; Earley, 1998). School inspection is for many teachers the single most significant evaluation of their work and is most resented when it lays claim to impartiality or objectivity. OFSTIN, the self-appointed body for monitoring standards of inspection, found:

> *a set of previously-agreed expectations and issues, which unduly influenced interpretation and judgement. Others were surprised by how quickly, and how early in the process, judgements appeared to form, and how frequently these were influenced by prior subjective expectations. (Boothroyd et al. 1997, p. 11)*

The so-called 'new sciences' have dramatically overturned century-long beliefs about measurement, and many writers in the field of new leadership draw parallels from the worlds of the physical sciences. One of these, Margaret Wheatley (1994) comments that when we observe, whether in the sub-atomic environments or in the world of people, we participate in the creation of the reality we see.

> *If quantum matter develops a relationship with the observer and changes to meet his or her expectations, then how can there be scientific objectivity? If the scientist structures an experiment to study wave properties, then matter will behave as a wave. If the experiment is to examine particles, matter shows up in particle form. (p. 65)*

Organisational reality is similarly determined by what we pay attention to. What we see is what we look for and what we worry about is what we have decided to worry about. If we acknowledge the part we play in the process, it changes the nature of the things we talk and argue about.

Evaluation is not a simple linear process. It has many facets and manifold purposes. Among them we can distinguish an overtly political purpose, an accountability purpose, a diagnostic purpose, a formative or developmental purpose, a marketing or public relations purpose. Evaluation is, however, rarely pursued single-mindedly, but rather with a mix of intentions. The danger is that these purposes are so intertwined that whether one is a participant or the intended audience of evaluation, it is difficult to unravel the tangled skein. Consequently what is reported may be accepted without demur or, on the contrary, provokes protracted discussions of validity, reliability and applicability. Yet evaluation is critical in moving us towards a deeper understanding of leadership. A useful starting-point is the issue of audience. Who is evaluation for?

The importance of audience

In order to disentangle the various intentions of evaluation, it is important to be aware of the audience, to identify who evaluation is for and what immediate or longer-term purpose it is designed to serve. What, for example, is the purpose and primary audience for school effectiveness studies; of quality assurance reports by the local authority; of international comparisons of country-by-country performance?

One of the largest growing 'industries' in recent years is that of international comparison. The reports have a direct and highly significant impact on policy-making and far-reaching effects on the work of school leaders and classroom teachers. For example, the Third International Mathematics and Science Study (TIMMS), the OECD's education indicators, the EC's Eurydice's 'key data' on the performance of educational systems, have as their primary audience policy-makers and are explicitly designed to inform national priorities in decision-making. But in the construction and reporting of data considerable care is given to another audience, that is the media, because it is recognised that newspapers and television play a critical role in shaping public opinion and educational policy. These international studies are powerful sources of evaluation data but are rarely seen by teachers and largely unknown to school or authority leaders. Yet it is authorities, heads and teachers who are required to 'deliver' on the basis of those policies and ought, therefore, to be one of the most informed and critical of audiences.

This applies in equal measure to a form of evaluation that touches teachers more directly, that is, the school inspection report. OFSTED reports address multiple audiences, but what is their primary readership? Who are they written *for*? – the headteacher and school management team? the whole school staff? the local authority? the governors? parents? a wider public? the media? the DfEE? OFSTED itself? It would be an interesting and educational exercise to ask a group of teachers, parents, or school students to rank in order of priority the audiences which they see as the targeted readership of the OFSTED report.

Clues to audience can be found in the register, language and 'coding' of the report. The following is an example of an OFSTED report.

> *The school is outstandingly led by the headteacher, strongly supported by her senior management team and governors who are well informed about the organisation of the school. Notable strengths in leadership are the clear enunciation of the aims and purposes of the school; high expectations; the involvement of all members of the school community in decision-making and planning for improvement.*

One of the first audiences for this report was the headteacher, for whom it was a ringing personal endorsement of her efforts to take the school forward into a new era. However unwelcome an inspectorial visit was in prospect, in retrospect it was gratifying and affirming for good practice throughout the school to be so publicly recognised. It was reassuring for those parents who actually read the report and for those who became aware of it through the local press. Although the audience of this report appears on the surface to be limited to a group of local interested parties or 'stakeholders', its messages extend much wider, to the local authority, to other schools, and become assimilated into a canon of good practice. The comments on one school in fact send out more far-reaching signals and are addressed to much wider audiences. The notion of the 'beacon school' leans on this metaphor (or semaphore).

OFSTED inspections

Three aspects of OFSTED reports are worth examining in more depth if we are to understand how leadership is evaluated and if we are to gain clearer insights into what schools can do to become more expert in evaluating leadership for themselves. The three aspects we will examine in turn are:

- the content – the explicit reference points for judging effective leadership
- the medium – the style and register of reporting
- the evidential base – the transition from evidence to definitive judgement.

Matters of content

Lying behind the reporting of school, and leadership, performance lies an implicit, and increasingly explicit, view of what makes for effective schools and effective leadership. The spelling out of these in OFSTED's *New Framework for School Inspection* (1995) has been widely welcomed as it helps schools to know more clearly on what basis they are being judged.

In his Annual Report, OFSTED's Chief Inspector lists five main aspects of leadership and management. One of the five categories is simply called 'leadership', while the other four categories describe what can be inferred about leadership and management from the following: the school's ethos; implementation of school's aims, values and policies; development planning, monitoring and evaluation; and support and monitoring of teaching.

Evaluating the quality of leadership in the nation's primary schools, the Chief Inspector arrives at the judgement that three-fifths of primary schools are 'well led'. This is based on a score of 58 per cent of heads being rated in the good/very good category as giving 'clear educational direction for the school'. However, on those other four areas from which the quality of leadership is inferred, only 26 per cent are deemed good/very good on support and monitoring of teaching, 32 per cent get a good/very good grade for development planning, 53 per cent for implementation of aims and policies and 76 per cent for ethos. These gradings for different aspects of the school's 'performance' are then aggregated to arrive at a final judgement of the leadership. So, for example, management and leadership was judged to be good/very good in 50 per cent of primary schools and 56 per cent in secondary schools.

Knowing the nature of the criteria by which leadership is judged by inspectors is an important step forward and widely welcomed by senior management of schools. However, these criteria should be no more than a starting-point for a critical appraisal by school staff as to their value and relevance. Some of these features and hallmarks of effective leadership may reflect the contemporary culture and current political context. Some criteria will be suggestive rather than definitive, ephemeral rather than timeless. Some have stood the test of time while others are, no doubt, still to be invented.

Matters of language and register

Just as important as the content of reporting is the medium through which messages are relayed to a wider public. The style of OFSTED reporting has been described as 'objectivisation', in other words, categorical judgements presented as if they represented an objective reality and as if inspectors, on the basis of a one-week visit, could arrive at such definitive conclusions. OFSTED school reports have an unequivocal register. They eschew the coded language redolent of reports of years gone by which, as often as not, were likely to provoke the question – is this good or bad? The newer language and register is designed for a broader public. It is the blunt speaking that mimics the tabloid press – simple and direct. It is also quite explicitly seen as a model for other countries seeking to evolve models of accountability, quality assurance and public reporting.

The clarity, accessibility and forthright nature of school reports is in many ways a move forward. The emphasis on 'plain English' in Scottish Office documents has won them the prized quill-pen hallmark. Plain speaking and plain writing bring greater transparency to the evaluation of school performance. They help to develop a public vocabulary and perform an educative function.

What is concealed within the prose, however, is of critical relevance for how parents, teachers, pupils and the wider public evaluate schools and judge the quality of their leadership. The issue is one of 'voice'. Whose voice is being heard? How trustworthy is it? How can we know? How can we test its truth and the honesty of its intent?

Michael Fielding (1998) warns of the hidden agendas in speaking on behalf of others:

> *in speaking about others, even in the sense of describing what you take to be the case, you may, in effect, be seeking in their place, that is, speaking for them. The very language you use in your description is likely to be saturated with values, frequently your own. (p. 8)*

Quoting Alcoff, he writes:

> *In both the practice of speaking for as well as the practice of speaking about others I am engaging in the act of representing others' needs, goals, situation, and in fact* who they are. *(p. 8)*

Allowing authentic voices to emerge through the reporting of others' experience is the hallmark of good research studies, illuminating biographies and the most engaging fiction. It is what good external evaluation can do, providing an account in which people can recognise their own experience.

From observation to judgement

The third aspect of OFSTED reporting, linked closely to the other two, lies most deeply beneath the surface of what is written about school performance. What is the nature of the evidence from which inferences and conclusions are drawn? What is the reliability and validity of that evidence? What are the intermediate steps from evidence to judgement? How summative conclusions are finally arrived at is far from transparent yet is the most important and useful information for school leadership because it addresses itself to processes, relationships, expectations, ethos – the very stuff of good schools and astute leadership.

Inspectors' evaluations of leadership are subjective and based on inferential judgements by a team of people over the course of a week or so. This is true not simply of OFSTED but of many quality assurance procedures, local authority and private sector validation. Commonly they draw on four main sources of evidence: one is the self-report (explicit and inferred) by the headteacher herself; the second source is documentation – of plans, policies and communications; the third source is the direct evidence from stakeholders – teachers, pupils, parents; the fourth, observation and inference made from walking around, visiting classrooms and through informal encounters.

The first of these four sources is the head herself. Her self-presentation and behaviour over the course of the week and in pre-inspection meetings is one of the bases for judgements. For example, she presents a picture of herself through her chairing of a briefing or report-back meeting; the way in which she speaks to, listens to or includes staff in discussion; her casual encounters with staff or pupils and her apparent familiarity with them and their names; the nature of formal as well as passing discourse; how the head approaches visits to classrooms, participates in the teaching or teaches herself. Some of this is fairly open to objective analysis and description – the choice, nature and tone of language, listening skills, styles of communication and decision-making. However, this is rarely conducted in any systematic way with the kind of concern for evidence that would satisfy a research student. Many of the individual competencies, and competences, are 'picked up' through subliminal cues, things not said, body language, interpersonal chemistry.

A second source of inference on the quality of leadership is the documentation provided by the school. Qualitative judgements are made about the nature and content of the documents seen. Much of this is open to quasi-objective analysis – for example, issues of presentation, readability, language, tone. Judgements can be made about the coherence and relevance of policies, the sophistication of development plans, the level of explicit understanding of self-evaluation; and the more these judgements of 'quality' can be tied to discussible evidence, the more helpful it is for developmental purposes. While the nature of an inspection event makes it difficult to engage in such formative discourse, time and space can be created for this, and where it happens it can immeasurably enrich the process.

The third source for the quality of leadership is from other 'witnesses' who are members of the school community – teachers, pupils and parents. Some of that evidence is gathered systematically, for example through questionnaires distributed to a sample of parents, or through interviews with teachers and pupils. Again, much that is garnered is in the space between words, what is not said as much as what is said, the subtle cues for which reciprocal antennae have been trained. How these impressions and pieces of evidence come together to form a summative judgement remains to some extent a mystery. When inspectors report their findings to the school leadership, possibilities of open dialogue are constrained by the fact that they can neither reveal the sources of their data nor are able to quantify them. For example, as one head-teacher reported:

> *I was frustrated by it because I couldn't tell if the criticism made of me – 'never being out of my office' – was the voice of the majority, picked up from one, two or a minority of staff, or perhaps even from a small group of pupils in a particular year group.*

The issue of voice is again to the fore. The authentic voice is inaccessible. It is mediated through the perceptions and interpretation of an inspector, or inspectors, speaking on behalf of others.

The same issues are amplified with regard to the fourth source of evidence – the organisation and ethos of the school. This can be made objective and systematic to some degree, for example, focusing on the match between planning and implementation, the congruence between policy and practice, the degree to which self-evaluation is visible and embedded in day-to-day school and classroom practice, the overall level of comfort, challenge or satisfaction as reported by people themselves. Much of the weight of judgement about effective leadership is, however, inferred from the overall climate as experienced by a visiting team. Such intuitive assessments may be highly insightful and valuable to a school, but only when they are presented in a way that can engage a dialogue and generate a concern for evidence and further inquiry.

OFSTED's Chief Inspector claimed in an off-the-cuff statement that all he needed was one day in a school to form judgements about its quality. It brought a swift rejoinder from the NUT to the effect 'Why spend a week on inspections, then?' There is a common-sense 'truth' in the Chief Inspector's remark, because some schools 'feel' comfortable and inviting while, in others, the tension is almost palpable. However, the culture, rhythms and patterns of organisational life lie much more deeply buried. They are only discernible over time, and are never static enough to be pinned down with precision. That is why inspection works best and is most positively received when feedback is given not as something definitive and objective, but as an agenda for discussion. Inspection is most effective when it offers opportunities for school leaders and inspectors together to reflect critically and openly on those deeplying, but highly significant, aspects of school quality.

The example of the 'Beacon' school

There is a lesson about external evaluation to be learned from the development of Beacon schools. The term 'Beacon school' was designed to convey an image of shining models of good practice. The first cohort of schools was selected on the basis of OFSTED reports – exemplary schools from which others could learn. However, this was not, by and large, how Beacon schools evaluated themselves. They recognised their own strengths and weaknesses and acknowledged that it was not a matter of 'teaching' other schools, but engaging in a dialogue with them. A critical feature of that dialogue was evaluation, finding a meeting-ground for the external and internal perspectives. They did not see their role as showing off to others, but as developing collegial relationships in which there was mutual learning among networks of schools, recognising where their own strengths lay and acknowledging their own weaknesses. The suspicion, or hostility, of other non-Beacon schools was only overcome when schools presented themselves as learners and collaborators rather than models, teachers, or definitive sources of reference.

Someone who has had considerable involvement with Beacon schools is David Hargreaves, who from their very first conception has been critical of the loose terminology of 'good practice'. In common usage good practice, he argues, may be no more than a nice idea, but in order for good ideas to become validated as 'good practice' they need to be subjected to a sterner test of evidence than the judgements of an inspection team, however astute.

Jean Rudduck, addressing Beacon schools in May 1999, offered them lessons from her own study in which she illustrated the dangers of the 'grand design', the simplistic borrowing of others' practice, and the vital importance of 'contexting'. Quotes from teachers and headteachers interviewed in the course of her research illustrate these issues:

> There is an incredible tendency in the education service to want the Grand Design – you know, this is the huge model that we must apply to everyone.

> There's a potential for every school to be a Beacon school in something or other.

> I feel at times there is a danger of getting to believe that the good practices are everywhere else and that the host school has got everything right and that we've got to learn from them rather than it being a two way process.

> (From address by Jean Rudduck to Beacon Schools, York, May 1999)

These issues have a direct and significant implication for the evaluation of schools. In well-managed inspection teams much time is invested in sharing experiences, discussing and testing the basis of judgements and evidence, working closely together to ensure some commonality and consistency. In effective teams there is a recognition that judgements must be tentative and exploratory and that the nearest we can get to a valid account is by engaging in an open and searching dialogue and through a confluence of internal and external evaluation.

A Scottish example

Although different in many fundamental respects, the Scottish system shares some features with OFSTED. A four-point scale (Figure 7.1) is used to assess the quality of leadership in a range of areas, in many respects similar to those of OFSTED, but arrived at in discussion with heads and subject to prior self-evaluation by the school on the basis of 33 indicators published in the policy document *How Good is Our School?* (SOEID, 1997).

In the 1999 HM Inspectors of Schools Report, *Quality and Standards in Scottish Schools*, this was reported. 'Headteachers' leadership skills were very good or showed more strengths than weaknesses in 80% of primary and 85% of secondary schools.' Strengths singled out by HMI were:

4 = major strengths
3 = more strengths than weaknesses
2 = more weaknesses than strengths
1 = unsatisfactory

Figure 7.1: The Scottish four-point scale

- commitment and vision
- communication
- being well regarded within the school and wider community
- good working relationships and teamwork
- a supportive ethos.

Main weaknesses highlighted in primary schools were:

- too little attention to ensuring that staff followed school policies
- lack of focus on managing the curriculum
- lack of systematic monitoring of learning and teaching and feedback
- poor use of the strengths of staff in making planned improvements
- too little attention to raising pupil attainment as a main priority of the school.

Main weaknesses highlighted at secondary level were:

- not enough emphasis on focus on raising standards of achievement
- not setting high expectations for pupils' work
- not raising expectations of staff
- failure to involve senior staff more directly in monitoring the work of the school and departments.

Common to the English and Scottish models is the emphasis on policy and planning, ethos, support and monitoring of teaching, and allied to this the underpinning premise that the ultimate test of leadership is raising standards of achievement.

In Scotland an inspectorate team gathers information from a variety of sources, some formally and some informally. The education authority provides one piece of the jigsaw, forming a backdrop and set of predispositions to the judgements that will be made during the school visit. A key element in the HMI visit is the presentation by the headteacher to the visiting team. This adds a further piece to the picture being assembled, perhaps even a crucial centrepiece as it lays out the vision, the philosophy, strategy, planning, professional development and other key aspects of the school's organisational life. However, as in interviewing or public speaking it is not only the content of the presentation that is being evaluated. Also important is the effectiveness or impact, the apparent conviction the presentation carries with it, the quality of communication, its congruence with other messages being picked up by the inspectors, the headteacher's 'style'. Inspectors are expected to have keen antennae and it is the subliminal messages picked up in these interpersonal encounters that play a part in colouring and shaping their final judgement.

The inspection team will spend four hours or more in direct interview with the head (although generally less in a primary school) at different points over the week, checking out the fit between what is said and what is done.

A further important element is the systematic negotiation of inspectors' judgements with the school's senior management team. Going through the performance indicators in turn, both sides challenge the basis of evidence for judgements on a scale of 1 to 4. It is the process itself which is, again, one of the most revealing aspects of leadership. The ability of the head or senior management team to be self-critical and engage constructively in the debate tells its own story. As one inspector put it:

> It is quite common for a headteacher to run down the list of P.I.s (performance indicators) and to say 'We have done that. We have done that. So we should get a 4.' But the very act of seeing evaluation in this mechanistic way is in itself evidence of an inadequate approach to the issue.

At its best this collaborative pursuit of evidence tests the quality of thinking about management, leadership and effectiveness, and this forum for negotiation is seen by the Scottish Inspectorate as a seminal aspect of the quality assurance process, not only in arriving at some summative assessment but as a model in its own right for school self-evaluation.

Scottish inspectors are the first to admit to the difficulty in making categorical judgements. While a '4' (major strengths) is very often obvious and unambiguous, the borderlines between '2's and '3's and '1's and '2's is less clear-cut and more open to discussion, negotiation and a press for evidence.

The end result of the Scottish inspection may be a high commendation or an expression of serious concern about the head's ability to give appropriate leadership to the school. A grade of '1' (major weakness) may either call for an urgent and high level of support from the authority or an agreement between HMI and authority that the headteacher should be swiftly replaced, a process that it is rarely easy and never undertaken lightly. It has long been said that Scottish inspectors 'work in the spaces' and they do so usually quietly, sensitively and with respect for the incumbent rather than publicly or punitively.

Headteachers who are given a '1' or '2' in school reports are in a minority, accounting for between 5 and 15 per cent of all schools. This is, none the less, a significant proportion, and Scottish inspectors are at pains to emphasise the high-stakes nature of that assessment and the careful and scrupulous collection of evidence that needs to be gathered before final judgements are made. Scottish inspectors are also keen to emphasise that the structure of the Inspectorate, with its internal accountability, monitoring and striving for consistency, is designed to inspire confidence in the quality assurance process. Scottish inspectors bring with them a broad national experience and, by virtue of geographic scale and frequent in-service training, a consistency of approach which is not available to OFSTED-contracted teams. Self-evaluation within inspectorate teams is seen as an important modelling of what is expected of schools, and the question 'How good is our Inspectorate?' is pursued systematically along with the question 'How good is our school?'

However much the inspectorate strives for fairness and uniformity, its value will ultimately rest on the degree to which it is able to complement the school's own internal evaluation and to strengthen the capacity of the school and school leadership to be self-evaluating and self-improving. It was in recognition of this that in 1992 school self-evaluation was made a central plank of policy, and in the 1997 the new policy document *How Good is Our School?* with emphasis on the pronoun at the heart of the question signalling where the ownership of evaluation ought to lie. HGIOS, as it is known in Scotland, grew out of the good practice that had developed from the bottom up and, as that document says in its introduction, 'this came together quite naturally' – the document wrote itself.

Schools speaking for themselves

It was the experience of self-evaluation in Scotland that motivated the National Union of Teachers to commission a project aimed at developing a similar framework for schools in England and Wales. Since the publication of that study in 1996 (MacBeath *et al.*), self-evaluation has been high on the NUT policy agenda and in 1999 it co-sponsored the publication of *Schools Must Speak for Themselves*. The book (MacBeath, 1999) contains this passage:

> There is an emerging consensus and body of wisdom about what a healthy system of school evaluation looks like. Its primary goal is to help schools to maintain and improve through critical self-reflection. It is concerned to equip teachers with the know-how to evaluate the quality of learning in their classrooms so that they do not have to rely on an external view yet welcome such a perspective because it can enhance and strengthen good practice.

> In such a system there is an important role for an Inspectorate or Office of Standards. It is to make itself as redundant as possible. It does so by seeking to reinforce the foundations of self-review and by helping schools to build more effectively on those foundations. (p. 1)

This role of an external inspectorate is strengthened rather than diminished by strong internal evaluation. This is increasingly being acknowledged by OFSTED in their move to a 'lighter touch' and a more selective approach to inspection. In the OFSTED publication *Evaluation Matters* (1997) the Chief Inspector's introduction begins with the question 'How Good is our School?', emphasising the importance of self-evaluation. It is to that issue that we turn in the next chapter.

8

■ ■ ■

Evaluating Leadership – from the Inside

To avoid speaking on behalf of others, schools need to be able to speak for themselves. School leadership needs to have the criteria, expertise and tools for self-evaluation, to extend the scope of inquiry beyond a limited group of stakeholders and to see evaluation not as something occupying an intensive week but as extensive, internal and integral to the day-to-day life of the school.

How good is leadership in our school? The question may be answered with the same two foci taken by the Inspectorate. On the one hand, the focus could be specifically on those people who occupy formal positions of leadership within the school trying to evaluate how effective they are in carrying out their job and meeting their goals. On the other hand, the school could attempt to assess how leadership impacts on the school as a whole and is refracted through day-to-day aspects of school life.

There is a third way, and one which tends to be less addressed by external inspection. It explores the issue of leadership in a more inclusive way. It works from a wider definition. It engages in a deeper search for leadership in the myriad aspects of classroom and school life, and in shared collaborative leadership. It seeks out instances of initiative exercised by individuals and teams and looks for networks from which new leadership arise.

The school can, of course, adopt the approach that best fits the context and purposes of evaluation. In this chapter we offer some strategies. We will start with the people who hold formal positions of leadership, before moving on to examine the wider expressions of leadership.

Evaluating headship

This has two aspects: the first focuses directly on personal qualities (competencies and competences); the second infers the quality of headship from aspects of school organisation, climate and relationships.

In the 1997 version of the Scottish Office document *How Good is Our School?*, one of the 33 indicators by which schools are expected to evaluate themselves is '7.4 *Effectiveness of leadership*' (Figure 8.1). These indicators can easily be turned into a self-evaluation instrument as illustrated in Figure 8.2, allowing the headteacher to reflect on his/her performance in relation to each of the categories. This has its limitations, of course, and can be open to self-deception. The headteacher might need another perspective, perhaps that of a member of the senior management team, a head from another school, or a member of staff?

The bravest of headteachers may use this instrument in a more systematic way to get feedback from a larger sample or from a number of different viewpoints. For example, the form may be given, anonymously to:

- the senior management team
- all (or a random sample of) teachers
- the governors
- a sample of parents
- a sample of students.

It is our experience that a brave and confident head who exposes herself to this is not only prepared to see herself as others see her but will take steps to address the issues that this raises.

An instrument with a similar purpose but a somewhat different format is shown in Figures 8.3 and 8.4. This comes with two separate forms. Each carries the same items, the only difference being that one is headed 'Me as I am', while the other is headed 'Me as I would like to be'. The headteacher, or anyone else for that matter, filling out the form starts with 'Me as I am' and works down the list, scoring herself 1 to 5 on the 5-point scale. Having got to the bottom, she joins the circles to give herself a profile. She then repeats the process with an identical form, this time, however, completing the items with a focus on 'Me as I would like to be'. This gives a second, and usually quite different, profile. If the two profiles are completed on thin paper, one can then be superimposed on the other and held up to the light to see where the largest disparities lie. If they are completed on overhead transparencies or translucent sheets they can be overlaid one on top of the other. The gaps that appear illustrate the areas to be worked on as identified by the headteacher herself.

The gaps are, of course, as seen from the perspective of the individual herself and might well be different if looked at from another viewpoint. A headteacher might, therefore, wish to have another perspective – from a partner,

Performance Indicator 7.4

Effectiveness of leadership

This performance indicator is concerned with the following themes:

- professional competence and commitment;
- leadership qualities; and
- relationships with people and development of teamwork.

It refers to the headteacher of a primary, secondary or special school, the head of a secondary department or others with leadership responsibilities.

Level 4 Illustration

- He or she demonstrates a high level of professional competence and commitment based on wide-ranging up to date knowledge and skills, including the ability to initiate, direct, communicate, manage staff and their development and delegate effectively. Where applicable, his or her teaching is a model of good practice.
- He or she has a wide range of relevant personal qualities, including the ability to create confidence and inspire others; he or she is a positive influence on his or her area of responsibility. He or she has the ability to evaluate objectively the qualities of staff and their contributions to teamwork. He or she demonstrates breadth of vision and can take difficult decisions effectively when necessary.
- He or she has very good relationships with pupils, parents and staff. There is a planned development of teamwork, staff are involved in policy development and his or her dissemination of information is clear and prompt

A performance broadly equivalent to that illustrated above would merit a Level 4 award.

Level 2 Illustration

- He or she demonstrates a degree of professional competence based on relevant knowledge, although this is not always successfully applied in practical contexts. There are difficulties in communicating and/or delegating effectively and attempts at initiating and directing are only partially effective. Where applicable, their teaching provides a good model in a number of respects.
- He or she demonstrates leadership but is not wholly successful in inspiring confidence in others and a number of staff do not respond to his or her management style, either because he or she is not wholly successful in inspiring confidence or does not provide a clear sense of direction. He or she lacks breadth of vision and tends to avoid difficult decisions.
- Difficulties arise at times in his or her relationships with pupils, staff and/or parents. He or she has difficulties at times in creating a team approach and while there are attempts to do so, in practice there are only occasional instances of effective teamwork and dissemination of information is not always clear or prompt.

A performance broadly equivalent to that illustrated above would merit a Level 2 award.

Figure 8.1: Effectiveness of leadership

children, or from friends or colleagues. One head who had taken the form home to be filled out by his wife, reported:

There wasn't a very close match between what I had done and her version of me. We had a most enlightening discussion on the subject which ended up with her saying 'Well all I can say is that you may be that person when you are in school, Harry, but that's not the person you are when you come home to me.'

	1	2	3	4	Management? or Leadership?
Commitment					
Up-to-date knowledge					
Ability to initiate					
Ability to direct					
Communication skills					
Manages staff effectively					
Supports staff development					
Delegates effectively					
Models good teaching					

Creates confidence in others					
Inspires others					
Has a positive impact on practice					
Ability to evaluate others effectively					
Demonstrates breadth of vision					
Takes decisions effectively					
Maintains good relationships with staff					
Maintains good relationships with pupils					
Maintains good relationships with parents					
Involves others in policy development					
Disseminates information promptly and effectively					

Figure 8.2: Qualities of leadership

When people go through this exercise they very commonly say 'It depends on where and when I fill this out. I am tough in a school context but tender in the family situation. I am assertive with people in positions of power over me but deferential to those beneath me in the formal hierarchy.' In other words, these are not fixed competences but personal qualities which may express themselves differently in different contexts. It again underlines the point made in Chapters 2 and 3 that we are, in fact, different people in different contexts and within different relationships. The headteacher in Chapter 3 who described herself as 'compassionate, gentle and thoughtful' but also 'strategic, innovative and astute', recognised the importance of context in determining how she would behave and, in a sense, who she was.

It is a virtue rather than a flaw of a self-evaluation protocol such as this that it is context-dependent. When the exercise is engaged with in a professional development context, therefore, it can provide an excellent tin-opener, disclosing issues

	1	2	3	4	5	
rule breaker	1	2	3	4	5	rule observer
efficient	1	2	3	4	5	inefficient
radical	1	2	3	4	5	conservative
share power	1	2	3	4	5	hold power
authoritarian	1	2	3	4	5	democratic
charismatic	1	2	3	4	5	reserved
pursue long-term goals	1	2	3	4	5	pursue short-term goals
forgiving	1	2	3	4	5	unforgiving
competitive	1	2	3	4	5	uncompetitive
delegate a lot	1	2	3	4	5	delegate very little
like change	1	2	3	4	5	dislike change
confront bad practice	1	2	3	4	5	tolerate bad practice
gentle	1	2	3	4	5	tough
reliable	1	2	3	4	5	erratic
strong values	1	2	3	4	5	open-minded
attend to detail	1	2	3	4	5	careless about detail
gregarious	1	2	3	4	5	private
size up people well	1	2	3	4	5	bad at sizing up people
demanding	1	2	3	4	5	undemanding
individualistic	1	2	3	4	5	team player
inflexible	1	2	3	4	5	flexible
optimist	1	2	3	4	5	pessimist
fight for beliefs	1	2	3	4	5	back off from a fight
entrepreneurial	1	2	3	4	5	cautious
predictable	1	2	3	4	5	unpredictable
take risks	1	2	3	4	5	avoid risks
take decisions easily	1	2	3	4	5	difficulty in decision-making
assertive	1	2	3	4	5	unassertive
manipulative	1	2	3	4	5	straightforward
easily influenced	1	2	3	4	5	unbending
low profile	1	2	3	4	5	high profile
idealistic	1	2	3	4	5	pragmatic
listen more than talk	1	2	3	4	5	talk more than listen
lead from the front	1	2	3	4	5	lead from the back
....	1	2	3	4	5	....

Figure 8.3: Me as I am

for wider discussion within the group. The exercise can be undertaken explicitly with reference to specific contexts or time of the year, week or day, for example:

Me as I am:

- in management team meetings
- in whole-staff meetings
- leading training sessions
- observing teaching in classrooms
- conducting appraisals
- engaging in an OFSTED inspection
- at an informal staff function
- at a local authority conference.

	1	2	3	4	5	
rule breaker	1	2	3	4	5	rule observer
efficient	1	2	3	4	5	inefficient
radical	1	2	3	4	5	conservative
share power	1	2	3	4	5	hold power
authoritarian	1	2	3	4	5	democratic
charismatic	1	2	3	4	5	reserved
forgiving	1	2	3	4	5	unforgiving
competitive	1	2	3	4	5	uncompetitive
delegate a lot	1	2	3	4	5	delegate very little
like change	1	2	3	4	5	dislike change
confront bad practice	1	2	3	4	5	tolerate bad practice
gentle	1	2	3	4	5	tough
reliable	1	2	3	4	5	erratic
strong values	1	2	3	4	5	open-minded
attend to detail	1	2	3	4	5	careless about detail
gregarious	1	2	3	4	5	private
size up people well	1	2	3	4	5	bad at sizing up people
demanding	1	2	3	4	5	undemanding
individualistic	1	2	3	4	5	team player
inflexible	1	2	3	4	5	flexible
optimist	1	2	3	4	5	pessimist
fight for beliefs	1	2	3	4	5	back off from a fight
entrepreneurial	1	2	3	4	5	cautious
predictable	1	2	3	4	5	unpredictable
pursue long-term goals	1	2	3	4	5	pursue short-term goals
take risks	1	2	3	4	5	avoid risks
take decisions easily	1	2	3	4	5	difficulty in decision-making
assertive	1	2	3	4	5	unassertive
manipulative	1	2	3	4	5	straightforward
easily influenced	1	2	3	4	5	unbending
low profile	1	2	3	4	5	high profile
idealistic	1	2	3	4	5	pragmatic
listen more than talk	1	2	3	4	5	talk more than listen
lead from the front	1	2	3	4	5	lead from the back
....	1	2	3	4	5	....

Figure 8.4: Me as I would like to be

The more we move away from static competences to more fluid contextual behaviour, the more useful the evaluation instrument becomes as a diagnostic or formative tool. If we can find simple tools that combine Jerome Bruner's twin principles of economy and power, insights to be gained can have an immediacy and spontaneity without losing the cutting-edge that effective evaluation requires.

The simple pie chart in Figure 8.5 exemplifies economy taken to its most pristine form, but is also a relatively powerful device. The headteacher is asked to make an intuitive judgement about her management style. What is the balance among command, consultation and consensus? The 'talking heads' in Chapter 3 who described their style would have responded to this very differently, some with a fairly high degree of command, all with a large degree of consultation and at least one with a virtually full circle on consensus.

In the example shown in Figure 8.5 the headteacher sees herself primarily as consultative, seeking consensus much of the time and only occasionally in the command mode.

The economy of this instrument, some might say, is too simplistic by half, but its real power comes when used with others, asking for their judgements of how decisions come to be made in the organisation. Figure 8.6 gives three different versions from the same school, except that it is clearly not the 'same' school for its different members.

While the differences of perception which this instrument can engender may lead to useful and challenging debate, it provides an opportunity to go beyond opinion and counter-opinion with a more rigorous analysis. It can be a first step in clarifying the language of the 'three Cs'. What is 'consultation' to me may not be consultation from where you stand. What I see as 'consensus' may be for you majority vote, or even thinly disguised 'command'. Evaluation can then move beyond this to look, for example, at recent crunch decisions, which can be revisited and unpacked again. Or it can focus on a decision about to be made (say, over the forthcoming week), so providing a prospective, rather than a retrospective, record. Analysis might be undertaken by the headteacher herself, primarily for her own enlightenment, or it may be undertaken with the management team as a whole or, with still more risk attached, involving a whole staff or small representative group of staff.

Figure 8.5: Command, consensus and control

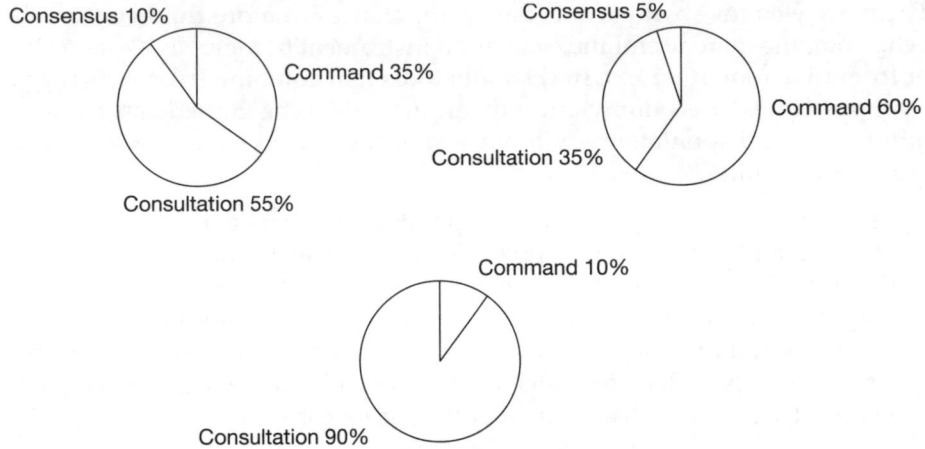

Figure 8.6: Command, consensus and control from three different perspectives

Values and time

Another fairly economical but potentially powerful device is the one-day diary. It was used to great effect in the Effective Leadership study, not only from the point of view of generating interesting research data but for the revelations it provided for the participating heads themselves. The researchers asked heads to think about what was important to them and to prioritise these values, say in order from 1 to 7. They were then asked to keep a detailed diary over the course of just one day, noting actions – where they took place, with whom, with what outcome, with what purpose. The completed diaries were then set alongside the value priority list to examine the closeness of fit (see Figure 8.7).

Values	Time
What is most important to:	• What? • Who with? • Where?
• Me? • The school?	• With what outcome? • With what purpose?

Figure 8.7: Values and time

This proved to be both a confirming as well as a challenging exercise. Headteachers were, on the whole, relieved and pleased to find a fairly close match between the values they professed and the time they invested, but this was not always the case, and the mismatch between intention and actuality was not only thought-provoking but led to some hard-headed discussion about how to bring these into closer conjunction.

The four quadrants

A companion exercise which might help to move insights a little closer towards action is the urgency/importance matrix. It is familiar to many head-teachers as a staple on management courses. It is sometimes dismissed as irrelevant in a school context of constant surprise and unpredictability. It can, however, be very useful as a starting-point for examining values and action or as a sequel to the values/diary exercise. The four quadrants shown in Figure 8.8 allow headteachers (or other members of the school community) to put tasks, events and actions into whichever of the four quadrants is most appropriate. Every letter, phone call, memo, interview or visit in a given period of time is recorded in one of these categories.

Stephen Covey (1989), the chief advocate of this tool, argues that the large bulk of leaders' time should be in quadrant 2. Where this isn't the case, he suggests, it is a time for some reflection, replanning and intensive review. He describes the four quadrants as in Figure 8.9.

As a developmental tool this can be used at any level from the classroom teacher to pupils organising their leisure, study and personal lives.

Quadrant 1	Quadrant 2
Urgent and important	Important but not urgent

Quadrant 3	Quadrant 4
Urgent but not important	Not urgent and not important

Figure 8.8: The four quadrants

Quadrant 1	Quadrant 2
Crises Pressing problems Deadline-driven projects and meetings	Preparation Prevention Values clarification Relationship building Empowerment Relaxation
Needless interruptions Unimportant meetings, phone calls Other people's minor issues	Trivia, busywork Time wasters Escape activities Irrelevant mail Excessive relaxation
Quadrant 3	Quadrant 4

Figure 8.9

Sketches of leadership

Another economical and powerful device used in the Effective Leadership study was the freehand spontaneous drawing of leadership as seen from a number of perspectives. At the start of the project, participating headteachers were given the freedom of a large A2 sheet of paper to depict themselves in relation to their job. Figures 8.10(a) and (b) give two examples of those art

Figure 8.10a

Figure 8.10b

works. Their illustrations sparked extended and significant discussion, so much so that the research team later published the taped record of these, together with drawings, as *Images of Leadership* (MacBeath *et al.*, 1994).

The second stage of the exercise was to go through a similar exercise from a pupil viewpoint. This produced a range of colourful and sometimes idiosyncratic views of headteachers. Examples of these are illustrated in Figures 8.11(a) to (d).

The card sort

Another device used in the Effective Leadership study was the card sort. After some discussion and piloting with different stakeholder groups, a set of cards was devised, each card bearing one statement about the role or possible functions of the headteacher. Groups (pupils, parents, teachers) were then asked to lay the cards out in front of them on the table and, as a group, to agree on the most and least important ones and arrange them in order of priority.

Figure 8.11a: What does a Headteacher do?

Figure 8.11b

*The headteacher visits classrooms and says
'well done' to the boys and girls*

Figure 8.11c

*The headteacher stays behind after school
and dances in the hall*

Figure 8.11d

Another approach to prioritising used in the same project was a more conventional one, a five-category response sheet asking people (governors, parents, teachers) to choose their most and least preferred models of leadership. The differences within and between groups led to rich and useful debate in return for a very small investment of time. A copy of this instrument is shown in Figure 8.12.

The critical-friend interview

In Chapter 6 the role and functions of the critical friend in supporting self-evaluation are described. In the European Project *Evaluating Quality in School*

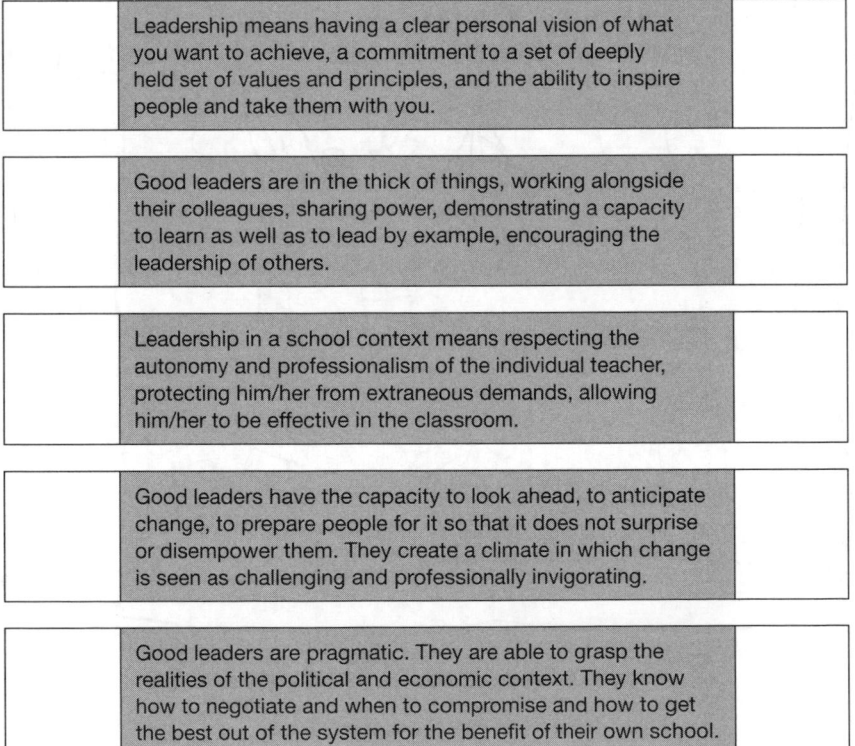

Which of the following five definitions of leadership is the closest to your own view? Please put a tick (✓) in the appropriate box.

Which of the above five definitions of leadership is furthest away from your own view? Please put a cross (✗) in the appropriate box.

	Leadership means having a clear personal vision of what you want to achieve, a commitment to a set of deeply held set of values and principles, and the ability to inspire people and take them with you.	
	Good leaders are in the thick of things, working alongside their colleagues, sharing power, demonstrating a capacity to learn as well as to lead by example, encouraging the leadership of others.	
	Leadership in a school context means respecting the autonomy and professionalism of the individual teacher, protecting him/her from extraneous demands, allowing him/her to be effective in the classroom.	
	Good leaders have the capacity to look ahead, to anticipate change, to prepare people for it so that it does not surprise or disempower them. They create a climate in which change is seen as challenging and professionally invigorating.	
	Good leaders are pragmatic. They are able to grasp the realities of the political and economic context. They know how to negotiate and when to compromise and how to get the best out of the system for the benefit of their own school.	

Figure 8.12: The meaning of leadership

Education (MacBeath *et al.*, 1999), it was seen by schools as the most valuable ingredient in helping them to become more aware, critical and self-improving. Critical friends were outside consultants – industrialists, university lecturers, board members, or sometimes parents – allocated to the school (or chosen by them) to work with teachers, the management team or with the headteacher specifically. Their role was to be both supportive and challenging. In one of the Finnish schools in the project the head described her relationship with the critical friend as of one of the most difficult but fruitful episodes of her 32-year career. Her critical friend had cleared an afternoon with her, then started the interview off with the request 'Tell me about your job.' The session lasted four hours and although the critical friend spoke very little she helped her, in the headteacher's words, 'travel a path I had never travelled before'.

The critical friend can play a valuable role in supporting the process of self-evaluation, offering the challenge to complacent, uncritical, or over-generous self-assessment. This may be through the kind of open-ended interview described or by using some of the self-assessment tools as a focus for the dialogue. The critical-friend role is one that can affirm, surprise, and reveal unrecognised depths and unsuspected assets. It is a sensitive and complex role about which comparatively little has been written. The range of skills described by heads who had evaluated the impact of the critical friend in the European Project is shown in Figure 8.13.

Collegial consultancy

Collegial consultancy can provide a different kind of in-depth evaluation. It may take many different forms, but the one that follows has proved itself in a range of different contexts. It works as now described.

Anything from five to fifteen leaders form a circle. One has volunteered beforehand to prepare a five- to ten-minute talk on a challenge she is currently facing. She starts by sketching the background of her school. She then goes on to describe how she sees the issue she is currently wrestling with. The task of the group is to listen as sensitively and accurately as possible so that they can follow up with intelligent and probing questions. The essential elements of the protocol are:

- seek first to understand
- try to get inside the issue from the speaker's standpoint
- ask questions that are designed to help her think through the issues
- don't preach
- don't anecdotalise
- don't offer suggestions as to what you did in your school.

Role	Skills
Adviser	• provides useful advice • offers a clear picture of the school's strong and weak points • gives information and materials about self-evaluation and development planning • suggests methods and other forms of support • gives clear guidelines on how to implement proposals.
Organiser	• moderates meetings • keeps time • structures the process • helps organise the work • provides guidelines for actions • prepares meetings or whole school activities • comments on strategic discussions • sets out clear objectives • directs working parties effectively.
Motivator	• gives reassurance and encouragement • is a good listener • gives reassurance and encouragement • creates a sense of importance of the project in the school • demands more from the school • is inspiring and encouraging • stops people from becoming too ambitious • makes self-evaluation understandable • helps in finding new ideas • keeps the work going • proceeds by small steps • gives an idea of where thing lead to • promotes ongoing activities • helps bridge gaps • helps in focusing • encourages a positive approach to collaborative work • helps to motivate the pupils and parents to co-operate in the project • prompts the action groups to recast the working tools.
Facilitator	• handles emotions • keeps the balance between personal and professional matters • lays fresh emphasis on the context-related aspects of the learning process at school • asks questions about interpersonal relations.
Networker	• builds networks • suggests possible partners outside/from other schools • helps in team-building • strengthens the co-operation between school and work • acts as a contact person with students of the teacher training college and the university.
Outsider	• brings in an outside view • is critical of the 'ordinary' • occasionally brings in counter arguments • creates multiple perspectives • mirrors one's own perceptions • enhances coherence among diverse viewpoints • calls the school into question in terms of its organisational aspects • analyses the school having the perspective of another enterprise.

Figure 8.13: The roles and skills of the critical friend

While this process does not preclude advice, it tends to be given or asked for only after the speaker's context has been grasped by the group and then offered in the form of 'Have you thought of . . .?', 'have you tried. . .?'

The technique was used to great advantage in the context of a seven-country study by the Bertelsmann Foundation. In one session a Dutch school leader talked about her difficulties in getting the teaching staff to change their life-time-ingrained habits. When it came to the 'Have you tried/have you thought of . . .?' questions her answers were 'Yes, we've done that. Yes, we have a school council. We have a newsletter. Yes, we do have praise systems for students. We have working parties. Yes, we have a mission statement, a school development plan, a system of review. Yes, we have staff appraisal.' Thirty-five minutes into the session a group member remarked, 'You seem to have everything. Yet I get a sense you have nothing.' This struck a chord with the headteacher in the hot seat. She didn't reply immediately but wrote silently. In the fifteen seconds or so of silence that ensued within the group the true nature of the issue was being grasped. It was eventually articulated by another head who said:

> It has brought something home to me. I have got the structures but never really deeply tackled the culture issue. In fact the more I think about this the more I see the structures as an impediment, not a support.

In these sessions the last five to ten minutes are given over to reflection on what has been learned by the participants. Each participant in turn says one thing that they have learned until finally it is the turn of the incumbent of the hot seat to reflect on what she has gained from the session. Articulating this and sharing it with the group, which has been through a common experience, proves to be an important part of the summary and closure of the session. In our experience a session like this can easily last for an hour and a half or more. It is an important aspect of planning to allow that kind of space and time so that the session can develop its own equilibrium and its own momentum.

These sessions have a special quality, a thoughtful, unhurried, reflective ethos. At the end of the session described above, a Norwegian headteacher, summarising what she had learned, said:

> For me it was like turning the pages of a book. With each page we moved deeper and deeper into the heart of the story. The mystery deepened. But as we got deeper and deeper the mystery also began to unravel. We began to see the light and find a happy ending.

This in-depth analysis often crosses the threshold from evaluating the individuals in formal leadership positions to leadership as expressed through the culture and character of the school. Leadership comes to be seen as a moving, restless, dynamic process. The quality of leadership is refracted through the facets and fragments of school life. It is seen in the corridor traffic, the entry and exits from classes, to brief encounters in hallways and on staircases, in the rhythm of classroom life and the harmonies of relationship.

Evaluating shared leadership

In evaluating leadership through the organisation and ethos of the school we might ask questions such as these:

- Where does the school get its energy from?
- Is there a sense of purpose and direction?
- Where and from whom does that sense come?
- How are decisions made?
- Where are the networks?
- What are the shared norms?
- How do norms change over time?

When we ask these kinds of questions and probe carefully for the answers, we will probably arrive at a highly complex view of how change, power and authority work. These questions unveil informal status, assumed rather than conferred. They illuminate shared vision and authority, emergent decision-making, currents and cross-currents of influence, push and pull, public and private authority, high-profile vacuity and low-profile effectiveness. Answers to these questions may reveal the nature of informal networks and their significance in sustaining people in times of pressure and stress.

When we change the focus from the person of the headteacher to the ethos of the school we can revisit some of the tools described earlier but with a different focus. We may, for example, reframe the 'Me as I am' instrument to become an organisational probe. It might look something like Figure 8.14. This may be used to help dig a little deeper into those subjective but none the less significant impressions, the 'feel' of the school. The dialogue that it stimulates can lead deeper and deeper into an examination of what lies beneath those surface characteristics of school ethos.

Development analysis interview

The development analysis interview has been used by researchers to explore the school's capacity for change. In this particular model researchers conduct two-handed interviews, with the headteacher and someone else in the school who brought a different perspective on recent developments. The two interviewees are asked to focus on a change or development that the school has been through in the last year or more. The task of the interviewer is to lead them back through the change process in careful detail, eliciting not only what was done and by whom, but the intentions, feelings and impact of the change. A substantial amount of qualitative data can be accumulated from such an interview, lasting up to an hour and a half. The task of the interviewer, or criti-

tidy	1	2	3	4	5	untidy
warm	1	2	3	4	5	cold
parent-friendly	1	2	3	4	5	parent-unfriendly
colourful	1	2	3	4	5	drab
authoritarian	1	2	3	4	5	democratic
comfortable	1	2	3	4	5	uncomfortable
orderly	1	2	3	4	5	disorderly
sensitive	1	2	3	4	5	insensitive
strict	1	2	3	4	5	easy-going
high stress	1	2	3	4	5	low stress
pessimistic	1	2	3	4	5	optimistic
tense	1	2	3	4	5	relaxed
helpful	1	2	3	4	5	unhelpful
competitive	1	2	3	4	5	uncompetitive
formal	1	2	3	4	5	informal
reactive	1	2	3	4	5	proactive
likes change	1	2	3	4	5	dislikes change
stimulating	1	2	3	4	5	boring
pupil-friendly	1	2	3	4	5	pupil-unfriendly
inflexible	1	2	3	4	5	flexible
clear values	1	2	3	4	5	no clear values
avoids conflict	1	2	3	4	5	responds well to conflict
adventurous	1	2	3	4	5	cautious
uses time well	1	2	3	4	5	time used badly
risk-taking	1	2	3	4	5	avoids risks
open to new ideas	1	2	3	4	5	sceptical of new ideas
idealistic	1	2	3	4	5	pragmatic
pursues long-term goals	1	2	3	4	5	pursues short-term goals
looks to the past	1	2	3	4	5	looks to the future
....	1	2	3	4	5	....

Figure 8.14: Ethos indicators

cal friend, is then to categorise and 'score' these data to give a judgement of the school's capacity to handle change. So, on the basis of how the two significant actors in the school conceptualise change, inferences can be made as to whether the development is seen as reactive or proactive, simplistic or sophisticated, or revealing a capacity for self-reflection and self-improvement.

The interviewer or critical friend has to come to the exercise with objectivity and critical distance, and school staff need to be prepared for a level of analysis and feedback that is highly challenging.

The quadrant

The matrix in Figure 8.15 is one that has been used by commercial companies to categorise their employees on two intersecting scales – positive to negative and high to low energy.

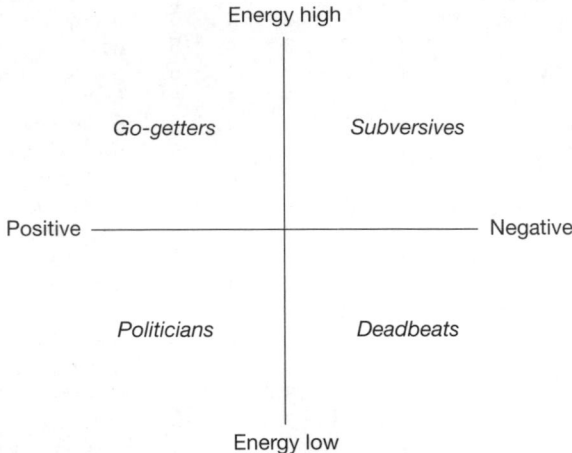

Figure 8.15: Evaluating staff – energy and attitude

It isn't difficult for headteachers to start writing names of their staff into the four quadrants. To put people into boxes like this does, however, rest on two assumptions: (1) that the vantage-point – your own as a headteacher – provides a good or accurate view of the terrain; (2) that qualities – of energy and positivity – actually belong to the individuals, that they are inherent and fixed.

It is instructive, therefore, to test these two assumptions. One way is by changing the viewpoint or viewer. The same instrument in the hands of a fellow trade union member, the secretary of the angling club, a fellow football supporter, or someone's children might give a very different picture of energy and positivity. Within the school context we might test some of the assumptions of the 'human qualities' models by focusing on the context and conditions which create go-getters out of deadbeats, which allow politicians to find new energy and encourage subversives to channel their energies into new constructive outlets. The following is one way in which this can be used as a staff development activity.

Think back over the last term of school. Now think of times, places, relationships in which you were highly positive and full of energy. Write them in quadrant 1.

Now think of times when you felt like a real deadbeat, negative and devoid of energy. Write them in quadrant 4.

Now think of times when you had a strong negative feeling (for example, about the school or the authority or the government) and were so energised by it that you took some action (a complaint, a letter, a phone call). Write these in quadrant 2.

Now think of times when you felt no enthusiasm or energy for what was going on but put a good face on it, accepted or even endorsed something for the sake of a quiet life. Write these in quadrant 3.

As a development exercise this can help everyone to reflect on the school as an energy system, producing or draining off energy in different places, at different times of the year, and depending on the ebb and flow of relationships. Understanding the ecosystem of the school tells its own story about contexts of leadership. To what extent are these places created and recreated by effective leadership? To what extent do they have a life and momentum of their own? As a self-evaluation tool the quadrant exercise can lend insights into the organisational life of the school and help to spotlight what might be changed for the better.

Photo-evaluation

A thermal imaging camera would be able to capture the hotspots and cold blue places in the school's energy system, showing where energy is created and entropy doing its dirty work. Taking photographs is the closest we can approximate to this, but may offer some more far-reaching insights than the high-tech equivalent. The headteacher of a Scottish primary school, Susan Ross (1995) describes what she did to involve parents in the evaluation of their school through the use of this approach.

> *A further opportunity to extend the discussion with parents was offered by the decision to photograph 'a day in the life of Coalsnaughton Primary'. John MacBeath, who was still working with the school, acted as the proverbial 'eye' for the course of one day, providing a collection of photographs which gave a comprehensive insight into the ethos of the school.*
>
> *Here was visual evidence of relationships, pupil–pupil and teacher–pupil, giving us another focus to assess the ethos of the school and to deepen discussion on the school's main purposes and values. What did the photos say about the ethos we were trying to create? How could that ethos support and enhance pupils' ability to learn? A second parents' evening was held. With the questionnaire results as a backdrop to discussion, parents were asked to work in small groups, listing all the things they thought made a 'good' school. They then had to select and agree on ten. Their next task was to look through the photographs and see if they could find evidence in Coalsnaughton school to match their criteria of a 'good' school. (p. 28)*

Two Austrian researchers, Ulrike Steiner-Löffler and Michael Schratz (1996) have extended the use of this technique. They give cameras to groups of students, inviting them to plan together and then, on camera, to capture places, people, events that to them say something significant about the school, whether in terms of physical provision, ethos, or teaching and learning.

One of the photographs they cite as an example is the closed door to the head-teacher's study. They ask, 'From a student perspective, what messages are being sent out from that inanimate object? What kind of energy system lies behind that door?' When discussion is embarked on with students, familiar places become invested with new meaning – the head's office is no longer the administrative centre of the school, but seen as a door behind which dangers lurk. The staffroom is seen, not as teachers see it, a retreat, a respite centre, but as 'the place where boring lessons come from'.

Diaries and logs

Headteachers, teachers and students often keep diaries on an informal and voluntary basis but the 'log' or diary can be put to systematic use to focus on an aspect of the school at a given time or with a specific theme. The homework log is an example of record-keeping that has been used to give an insight into what happens when students are left on their own to do their homework or study.

The approach is quite simple. A class or year group is asked to keep a careful record over the space of a week of what they did from the time of arriving home until bedtime and for the whole day on Saturday and Sunday. Carried out in a climate of trust and honest 'research', this has a number of benefits. It provides a view for students themselves of how they divide their time and how effective they are in using their time and resources. The greater value comes from the process of sharing and discussing the data in groups, with teachers, team leaders and senior management. It can be a useful tool for making homework or study more efficient and effective but, like all good tools, it can be put to other purposes such as classroom and school-wide learning.

Spot checks

The spot check is a way of ascertaining, at a given moment during the lesson, what is happening. It is in a sense like lifting a single frame from a moving picture at a totally arbitrary moment. One simple, easy-to-use version of this is for the teacher to stand back from the lesson and ask three questions:

- What are the students doing?
- What are they learning?
- What am I doing?

To this may be added a fourth, formative, question: 'What am I going to do next?' This exercise is obviously best undertaken when students are engaged in some activity and the teacher is free to observe. The answer to the question

'What are they doing?' may have a simple reply – writing in their books. But a little deeper probing might reveal some more complex and varied activity – some writing, some copying from their neighbour, some stuck and looking for help. The deeper question, 'What are they learning?' might require a sampling of the quality of work or some questioning of an individual student. When teachers do this they are sometimes shocked to find the misconceptions that students are working on and the lack of any deeper level of understanding.

A study in Singapore classrooms (Tay-Koay Seiw Luan, 1997), in which students in their final year of secondary school were asked to report about their thinking during a lesson, revealed the data shown in Figure 8.16, disaggregated by the ability of the student.

Probing still further into their learning processes, students were asked what was actually going on in their minds during a lesson, in an attempt to identify the intellectual skills that were being exercised. See Figure 8.17 for the findings.

These kinds of results were repeated across a number of different observed lessons. They paint a disappointing picture for a country at the apex of international league tables of attainment, but not an unexpected one. Headlines in Singapore's *Straits Times* about 'the overtaught Singapore student' and calls for a deep cut in curriculum content are a response to growing evidence from employers and universities that students have acquired exam-passing skills at the expense of thinking skills and aptitudes for lifelong learning.

As a self-evaluation tool, a spot-check instrument, which asks students to reflect on their thinking, can offer to both teacher and pupil insights into the quality of learning as well as a conceptual vocabulary to raise awareness of metacognitive skills – thinking about how we are thinking. Self-reporting of this nature requires of students some high-level language skills as well as conceptual skills, but it is a way of introducing them to a higher level of self-analysis, or 'metacognitive' activity. For teachers to use in their own classrooms to help students monitor their own learning strategies, it can be an invaluable development tool.

	Low ability	Average ability	High ability
Not thinking actively	29	16	14
Lesson-irrelevant thinking	26	23	33
Lesson-relevant thinking	36	45	30
Lesson-relevant and -irrelevant thinking	9	16	24

Figure 8.16: What were they thinking
(*Source*: Tay-Koay Seiw Luan, 1997.)

What pupils were doing	% of pupils self-report on lesson
Note taking	21
Responding to questions	9
Trying to understand	45
Visualising	6
Assimilating	7
Applying	1
Hypothesising	2
Analysing	5
Evaluating	3

Figure 8.17: What were they doing?
(*Source*: Tay-Koay Seiw Luan, 1997.)

A variation on this theme came from a school in the Socrates Project 'Evaluating Quality in School Education' (MacBeath *et al.*, 1999). Students armed with tape recorders dropped into classes at random and picked a student to question about her learning at that moment. At that school it also became apparent that many students lacked the conceptual language to describe their learning or thinking. The awareness of this is a valuable starting-point for growth.

Shadowing

Shadowing is a simple, economic, but potentially rich technique for getting an insight into a slice of school or classroom life. In a secondary school, for example, an individual student may be followed over the course of a day, as she moves from class to class, through breaks, lunch hour, games or library times. The intention is to 'see' the school through the eyes of the student. Shadowing can be done by a teacher, headteacher, parent, member of the governing body, a teacher in training, or a school student. There are three key considerations to bear in mind:

1 The presence of the shadower will affect how typical the school day is. The status of the shadower will have the deepest impact. A headteacher is unlikely to see a representative example of a lesson or school day. A school student is likely to create less 'disturbance' to routine events.

2 Seeing the familiar as unfamiliar may be more difficult for a school student immersed day to day in the environment of the school.

3   A clear task focus and preparation are critical. Unfocused observation is likely to bring minimal returns. Things to look for and questions to ask are crucial. A set of questions can be provided for the shadower to debrief the student at regular intervals.

Shadowing may be of a student, a teacher, a headteacher, a member of office or technical staff, or a member of the governing body.

The purpose and audience for the results needs to be clear beforehand. The audience may, for example, be the senior management team, the whole staff, parents or a joint parent–teacher meeting.

Interviews

Interviewing is one of the most common ways of gathering data. It is potentially the richest source but also the most time-consuming and complex. For school self-evaluation, consideration has to be given to the following:

- What is the purpose?
- Who will be involved?
- How can representativeness be assured?
- What is the best – individual or group interview?
- How long will each interview last?
- Who will conduct the interviews?
- How will confidentiality or anonymity be ensured?
- Where will interviews be held?
- How will they be recorded (tape or notes?)
- Will they be structured, semi-structured or open-ended?
- Who will analyse the data?
- What will the costs be?
- Will the return repay the investment of time, energy and resources?
- Are there other more economical alternatives?

Many of these seem obvious and even trivial questions, yet simple things like time and place are extremely important. The setting may be comfortable, relaxing, or intimidating to the interviewee. The headteacher's study, for example, may inhibit any frank discussion. Time, too, has to be allowed for people to establish trust and gradually express their real feelings. In the right setting and with the right climate the success of the interview also then relies on the skills of the interviewer in allowing time for reflection, prompting and probing sensitively, reading and responding to the feelings of the interviewee.

With children, especially younger ones, it is often preferable to have a group interview with three or more present. This helps to ease the tension for children who find the interview situation unfamiliar and threatening. They'll feel more free to speak if there are others of their age present. As with all of these techniques, piloting beforehand is important in testing and refining the interview protocol.

Focus groups

Focus groups are a more economical way of getting a great deal of information quickly. The focus group may, theoretically, be any size. If it is a face-to-face group it will probably be around ten or twelve people, chosen to represent different viewpoints, age or status. In a school it might consist of students of different ages and both sexes. Or it might be a mixture of students and teachers. Its function is to provide information in as open and honest way as possible, allowing the group to debate and distil the issues, arriving at consensus where there is genuine agreement and identifying differences where those differences are significant.

A school focus group might be asked to take a broad view of the organisation as a whole or to provide feedback on specific aspects such as homework, discipline, learning and teaching, parent meetings or professional development, for example. Running the group, keeping it on task, creating the right kind of climate and encouraging participation require expert skills, and it may be best for a school to secure the services of an outside person for this purpose unless it has an inside person with that role and relevant expertise.

Profiling

Focus groups may provide the forum for the use of profiling techniques. These can take many forms and be used in many different ways and for different purposes. The profile consists of a set of criteria (perhaps ten or a dozen) which people use to evaluate the school as a whole or specific aspects of it. A good example of the profile comes from the Socrates Project 'Evaluating Quality in School Education'. In this project the 101 participating schools all used the same profile of twelve characteristics as reproduced in Figure 8.18. Four groups of stakeholders (students, parents, teachers and governing bodies) were involved in assessing their school on each of the twelve categories using a four-point scale plus a judgement on improvement, decline or

	+ +	+	−	− −	↗	↔	↘

Outcomes

	+ +	+	−	− −	↗	↔	↘
Academic achievement							
Personal and social development							
Student destinations							

Process at classroom level

	+ +	+	−	− −	↗	↔	↘
Time for learning							
Quality of learning and teaching							
Support for learning difficulties							

Process at school level

	+ +	+	−	− −	↗	↔	↘
School as a learning place							
School as a social place							
School as a professional place							

Environment

	+ +	+	−	− −	↗	↔	↘
School and home							
School and community							
School and work							

Figure 8.18: The school self-evaluation profile

stability. Each of the four groups then sent two of their members to a school evaluation group whose task it was to reach consensus on the twelve criteria. This proved in most cases to be difficult but, in the process of discussion and negotiation, brought to the surface clear differences of opinion. It required people to listen more carefully to perspectives and experiences quite different from their own.

Following the evaluation by the group, a number of key areas for further evaluation or action were agreed on. The profiling instrument (Figure 8.18) provides a target over the course of the next year for the school to work towards.

Critical incident analysis

The critical incident analysis focuses on a micro-event in the life of a school. It might be a confrontation between a teacher and student, a complaint from a parent, or a communication difficulty in a senior management meeting. The purpose of the analysis is to unpack the incident in as much detail and depth as possible to throw light on school procedures, attitudes or capacity to handle conflict. The ultimate purpose is to identify what could be done to avoid a similar happening in the future or, more positively, to develop more effective communication, a more resilient culture or more widely agreed norms. Figure 8.19 gives an example from an analysis by a group of fifteen-year-old students of a disciplinary incident in one classroom.

The value of the analysis is not only in reaching a deeper level of shared insight, but in examining points at which action could have been taken to avert the escalation of trouble. The student group were able to identify a number of

Pressure and lack of time

The student recognises that the teacher is stressed and under pressure. She recognises that both she and the teacher have overreacted but they didn't have the opportunity to sort it out before it all spiralled out of control.

Authority and respect

The student recognises in retrospect that she had undermined the teacher's authority in front of the class. She also feels that her own authority was being diminished in front of her classmates. She feels greater mutual respect might have averted it.

Figure 8.19: A spiral of trouble

things that could have been done by the student herself, by other students or by the teacher. The critical incident analysis is also useful to the teacher who is better equipped to deal with the situation next time and has a common reference point with the class.

In conclusion

The quality of leadership in a school is tested most stringently by the nature and experience of a school's day-to-day life. Schools have at their disposal a large array of tools and strategies for self-evaluation which, when used systematically and with thought as to purpose and audience, can go beyond awareness-raising to a wider sharing of leadership.

Before embarking on pupil shadowing
- is it appropriate to stay with the pupil (teacher/head) during break and lunchtime?
- should the teacher/pupil match be the same sex and ethnicity?
- how do you communicate to all staff concerned that the purpose of the exercise is not to check on them?
- what do you report back to staff and pupils on your experience?
- how do you ensure that the exercise is used to improve school practice?

While pupil tracking
- what sort of range of teaching styles does your pupil encounter during her day, e.g. whole class/group work?
- does the content of the curriculum in any way reflect her experiences or heritage?
- is she encouraged to be an independent and responsible learner?
- does she have an opportunity to participate in oral work in the classroom? If so, does she do so?
- how many interactions does she have with teachers during the day? are they generally positive? is she called by name in the classroom or corridors?
- how does the pupil relate to her peer group?

After pupil tracking
- if relevant, what was the extent and effectiveness of learning support?
- were there connections between subject areas? were they made apparent to the pupil?
- did the day appear to have coherence?
- did the pupil receive mixed messages from the different adults she encountered?
- how did she spend her day out of classroom time? was there somewhere appropriate for her to go? were the corridors safe?
- what did she think of her schooling in general and the day you have observed in particular?

Guidelines for shadowing or 'tracking'

Divide participants into small groups (5 – 6 per group). Assign them the perspective of students, tutors, parents. Ask them to agree on five key indicators of a good school (or classroom, or learning). (10 minutes)

Create three new mixed groups of three (one from each) or group of six (two from each).

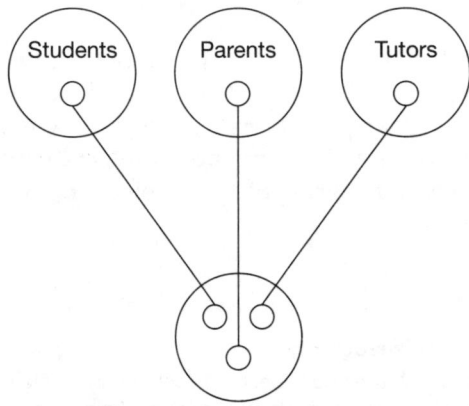

Task

Agree on seven key indicators. Discuss how evidence might be gathered as to the achievement of these. Discuss some kinds of instruments which might be used. (20 minutes)

Plenary

Facilitator brings ideas together. Compiles common list of indicators. Probes, challenges on precision, focus, measurability. Discusses notions of qualitative and quantitative approaches. Clears up common confusion over the two (see suggested reading).

School speaking for themselves – the process

Consider the main purpose, or purposes, of different kinds of evaluation, what form they take and the audience for whom they are intended.

Purpose	Form	Audience
political		
accountability		
diagnostic		
formative or developmental		
marketing or public relations		
other		

Evaluation – a question of purpose

References

■ ■ ■

Acker, S. (ed.) (1989) *Teachers, Gender and Careers*, London: Falmer.

Adler, S., Laney, J. and Packer, M. (1993) *Managing Women*, Buckingham: Open University Press.

Arygris, C. and Schön, D. (1978) *Organisational Learning: A theory of action perspective*, Reading, MA: Addison Wesley.

Barber, M. and Brighouse, T. (1992) *Partners in Change: Enhancing the teaching profession*, London: IPPR.

Bennett, A.E., Bryk, A.S., Easton, J.Q., Kerbow, D., Luppescu, S. and Sebring, P. (1992) *Charting Reform: The principal's perspective*, Chicago: Consortium on Chicago School Research.

Bennis, W. (1997) *Organizing Genius: The secrets of creative collaboration*, London: Nicholas Brealey.

Bennis, W. and Nanus, B. (1985) *Leaders: the strategies for taking charge*, New York: Harper & Row.

Bernstein, B. (1970) 'Education cannot compensate for society', *New Society*, 387, 344–47.

Binney, G. and Williams, W. (1997) *Leaning into the Future: Changing the way people change organisations*, London: Nicholas Brealey.

Black, J. (1994) *Mindsfore*, London: Thorsons.

Bohm, D. (1983) *Wholeness and the Implicate Order*, New York: Ark Paperbacks.

Bolman, L.G. and Deal, T.E. (1991) *Reframing Organisations: Artistry, choice and leadership*, San Francisco, CA: Jossey-Bass.

Boothroyd, C., Fitz Gibbon, C., McNicholas, J., Thompson, M., Stern, E. and Wragg, T. (1997) *A Better System of Inspection?* Northumberland: OFSTIN.

Boylett, I. and Finlay, D. (1996) 'Corporate governance and the school headteacher', *Public Money and Management*, April–June, pp. 31–38.

Brighouse, T. and Woods, D. (1999) *How to Improve Your School*, London: Routledge.

Cave, E. and Wilkinson, C. (1997) in Kydd, L., Crawford, M. and Riches, C. (eds.) *Professional Development for Educational Management*, Buckingham: Open Unversity Press.

Coleman, P. (1998) *Parent, Student and Teacher Collaboration: The power of three*, London: Paul Chapman.

Cooperrider and Srivasta (1999) quoted in Brighouse, T. and Woods, D. (1999) *How to Improve your School*, London: Routledge.

Cornog, G. (1970) 'To care and not to care', in Ryan, K. *Don't Smile Until Christmas*, Chicago: University of Chicago Press, pp. 1–24.

Covey, S. (1995) *Principle-centred Leadership*, New York: Houghton Mifflin.

Covey, S. (1989) *The Seven Habits of Highly Effective People*, New York: Simon and Schuster.

Covey, S. and Merrill, R.A. (1994) *First Things First*, New York: Simon & Schuster.

Csikszentmihalyi, M. (1990) *Flow: the psychology of optimal experience*, New York: Harper Perennial.

De Lyon, H. and Widdowson Migniuolo, F. (eds.) (1989) '"Miss is a Lesbian": The Experience of a White Lesbian Teacher in a Boys School' in *Women Teachers. Issues and Experiences*, Buckingham: Open University Press.

Dempster, N. and Logan, L. (1998) in MacBeath, J. (ed.) *Effective School Leadership: Responding to change*, London, Paul Chapman.

Dempster, N. and Mahony, P. (1998) in MacBeath, J. (ed.) *Effective School Leadership: Responding to change*, London, Paul Chapman.

Dimock, C. (1996) 'Dilemmas for school leaders and administrators in restructuring,' in Leithwood, K., Chapman, J., Coson, D., Hallinger, P. and Hart, A. (eds.) *International Handbook of School Leadership and Administration*, Vol. 1, Dordrecht: Kluwer.

Earley, P. (ed.) (1998) *School Improvement after Inspection? School and LEA Responses*, London: Paul Chapman.

Epstein, D. (ed.) (1994) *Challenging Lesbian and Gay Inequalities in Education*, Buckingham: Open University Press.

Epstein, D. and Johnson, R. (1998) *Schooling Sexualities*, Buckingham: Open University Press.

Evetts, J. (1994) *Becoming a Secondary Headteacher*, London: Cassell.

Feuerstein, R., Rand, Y., Hoffman, M.A. and Miller, R. (1980) *Instrumental Enrichment: An intervention programme for cognitive modifiability*, Baltimore, MD, University Park Press.

Fielding, M. (1998) 'Making a difference', paper presented at International Congress on School Effectiveness and School Improvement, Manchester, January.

Franks, S. (1999) *Having None of It. Women, Men and the Future of Work*, London: Grant.

Fullan, M. (1997a) *What's Worth Fighting for in the Principalship?*, Mississauga: Ontario Teachers' Federation.

Fullan, M. (1997b) 'Emotion and hope: constructive concepts for complex times', in Hargreaves, A. (ed.) *Positive Change for School Success*, Alexandria, VA: ASCD 1997 Yearbook.

Galton, M., Hargreaves, L. and Pell, A. (1997) *Class Size, Teaching and Pupil Achievement*, London: National Union of Teachers.

Gardner, H. (1997) *Leading Minds: An anatomy of leadership*, London: HarperCollins.

Gilligan, C. (1982) *In a Different Voice*, Cambridge, MA: Harvard University Press.

Goleman, D. (1996) *Emotional Intelligence*, London: Bloomsbury.

Grace, G. (1995) *School Leadership, Beyond Education Management*, London: Falmer.

Gray, J. and Wilcox, B. (eds.) (1995) *Good School, Bad School: Evaluating performance and encouraging improvement*. Buckingham: Open University Press.

HM Inspectors of Schools, Audit Unit (1999) *Quality and Standards in Scottish Schools*, Scottish Office Education and Industry Department, Edinburgh, HMSO.

HM Inspectors of Schools, Audit Unit (1997) *How Good is Our School?*, Scottish Office Education and Industry Department, Edinburgh, HMSO.

Hackman, J.R. and Oldham, G. (1976) 'Motivation through the design of work: A test of theory', *Organisational Behaviour and Human Performance*, 16 (2), 250–79.

Hall, G. and Hord, S. (1987) *Change in Schools: Facilitating the process*, Albany, New York: State University of New York Press.

Hall, V. (1996) *Dancing on the Ceiling. A study of women managers in education*, London: Paul Chapman.

Hampden-Turner, C. and Trompenaars, L. (1993) *The Seven Cultures of Capitalism*, New York: Doubleday.

Hannon, P. (1993) 'Conditions of learning at home and in school', in *Ruling the Margins*, London: Institute of Education, University of North London.

Hargreaves, A. (1995) *Changing Teachers, Changing Times*, London: Cassell.

Hargreaves, D. (1999) Creative Professionalism: The role of teachers in the knowledge society, London: *DEMOS*, pp. 29–32.

Hargreaves, D. (1997) 'Equipped for Life', ESRC paper, Cambridge: School of Education, University of Cambridge.

Hargreaves, D.H. (1998) 'The knowledge creating school', Paper delivered at the *British Educational Research Association*, Queen's University, Belfast: August.

Heifetz, R.A. (1994) *Leadership Without Easy Answers*, Cambridge, MA: Harvard University Press.

Herbert, C. (1992) *Sexual Harassment in Schools. A guide for teachers*, London: David Fulton.

Herndon, J. (1968) *The Way it Spozed to Be*, New York, Wiley.

Hertzler, J.O. (1940) 'Crises and Dictatorships', *American Sociological Review*, 4, 157–69.

Hill, N. (1928) *Secrets of Success*, New York: Schuster.

House, E. (1973) *School Evaluation: The politics and process*, San Francisco: McCutchan Publishing.

Illich, I. (1971) *Deschooling Society*, New York: Harper and Row.

Jarvis, P. (1997) 'Learning practical knowledge', in Kydd, L., Crawford, M. and Riches, C. (eds.) (1997) *Professional Development for Educational Management*, Buckingham: Open University Press, pp. 26–36.

Kotter, J.P. (1996) *Leading Change*, Boston, MA: Harvard Business School Press.

Kotulak, R. (1996) *Inside the Brain: Revolutionary discoveries of how the mind works*, Kansas City: Andrews McMeel.

Kydd, L., Crawford, M. and Riches, C. (1997) *Professional Development for Educational Management*, Buckingham: Open University Press.

Leithwood, K. (1999) *Educational Accountability: The state of the art*, Gütersloh: Bertlesmann Foundation.

MacBeath, J. (1999) *Schools Must Speak for Themselves*, London: Routledge.

MacBeath, J. (1998) (ed.) *Effective School Leadership. Responding to change*, London: Paul Chapman.

MacBeath, J., Boyd, B., Rand, J. and Bell, S. (1996) *Schools Speak for Themselves*, London: National Union of Teachers.

MacBeath, J., Kruchov, C. and Riley, K. (1994) *Images of Leadership*, Glasgow: University of Strathclyde.

MacBeath, J., Mearns, D. and Smith, M. (1986) *Home from School*, Scottish Education Department, Glasgow: Jordanhill College.

MacBeath, J., Meuret, D., Schratz, M. and Jakobsen, L. (1999) *Evaluating Quality in School Education*, Brussels: European Commission.

MacBeath, J. and Mortimer, P. (1994) 'Improving School Effectiveness: A Scottish Approach', paper presented to the British Educational Research Association annual conference, Oxford University, September.

Macdonald, A. (1998) 'Postscript', in MacBeath, J. (ed.) *Effective School Leadership: Responding to change*, London: Paul Chapman.

Macdonald, J. (1989) 'When outsiders try to change schools from the inside', *Phi Delta Kappan*, 71 (3), 208.

MacGilchrist, B., Mortimore, P., Savage, J. and Beresford, C. (1995) *Planning Matters*, London: Paul Chapman.

Marshall, J. (1984) *Women Managers. Travellers in a Male World*, Chichester: Wiley.

Martin, P. (1997) *The Sickening Mind*, London: Flamingo.

Mead, M. (1949 rpt 1981) *Male and Female: A study of the sexes in a changing world*, Harmondsworth: Penguin.

163

Mintzberg, H. (1994) *The Rise and Fall of Strategic Planning*, New York: Prentice Hall.

Mortimore, J. and Mortimore, P. (1991) *The Secondary Head: Roles, Responsibilities and Reflections*, London: Paul Chapman.

Mortimore, P. and Whitty, G. (1999) 'Can school improvement overcome the effects of disadvantage', in Cox, T. *Combatting Educational Disadvantage*, London: Falmer.

Myers, K. (1995–1998) 'Talking Heads', series of articles in the *Times Educational Supplement*, London.

Nias, J., Southworth, G. and Yeomans, R. (1989) *Staff Relationships in a Primary School: A study of organisational cultures*, London: Cassell.

Office of Standards in Education (1995) *New Framework for School Inspections*, London: Department for Education and Employment.

Ouston, J., Fidler, B. and Earley, P. (1998) 'The educational accountability of schools in England and Wales', *Educational Policy*, 12 (1), 111–23.

Ozga, J. and Walker, L. (1999) 'In the company of men', in Whitehead, S. and Moodey, R. (eds.) *Transforming Managers: Engendering Change in the Public Sector*, London: Taylor and Francis.

Paul, R. (1996) Dialogical thinking: Critical thought essential to the acquisition of ritual knowledge and passions, unpublished seminar paper, University of Glasgow.

Pinker, S. (1998) *How the Mind Works*, London: Penguin Books.

Rafferty, F. (1995) 'Football governors attacked by the head', *Times Educational Supplement*, 2 June.

Rallis, S.F. (1988) *Dynamic Teachers: Leaders of change*, Thousand Oaks, California: Corwin Press.

Reay, D. (1993) 'He doesn't like you Miss: Working with boys in an infant classroom', in Claire, H., Maybin, J. and Swann, J. *Equality Matters: Case studies from the primary school*, Clevedon: Multilingual Matters.

Reeves, J. and Dempster, N. (1998) 'Developing Effective School Leaders', in MacBeath, J. (ed.) *Effective School Leadership: Responding to change*, London: Paul Chapman.

Reeves, J. and MacGilchrist, B. (1997) 'Gauging the impact of improvement strategies'. *Paper presented at the British Educational Research Association, University of York*, York: September.

Riehl, C. and Lee, V.E. (1995) 'Gender, Organisation and Leadership', in Leithwood, K. *et al.* (eds.) *International Handbook of Educational Leadership and Administration*, Dordrecht: Kluwer.

Rosenblum, S., Louis, K.S. and Rossmiller, R. (1994) 'School leadership and teacher quality of work life', in Murphy, J. and Louis, K.S. (eds.) *Reshaping the Principalship*, Newbury Park: Corwin Press.

Ross, S. (1995) 'Using ethos indicators in a primary school', *Managing Schools Today*, pp. 26–30.

Rutter, M., Maughan, B., Mortimore, P. and Ouston, J. (1979). *Fifteen Thousand Hours: Secondary schools and their effects on children*, Cambridge, MA: Harvard University Press.

Salomon, G. and Perkins, D. (1998) 'Individual and social aspects of learning', *Review of Research in Education*, 23.

Schratz, M. and Steiner-Löffler, U. (1998) *Die Lemende Schule*, Weinheim: Beltz Verlag.

Scottish Office Education and Industry Department (1998) *Standards and Quality 1995–1998*, A Report by HM Inspectors of Schools, The Audit Unit, Edinburgh: SOEID.

Senge, P. (1992) *The Fifth Discipline: The art and practice of the learning organisation*, Sydney: Random House.

Sergiovanni, T. (1998) 'Leadership as pedagogy, capital development and school effectiveness', *International Journal of Leadership in Education*, 1 (1), 37.

Sergiovanni, T.J. (1992) *Moral Leadership: Getting to the heart of school improvement*, San Francisco, LA: Jossey-Bass.

Shakeshaft, C. (1989) *Women in Education Administration*, New York: Sage.

Simkins, T., Ellison, L. and Garrett, V. (1992) 'Beyond market and managerialism? Education management in a new context', in Simkins, T. *et al. Implementing Educational Reform: The early lessons*, Harlow: Longman.

Sobel, D. (1997) *Longitude*, London: Fourth Estate.

Southworth, G. (1995) *Looking into Primary Headship: A research based interpretation*, London: Falmer.

Spencer, L. (1978) *Soft Skill Competencies*, New York: McBer.

Spencer, L.M. and Spencer, S.M. (1993) *Competence at Work: Models for superior performance*, New York: Wiley.

Steiner-Löffler, U. (1996) 'Pupils evaluate school culture: a photographic approach', Paper presented at the European Educational Research Association, Seville, September.

Tay-Koay Seiw Luan (1997) 'Students' reports of their cognitive processes and level of understanding during regular classroom instruction', in Tan, J., Gopi, S., Nathan and Kam, Ho Wah. *Education in Singapore*, Singapore: Prentice Hall, pp. 187–204.

Tiana, A., Scheerens, J., MacBeath, J., Thomas, S. and Smees, S. (1999) *Innovative Approaches to Evaluation*, Brussels: European Commission Report.

Trenchard, L. and Warren, H. (1984) *Something to Tell You*, London: Gay Teenagers' Group.

'V' (1996) *The Mafia Manager*, New York: St. Martin's Griffin.

Varlaam, A , Nuttall, D. and Walker, A. (1992) *What Makes Teachers Tick? A survey of teacher morale and motivation*, Clare Market Papers No. 4, Centre for Education Research, LSE.

Walkerdine, V. (1987) 'Sex, Power and Pedagogy', in Arnot, M., Weiner, M. and G. *Gender and the Politics of Schooling*, London: Hutchinson in association with the Open University.

Waller, W. (1932) *The Sociology of Teaching*, Wiley: London and New York.

Wheatley, M. (1994) *Leadership and the New Science*, New York: Berrett–Koehler.

Wilcox, B. and Gray, J. (1996) *Inspecting Schools*, Buckingham: Open University Press.

Wilhite, M. and Basnet, L. (1999) 'Teaching excellence', *POD Network Newsletter*, 10 (5).

Winkley, D. (1989) 'An analytical view of primary school leadership', *School Organisation*, 3 (1).

Wragg, T. (1998) 'What Do We Really Mean by Incompetent Teachers?', *Parliamentary Brief*, p. 52.

Index

■ ■ ■

Walking Home From Mongolia

Also by Rob Lilwall

Cycling Home From Siberia

Rob Lilwall

Walking Home From Mongolia

Ten million steps through China
from the Gobi Desert to the South China Sea

HODDER &
STOUGHTON

First published in Great Britain in 2013 by Hodder & Stoughton
An Hachette UK company

1

Copyright © Rob Lilwall 2013
Illustrations copyright © Tim Steward
Maps copyright © Rodney Paull

A CIP catalogue record for this title is available from the British Library

ISBN 978 1 444 74528 3
EBOOK ISBN 978 1 444 745290

Typeset in Monotype Sabon by Palimpsest Book Production Limited,
Falkirk, Stirlingshire

Printed and bound by CPI Group (UK) Ltd, Croydon CR0 4YY

Hodder & Stoughton policy is to use papers that are natural, renewable
and recyclable products and made from wood grown in sustainable
forests. The logging and manufacturing processes are expected to
conform to the environmental regulations of the country of origin.

Hodder & Stoughton Ltd
338 Euston Road
London NW1 3BH

www.hodder.co.uk

Contents

千里之行，始于足下

A journey of a thousand miles begins with a single step.

For Mum and Dad
Thank you for the home you gave me.

Author's note

This book is written from a mixture of memory, notes scribbled in diaries and a few promptings from photos and video footage. In some places I have abbreviated or reconstructed the wording of conversations, and in others I have probably got details slightly wrong. Occasionally the order in which things happened has been altered to help the narrative flow. But aside from this, I believe it is an accurate portrait of what happened.

For prices, the Chinese Renminbi (RMB) currency has been converted to the British pound at a rate of 10 RMB to £1 (the rounded rate at the time of the expedition).

Although most people in Mongolia and China speak in terms of kilometres, all distances have been given in miles. Because we often walked on unmapped trails, many distances are based on my best estimates, and generally rounded down.

Preface: The danger of atlases

Winter was at hand and the Siberian snows were beginning to scatter their way south into Mongolia when Leon McCarron and I set out to walk from the Gobi Desert to Hong Kong. Initially, we had intended to start in late summer, or at least early autumn, but preparations had spiralled out of control and we ended up taking our first steps into the desert in mid-November.

This was my second major expedition, and in many ways it was connected to the first. That journey had begun seven years previously when, aged twenty-seven, I packed in my job as a geography teacher in order to ride across the world on my bicycle. Rather than starting from England, I had flown just about as far away from home as I could think of – to northeast Russia – and then spent the next three years cycling back again. I called the trip 'Cycling Home From Siberia', and it became a rite-of-passage adventure, taking me through countries as far-flung as Japan and Papua New Guinea, Australia and Afghanistan. Before I got back to London, I had been robbed at gunpoint, struck down by malaria and knocked over by cars. However, it was the positive experiences that deeply affected me, especially the hospitable people from dozens of cultures whom I met as I travelled. And, best of all, while I was stuck in Hong Kong trying to hitch a boat ride across the South China Sea, I got to know a beautiful Chinese girl called Christine.

When I eventually got home I found my life would not continue where I left off. Rather than returning to teaching as I had planned, I ended up writing a book and giving lectures about the trip, and a TV network picked up my self-filmed video footage and made a series. Christine, meanwhile, was now working in London. Eighteen months after my return home, I proposed to her over a game of Scrabble in Kew Gardens.

Once we were married, we decided to move to Hong Kong, the city where we had first met – Christine's home, and now my new home. We settled into a flat on a leafy outlying island, a half-hour ferry ride from the skyscrapers. We had volunteered to set up a fundraising office for a children's charity we really believed in called Viva, and I continued to pay the bills through freelance speaking and writing work.

Life was going well. Yet, at the same time, I was getting itchy feet once more. A feeling deep inside was urging me to embark on a new expedition, something long and tough, that would test me to my limits all over again. I started casually browsing maps and atlases – always a dangerous activity – and before long I became fixated on the idea of a big trip through Mainland China.* I had loved the stretches of my bike ride that passed through the eastern and southern parts of the country. Now I was dreaming of exploring China's interior, with its lonely deserts, wild mountains and magnificent rivers. And there is much more to China than just its physical geography. It is the oldest continuous civilisation in history with the Great Wall and multitudes of other extraordinary historical sites. In recent decades, China has risen to prominence on the world stage, and now pundits proclaim that it will not be long before China rules the world. To top it off, my wife is Chinese. I wanted to get to know her, and Hong Kong's, motherland better.

But if I was going to explore China, how should I do it? After being asked at almost every dinner party since the cycling trip, 'How many punctures did you get?', I felt it was time to try a new, more challenging mode of transport. And so the idea of a walk started to ferment in my mind. Walking would be much slower, and

---

* Hong Kong is a part of China, but distinct from the mainland, culturally, economically and politically. It has its own currency, its own border crossings, and is known as a Special Administrative Region because it is governed under different rules.

physically harder, especially because I would have to carry all my heavy gear. But travelling on one's own two feet was also the most ancient means of transport – the way that the majority of people through history had encountered their world.

I mulled on possible routes, and began to think that traversing China on its vertical axis would be more interesting than going across its horizontal one: it would take in greater historical and scenic diversity. I also wanted to stay away from China's booming coastline, and instead journey inland, far from where most foreigners visited. I would pass through its core, at ground level, and see how China changed from top to bottom.

Then, as I lay in bed one night, the whole shebang came together in a single thought: 'Walking Home From Mongolia'. I was suddenly wide awake. I would start in the Gobi, and walk back to Hong Kong. It would be a long way – roughly the equivalent to walking from London to Kazakhstan, or from Los Angeles to New York. My mind started to fill with images of striding across windy deserts, climbing over misty hillsides, and camping in jade-green terraced fields; of braving epic storms, jumping in tranquil rivers, and meeting smiling people. The expedition took a hold of my mind. And, once that had happened, I could not shake it off.

I broached the idea with Christine during a walk up our local mountain. She listened quietly and, when I finished, we stopped walking and looked out across the bay. A ferry was chugging in towards the terminal, and tropical clouds filled the sky above the South China Sea.

'How long would it take?' she said, following my gaze, then glancing up at my face.

'Three to four months, I think.' I hoped. 'But I will only do it if you agree.' While cycling home from Siberia I'd been footloose and fancy-free, accountable to no one, and able to choose my route, my timing, my style. But I was no longer young and unmarried. This time I would need Christine's blessing.

'Hopefully, building on the profile from the last trip,' I continued, 'I can also get a TV network and sponsors to back it.' I knew I could not justify such a long trip purely for the fun of it. So I also had aspirations to film the expedition and do some freelance writing as I went. This would help cover the costs, and give it a professional rationale too.

Christine was quiet. 'I guess I am open to it,' she said eventually. She knew that I loved going on these crazy expeditions, yet as her eyes held mine for a moment, I saw she was frightened. We knew that she would not want to come with me because, although she liked a challenge (two years previously she had left a promising legal career to work in the charity sector), she enjoyed neither pain nor going for days without a shower, both of which would make up the bread and butter of the journey.

'We can use it to raise money for Viva,' I added. 'I think it will be a great platform for the charity.' I also hoped she could fly out to meet me two or three times, when I was taking some days off. We would thus not be entirely apart.

Christine looked vulnerable, bracing herself for the storms to come. It would be hard for both of us. 'OK,' she said, 'if this is what you really want to do.'

I've seen grown men reduced to little boys as their wives dismiss their deepest dreams as immature nonsense, but here was my wife giving me her permission, knowing the sacrifice. My mind swirled with gratitude and excitement. I could not believe that I was going to try and walk, quite literally, the length of China.

Part One

Into the Gobi

Хүний эрхээр зовохоор өөрийн эрхээр жарга

Better to suffer in liberty than delight in captivity.

I

Start line in the emptiness

Distance to home: 3,000 miles

14 NOVEMBER

Standing outside the rundown hotel under a crisp blue sky, I fumble to attach the four ropes and carabiners to my rucksack. Then I hoist it onto my back, pick up my brand new walking poles and hurriedly put my gloves on. The air is cold, and the world is silent. Taking my first step, the ropes jerk taut and the steel trailer to which I am attached starts to roll along behind me. The wheels start to squeak. Molly Brown is loaded with 100 kilograms' worth of camping gear, camera equipment, food and water supplies. The harness lines tug at my waist and I step off the pavement, onto the road, and the wheels bump down behind me.

I look round. My expedition partner and cameraman, Leon, walks past, also wearing a rucksack, but without a trailer. We will be taking turns to pull Molly Brown, and I am going first. Leon holds a camera in his right hand and I let him stride ahead for a few metres until he stops and turns to film. I start moving again.

We are on the main street of Sainshand, a small town in Southern Mongolia in the middle of the Gobi Desert. This little town is our starting point, and my home in Hong Kong is over 3,000 miles' walk away to our south. Today is day one.

Like most towns in Mongolia, Sainshand bears the marks of a nation that was a Soviet puppet for much of the twentieth century. Both sides of the street are lined with unimaginative apartment blocks. They have now been repainted in garish colours, yet the uniform, communist windows still stare out at us, bitter and disinterested. A large grey chimney spouts black smoke into the dry, frozen air. The cracks of land between every building are filled with brown Gobi dust. We still cannot see the open desert because Sainshand is surrounded by a small ridge, and the first hour of the expedition will be spent walking to get beyond it.

A handful of Mongolians wrapped in thick coats and scarves walk past. Their rugged, serious faces break into bemused smiles as they look at me pulling Molly. Cars slow a little to chug alongside us, with their drivers and passengers also staring. I feel strangely detached from the world. I cannot believe that we are finally setting off. I have no idea of what lies ahead – what places we will see, what people we will meet, what adventures we will have.

Reaching a red traffic light, I stop and wait beside the line of cars. A couple of middle-aged ladies start crossing the road and, when I look up at them, they giggle. I smile back, sheepishly. I feel like a pantomime horse-drawn carriage, with me as the horse. As the lights turn green, most of the cars go straight on. But Leon and I turn left, south, out of town, towards the emptiness.

The road surface, still asphalt, curves through a gentle depression before climbing to an opening in the ridge. We pass a few wooden shacks and walled compounds on the outskirts of town. I am getting into my stride and, as I lean into the harness, Molly rolls forward and lurches back again with each step. My boots feel comfortable yet unfamiliar, and I hope I have worn them in enough. The cold sun is blazing above us, and the only sounds are the continued squeaking of Molly's wheels, and the clink, clink, clink of my poles on the tarmac.

As the road starts to tilt gently uphill, I gasp at the effort of pulling Molly. The frozen air cuts my lungs. It is only 14 November, hardly deepest winter, yet it is −10°C. This is warm compared to what we are expecting in the months to come.

Leon, who has been hanging back to do some extra filming, catches up, and a few minutes later we reach the gap in the ridge. We stop together and look out onto the Gobi Desert. It is a titanic plain of brown dust and gravel, as wide and long as an ocean, rumbling brazenly away from us in all directions. I can just make out a faint line of hills and ridges running along the horizon, beyond which the whole world melts into nothingness.

I shake my head. 'Crumbs, that looks big. Do you feel like walking across it?'

'We might as well, now we're here,' Leon says in his Northern Irish accent, smiling. He has floppy brown hair and a youthful, freshly shaven face. At twenty-five, he is nine years younger than me. He puts his poles down, and starts to set up the tripod.

I find it hard to grasp how far this land stretches and how long it will take us to walk across it. A week ago, on our flight to the Mongolian capital of Ulaanbaatar, I had looked down on the ruffled plains and worked out that for every minute it was taking us to cross the desert in a plane, it would take us half a day of marching.

I see, however, that in the foreground it is not entirely empty. The asphalt road continues southwest, but now we will be bearing away from it, southeast, on one of the dusty jeep tracks that scythes across the plain. I hold up my compass and confirm that the most prominent jeep track is heading in roughly the right direction. I also see that half a mile down this track there is a white felt tent – a nomad's ger.* It stands alone, defiant, as if it were the final outpost of civilisation.

Leon is still stooped over his camera. I wait until he has finished shooting a wide panning shot.

'Shall we go?' I say.

'I'm going to do some more filming, you go ahead.'

Silence hangs in the air for a moment. So this is it, our start line in the emptiness. After the months of hectic planning, there is nothing else to say, no more waiting, no more preparing. I take a deep breath and lean forward in the harness. Molly's wheels start rolling. We bump off the asphalt and onto the brown earth. The journey of ten million steps has begun.

---

* Known as a yurt in Central Asia.

2
The ger

14 NOVEMBER

Molly's wheels scratched the gravel behind me as I took my first slow paces into the desert. Although the Gobi was a bleak and hostile environment, I now saw that its floor was covered in patchy clumps of dry grass, and in the distance I caught sight of some large brown animals. Perhaps they belonged to the lone *ger* up ahead.

As I drew slowly nearer, a man emerged from inside, climbed on a motorbike and started to bounce through the dust in my direction. He crunched to a halt beside me. He was about thirty, with a faint beard, and a face that, to my unaccustomed eye, reminded me of Genghis Khan.* He was wearing a long green robe tied with an orange sash around his waist, and on his head he wore a red baseball cap, on top of which was perched a lopsided yellow builder's hat.

I smiled, and nodded my head. 'Hi,' I said.

He squinted at Molly, and looked me up and down. I was wearing a synthetic windproof coat and trousers from Hong Kong, a cheap pair of sunglasses, and a Mongolian rabbit fur hat from a market in Ulaanbaatar.

'*Ger, ger*,' he shouted above the noise of his engine. Then pointing to the *ger*, '*Jid, jid.*'

I concluded that he was inviting me to his *ger*, though I was not entirely sure.

'Thank you, I'll come in just a few minutes,' I said in English, gesturing to Molly.

---

* Chinggis Khan is more phonetically accurate, but throughout this book the more familiar Genghis will be used.

The man grunted and flicked his head, before revving his bike and driving towards Leon, who was walking two hundred metres behind me. Just before I reached the *ger*, the bike overtook me again. I saw the man waving at me to hurry up before disappearing through the *ger*'s low doorway.

'I think this guy is inviting us for a cup of tea,' I said, as Leon caught up.

'Yeah, that's what I thought too. I know we were hoping for some Gobi hospitality, but I wasn't expecting it so soon.'

I unclipped myself from Molly and lowered her to the ground. The greyish-white tent was perfectly round, two and a half metres high, and six metres wide. It did not seem to have ropes holding it up, but the whole structure must have been very stable – the Gobi is famed for powerful storms that, according to old travellers' tales, can rip a tent to pieces. A small crowd of white chickens pecked the earth around the entrance as Leon and I ducked inside.

We found ourselves in a warm, cosy, circular space, which smelled faintly of sweet milk. I pushed my sunglasses onto my head and my eyes adjusted to the light. Cluttered around the edges were several beds, tables and chests, all painted with colourful, angular shapes. Wooden staves weaved in zigzags up the walls and met in the middle of the roof, where the chimney, running up from the central stove, exited. Beside the stove sat a bucket of dry dung. A middle-aged couple were sitting to one side, watching a Mongolian soap opera on an old colour television.

The motorbike man gestured us to a bench, and as we sat down he slopped two cups of lukewarm tea on the table.

He sat down beside us. 'My name is Sahana,' he said, pointing to himself. He pointed at us and said, 'My name is?'

'My name is Rob,' 'My name is Leon,' we said.

'Rob . . . Leon,' repeated Sahana. Then he said, 'Hourse, hourse.'

'Yes, horses,' I said, assuming the animals I had spotted in the distance were Sahana's horses. 'How many do you have?' I started counting on my fingers.

Sahana did not understand, but said 'Yes, yes, hourse,' and pointed to the floor.

Perhaps he was saying that this *ger* was his house? Making conversation over our cups of tea was proving a little tricky. As the majority of the journey before us would be in China, we had concentrated on learning Mandarin beforehand. The only Mongolian word we knew was *biacla* (thank you). But we did have a letter translated into Mongolian that explained our journey. I had often used such letters on previous expeditions – I called them my 'magic letters', because once people understood what I was doing, they usually became less suspicious and more likely to help.

I dug out the letter and handed it to Sahana. He snatched it, looked at it briefly, and set it on the table. Perhaps he could not read, or perhaps he preferred talking. I pulled out a photocopy of a map and tried again to explain our plan.

'We are walking to Zamiin-Uud,' I said, wiggling my index and middle fingers in a walking movement. Zamiin-Uud was the border town with China, about 150 miles, or two weeks' walk south from here. I tried to indicate it on the map.

'Zamiin-Uud, ummh.' Sahana nodded. He looked across at Leon, who was pointing the camera at us.

'Is it OK to film you?' Leon asked.

'No, no,' Sahana said, shaking his head and waving for Leon to put the camera away. Leon lowered the camera. The lady who had been sitting watching us stood up and changed the TV channel.

We looked at the map again, and with my finger I traced the route we planned to take. After the Mongolian border we would be crossing into China, but this did not mean the end of the Gobi, for the desert continued south into Chinese territory for almost another month of walking. Eventually, we would breach the Great Wall and definitively enter what has sometimes been referred to as 'the core' of China – the heartland of its ancient civilisation. Then we would veer west, along the Great Wall for a while, before turning south once more and following the heavy torrent of the Yellow River towards the old capital of Xian. From here, we were heading due south all the way – through Southern China's uncountable lines of mountains, valleys, cities, forests and fields – until we reached the sea and Hong Kong. I was now expecting the journey to take us about five months.

This was a bit of a mouthful, so I simply said, 'Through China.'

'China!' Sahana scowled and shook his head. He seemed agitated, and started to make a throat slitting gesture.

'Throat slitting,' I said, turning to Leon. 'Is that what this guy would like to do to the Chinese, or what he thinks the Chinese will do to us?'

'I'm not sure,' said Leon, 'perhaps both?'

Sahana, seeing I did not fully understand, suddenly leaned across the table and grabbed my neck, his strong fingers tightening around my throat. I spluttered and nodded in a panic, 'Yes, OK, you do not like China.'

The rugged Mongol nomads of the grassy steppe* and arid desert differed deeply from the settled agriculturalists of China, the Middle Kingdom, and had been enemies down through the ages. Both disdained the other's way of life. The silk- and poetry-loving Chinese had viewed the nomads as uncivilised, illiterate barbarians, half-men, half-beasts, who wrestled, drank fermented mares' milk and sang throatily. The nomads had considered the Chinese to be rich, oppressive tax collectors and used their swift, superior skills in horsemanship to raid and pillage their enemies' land on a regular basis, sometimes with astounding success. However, in the 1600s, China had annexed Mongolia as its own territory for several centuries, and perhaps it was about this that Sahana was still bitter.

As if reading my mind, Sahana suddenly said, 'Genghis,' with his thumbs up. Then he said 'China' and leaned towards my throat once more.

From the moment we had landed in Ulaanbaatar the previous week, we realised that Genghis Khan, the greatest pillager of all, was something of a national hero. The capital's airport was named after him and there was a grand statue of him against the Parliament building. Vodka brands and banknotes alike bore his image.

'Ah, I see,' I said, nodding and pulling back. 'You like Genghis, and you like the way he went and conquered China.'

---

* Steppe is the name given to an eco-region of grassy plains found across Central and Northern Asia.

Although Sahana had been kind to invite us into his *ger*, the more time we spent with him, the more he seemed to resemble Genghis: he looked like Genghis, he liked Genghis, and grabbing me by the throat was just the sort of thing Genghis might have done. Genetic studies have shown that 0.2 per cent of the world's population, and 10 per cent of Mongolians are Genghis's living descendants. Perhaps it was a reasonable hypothesis that friendly but gruff Sahana, who kept grabbing my throat, was one of them.

Sahana's behaviour was becoming increasingly erratic the more we talked, and I started to wonder if he had been drinking. He growled at me, staring intensely. Then he started making a howling noise, followed by more throat-slitting gestures.

'Ah, wolves!' I said. 'Well, we have our poles.' I gestured that we would fight them off. I knew that although there were a few wolves, and even snow leopards and bears in the Gobi, the chances of seeing any of these creatures, let alone being eaten by them, were distinctly remote.

Sahana was unimpressed, and shook his head at me again with a mutter. It felt like time to leave.

'We should get going,' I said to Leon.

He nodded.

We said '*biacla*', grabbed the magic letter and stood up. Sahana followed us outside. As I reattached myself to Molly, he pointed south.

'Khamariin Khiid,' he said, emphasising the kh sound like a cough, his face relaxing slightly.

Khamariin Khiid was a Buddhist monastery in the middle of the desert. We were hoping to reach it in about three days' time to fill up our water bottles. Sahana's pointing seemed to confirm that the jeep tracks we had chosen were going in the right direction. By this, at least, we were reassured.

We shook Sahana's hand, said '*biacla*' a few more times and started walking away. He stood watching us leave, until a few minutes later I looked over my shoulder and his *ger* was just a small white shape, blurring into the vast expanse that had now become our home.

3
The first night

14 NOVEMBER

It was already mid-afternoon, and the white sun had started its trajectory towards the western horizon.

'What did you make of that?' said Leon. He was walking alongside me, planting his poles firmly in the gravel with each pace. He looked determined but relaxed.

'I'm not quite sure,' I said. 'It was a bit of a shock when he kept grabbing my throat.' We laughed nervously.

In my past travels, I had been fortunate enough to be invited in for tea by strangers all over the world. But if I was honest, Sahana's fierce manner had alarmed me. In Hong Kong I had met up with a man who had driven through Mongolia the previous year. While he was in the desert outside Sainshand taking photos, two drunk Mongolians on a motorbike had tried to mug him with a knife, though luckily he had been able to escape unharmed. I recounted this to Leon, and suddenly we were suffering from first-day jitters.

'I think it might be a good idea to keep out of sight when we camp tonight,' I said. The whole of Sainshand must have seen us leaving town, and we might be a bit of a tempting target with our big cameras.

At that moment, we saw a motorbike streaking along a parallel dusty track. We breathed a sigh of relief when it passed without stopping.

'We should try and make it to that next ridge,' said Leon. 'We'll be less conspicuous there.' Up ahead, the second small ridge was slowly becoming more defined and we could just make out where our jeep track cut through it.

We had been walking for two hours since leaving the town centre, and it was Leon's turn with Molly. I unshackled my rucksack, he shackled on his, and the three of us rolled off again. A column of telegraph poles ran through the desert ahead of us, and a few jeeps blazed across the skyline.

The sun disappeared in a flare of orange as we reached the ridge, and I got behind Molly and helped push her up the steep incline. By the time we reached the top it was dark, so we turned on our head torches as we skirted sideways until we found a clear patch of land. The temperature, meanwhile, had dropped into the minus teens. We threw on some extra clothes and stamped our feet to warm up, then pulled out our two little tents and pitched our first camp. I climbed into my tent and sleeping bag, and leaned outside to light the petrol stove – I was taking first turn with cooking duty. The flame burst upwards for a moment before stabilising. I put on our single pot to heat, and poured in water, instant noodles and tinned beef. Twenty minutes later, with the concoction boiling, I slopped half into the lid of the pan, which acted as our second bowl, and passed it across to Leon's tent. 'Dinner is served,' I said.

'Thank you,' said Leon, though his face betrayed a slight concern when he shone his head torch on the resultant mush. Leon was usually a vegetarian, but forced himself to eat meat when on expeditions. 'What is this stuff?' he said as he started eating.

'It's supposed to be beef, but I think it might actually be dog food,' I said.

'Better than dog meat, I guess.'

'Dog doesn't taste bad actually. It's certainly nicer than this.'

There was a brief but noticeable silence from Leon's tent before he continued eating.

I sat hunched in my sleeping bag, eating with my spoon. The feeling of being out here under the stars seemed strangely familiar, though it had been a good year and a half since I had last camped in the wild. At the same time, I felt exhausted, even though it was just 7 p.m., and we had only covered ten miles today – about 0.3 per cent of the way home. After I finished eating, I pulled out my diary and started to scribble.

Well, we have set off. Finally. Me pulling Molly. It's quite hard work – I think we are in for some sore muscles. This is going to be such a hard expedition – mainly because it is in winter. It is so far, so very far, to get home.

I found it hard to believe that just a few days ago we had been running between last-minute meetings like headless chickens in balmy Hong Kong. In fact, it felt as though I had been running around like a headless chicken for the past four months.

Almost a year previously, after getting the go-ahead from Christine, I had waded into the intimidating world of TV networks, and started trying to persuade someone to back the trip. There was some interest, but I was naïve in my approach, and the negotiations became both protracted and complicated. It was eight months before a network said yes, by which time it was almost July. With this green light, Leon and I could at last launch into serious preparations, which would take another four months. But the amount of time it had taken to get to this point also meant that we had to abandon the initial idea of a summer–autumn journey. Instead, we set ourselves a start date of 1 November – the absolute latest if we were to stay ahead of the winter.

Leon was based in London and I was in Hong Kong, so we worked remotely on our numerous preparations: getting fit, learning Mandarin, building a website, finding sponsors for our gear, sorting out visas and flights, researching the route and, importantly, doing a practice trip.

The months passed quickly with a deluge of emails and meetings. Gradually some things came together, but at the same time, others began to unravel. During our fitness training, Leon struggled with a shoulder injury and I got sore knees; we built a website, but it kept malfunctioning, so we had to build another one; some companies generously came forward with sponsored gear but, at the eleventh hour, a couple of the key ones backed out. There were also delays with finalising the TV contract, and as the network outlined their strict filming requirements, we began to think that we might have bitten off more than we could chew.

In the end it had been two weeks after our 'absolute latest start date' that flustered, exhausted, and having had no time to do a practice expedition, we finally boarded a plane bound for Mongolia.

I put down my diary and rummaged around for my toothpaste. The tube was partially frozen, but I managed to squeeze some out; after brushing my teeth, I unzipped the tent door to spit. The moon was casting a pale glow over the desert, and I could see a few lights on the ridge of Sainshand, twinkling in the distance. Sitting alone in my tent, the Gobi wind blowing in my face, with the manic, stressful months of preparation now behind me, I had a long overdue moment of peace and quiet. The scale of what lay before us began to dawn on me. It was one thing to dream up fun trips from the comfort of home, another to actually embark on them. We were about to walk across one of the coldest deserts on earth, and then trek the length of the world's fourth biggest country. We were fairly fit, but we were not Ironman triathletes. We were supposed to film the walk for a major TV network. We did not have a support crew or back-up if something went wrong. We could easily get lost, injured, or in trouble with the Chinese police.

I shivered. I'd camped in the extreme cold before, but tonight's relatively warm −15°C felt colder than I remembered it. The infamous Gobi winter was already setting in. We were going to have to move fast to stay ahead of its plummeting temperatures.

4
Leon

Distance to home: 2,986 miles

'So which way do you think to Khamariin Khiid?' asked Leon.

It was the morning of day two, and we were standing at a jumble of jeep tracks that headed in almost every direction across the wide Gobi plain before us.

'I have no idea,' I said. 'How does it look on the maps?'

For navigation, we had bought some topographical maps in Ulaanbaatar, but these showed only a handful of the many jeep tracks. We had also cached some Google Maps satellite images on our iPhone, but these showed all the jeep tracks and it was impossible to figure out which was which, now we were here on the ground. There were several more prominent tracks, but many jeep drivers had evidently grasped the liberating idea that there was nothing to stop them blazing their own new trails, like ships at sea. We debated the matter for several minutes, nervous about the possibility of getting lost so soon. The white exhaust of a jet cut silently through the sky far above. I felt very small, standing alone with Leon in the middle of this vastness.

Thankfully, a moment later, a jeep appeared in a cloud of dust behind us. We waved it down, and Leon ran over to speak to the driver. The driver knew Khamariin Khiid and pointed confidently to the broad, right track. The jeep roared away, and we walked onwards. I had taken first turn with Molly again this morning, though it felt harder work than yesterday. This was partly because the novelty and adrenaline of day one were gone, and partly because the jeep tracks were often corrugated and bumpy, which made Molly and her heavy load rattle and jolt.

While preparing for the trip, some veteran explorers had impressed on us the need to take only the minimal gear, ten kilograms or less. However, this turned out to be an impossible aspiration, because firstly we needed a lot of warm camping gear and clothes for the winter, and secondly we had a whole load of camera and technology gear for the filming. Moreover, on the initial desert stage of the expedition, we would have to carry plenty of food and water. In the twelve days it would take to walk to the border town, we were hoping to partially resupply at the Khamariin Khiid monastery, as well as a hamlet we had spotted on the map, and possibly also at a few nomad camps. However, we did not know how often we might encounter the camps. We initially planned to carry five days' worth of supplies, but in the end decided to take eight:

- Instant noodles x 30 (4 packs a night)
- Tins of meat x 8 (1 tin a night)
- Tins of peas x 4 (1 tin every other night)
- Bags of biscuits x 8 (1 pack a day)
- Slabs of chocolate x 24 (3 bars a day)
- 1.5-litre bottles of water x 36 (7 litres a day, including cooking)
- Loo roll x 2 (one each)

Together with a few luxury items to keep our morale up (an iPod, Kindle and diary each), we had well over 100 kilograms of stuff, making this leg of the journey equivalent to dragging a very large human corpse across the desert, slowly eating it as we went.

This was too much weight to carry on our backs. During our preparations, therefore, we had considered ways of pushing or pulling the load on wheels. My first idea had been to buy a couple of rugged baby buggies.* Leon, on the other hand, had sought advice from the great desert explorer Ripley Davenport. As it happened, Ripley had walked across the Gobi the previous year,

---

* While cycling across the Nullarbor Plain in Australia, I had met a cheerful Japanese gap-year student employing this very method, his buggy loaded up with biscuits and water as he walked across the country.

dragging a trailer. He had named the trailer Molly Brown after the *Titanic* survivor Margaret Brown, who had urged her lifeboat to go back to look for more passengers still in the water. He had finished his expedition in Sainshand and left Molly behind when he flew home. 'Assuming you can find her,' Ripley had said to Leon, 'you can have her.'

Our train had arrived in Sainshand at night, and Ripley's friend, Nassa, had been on the platform waiting to meet us. Nassa had taken us back to her little house by taxi, and we had walked through the darkness to a shed at the bottom of her yard. And there, beneath a couple of old mattresses and a bicycle, Molly sat waiting for us. She was made from welded steel, with four solid wheels, and she seemed relieved to have been rescued from premature retirement. When we loaded her up, our heaviest items were our bottles of water. We stored these inside pairs of woollen tights, which in turn were packed into cardboard boxes, in the hope of stopping the water from freezing too quickly. We piled these boxes, plus the other bags of food and gear, onto her chassis and strapped them down with ropes. Molly would be a difficult companion to haul across the Gobi, but we needed her.

The chain of events that had led me to invite my other expedition companion, Leon, had begun two years previously, under very different circumstances. Christine and I had been in New York and, although I was not a regular Twitter sort of guy, I had posted a short tweet about how this was 'a city that actually makes me want to get up early'.

It happened that Leon was in town, working as a camera intern for a well-known documentary maker. He was planning to set off on his own bicycle ride across the world and, since meeting me briefly at an event in London, he had been following my irregular tweets. When he saw I was in New York, he emailed asking if we could meet for a coffee.

It did not take long to spot young Leon in the café on Park Avenue. As we sat down, he explained the route he hoped to ride through America, Australia and Southeast Asia, finishing in Hong

Kong a year later. Christine and I had recently decided to move back to Hong Kong, and as Leon seemed like a nice guy, we invited him to come and stay with us when he arrived.

A year later, in Hong Kong, I was beginning to talk with TV networks about making a programme based on my Mongolia trip. On my cycling expedition, I had simply filmed myself, but this time I wanted higher-quality footage. However, I still wanted a self-sufficient expedition, without a support crew driving along with me. So I needed someone who was good with a camera and able to walk 3,000 miles. Initially I asked my oldest adventuring friend, Al Humphreys. Although Al said yes at first, a few months later, just as the TV network started to get interested, he emailed to say that he could not come after all. I was rather stumped. I did not know anyone else who fitted the bill.

That very weekend, Leon arrived in Hong Kong, and Christine and I went to meet him on our village waterfront. In contrast to the fresh-faced youngster we had met in Manhattan, he now sported a magnificent Crusoe-esque beard, and straddled a bike loaded with panniers and 10,000-miles' worth of stories. He had made it, and from here he would fly home.

Sitting on our sofa drinking beer that night, I asked Leon why he had done his cycling adventure – a question I had been asked a thousand times myself, and had never been good at answering.

'When I left university,' he said, swigging from his bottle, 'I realised that I liked adventure, and I liked camerawork. So I decided to go cycling and film it along the way too. I thought it would be a great start to a career as an adventure cameraman.'

My ears pricked up.

'I've enjoyed this trip so much, and I really want to do something in China again soon. I'd also love to go to Mongolia – that place looks really cool.'

I had at this point not even mentioned the walk to Leon. But as I got to know him better in the next few days, I realised that behind his beard he was clearly intelligent (he had received a first-class degree in film studies), and he was good expedition material (his recent bicycle trip proved that). We also seemed to share a reasonably laid-back temperament. I felt we would get on well.

So the day before Leon had left Hong Kong, I had asked him to come on the walk with me as cameraman. I was not sure Leon would accept my proposition, but after he had flown home and discussed the idea with his long-suffering girlfriend Clare, he had emailed me to say he was in.

For the next two days we moved onwards across the plain at our maximum speed of two miles per hour and another ridge came slowly into sight. Just before we reached it, mounds of dung appeared on the track. They looked fresh, and a few hundred metres later, we spotted the owners: Bactrian camels. These huge brown beasts, with their single humps and implausible faces, were gathered around some kind of well. As we drew closer, one of them, presumably the chief, turned to face us. He was ten feet tall.

We stopped and Leon set up the tripod to film. 'Did you know that George Lucas actually based the planet Tatooinne on Mongolia,' he said. 'I keep thinking about it when I look out across the desert, and think of the *gers*, which look like Luke Skywalker's house. And look at these camels, they're just like aliens.'

'Yes, they do look quite alien-ish,' I said, squinting at the chief camel. He stared back at me. 'Shall we walk through them, it might make some nice filming.'

'I don't think that would be a good idea.'

At that moment, the chief started to stomp forwards, his huge shoulders hunched like a gladiator's. These camels were not completely wild, but they were untended, and it would not be an amusing experience to have them butt us to the ground and stamp on our heads. The other camels raised their necks and turned to see if we dared take on their lead fighter. We did not, and instead veered sharply around them. I tried not to look nervous as I talked to Leon's lens about the approaching beast before we hurriedly walked away from his turf.

An hour later, with Leon in the harness, we began to climb the next ridge. The terrain grew soft and steep, and we wound into a series of hillocks, surrounded by wave-like rocks streaked with reds and browns. Ascending onto a broader hill, we saw two short, wide pillars made from stone and concrete. A string of blue prayer flags fluttered in the wind between them. A dog trotted past with a dead bird in its mouth – our eyes followed it down a track until, suddenly, from amid the rounded hill tops, we saw a huge white dome and golden stupa rising out of the earth. Behind it were a small scattering of huts and several dozen *gers* lined up in rows. We had reached the desert monastery of Khamariin Khiid.

5
The desert monastery of Khamariin Khiid

Distance to home: 2,957 miles

16–17 NOVEMBER

> Is there wine? Then drink!
> Is there a song? Then sing!
> Are there thoughts? Then talk!
> Is there brandy? Then drink!

So wrote Danzan Ravjaa, the eccentric Mongol Buddhist saint of the Gobi almost two centuries ago. The day before the expedition started, we had seen his statue in Sainshand – a grey figure levitating in the lotus position, with a submissive scorpion perched on his shoulder. His middle-aged and beardless face looked serene, and he wore a large pointy hat with a small skull at its tip. It was he who had made the site of Khamariin Khiid one of the most important spiritual centres in the country.

We rolled down into the monastery encampment. After two days in the emptiness, we found ourselves staring, wide-eyed, at the huge white dome with its golden stupa. We were elated to have made it here, because we needed to fill up our water bottles, and we were also excited by the thought of spending a night in one of the cosy pilgrim *gers* that we had heard were available for rent. It was almost evening, so we decided to postpone our look around the monastery until the following morning.

A middle-aged couple appeared and, after a bit of haggling, showed us to a *ger*. We spread our stuff on the four empty beds, and waited for the camel-dung stove to heat up. We felt a strong sense of relief to be back in the warm. There were also some electrical sockets, so Leon plugged in the camera batteries to charge and took out the laptop. Besides filming, walking and carrying half our gear, Leon was also responsible for technical administration, which included backing up and checking the footage we had taken. I leaned back on my bed, and reflected that Leon had a much harder job than me. Something else that had not made his life any easier was that he had had very little time to get to know the filming equipment before we set off. After waiting many months for some promised cameras from a key sponsor, they had pulled out at the last minute. We had therefore had to scramble to buy our own just a few days before we left.

We ate our noodles and dog food with our eyes glued to the little laptop screen, while it played back what we had filmed so far. We were reasonably happy with what we had shot, though I did some-times look tense on camera, and Leon spotted some dust on the lens that he would need to clean off the following morning.

We finished eating, and Leon pulled out a small silver hip-flask.

'We've made the first landmark. I think we deserve our first swig,' he said.

He held the flask to his nose for a moment, closed his eyes, and tipped it back for a split second.

'Time for you to become a real man, Rob.' He handed it to me.

Leon's one luxury on expeditions, it turned out, was his hip-flask of whisky. I had never been much of a whisky man, but as Leon expounded how the dark, ambrosial liquid had spent decades maturing in oak sherry barrels in the Scottish Highlands, I followed his example, and tipped the flask back.

'Only one swig?' I said, coughing a little as the liquid burned pleasantly down.

'Yes, one for minor celebrations. We need to save the double swigs for major celebrations, and for when things get really bad.'

'Fair point,' I said, handing it back.

However, despite the hard liquor to wash down my dinner, my stomach did not feel great. Our diet thus far – noodles, beef, choc-olate and biscuits – contained little fibre. My guts were not working very smoothly. Before bed I took a laxative pill, hoping that it would not kick in until the morning – the temperature was down to the low minus teens outside.

I woke just after 5 a.m. with a gurgling stomach and stumbled hurriedly out into the dawn. Scrambling onto the other side of a frozen ridge, I squatted down and enjoyed the sunrise in total privacy as a loud, satisfying explosion resounded across the emptiness. When I got back to the *ger*, Leon was up and cooking breakfast. He noticed the relieved expression on my face, and requested a laxative tablet for himself.

We walked back up to the monastery for a proper look, now noticing numerous golden statues of the Buddha, dotted on the hillsides and shimmering in the morning sun. Mongolia had been a predominantly Buddhist land for centuries, and followed Tibet's distinctive lama strand of Buddhism. Lama Buddhism includes the belief that its deities are regularly reincarnated in human form as lamas – as, for example, the famous Tibetan line of Dalai Lamas. In Mongolia, the best known are the Noyon Lamas, said to embody a powerful Indian tantric deity. Danzan Ravjaa, the Mongol saint whose statute we had seen in Sainshand, and who had made Khamariin Khiid such an important place, had been the fifth reincarnation of the Noyon Lama.

Leon and I reached the dome shaped building and, entering through a large doorway, found ourselves in a huge white cavern, spotlessly clean, and pristinely decorated with Buddhist paintings and shiny artefacts. It felt strange to have suddenly moved from the wild Gobi into such a tame and serene sanctuary, and we whispered to each other, feeling out of place in our dusty expedition clothing. Before we had a chance to look around properly, and as if to confirm our sense of not belonging, a middle-aged female caretaker appeared and told us to leave.

Back outside, we climbed a wide set of stairs onto the roof. A group of local children, weather-beaten but smiling, had gathered. A couple of them had skateboards, and they darted around us, laughing and shinning down the steep parapets as if this was a playground, happily oblivious of the ten-metre drop if they slipped.

Danzan Ravjaa had himself spent his early childhood in poverty in the Gobi. But the local monks had recognised the little boy's divine attributes; he was soon hailed as the next Noyon Lama and sent to a monastery for training. As he grew up he displayed both wit and mischief, traits that grew with age, and in adulthood quickly gained a reputation – not so much for discipline and devotion as for being a brilliant playwright and poet, a heavy-drinking woman-iser, and a somewhat bizarre miracle worker.

Though these may seem strange qualities for a saint, he was widely loved, and in many respects a man ahead of his time, advocating more equality for women and education for children. Amid the rocky hollows around the monastery lay the remains of a three-storey theatre that he had built, and to which thousands of nomads used to flock to watch his plays. The performances were not for entertainment only, but were also filled with political satire against the oppressive forces at work in the nation. It was during a play that Ravjaa was said to have performed one of his more eccen-tric miracles: making his pee levitate in mid air as he stood on top of a hut. It was enough to make the raucous crowd behave itself. On his darker side, like many tortured artistic souls, he had a quick temper, and his disinclination to show self-restraint earned him enemies. Accounts of the final years of his life give the impression of a rather pitiful alcoholic with deteriorating health. It is thought that he eventually died after being poisoned, possibly by a spurned lover.

After his death in the mid-1800s, his disciples continued to dwell in Khamariin Khiid, until in the 1920s and 1930s Stalin's puppet government purged Buddhism across the country – hundreds of monasteries were destroyed, and tens of thousands of monks were executed or sent to labour camps. However, just hours before the army arrived to tear Khamariin Khiid to pieces, some loyal monks managed to bury over fifty chests full of Ravjaa's artefacts and works.

The decades passed and, with all evidence of Rajvaa gone, some began to say that the merry-making lama of the Gobi was only a legend. But knowledge of the whereabouts of the chests was passed down from father to son. With the collapse of the Soviet Union in the early 1990s, Mongolia regained full independence, and the latently practised Buddhism began to resurface. A man named Atangerel, a descendant of the original chest burier, now faithfully dug up the old chests, thus bringing to light Ravjaa's poems, plays, clothing and furniture. Not long after, Khamariin Khiid was rebuilt, becoming a popular destination once more for devout pilgrims, and for foreign tourists too.

As Leon and I stood looking out on Ravjaa's old stomping ground, a convoy of four jeeps roared up beside the dome and half a dozen Mongolian tourists piled out. They were wearing flashy clothes and were abuzz with mobile phones and cameras. A monk appeared and led them inside. A few minutes later they re-emerged, and started taking photos of almost everything in sight before leaping back into their vehicles and disappearing in another cloud of dust. It had probably taken them about an hour to drive here from Sainshand, twenty minutes for the photos, and it would take an hour to drive back again. A whole pilgrimage in less than two and a half hours – not bad.

Molly, Leon and I marched back into the wilderness, and the stupa and domes of the monastery gradually disappeared into the grit behind us, as if they had only ever existed in our imaginations. I thought more about the jeep-borne pilgrims we had briefly met. I wondered what they had been hoping to gain from their visit. Perhaps it was just a fun excuse for a jaunt through the desert, or perhaps they were in search of something more.

The concept of pilgrimage was a hard one to define, and even dictionary definitions are decidedly vague. Maybe the word has been devalued in recent decades, as planes and luxury tours have made travelling effortless. I preferred to think of pilgrimage as something that has a meaningful end-point, whether that be religious or personal, but also as something that tests the pilgrim and their commitment to reach that place. In this sense, it was a helpful framework for me to understand my own, often opaque, motivations for adventures.

On this expedition, I was trying to get home – a meaningful place, for sure. En route to this meaningful place, I hoped to have some fun, learn about the places I went through, and also to catch glimpses of the beauty and holiness that suffuse the world. But I realised now that wanting to face the tests of the road was also a strange – but significant – part of my motivation.

Undoubtedly, I would face physical tests – with ten million heavy footsteps to be taken; and there would be professional tests – with a TV programme to be shot. But there would also be tests of character and heart: who I was deep down, and who I was becoming. If the expedition failed, it would be a huge disappointment and a financial catastrophe, but not the end of the world. If, however, when I found myself in the thick of hard times, I let my heart become embittered and turned to stone, that really would be a failure. A big source of strength in my life, and something that gives my life meaning, is my Christian faith, which I had grown into as a child. I hoped that this would help me in these tests of heart and character. I sometimes liked to think of the whole of my life as a kind of pilgrimage, in search of the mysterious Christian God, whether I was on a literal journey or not.

And so as I walked, I prayed, with the pilgrims of old, that the king with his scarred hands and feet would walk with me, and keep my heart soft, and stop the expedition from becoming mere vanity. As the Celts used to say:

> To go to Rome
> is much trouble, little profit
> The king thou seekest there
> Thou wilt not find
> Unless he travels with thee

My spiritual musings were rudely interrupted, by the sort of thing I imagined those of many pilgrims through the ages have been, when Leon and Molly stopped abruptly up ahead.

'Are you OK?' I called out to my brother pilgrim.

Leon was frantically disentangling himself from his rucksack and rummaging around in it. Suddenly triumphant, he pulled out some loo roll.

'I think the laxative is kicking in,' he shouted over his shoulder as he ran into the desert. 'Keep going, I'll catch you up.'

6

Winter cometh

Distance to home: 2,942 miles

18 NOVEMBER

We emerged from our tents the next morning to see a blanket of grey cloud had rolled across the sky. The temperature was now pushing towards −20°C, and by the time we set off it had started to snow. A white layer quickly dusted the floor and the visibility dropped to a few hundred metres. The sun glowed through only as a pale halo of white, and to the south I could see the dark shadow of a mountain looming through the snowfall. I pulled my scarf tightly round me to stop the snowflakes going down my neck, and we moved as fast as we could to keep warm.

In mid-morning the sound of an engine drifted through the semi-whiteout behind us – a motorbike. It was driven by a man in a bright red jumpsuit and he stopped when he reached us.

'Hello,' he shouted with a smile.

'Hello,' we shouted back. He had a young, clean-shaven face, and his outfit stood out like blood against the white landscape.

'My name is Tagwar,' he said in English. 'What is your name?'

'Rob and Leon,' we introduced ourselves. 'Nice to meet you.'

'What?'

'Nice to meet you.'

'What?'

'Err, never mind. We are going to Zamiin-Uud. Is this the right way?' I pointed along the road. We were heading east and hoped soon to intercept the main track heading south to the border town.

'Yes, yes, yes. Next?' said Tagwar.

'What?'

'Next?'

'Oh, err, Erlian.' The first town across the border in China.

'Next?'

'China.'

'Next?'

'Hong Kong.'

'OK, OK, OK,' he said, smiling and pointing to confirm we were going the right way. He started to wave his hands enthusiastically in a flat motion and exclaimed, 'ROAD, ROAD . . . LET'S GO . . . LET'S GO . . . LET'S GO ROAD!'

'Ah, a "Let's Go Road",' we nodded. Leon said that perhaps he meant an asphalt road – someone in Ulaanbaatar had told us of a rumour that one was being built down this way, though it must have been very new as it was not visible on the one-year-old Google satellite images.

Tagwar patted the back seat of his motorbike, offering me a lift.

'Err, sorry, we are not allowed to take lifts,' I said, 'and I will probably fall off as I am attached to Molly.'

'OK, OK,' shouted Tagwar, before letting out a final cheerful, 'Let's go!' and roaring away, at probably twenty times our walking speed.

Shortly afterwards, a *ger* appeared out of the whiteness. Outside it stood half a dozen camels, a flock of goats, a truck and Tagwar's motorbike. We could hear some dogs starting to bark and we hoped our poles would be enough of a deterrent. But as we drew closer, Tagwar and an older man emerged, subdued the dogs, and welcomed us inside with broad smiles.

Entering a *ger* during a Gobi blizzard was like stepping through a magical doorway. The land of bitter wind and swirling snow was suddenly replaced by an enchanted world of colour and shelter. I sat down next to Tagwar on one of the beds and took in my surroundings. The layout of the *ger* was similar to Sahana's, and a patter of snowflakes fell gently through a section in the roof where the felt had been folded back for ventilation. Two little girls, aged about two and six, sat on the patterned floor, staring at us with open mouths. A lady in her thirties with a pink scarf wrapped around her head smiled, stoked the stove and spoke to the older man in gentle, staccato tones. The man poured some milky tea into small china bowls and handed them to us.

'Camel milk,' said Tagwar.

'Thank you,' we said, beaming and gulping down the hot liquid. The lady offered us a bowl of fresh, deep-fried dough cakes, and I felt the warmth returning to my cold bones. Tagwar explained that these people were his friends, and he was on his way to Urgan, a town near Sainshand.

'Me,' he said, pointing to himself, 'wrestling teacher.'

He took out his mobile phone, and showed us a photo of him, or at least we assumed it was him, in a contorted, semi-inverted position on a wrestling mat, holding someone in a headlock. Since pre-Genghis days, there had been three main sports in Mongolia – archery, horse racing and wrestling. An early source recounts a wrestling match between two key champions, at the end of which Genghis demanded the victor break the back of the defeated champion. Today, although archery and horse racing are still practised at the annual summer games in Ulaanbaatar, it is wrestling that is the Mongols' greatest talent. Wrestling competitions sometimes attract over 6,000 contestants. Mongols have even branched into Japanese sumo wrestling, and in recent years have frequently become world champions.

The two girls continued to stare at us, and the older one produced an exercise book and proudly showed us neatly written lines of English handwriting. Somehow, they were getting an education out here, quite literally in the middle of nowhere. Leon had the camera out, and he flipped the LCD screen round. The girls were mesmerised by the images of themselves. The six-year-old posed excitedly with a victory sign. The two-year-old looked intently at herself and said 'Mama', before suddenly getting a shock and bursting into tears. Her big sister grabbed her and gave her a hug. We produced a bag of sweets and the older girl shyly took one. Her little sister was unable to decide on a sweet and instead took the whole bag and carried it off to her mother, who laughed gently.

'Sunglasses?' said Tagwar, indicating mine. He looked very proud as he tried them on; I guessed he was thinking how perfect they would be for keeping the snow out of his eyes while riding his motorbike. I had a spare pair, so I said he could keep them.

After about an hour, the warmth had started to make us feel drowsy and content. But we had to keep going, there was a winter on our tails, and it was not going to make life any easier if we started taking long tea breaks. Back in the cold, the older man beckoned us over to a Bactrian camel and invited me to climb on. I swung a leg over its back, and felt its muscles strain with immense power as it stood up, back legs first. Ten feet off the ground, for the next few moments I felt like a king – this would surely be the way to cross the desert in style.

We said our farewells and, as we got moving again, we saw a little blue coat bobbing up and down amid the huge herd of goats. It seemed that as well as practising her handwriting and looking after her sister inside the *ger*, the six-year-old girl also had the job of looking after 200 goats in a Gobi winter.

Plodding onwards through the whiteness, Molly and I drifted behind Leon; I tried to keep sight of him, despite the low visibility. Sometimes I saw his footprints in the snow ahead of me. At 5 p.m. the sky started to darken and the temperature dropped fast – even while pacing hard with Molly, I was still feeling cold. I saw the silhouette of Leon up ahead, standing beside a small embankment, stamping his feet. Suddenly, from nowhere, a truck hurtled into view, flew along the top of the embankment and disappeared into the sea of hills to the south.

'Well, here's the Let's Go Road,' shouted Leon, 'and it's definitely asphalt.'

7
The Let's Go Road

Distance to home: 2,927 miles

19 NOVEMBER

'How did you sleep?' Leon asked, as we set out fast down the Let's Go Road the next morning. The clouds had gone and the sky was a deep, cold blue.

'Not bad, but not great,' I said. 'The side of my body lying against the air mat kept going numb.'

'Sorry about that. It actually took me weeks to get them from the sponsor.'

We had camped the previous night in the lee of the Let's Go Road; for the first time, the temperature had dropped into the −20°Cs. Half the knack of camping comfortably in the extreme cold is to have a decent insulated mat to protect one's body from the frozen ground. We had somehow overlooked this in our preparations, and now were stuck with a couple of weedy air mats. In my desperation the previous evening, I had ripped up one of our disintegrating cardboard boxes to use as a bed.

And the cold was not just affecting our sleep. When cooking the previous night, I had found that our tins of so-called beef were frozen solid. I had to put the whole tin into the pot of brewing noodles to defrost before I could get the tin opener into it. Then, overnight, my breath had condensed into ice crystals on the inner tent, and when I sat up in the morning I was greeted by a shower of icicles down the back of my neck. As I got out of the tent, my feet were numb before I had my boots on, and as we packed we noticed that the water in our remaining bottles was three-quarters frozen. It was only our sixth day, and winter had well and truly arrived.

The Let's Go Road – with its jet-black ribbon of tarmac – unfurled before us, cutting a sharp line across the bright, snowy land. Its smooth surface allowed us to move considerably faster than normal, perhaps even at three miles per hour. But it was not only us moving faster – cars and trucks sped past sporadically, all seemingly out of control. Until very recently, Mongolians had been used to the bumpy desert tracks that acted as a natural speed check. This new road, combined with a bit of ice, and perhaps a drop or two of Genghis Khan vodka, seemed a perfect recipe for terrible crashes.

The white expanse around us, meanwhile, now looked more like tundra than desert. Tufts of grass broke through the thin carpet of snow, and in mid-morning we spotted several groups of camels, cows and beautiful black horses grazing on the hillsides. Although they were free to roam, these animals were all owned by nomads, whose *gers* were either invisible in the whiteness, or tucked away just over a neighbouring hillside.

During a short break, we stuffed biscuits into our mouths and gulped at our half-frozen water. 'If we find one, let's try and stay in a *ger* tonight.' We agreed, shivering.

As evening approached, we were relieved to spot two *gers* half a mile off the road. We walked across and met a pair of middle-aged goat herders herding their goats into a pen. They spoke no English, but we showed them our magic letter, and they immediately said we could stay in their spare *ger*. The stove was lit, and after Leon and I had brought in our frozen water bottles to melt, we sat down in a daze of relief and removed our boots. Desert hospitality was a wonderful thing.

An hour later we were beckoned through to the main *ger*, and treated to an amazing feast of hot, fatty stew with goat meat and tagliatelle-like pasta. It was a welcome change from our usual diet, though interestingly there were still no vegetables in sight. We grinned across at the two men, with their weather-beaten faces. As we ate, I wondered how they coped without laxative tablets. They grinned back. No, it did not look like they were in need of laxatives.

On a more serious note, this was the third nomad *ger* that we had visited, and I felt frustrated that we could not communicate better. I wondered what their lives were like. How often did they move camp? What did they make of the outside world? What had they seen during their lives out here in the desert? It was easy to romanticise the nomadic way, but it was probably a very tough life.

Traditionally, a nomad's livestock would have provided almost everything they needed to survive: meat, dairy products, chair coverings, clothing and transport. Only supplies of staple wheat or rice, and wood for building structures such as the *ger* frame, would need to be bought or bartered for. However, there was evidence that life was changing. Even right out here, in this *ger*, there was a TV on the table, and a couple of mobile phones tucked under the wooden stays in the roof. Outside we had spotted solar panels and a rudimentary satellite dish. However, tonight the TV was not working, and the older of the two men seemed to be missing his favourite show, as he was continually fiddling with the controls, and heading out to adjust the dish.

Although there are still tens of thousands of nomads using the desert as a low-grade common for their flocks, the nomadic life is increasingly under threat. Mongolia's population has increased sixfold in the past century, leading to serious concerns about overgrazing. Hundreds of thousands of nomads have moved to Ulaanbaatar, partly to look for more settled work, and partly because extreme winters have decimated livestock in recent years.

Leon and I had seen the consequent '*ger* city' – tens of thousands of *gers* – around the outskirts. The migrants' practice of fuelling their stoves with garbage and cheap coal (rather than camel dung) is creating some of the worst urban air pollution on earth. But although there is extensive poverty and pollution, Ulaanbaatar's city centre is starting to boast more and more flashy designer shops, shiny offices and new apartment blocks.

We had come to a country on the cusp of monumental change. The colossal Oyu Tolgoi mine, just a few hundred miles from where we were walking, was due to begin production shortly. It is thought to be the biggest unexploited reserve for copper, silver and gold in the world, and is forecast to add up to 30 per cent to the country's

GDP, and bring in US$8 billion a year for the next fifty years. As a result of this and other resources, foreign investment was soaring. Mongolia's economy had recently become the fastest-growing in the world.

'This country is so rich in resources, and the population is so small,'* an expat had told us, 'that in a decade or two this place could become the next Dubai.'

And now, here in the Gobi, was the new 'Let's Go Road'. When finished, it would link Mongolia with China, the ancient enemy, but now the keenest customer for millions of tonnes of raw materials. Sitting in that warm, hospitable *ger*, as the temperature dropped into the low −20°Cs again outside, I thought of the two little girls we had met the day before. It was strange to imagine how much their lives might differ from those of their parents.

* With only three million people in the world's nineteenth largest country, Mongolia's population density is the lowest in the world.

8

The incident of the fallen poles

Distance to home: 2,909 miles

The two nomads fed us a beautiful hot breakfast of tagliatelle stew, but adamantly refused the money we offered them. 'We've got a lot to learn from guys like that,' Leon and I said to each other as we walked through the bitterly cold morning and back to the Let's Go Road. Just before we reached it, Leon decided to stay back and film a long-distance shot. I strode onwards. Half an hour later, I heard someone shouting and turned to see the lone figure of Leon waving against the bleak white backdrop. I stopped, and when he reached me he did not look happy.

'Why didn't you wait?' he said. 'I can't walk with the tripod, it's too awkward.'

'Sorry, I thought you would easily catch up.'

Leon looked down at Molly. 'Where are my poles?' He had balanced them on all the bags when he sent me ahead, but they were no longer there.

'They must have fallen off, didn't you see them when you came down to the road?'

'No, I cut the corner to the road.'

We stood squaring off for a moment, and then Leon huffed and said he would go back and look for them. He put down his pack and the camera by the roadside and marched back, retreating over our hard-won ground. I started pacing to keep warm, fuming in my head about Leon – the accusatory tone that he had just used had particularly grated on me. I grabbed the camera and filmed a video diary entry reflecting on what had just happened.

Although we were getting on well most of the time, it should not have been a surprise that we were beginning to annoy each other. From the moment it starts, an expedition combines frequent difficult decisions with long, intense periods of exhaustion, fear, stress, pain and boredom. Throw into the mix the fact that adventurers are usually strong-willed and stubborn, with over-inflated egos, and you have a great scenario for relationship meltdown. For this reason, the godfather of modern expeditions, Ranulph Fiennes, describes how vital it is 'to do a huge amount of careful preparation and selecting when recruiting the team for an expedition. People need to be physically strong, but you also have to test them mentally and test their character very carefully.'

However, in contrast to such careful tests of ability and character, I had recruited Leon on the basis of intuition, having known him for just a few days. During our four intensive months of preparation, we had communicated only by Skype. We had hoped to go on a two-day expedition in Hong Kong to practise working as a team and getting used to our gear, but as tasks spun out of control, we simply did not have time.

Half an hour later, Leon reappeared with poles in hand. We started walking again, side by side, in silence. At first the silence felt awkward, but it was good that we had both had some time to calm down. As we continued onwards, I realised we had to talk. We could not afford to let annoyances like this go unresolved, or else they would fester into resentment, and a downward spiral from there. It was not so much that we were about to have a massive punch-up or walk off our separate ways – though, given how long the trip was, we should not discount that as a risk. Rather, on this expedition, we were not merely trying to complete it together, but to film it together. And to film it well, we needed to remain friends – a cameraman filming or a presenter presenting before someone they disliked was hardly likely to produce good material.

Suddenly, before I had said anything, Leon spoke up.

'Rob, I'm sorry that I shouted at you. It was really hard to catch up with you when I was carrying the tripod.'

I was impressed that Leon had initiated the conversation and been the first to apologise. I felt slightly ashamed. Wasn't I supposed to be the older, more mature one?

'Yes, sorry I kept walking,' I said. 'I just thought you were doing some extra filming, and that you could put the tripod away in your pack.'

We talked on through the 'incident of the falling poles', sharing our perspectives, and acknowledging that we both had reasons to be annoyed and that, in this case, it basically came down to bad communication. We had to stop making assumptions that the other person had the same understanding as we did, and instead we needed to overcommunicate. If Leon wanted me to wait and keep an eye on his poles, he needed to tell me. If I wanted Leon to put away his tripod and catch up with me while I made headway with Molly, I needed to tell him. We talked about how we were bound to annoy each other on a regular basis. 'Clearing the air' conversations like this were going to be vital.

We were starting to run low on food, because it turned out that the Let's Go Road had bypassed the hamlet where we had been hoping to resupply. However, the two nomads who had hosted us had indicated we would soon reach a *ger* restaurant beside the road, and we were relieved when we finally reached it at lunchtime the next day. The husband and wife who owned the *ger* served us bowls of wonderful hot noodles, while their little boy played on the floor with a few toys. Their business would do well with the new road, and increasing traffic, and their ability to just pack up and move to better locations.

A couple of truck drivers, one chubby, one thin, and both wearing tatty, ex-military clothing, sat at the adjacent table, and I noticed a small handgun on their table. 'Wow, this really is the Wild East,' I marvelled to myself, guessing that the route must be vulnerable to bandits.

Leon, meanwhile, was busy fixing his sunglasses, which had cracked in the cold (we had no more spares). He finally finished, put them on, and asked me what I thought.

'You look like some kind of demented desert pirate,' I laughed, explaining that I could hardly see one of his eyes, there was so much tape wrapped around the frame.

The chubby truck driver with the gun looked over at us and grunted. We jolted to attention. He nodded and passed his own sunglasses to Leon. The driver watched carefully as Leon nervously tried them on, then insisted that he keep them. Leon said an extra-polite thank you.

'Cool,' I thought, 'Leon just got given some sunglasses by a gun-wielding trucker.'

The truck drivers got up and left, but the gun remained on their table. Tentatively I leaned over to examine the deadly weapon.

It felt very light, and I realised it was one of the little boy's plastic toys.

9
Genghis

Distance to home: 2,894 miles

21 NOVEMBER

The Let's Go Road was still not complete, and it soon petered back into the desert, forcing us to press onwards on a grit track. There were, however, still regular trucks rumbling past throughout the day, carrying manufactured goods up from China, or raw materials the other way. Although we were still in the middle of the Gobi, our route was now, broadly speaking, the highway to Beijing. It was a route that had been in use since ancient times, and through the centuries it had seen the passage of fearless traders, devout pilgrims, promised princesses and ferocious raiders, as well as – of course – Genghis and his armies on their way to unleash hell on the world.

I still found it hard to believe that the stories of Genghis's life and achievements were real; even his childhood was the stuff of Hollywood legend. He had been born with the name Temujin, about 800 years ago on the grassy steppes northeast of Ulaanbaatar. At that time, the Mongol people were a series of scattered, competing nomadic tribes: hardy, wild, often fighting. Temujin's father, an important chief, had died shortly after he was born. His mother was left destitute and had to fend and provide for the family herself.

Temujin and his siblings grew up in a dangerous world – and with no shortage of sibling rivalry. This escalated severely when, at thirteen, Temujin got into an argument with his older half-brother about the rightful ownership of a lark and a minnow they had caught. Later that day, Temujin murdered his brother. Not long after this he was kidnapped and held hostage by a neighbouring tribe.

He managed to escape, hiding in an icy river to avoid recapture, and befriending one of his former captors to help him make it safely home.

As he reached manhood, Temujin took up the leadership of his local tribe and, after two decades of fighting and politicking with other tribes, managed to unite them all behind him. He now took the name Genghis Khan – Ruler of All – and from this new position of authority marshalled the most loyal and well-coordinated force of nomads that the world had ever seen.

And a force they were indeed. For more than a century, they swept south like a perfect storm in their tens of thousands, destroying anyone who stood in their way. Impregnable cities fell, armies ten or twenty times bigger than them were routinely defeated. Under the leadership of Genghis's sons and grandsons, the onslaught spread further and further – from Korea to Indonesia, from Persia to Poland; all collapsed before them.

The Mongol's victims in far-flung lands barely knew who or what had hit them. When Christendom first heard about an army on horseback, smashing the Muslim peoples of the Middle East, they thought it was the legendary Christian King, Prester John, coming to aid them in their dreadful Crusades. But the Mongols then encroached into Europe, and when the Christian knights of Poland and Hungary said their prayers and went out to face the horseback warriors, they fared no better – by day's end their entire force had been destroyed, princes and bishops included.

The Chinese, in contrast, knew their pillaging neighbours well, having endured conflicts with them for thousands of years. They had kept the nomads at bay through a mixture of defence (the Great Wall was built partly for that purpose), bribery, marriage alliances, meddling in tribal politics, and occasionally fielding huge armies. But they never thought that the nomadic raiders would be capable of taking the whole Chinese Empire for themselves. However, under the leadership of Kublai Khan, Genghis's grandson, the unthinkable did happen. The Mongols completed their conquest of China, and founded the imperial Yuan Dynasty, which would rule the Middle Kingdom for almost a hundred years.

And what was it like if the Mongols did come your way? Well, one of the great secrets to their success was the fear that came in their wake.* If you were lucky, they gave your city the option of 'surrender or die'. If you did not surrender, you would be caught in a whirlwind of massacre worse than your most infernal nightmare.

While cycling through Central Asia a few years previously, I had gone past many of the cities, or ex-cities, that the Mongol armies had laid to waste: Termez – after a two-day siege in 1220, everyone in the city was slain; in Merv, 700,000 were executed in a single day. In order to take the seemingly impregnable citadel of Bukhara, Genghis forced captives to march into the moats – the siege moved forwards on top of their mangled bodies. The death toll of the Mongol conquests, including lives lost as a result of subsequent famines and sieges, is thought to be between thirty and sixty million. If this figure is taken in proportion to the global population at the time (less than half a billion), the figure becomes even more staggering, amounting to around 10 per cent of the global population wiped out.†

* Other factors behind the Mongols' success included their skill and speed at firing arrows from the saddle; their strategy of fleeing and counter-attacking when in trouble; and their willingness to learn and recruit from those they conquered all across Eurasia.
† Even the Pax Mongolica (Mongol Peace), which enabled the land routes between Asia and Europe to be travelled in relative safety, had a dark side – for these routes eased the passage of the bubonic plague from Asia to Europe. On the other hand, during this time of marginally easier move-ment, a family of Venetian merchants was able to travel to China and back, and Marco Polo's subsequent account was the inspiration behind Columbus's discovery of the New World, and a whole new epoch of world history.

10

Total whiteout

22–23 NOVEMBER

I woke again and again in the night to the noise of my tent walls flapping in a rage. Outside, in the cold darkness, a storm was flinging itself down the valley like one of Genghis's thundering armies from eight centuries previously. As daylight dawned, the tent continued to shake violently; hunched in my sleeping bag, the thought of going out into this madness was not appealing. In the last few days I had been starting to feel increasingly tired from the continual walking and relentless cold. But we were short on food, our thermos flasks had cracked, and all the water in our bottles was totally frozen. We needed to keep moving to stay ahead of the winter that, evidently, was rapidly catching up with us.

'You OK Leon?' I shouted above the din, wondering if he was awake.

'Fine thanks, you?' he shouted back.

'Bit of a wind blowing outside.'

'Yes, I just had a look through my door and it's a total whiteout.'

I followed Leon's lead, and unzipped my tent for a peek. Gone was the sparse, open valley of the previous evening; instead we were enclosed in a prison of screaming whiteness, with a high-speed layer of snow dancing across the scrubby desert floor. The road we had been following yesterday was lost from sight.

Inside our tents, Leon and I stuffed away our things, and then, yelling like madmen, burst out into the storm. Immediately the tents tried to fly away. Leon sprawled himself on top of his, while I threw my rucksack inside mine. I suddenly remembered that we had previously discussed the importance of filming when things were most

43

desperate. I grabbed the camera, ran ten metres into the wind and turned it on.

Leon and I wrestled with our tents as the wind roared past. The coldest I had ever experienced had been −40°C in Siberia and with the wind chill, this was feeling almost as bad.

'How are your hands and feet?' I yelled. Frostbite and hypothermia were a real risk.

'Completely numb,' Leon shouted.

We needed to warm up fast. We dropped the bags, and started to run in wild circles, swinging our arms in windmills, doing kung-fu kicks in the air, and singing, 'I feel good' very loudly. After a few minutes the blood began to return to our digits. We quickly finished packing and followed the compass through the whiteout and back to the truckers' track.

As the morning progressed, even marching at full speed, we still felt cold in the blistering wind. To shield our faces, we put on our black balaclavas. They were the old-school 'terrorist' type, with holes only for the eyes and mouth.

Leon turned to me and asked, 'How do I look?'

I burst out laughing. 'You look like a member of the IRA who has taken a wrong turn and ended up in the Gobi.'

Leon smiled sheepishly, and looked even stranger.

The next few trucks coming down the road slowed to say hello, but when they saw our masked faces, they revved their engines and kept going. We were starting to feel thirsty, so we pulled off our balaclavas for the next truck and waved it down. The trucker first of all kindly offered us a lift, which we turned down. Instead, we asked for some water. He handed us a gloriously lukewarm bottle of water, which we gulped down quickly before it froze. In return we gave him one of our frozen bottles, which he could melt inside the warm cab on the way to the border.

As the whiteout gradually subsided, we realised that it was not actually snowing, but rather the gale was picking up snow from the ground and flinging it horizontally across the land. I had taken first turn with Molly, and when we switched round I jogged ahead to keep the blood pumping to my feet. It had been a crazy start to the day, but I thought we had coped well given the conditions. And I was especially happy that we had managed to capture much of the experience on camera.

The filming had been going reasonably well, and on average we had been shooting about an hour a day. In the cold, this was very time-consuming, and sometimes unpleasant, but it was what we had signed up for. I was gradually getting more relaxed when I presented, and Leon was increasingly nifty with the camera, though since the temperature had dropped into the −20°Cs on day five, he grimaced whenever he got it out.

'It's like holding a large block of ice,' he had said. 'All the plastic and metal are basically conducting the cold straight into my hands. They go completely numb, and it always takes an hour to warm them back up.' Our gloves were doing a good job at keeping our hands warm when we were walking, but they were not designed for holding blocks of ice.

When we reached the border in a few days' time, we would send back to Hong Kong a hard drive of the footage we had shot. The TV network that would broadcast the episodes had, at the last minute, outsourced the management and editing of the show to a small local production company – Tiberius Productions – and it was with them that we would have our main contact. We were looking forward to seeing what they thought of our desert filming.

We had met Tiberius just before we left, and found them to be a young, dynamic team; in our initial meetings, lots of creative ideas buzzed around the room. In addition to helpfully lending us a wireless mic and a second primary camera, they also gave us feedback on a test shoot, and took us shopping for extra gear. At the same time, though, it became evident that, as a production company, their priorities were different from ours. Their mandate was to focus on the technical aspects of the production. For Leon and me, the issue was much more about how we were going to pull off the expedition at all.

Leon and I had concerns about whether Tiberius understood our limitations. They would not be travelling with us, and it might be hard for them to grasp how – with our daily regimen of walking twenty miles a day while carrying all the gear, organising our own food, shelter and logistics, not to mention filming – we would not always be able to shoot the same quality of footage that was achieved on higher-budget expedition TV shows, with their convoys of support vehicles and fixers.

Conversely, Tiberius were unsure about whether we fully appreciated the high levels of filming standards that were required of us. Their main concern was with Leon's youth – it was unusual for someone of his age to end up as primary cameraman for an entire show. His main prior experience had been through his film studies at university, a handful of internships and freelance jobs, and the self-filming of his bike trip the previous year. However, Tiberius knew they had no choice: 'We're not exactly going to find another cameraman who is willing to walk across China,' they had joked.

Because our final two weeks in Hong Kong had been so busy with last-minute preparations, these production vs. expedition tensions were still somewhat unresolved when we departed. We certainly felt daunted by the filming pressure, and Leon's confidence was shaken. But I thought that as long as Leon pointed the camera in the right direction and remembered to take the lens cap off, it would all work out fine.

On our final two days before the border, the land flattened into long rolling hills, and the road widened to over a hundred metres. More and more convoys of trucks swerved past, waving and honking. One truck came over the crest of a hill too fast, and was obviously not expecting us. Out of control under its own momentum it came straight at me, and I had to dash sideways to get out of the way. The truck's roaring wheels missed Molly's rear end by less than a metre, and I realised that if she had been hit I would have had no time to detach myself and would have been dragged under too. My heart was beating in overdrive for the next half hour.

On our last night before the border town, Leon asked for another laxative tablet. I woke from my slumber to hear him making several panicked nocturnal outings. When I remarked on this the next morning, Leon laughed. He said he had just remembered a dream he'd had during the night.

'I was on the run,' he said, 'being chased by a man in a suit with dark glasses – like Mr Smith from *The Matrix*. I managed to hide behind some trees, and as I looked out I saw the agent hunting for me. I saw he had a name badge on, and when I looked more carefully, it said: Mr Lax!'

Leon and I were gradually generating slang for various aspects and procedures in the expedition, and from this point onwards, going for 'number twos' would be referred to as a 'Mr Lax'.

The first sign that we were nearing the border came with a sighting of the trans-Mongolian railway, with its absurdly long trains, clattering romantically past on the plain to the east. It was extraordinary to think these trains came all the way from Moscow. Shortly after this, some tall, rectangular buildings started to rise out of the far horizon. They looked peculiar to our eyes after all the emptiness. With civilisation so near, the exhaustion and hunger in my body suddenly felt more pressing. I was excited about having a hot shower, some vegetables, and a chance to talk to Christine.

Slowly, slowly the buildings drew nearer, and as they were starting to take on a clearer shape, we came to a large pile of stones, littered with bottles of vodka and beer cans and with a stake of wood coming out of it. It was an *oboo* – a sacred high point inspired by Mongolia's ancient shamanistic religions, and a site where people prayed for good luck on their journey through the emptiness. While we were filming, a car pulled up and two men climbed out. They drank a can of beer, walked a lap of the stones, jumped back in and drove off into the desert.

For us, the *oboo* was a marker that we had almost made it through the first stage of our long walk home. Distance-wise, we had only travelled about 5 per cent of the way. But walking across the Outer Mongolian Gobi was certainly not an easy way to start, and we had coped quite well, all things considered. As a team, we had had some arguments, but we had got through them without bitter feelings, and were steadily becoming friends. In terms of physical fitness, our bodies were tired and hungry, but in one piece – a satisfactory result given our state of exhaustion before we had even set off. And it had already been a fine adventure, with a few good challenges to overcome, and some wonderful encounters with the Gobi's hardy, hospitable people. I looked up at the *oboo* again, and said a prayer of thanks to my own God. Then I picked up Molly for the final time and set off towards the skyline of buildings on the ever-nearing horizon.

11

Mos Eisley

Distance to home: 2,830 miles

24–26 NOVEMBER
By the time we reached the outskirts of Zamiin-Uud, the sun was setting. The streets were grimy, and lined with an assortment of small concrete buildings and dirty *gers*, all mixed together. A large chimney spewed fumes into the icy air, and cars screeched and swerved down the narrow road. Welcome back to civilisation.

It took us an hour to reach the centre of the border town, and gradually more people were on the streets, all of them inhabiting very different worlds. A dad wheeled his toddler past in a baby buggy and smiled; two gruff-looking Genghises shuffled across the street, smoking; a teenage girl with lipstick and a smart handbag overtook us while writing a text message. Down in the gutter some little Chihuahua-like mongrels barked – too puny to be guard dogs, and too skinny to be eaten, they were simply left to breed and scavenge.

The town centre itself was bathed in murky light from a selection of half-working streetlamps. 'A wretched hive of scum and villainy if ever I've seen one,' said Leon, quoting Obi-Wan Kenobi's description of the space-port of Mos Eisley.

We hid Molly under a stairwell, checked into a cheap hotel and headed to the best restaurant in town, which as it happened did feel a little bit like the bar where Obi-Wan meets Han Solo, but without the cool band. As we sat down, the strange security and warmth of being inside a real building hit me. For a moment I felt giddy with euphoria, and I looked across to see Leon was grinning too. We ordered a feast of steak, chicken, vegetables and beer.

'Cheers,' I said. 'So far so good.' I took my first sip, and felt my cheeks flush.

'We've earned a couple of days off, that's for sure,' said Leon.

We looked out of the window. It was dark outside, and the iPhone showed that it would be in the low −20°Cs again tonight.

'And it's going to be nice to sleep inside.' Simple comforts had become the greatest of luxuries.

Back at the hotel, I took the much-dreamed-of, and very long hot shower. As I re-emerged from the bathroom, Leon told me he had just taken two phone calls from Christine. She was actually in the UK for work, and had gone there just before Leon and I left Hong Kong. A few minutes later she rang again. I felt emotional to hear her voice. She said that she had been coping OK, but now she was starting to dread the prospect of returning to our empty flat in Hong Kong the following week. I felt guilty, and said that hopefully we would be able to talk more easily in China, with its better mobile-phone coverage. It was also less than a month until we would meet up for Christmas.

In daylight Zamiin-Uud was less ugly, but still not somewhere one would stay longer than needed out of choice. Apart from a couple of small supermarkets, the shops were sparsely stocked, and most shopkeepers seemed a bit grumpy. We decided to save our main shopping for China. But before we crossed the border, we had other things to organise; in particular, we faced two potentially far-reaching decisions.

The first was about Molly. Although she had served us well and it was tempting to keep her for the upcoming Chinese section of desert, in China we wanted the freedom to go off-road. We also did not want to draw too much attention to ourselves from the Chinese authorities. Molly slowed us down, too – at our current rate it would take us three years to get home. Furthermore, there would be more regular settlements in China, so we would not need to carry the same heavy loads of food and water. We therefore decided, with a little sadness, that we should give her away.

The second decision was connected – what gear we could send home. Even without the food and water supplies, we still risked injury or over-exhaustion through carrying too much on our backs.

Anything not completely essential had to go. We therefore wrapped our spare camera, stove, batteries and clothes in a pink Mongolian blanket, and put it in a box. We added to this a hard drive of footage for Tiberius, and posted it all to Hong Kong.

Leon went to an internet café and I went back to the hotel and started work on my weekly newspaper article. I had been commissioned to write for a newspaper in Hong Kong; it was a privilege to have this writing opportunity, and it would help pay the rent while I was away. But my eyes were half shut in front of the laptop as I dug around my memories for some stories, and all I really wanted to do was lie down.

Our last task was to get rid of Molly. We wheeled her down to the train station car park. A young man was sitting in a shiny black SUV with his window rolled down. Western rock music was blasting from the stereo, and a huge pile of Chinese banknotes sat on the dashboard. Every few minutes, someone approached his window for a moment, before walking away again.

'Hello,' he called across to us, 'come and sit in my car – we can talk English and listen to music.'

We left Molly by the front of the car and hopped in. The man's name was Urult; it turned out that, despite appearances, he was not a drug dealer but a money-changer.

'I love Ooosis and Coolplay,' he said, putting on his favourite tunes, and then changing each track after they had only half played. Evidently not many people shared his musical taste around here, and he was glad to have a captive audience. Urult explained that his brother was some kind of big man in the town. 'He's a billionaire,' he said, though we thought he meant millionaire, and that he must be the local mafia boss, thus explaining both why the police overlooked this blatant black-market money-changing, and why there was no risk of robbery. Urult also said he could look after Molly, and that he would give her to the next desert explorer he met passing this way.

We could not have conceived it at this point, but those desert explorers would turn out to be Leon and me, returning to Mongolia three months later under the most unforeseen of circumstances.

Part Two

Into China

————

不怕慢 就怕站

*One is not so much concerned when he is slow
as when he comes to a halt.*

OUTER MONGOLIA

Zamiin-Uud
Erenhot

Mongolian farmhouse

Sonid Youqi

INNER MONGOLIA AUTONOMOUS REGION

N

Chahar Youyi Houqi

Jining

Fengzhen

Great Wall

Datong

Yungang Grottoes

SHANXI PROVINCE

⋯⋯⋯ route

country boundaries

provincial boundaries

0   100 km

0   50 mile

12
Welcome to China

Distance to home: 2,830 miles

27 NOVEMBER

We sat in the jeep and the driver grew in Genghis-like aggression as he slammed the door several times until it stayed shut. Then he jumped in, and we revved out onto the road.

Every expedition needs 'rules', and from the outset our basic rule was that we must walk every metre of the expedition unless officialdom or the police forced us to take a lift. Unfortunately, we had now reached such a moment, because the Mongolian–Chinese border had a strictly enforced 'motorised vehicles only' rule for crossing the two-mile border zone. Hence the jeep.

We drove into no-man's-land and joined a traffic jam of other beaten-up Russian jeeps, each driven by a chain-smoking Genghis. They were all constantly trying to overtake one another, as if they were fairground bumper cars. Our Genghis revved, laughed and lit cigarettes as he tried to barge into a position further up the line, and at one point we felt a scraping sensation along our side. He jumped out to observe that part of his bumper had fallen off, but was unabashed. Climbing back in, he growled something under his breath, leaned forward and revved into the side of the next jeep. Let the joust continue.

Eventually, we made it to the Soviet-era immigration terminal. We were unceremoniously stamped out of Mongolia and, with our adrenaline starting to flow, we entered the next building on which red letters proclaimed:

中国 二连	𐌰𐌰	Erlian* China
(Chinese)	(Mongol Script)	(English)

I held my passport tightly in my hands. I had been to China several times before, on bicycle trips and for work, and I had never had any serious problems with the police or bureaucracy. However, this time I was nervous because we had heard stories about our exact camera model being confiscated at the Chinese border, and if that happened the whole trip would derail. Leon had therefore packed it deep inside his rucksack and we hoped nobody would search us. We also had neither journalist visas nor filming permits, as we had understood that we would almost certainly have been turned down and, in any case, on journalist visas we would be subject to more regular police questioning. Therefore the only viable option was to enter China as tourists. We needed more than the usual one-month tourist visa, so we had paid an expensive visa agent in Hong Kong to fly our passports to Los Angeles and back. The Chinese consulate there was giving out multiple-entry visas, with a three-month stay allowed per entry. This was a lot better than one-month entries, but it still meant that halfway through China, we would have to somehow leave and re-enter the country to renew the visa.

'Good luck,' I said to Leon as we joined the queue.

'You too.' He looked nervous as well.

I reached the front and handed my passport to the officer.

Official (blank face): 'Where are you going?'

Me (broad smile): 'To Hong Kong.'

Official (furrowing his brow): 'You got your visa in Los Angeles?'

Me (smiling even more brightly): 'Yes.'

The official dithered for a moment before looking up and handing me back my passport.

'Welcome to China,' he said, squeezing a brief smile. I nodded back and walked on through into the Middle Kingdom.

* Erlian is a shortened Chinese name for the border town. The older Mongolian name is Erenhot, and the two seem to be interchangeable.

13
Dinos

Distance to home: 2,824 miles

27 NOVEMBER

After the Chinese took over the Mongol lands in the seventeenth century, they divided the majority of it into Outer Mongolia and Inner Mongolia for administrative purposes. Erlian, developed only as a tiny desert outpost for the trans-Mongol horse-relay postal system, lay on the border between these two provinces. But as the twentieth century arrived, the two Mongolias – caught like shrimps between the lumbering whales of Russia and China – were to have very different fates. Outer Mongolia achieved independence from China, becoming The People's Republic of Mongolia under Soviet lordship in 1923, and then the fully independent Republic of Mongolia in 1990.

Inner Mongolia, meanwhile, although making some fleeting attempts to unify with independent Outer Mongolia in the 1920s and 1930s, remained part of China throughout the tumult of Chinese Nationalist rule, Japanese invasion and civil war. When the Chinese Communist Party (CCP) won the civil war in 1949, Chairman Mao extended Inner Mongolia's boundaries to encompass much of China's northern frontier, and Erlian became an international border post. By the early 1990s it had grown from a relay station to a small town of 8,000 people, and in 1992, having opened up to international trade, the Han Chinese pioneers poured in. Its population today is pushing towards 100,000.

We were wide-eyed on our short walk into the town centre, gazing up at the ten-storey buildings and glass-fronted shops. The shops sold mobile phones, fast food, sports gear, sunglasses and computers. The streets were clean, cold, and buzzing with traffic. People scampered across the road looking upbeat and talking loudly, and many stared and laughed openly at us. I knew that a fair number of backpackers must pass through here by train, so we were not an entirely exceptional sight. Perhaps we did stick out, though, with our Mongolian fur hats and metal hiking poles.

While the young people were in jeans and branded jackets, the older men mostly sported green People's Liberation Army (PLA) coats, and PLA hats with rabbit-fur earflaps. We eyed the hats with envy – they looked even warmer than our Mongolian hats. Most faces were Han Chinese, but some looked more Mongol, with higher cheekbones and rosier cheeks.

We checked into a cheap hotel, and set out with the shopping list we had compiled in the desert. In search of new thermos flasks, we entered an odds-and-ends store on a side street. A young lady sitting with a baby on her lap was startled by our entry – evidently backpackers did not usually visit odds-and-ends stores. She called out and her husband appeared, and he looked startled too. But after I had said, '*Nihao, women shi yingguoren*' (Hello, we are British people) in my best Mandarin, their expressions softened. Very little English was spoken outside the main cities in China, and on past visits I had relied purely on a magic letter and sign language to communicate. Before this trip, however, I had been learning some Mandarin, and I was delighted that my first tentative efforts were being understood. There was a picture of Chairman Mao on the wall behind the desk, and the shelves were filled with pots, pans, cables, rice cookers, kettles and blankets. No sign of thermos flasks, though. Now came the challenge of explaining what we needed.

Digging deep into my memory banks, I said '*re shui*' (hot water), accompanying this with elaborate mimes of steaming water and some sound effects. The man watched me with devout concentration, and then suddenly smiled. He led me over to a shelf at the back with a line of silver thermoses. We haggled a little, and settled on 100 RMB (£10) each. We bade the shopkeeper and his wife a friendly goodbye and headed back into the street for the next items on our list.

To our delight, after only two hours of lively, jovial miming and haggling with a host of other helpful shopkeepers, we had managed to buy new prepaid SIM cards (for our one iPhone and one basic phone), lightweight blankets (to insulate us from the ground, instead of our cardboard), sunglasses, ice cream, a USB splitter, and PLA sheep's-wool mittens. For boys like us whose key goals when shopping were maximum speed and minimum pain, China was ideal. However, when we returned to the hotel and tried out the thermoses, mine was leaking. I headed back out, on a mission to get a refund from the friendly odds-and-ends store. The shopkeeper was still friendly, but he was not keen to give me a refund. Instead, he boiled a kettle, filled the thermos, gave the lid a very serious tightening and demonstrated to me that in fact it did not leak after all. It has been said before that Chinese shopkeepers are the most determined in the world. I admitted defeat and headed back with the same old thermos.

While Erlian's obvious claim to fame was its status as China's frontier-border town between Inner and Outer Mongolia, it also had another, arguably greater claim, going back to 1922. This was the year that American naturalist Roy Chapman Andrews set off from Peking into the Gobi, with a pistol in his belt and a small convoy of cars and scientists. No one had ever dug for fossils in the Gobi before, and their hope was to find some clues as to the origin of humans in Asia.

They stopped for the night in the tiny Erlian outpost, and a couple of Andrews' teammates went for a walk to do some preliminary digging. Before the sun set, to their astonishment, they stumbled on some fossils lying exposed on the surface of a dried-up salt lake. The fossils were not of early humans, but rather of some far older creatures, including an unknown species of Asian rhino and, most exciting of all, dinosaurs. Electrified by the find, the team crossed into Outer Mongolia and drove deeper into the desert, whereupon the discoveries kept on coming, with more species of dinosaurs, and even the first-ever dinosaur nests – complete with eggs. Although Andrews' fossils were all shipped off to America in the 1920s, thousands of new fossils have since been discovered in the Gobi.

'Woooooooow, look at those!' said Leon, pointing, as we walked into the enormous Erlian Dinosaur Museum Campus. I had recently discovered that Leon was a self-confessed dinosaur-super-nerd, and I had never seen him this excited. The path we were walking down – though Leon was almost skipping – was surrounded by long lines of life-size dinosaur models. The museum was in fact located very close to the site of Andrews' original finds, and we seemed to have the place all to ourselves.

As we entered the first building, robotic dinosaur models in the hallway roared and swayed their heads at us.

'This is so cool,' exclaimed Leon.

I remarked that one of them was sporting some effeminate feathers.

'Oh yes, more and more fossils have been found with feathers,' enthused Leon, 'and some people now believe that many – perhaps most – dinosaurs actually had them. How weird is that!' The feathers further established the link between birds and dinosaurs, which had originally been based on anatomic similarities. In fact, some have argued that we can go beyond saying that birds evolved from dinosaurs to assert that, actually, birds are dinosaurs.

We walked through to the main auditorium, which had a glass floor. Underneath it we could see a dig site packed with dinosaur bones and fossils. It was the same in the second room, though in here we also spotted a hole in the glass. As there was no one else in the building, we took it in turns to kneel down, put our hand through, and for a few magical seconds take hold of a large bone. It felt as if it would have been rather easy to steal, though neither of us wanted to add a dinosaur bone to our already overladen rucksacks.*

* In 2012 an American man was arrested for smuggling an impressive Tyrannosaurus skeleton out of Mongolia. It was sold for over US$1 million in an auction. At the time of writing he faces up to seventeen years in prison.

14
Police

Distance to home: 2,824 miles

28–29 NOVEMBER

'Left here . . .'

'Cross the road then right . . .'

This was a momentous day, our first of walking in China, and our first without Molly – I was excited to see how we would fare. Our packs weighed about twenty-five kilograms each, like an overweight check-in bag at the airport. I had tightened my waist-strap to bring 70 per cent of this weight off my back and onto my hips, but I could still feel the pressure bearing down through my whole body. There were still more than 2,800 miles to go.

'Left again . . .'

Leon glanced up and down from the iPhone, and gave directions as we weaved our way through the streets and out of the town. With our Chinese SIM cards we could zoom in on the satellite images from Google Maps, and a little blue dot showed precisely where we were as we walked. As we would not always have 3G reception, for a back-up map we had some pages torn out of a Chinese road atlas. Topographical maps would have been much better, but there were none available for most of China – not a surprise given its paranoid security policies.

In fact, after the Communists took over in 1949, foreigners were almost entirely banned from China until the 1980s. When Colin Thubron visited in 1986, he had marvelled at the unexpected suddenness with which China had opened up – for a well-travelled man such as himself, it was like 'discovering a new room in a house in which you'd lived all your life.' By the 1990s, floods of tourists were coming, and now, in 2011, there were only a handful of rumoured 'closed zones', which were still off-limits to foreign tourists. The trouble with the 'closed zones' was that their locations were also a bit of a secret. Leon and I could only hope that we did not accidentally stray into one.

'Cross this road, and left . . .'

We cleared the final few factories on the outskirts of town.

'OK, it should be straight all the way from here.'

Leon was not exaggerating, for we had arrived on National Highway 208, a smooth, new dual carriageway, blazing south, dead straight ahead of us to an empty horizon, a giant runway into China's heart. We would be more or less following this road until we left the Gobi in about 400 miles. It was already much busier than Outer Mongolia, with a car or truck passing us every few minutes. Half a mile away, running parallel, was the trans-Mongolian railway, and once or twice an hour an implausibly long train clattered past, bearing cargoes of passengers or coal.

Not long after setting out down this road, we found ourselves surrounded by a forest of wind turbines, standing thirty metres high, silhouetted against the big blue sky. The wind was gentle today so only a handful were actually spinning. At the turbines' feet was the familiar sight of life-sized dinosaur models. Tyrannosauruses rex and triceratops, diplodocuses and pterodactyls stood in static poses of fight or flight.

I looked ahead and my smile widened. There before us was a spectacle that we might have expected more in an eccentric corner of the USA than the northern frontier of China. A pair of sauropods (so Leon identified for me) reached their necks across the road and joined lips in a tender kiss. They thus created an archway ten metres high and thirty wide, under which all cars had to drive. Leon set up the tripod and we filmed ourselves walking back into the Gobi, framed by the love birds.

Because of the wind farms and the decent road, at first it had felt as though the desert in China was different to that of Mongolia. But as we went further we saw that we were surrounded by the same barren wasteland of grit, snow and small, defiant shrubs. The Google satellite images, however, showed that we could expect a steadily more developed and populated desert as we moved south. Numerous grey-black stains, like violent bomb sites, marked the presence of open-cast mines for which Inner Mongolia was becoming famous. And every twenty or thirty miles we could see clusters of buildings and settlements, the first of which we hoped to reach by sunset. Although we were slowly getting used to the cold temperatures, it would be good to find a place to stay if we could, especially tonight, as the temperature was forecast to reach −24°C. At the same time, I was in two minds about staying inside because I felt nervous about what the Chinese police might make of us. We were surely both conspicuous and suspicious with our rucksacks, cameras and our insistence on travelling by foot. I couldn't wait to see China properly, but my mind kept replaying worst-case scenarios of arrest, camera confiscation and deportation.

'What would you rather see,' I said, 'a dinosaur or an alien?'

'A dinosaur,' said Leon, without hesitating.

I said that although the combination of Leon's enthusiasm, and the chance to pick up an actual dinosaur bone were making me consider becoming a dinosaur nerd myself, on balance, I would still rather see an alien.

'Really?' said Leon, amazed. But then he wavered and started to ponder whether he might prefer to see an alien too, after all. He was deeply torn and we debated the matter for a while, eventually concluding that whichever we saw, the important thing was that we remembered to capture it on camera.

The sun was about to set, and we were distracted from our conversations by a settlement coming into view on the left-hand side of the road. However, as we got nearer, we saw not village houses, but a complex of faceless grey buildings surrounded by a tall grey wall, flying a large red Chinese flag.

'Uh-oh, are those military barracks?' said Leon.

We stopped. It would not be a good idea to try and sleep in a military village if we wanted to avoid attention from the authorities. We looked over to the right and saw something we had not noticed until now. The whole landscape was fenced off, and behind the fence there was a series of red 'keep out' signs. Behind the signs the desert was strewn with old tanks and large targets.

'I think that's a firing range,' I said.

We looked at each other. The sky was starting to darken, and a heavy, hushed cold was falling. I puffed out some misty breaths, while Leon scanned the iPhone. 'The airport is only four miles away,' he said. 'We could try and sleep there.'

Though it would not be ideal sleeping in an airport this near to a barracks, the wind was starting to numb our faces and the prospect of an airport floor seemed far preferable to camping. We set off at a brisk pace and, an hour later, turned up a side road and saw the small, modern terminal building shining like a little celestial inn out of the darkness. We walked past a couple of taxis and stepped into the light and warmth. Inside, it was sparklingly clean, and a handful of people sat waiting for the next flight.

We perched down next to them and wondered what we should do. It seemed suddenly obvious that such a tiny airport as this would be unlikely to stay open overnight. Two airport policemen started to approach, and my heartbeat quickened. It felt as if the whole terminal was watching us.

'*Women yao kan nimen de hujiao?*' they said in Mandarin, with straight faces.

'Err,' my vocabulary abandoned me and I sat grinning inanely at them. It was one thing shopping for thermoses in Mandarin, another to understand what a policeman was saying to me while I took refuge in a minor airport.

'*Women yao kan nimen de hujiao?*' they repeated.

'Ah!' I said, catching the key word, and translating for Leon, 'they want to see our passports.'

We handed them over. The policemen looked at them for a minute then, to our relief, gave them back. I explained that we were looking for a place to sleep, and they said something else I did not understand. A moment later, they walked away. Unsure what was going on, Leon and I went and sat in a little snack bar in the corner of the airport. It did not sell any cooked food, so for 4 RMB (40 pence) each, we bought some instant noodles which came in cardboard bowls, and a processed sausage (1 RMB, 10 pence). The noodles came with sachets of spices that could be added for flavour and, as we prepared to eat, I noticed Leon pouring all of the powder into his bowl.

'Are you sure you want to do that? That stuff is pretty spicy,' I said.

'Yes, real men eat all the hot powder,' Leon replied, stirring it in with his disposable chopsticks and smiling. I smiled back.

As we ate, we agreed that the Chinese processed sausage was a welcome upgrade from the tins of Mongolian dog food, though Leon's initially rapid pace of slurping noodles quickly slowed as the spice took effect. Mid-mouthful we looked up and saw the policemen heading towards us once more, this time accompanied by an older man wearing a police chief's cap.

'*Hujiao*,' (passports) they said in unison as they reached the table.

We produced them again and I glanced across at Leon. He was looking very solemn – the combined effect of the spices and the police. The chief said, 'The airport will be shutting soon, you cannot sleep here. But Erlian is only fifteen miles away, and there are plenty of hotels there. You can catch a taxi outside.'

We let out a small sigh and thanked the officers. Having filled our thermoses from a hot water machine, we stepped back into the cold. The sudden move from the pleasant terminal to the bitter cold outside felt like a slap in the face, but I was relieved that the police had not interrogated us further. They stood at the window, watching us go; I was not sure if they noticed that we ignored the taxis and simply walked back into the night. Perhaps they were just glad that we were off their turf and not their problem any more.

We spotted a little row of trees on the verge beside the firing range, so we scurried through them and put up our tents. It was illegal for foreigners to camp in China, but I was simply following my usual motto for camping in strange places – as long as nobody saw us and nobody expected us to be there, we would probably be fine.

But that night was our coldest night so far, and in the middle of the night I woke up almost shivering. I started to put on more clothes until in the end I was wearing almost everything I had: on my feet, two pairs of socks; on my legs, two pairs of tights, hiking trousers, and Gore-Tex trousers; on my torso, three thermal vests, a fleece, a windproof jacket and a puffa jacket; on my hands, thin gloves and wool mittens; on my neck, a buff and a scarf; on my head, a balaclava, a woolly hat, a Mongolian fur hat, and my spare boxer shorts. If the army had caught us that night they might have been somewhat surprised by the appearance of the British spy.

We were awoken by a couple of loud cannon booms, followed by some hearty male singing. It was the barracks up the road reporting for action. We packed up quickly and headed back onto the road before anyone saw us.

We marched hard and fast all day, until an hour before dark the next village came into sight. We hoped there would be some kind of basic hostel; spotting an old shepherd leading his flock through the desert, we scrambled across to intercept him.

'Excuse me,' I said, in Mandarin, 'we are British people, we are looking for a hotel.'

The shepherd stopped walking, looked at us for a moment, and then pointed a weather-beaten hand into the sky above the group of clay brick houses. It was hard to interpret exactly where he was pointing, but we said thank you and headed in that direction.

The village seemed deserted until we came to a little wooden shop. I walked in and three men stopped their conversation in mid-sentence and looked at me. I saw that the shelves were stacked with instant noodles, processed sausages, sweets and soft drinks. There were eggs and vegetables on the wooden counter and I was pleased that we were in the land of vegetables again.

'Excuse me, we are British people, we are looking for a hotel.'

One man led me outside and pointed his hand vaguely into the air, in a similar fashion to the shepherd. 'Chinese pointing', as Leon and I would come to call it, was usually like this – skywards and vague. As we set off again, the man called after us and acted out a climbing motion that was even more cryptic than the pointing.

We pressed on past more empty houses, and a chained-up dog barked at us. Two middle-aged ladies appeared and 'Chinese-pointed' for us to keep going, while again performing a mysterious climbing motion. We reached the railway line, clambered across it, and straddled a fence. 'Aha, the climbing,' we noted.

Another man led us to the next cluster of buildings and into a warm room full of tables, where a middle-aged lady said yes, this was the hotel (though it was evidently a pretty basic one). We beamed as we shed our packs and sat down. The lady brought us some snacks, and Leon laid his camera on the table while we waited to be shown to our room. The lady disappeared into the kitchen, and a moment later some dark shapes appeared at the window and half a dozen smartly dressed police officers walked in.

I groaned and realised Leon's camera was still on the table.

We stood and greeted them with a smile, though they remained straight-faced. They were mostly in their twenties.

'Passports please,' one of them said in Chinese.

We handed them over, yet again. While one officer copied our details onto a form, another stood by the table looking at the camera. This was what I had been worried about. Leon casually picked it up and played him some footage from the current memory card. Fortunately, this just showed us walking down the road, rather than the previous one that showed us camping beside the firing range.

After a short while the policemen started to relax and we joked with them about how beautiful and yet how cold China was, miming the freezing temperatures and the vast desert. One of the policemen challenged his colleague to pick up Leon's rucksack. The man took hold of the bag, but on his first attempt could not get it off the ground. This made Leon and I feel slightly less wimpish about our sore backs. In a second attempt, he squatted down underneath it and staggered to his feet. We all applauded and it was good to see some smiling. With our information copied down, the policemen handed back our passports, wished us luck and left.

We had been in China for less than sixty hours, and we had

already had two run-ins with the police. But we had survived the encounters unscathed and they had not seemed to care about the camera. Nonetheless, I hoped that we would not have to deal with the police every night on our long walk home.

15
Inner Mongolians

Distance to home: 2,789 miles

The next day we pressed on down the smooth asphalt. For hours the landscape of snowy, undulating plains hardly changed, though from time to time we saw more wind farms and farmhouses in the distance. Conspicuously, we did not see a single *ger*, although Inner Mongolia, too was historically a land of pastoral nomads. Such a way of life had continued even after the arrival of Chinese rule here four centuries ago, notwithstanding the slow tide of Han migrants who had begun to settle in certain parts of the region. It was only more recently, under Chinese Communism, that most Mongolians had been forced to end their itinerant ways. As Leon and I walked into the late afternoon, we wondered if the lonely brick houses dotting the horizon every five miles were inhabited by former nomads. Just before dark, with the temperature plummeting again, we spotted one a mile off the road, and decided to see if we could stay there for the evening.

We walked towards it across the dust; nearing it we saw a large, unchained dog pacing beside the porch and starting to bark. Leon zoomed in with the camera and we could see its breath forming mist in the air. The house was made from brick and concrete, with a glass-screened porch and corrugated-iron roof. A single red motorbike was parked outside, indicating someone was home. We shouted hello a few times. A teenage boy appeared, waved the dog quiet and walked over. He had a scruffy bowl haircut, thick black hair, and was clearly ethnically Mongolian rather than Han Chinese. He smiled, said hello in Mandarin, and led us past the dog and into the house.

We found ourselves in a dimly lit room, with a lone motorbike poster hanging on the bare walls. A bald man with rosy cheeks, presumably the boy's father, sat on a sofa watching television. He looked up, said a quiet hello, said something in Mongolian to the boy, and indicated that we should sit on the other sofa. We smiled and nodded and attempted to make conversation in Mandarin, our only medium of conversation. We tried to address both the man and the boy, but the man only glanced up from the TV occasionally and said very little. Leon and I took it in turns to do our usual party trick of explaining and acting out the walk and the cold. The man laughed a little, then turned back to the TV. It was screening some sort of Chinese obstacle-course game show.

The man muttered something to the boy in Mongol, who explained to us in Mandarin that he needed to go out to do something, though I did not understand what. A moment later we heard him roaring away on his motorbike. Leon and I looked at each other, wondering what we should do. Were we welcome here? It felt quite awkward. Maybe the boy had gone to get the police, like last night? I was really not in the mood to deal with the police again. Perhaps we should just cut our losses and set up camp? But it was unbelievably cold out there, and beautifully warm in here. The man continued to watch TV. It had been hard work trying to hold a conversation with him – perhaps he was shy, or perhaps he didn't want us here? Or maybe he just did not speak good Mandarin – though this seemed unlikely, because the Mongolian language had been banned for much of the Communist era. He must know some Mandarin.*

We did not know what to do and, paralysed by the warmth, we ended up sitting and waiting. Half an hour later we heard the motorbike returning, and the boy walked back in, smiling. Instead of the police, he had brought a hunk of meat, and he now stoked

---

* There was no point in us showing him the Mongolian magic letter because, while the people of Outer Mongolia read and write in a modernised Cyrillic version of Mongolian, the Mongolians of Inner Mongolia still read and write using the traditional Uighur script of Genghis's time.

up the stove and started to cook. I went outside to relieve myself. The cold was brutal, and the sun was setting almost purple on the empty horizon. I saw that the sheep pen, empty when we arrived, was now full of sheep and goats. The boy had been out shepherding in their flock, and getting some dinner.

Back inside, the boy was happily cooking away, and the man now smiled and said to Leon and I that we would be welcome to eat with them and spend the night. We expressed our immense gratitude, and a few minutes later, the boy was serving us with a tasty mutton soup and doughy buns to dip in it. I attempted a bit more conversation but, even with the boy, I was not able to get very far. We all smiled at each other, made appreciative noises about the food, and continued to watch TV.

I mused about the lives of our kind hosts. Where was the woman of the house?, I wondered. Before living in this little farmhouse, had they lived in a *ger* and owned cows, horses and camels, as well as sheep and goats? And what did they think of their Chinese rulers? The man would have been a child during the 1960s and the Cultural Revolution – Mao's megalomaniac attempt to reassert his power and bring the country under more central control. It had been the outer provinces of Tibet, Xinjiang and Inner Mongolia that had suffered the most. In Inner Mongolia, the focus of the terror was a campaign to root out an imagined Mongolian independence movement. Even official estimates admit to tens of thousands of ethnic Mongolians being killed, and hundreds of thousands imprisoned, maimed or injured.* Culture also suffered, with Buddhist monasteries destroyed, and both the Mongolian language and pictures of Genghis Khan being banned. No one who lived through the Cultural Revolution

---

* Dr Kerry Brown, an expert on the Cultural Revolution in Inner Mongolia, quotes reports of 'people being branded with hot irons, having their tongues and eyes ripped out, and being burnt alive'. The extent of the terror was such that 'a visiting soldier describes how, when he drove in an army jeep into one of the villages surrounding the provincial capital, Hohhot, people literally fled for their lives, believing him to be the latest in a constant stream of "clean up" patrols coming to get more victims'.

was unaffected, and in the end even Mao admitted there had been 'excesses'.

Since the 1970s, although such terrors had mercifully ended, a more deliberate policy of Han Chinese immigration into Inner Mongolia had swung into progress. By the 1980s, the Han Chinese were arriving in their hundreds of thousands, and the Mongolian people – who a century ago had been in a majority – were now outnumbered by more than four to one.* At the same time, the government was starting to promote the expansion of industrial zones and the exploitation of rich natural resources. In recent years, Inner Mongolia had become the fastest-growing economy in the whole of China.

Things had also improved somewhat for the ethnic Mongolians, as their culture had now become accepted, at least within officially sanctioned boundaries. The ban on their language had been reversed, to the point that it had become mandatory on all road signs – we had observed the indecipherable scrawls all down the highway. Genghis Khan, too, was no longer blacklisted. His picture was not only permitted, but statues of him had been built in many of the region's town squares. In an implausible volte-face, the Chinese government proclaimed that Genghis was actually a Chinese hero, not a Mongol one. After all, had his grandson, Kublai Khan, not been the founder of a Chinese dynasty? So of course he was Chinese.

However, despite the economic boom and renewed cultural affirmation, Chinese rule was still not a terribly positive thing for the Inner Mongolians. Many had been forced to settle down and cease their nomadic ways for good; most of the new wealth had gone to the Han, and the farming, industrial and mining developments were inflicting severe damage on the ecosystem.

I looked across the room at our host. His hospitality felt even more precious as I pondered what terrors he might have seen or experienced. Even though he must surely have reason to be distrustful

---

* The redrawing of the boundaries of Inner Mongolia also contributed to the proportionate rise in Han Chinese population.

of strangers, he had generously opened his home and shared a meal with us.

It was time for bed and, to top off their kindness, the boy showed us through a doorway and pointed to a bed on a platform that filled the width of the room. It was a *kang* – a special, centuries-old type of bed in northern China. Pipes, connected to the stove, run along beneath it, and so the bed is kept warm. This *kang* had a thin mattress on it, and all four of us climbed onboard and fell asleep side by side.

16
Dr Leon

Distance to home: 2,768 miles

We are walking onwards down the highway, day after day, from dawn until dusk, as fast as we can. The landscape around us shifts slowly from one empty panorama to another. Although we are moving south at twenty to twenty-five miles a day, the progress is almost indiscernible on our map of China, and we are clearly not outrunning the winter. It is December now, the night-time temperature is in the low −20°Cs, and it is unlikely that it will get much warmer until February.

But we are falling into a good routine and, whether we sleep inside, or camp, we dutifully rise with the sun and stagger back onto the road. We groan when we heave on our heavy packs, and we gasp with shock when we step into the cold for the first time each morning. But once we are moving, the crisp desert landscape, full of silence and majesty, makes us want to sing.

Time passes slowly, as we stride forwards, one step at a time. For the first few hours we usually walk and talk side by side. By the afternoon, we drift apart, lost in our own thoughts. Leon is proving to be slightly faster than me, both at packing up and at walking, but we always stay within a few hundred metres of each other because we need to work together on the filming. We now store the camera in a pouch on the back of his rucksack, while the tripod is strapped to the side of mine. When we need to film, we do not have to drop our packs, but simply help each other pull the camera and tripod out. We are ready to start recording in a matter of seconds.

We need to capture a wide variety of footage. Most of the time

I am the subject while Leon shoots, but sometimes we switch roles. We take many different types of shot, including scenic shots, inter-view shots, B-roll (shots of little details that bring a scene to life), buddy scenes and video diaries. I have also strapped our small GoPro sports camera to my chest. With the push of a single button I can turn this on to record exactly what I see in front of me. All being well, the huge mass of footage we take will eventually be edited down by Tiberius into a four-part series when we get back to Hong Kong, but that seems impossibly far away now.

While we are shooting, Leon also directs. Sometimes he makes me walk back and forth in front of the camera several times. Occasionally, his instructions are unclear, or I misunderstand. I walk too far or not far enough. We have to repeat the whole thing, both of us getting annoyed in the process.

But apart from getting in a mood with each other once or twice a week, we are mostly getting on well. We are both movie fanatics, and as we walk we often natter about our favourite and least favourite movies, scenes and stars, sometimes even straying into such highbrow topics as the relative merits of Orlando Bloom and Jason Statham. We agree that Orlando, in his role as an elf, has mastered the art of the 'middle-distance stare'. Meanwhile Jason (or Jase as we call him), England's skinhead tough guy in Hollywood, has three critical expressions underpinning his success: angry look, confused look and ready-for-action look.

Leon uses these insights as a basis for his own directing.

'Give us an Orlando,' he commands, as he films me standing at the roadside. I immediately raise my eyes to the horizon, with a slightly smug expression on my face, imagining Orcs.

'Give us a Jase,' says Leon, as he takes a shot from the front.

'Which one?'

'Ready-for-action.'

I strike a grimace, expectant of combat and head-butts.

Another part of our daily routine is stopping every one or two hours for a break. Both of our new Chinese thermos flasks are already leaking, so our tepid bowls of instant noodles supplemented with processed sausage are not as appetising as they could be. When we run out of hot water completely, we move onto stuffing copious amounts of cheap biscuits and peanuts into our mouths. Leon's appetite for peanuts, in particular, seems inexhaustible. Our breaks are also a chance to do our stretches, which we had been taught by our sports physiotherapists back home as the best way to prevent injury. My physio in Hong Kong has given me a little spiked rubber ball with which I am supposed to pummel my muscles. It is agony to use, and I call it my torture ball.

But though our bodies are doing fine overall, the aches and pains are gradually increasing. One day I start complaining about a mildly sore shoulder, and suddenly Leon pipes up and says it is just a tensed muscle, and that I should take some Ibuprofen and give it a self-massage with the torture ball.

'You sound like a radio agony aunt-stroke-doctor,' I say, heeding his advice, and rubbing my shoulder.

'Indeed, I am,' says Leon. 'Actually, you can call me Dr Leon.'

Over the coming months, Dr Leon will end up making many diagnoses of injury and prescriptions for treatment. His usual advice consists of confidently stating that the problem will probably just get better on its own, and it is best not to worry about it. On this point, I accuse Dr Leon of being no mere optimist, but rather a hopeavist, as in: 'I have no real basis for saying things will work out OK, but I certainly hope they will.'

17
Tones

Distance to home: 2,736 miles

3–4 DECEMBER
Mandarin is not an easy language for English speakers. Firstly, it has no linguistic connection to European languages, meaning words need to be memorised from scratch. Secondly, it does not use an alphabet, but thousands of different characters.* Thirdly, it is a tonal language, with four tones. You thus have to learn not only how to pronounce a word, but also to say it in the right tone. For example, *ma* ('first' high-pitched tone) means mother; *ma* ('third' down and then up tone) means horse. 'I love my *ma*' (first tone) or 'I love my *ma*' (third tone) would mean quite different things: depending on whether you are trying to express affection for your mother, or for your horse.

But I did not want to let any of this put me off, and my motto was 'to learn by making mistakes', meaning that I would speak as much as possible, and not worry about embarrassing myself. I had started teaching myself Mandarin only five months previously, though since we arrived in China I had also been listening to an hour or two of ChinesePod lessons on my iPod each day. Leon was also learning, but he had spent less time studying, and it was usually me who took on the 'communicator' role while he filmed.

So far, the Chinese seemed very forgiving and willing to repeat things, though they did gravitate towards using the same method as English people do abroad – assuming that by shouting the same thing louder and louder we would be more likely to understand.

---

* There is a system for reading and writing using a Roman alphabet – Pinyin – though this has limitations.

They were also happy to listen attentively to my attempts to speak, and to creatively interpret my eccentric sign language and noises when my vocabulary failed me.

My food vocab was particularly weak; in restaurants I would often be ushered through to the kitchen and shown a plethora of rice, meat and vegetables and I would have to point out what I wanted, with lots of '*hen hao, hen hao*' (very good, very good) encouragements when they suggested throwing them all in a wok and frying them up.

And it was not only us who were initiating conversations – the Chinese were usually very inquisitive about what we were up to, and were nearly always asking us the same questions:

Where are you from?

What are you doing?

Where have you come from?

Where are you going?

Are you married?

Do you speak Mandarin?

Do you have children?

What is your job?

How is China?

Which is better – China or England (or America)?

Why don't you cycle?

Why don't you catch the bus?

In his book about walking through China in the late 1990s, Canadian travel writer Bill Purves described a near identical list of questions. He referred to his rote answers, which he reeled off multiple times a day, as 'reciting his catechism'. Leon and I were getting used to reciting our own catechisms.

As well as my own self-study, Christine, who was fluent in Mandarin, had also helped me to practise before I left. However, this was sometimes frustrating for her because my pronunciation was terrible and I tended to get grumpy when she did not help me in the ways I wanted.

'Pass me the milk please,' Christine would ask over breakfast, in English.

'How do you say "milk" in Mandarin?' I'd ask.

'*Niu nai.*'

'How do you say "pass me"?'

'*Gei wo.*'

'How do you say "milk" again, I've forgotten?'

'*Niu nai.*'

'And "pass me" again?'

'Honey, just pass me the milk!'

During our second week in Inner Mongolia, Christine had arrived back in Hong Kong from England. She told me of the feeling of desolation that had hit her as she dragged her luggage up the stairs and through the door, and saw the empty flat before her. It then truly dawned that I would not be back for many months.

But at least it was now much easier for us to speak on the phone: we were in the same time zone, and the mobile phone signal in much of China, even the desert, was mostly good. Sometimes the conversations we had were comforting and encouraging, but sometimes they just reminded us how far apart we were, and for how long. Christine also gave me some help with my Mandarin on the phone or if I met someone while on the phone with her, she would listen in and correct me afterwards.

It was not unusual for cars that overtook us to stop and reverse back to take a better look, and perhaps ask some questions. One day, a man stopped beside us, and started to reel off questions to which we replied with our increasingly polished catechism.

In answer to the question 'What are you doing?', we replied by saying:

'*Women zuo qu Datong.*' 'We are walking to Datong', using the Mandarin word '*zuo*', which we thought meant 'walk'.

The man looked confused, but beckoned us to his car, offering us a lift at least some of the way.

'*Bu yong le, women zuo qu Datong.*' 'No thank you, we're walking to Datong,' we said.

He persisted a few more times, but after a while gave up on the two mad foreigners and drove off with a honk.

Christine overheard me on the phone and burst out laughing. She pointed out that the way I was saying 'walk' – using '*zuo*' instead of '*zou*' – actually meant 'sit down'. So Leon and I had in fact been saying, 'We are sitting down to Datong.' To avoid confusion, Christine said we should try the words '*bu xing*' for walking instead.

But even after this correction, there were more confused responses. And the next time Christine overheard, she laughed again and said we were now using the wrong tones, thus it sounded like 'not able to'.

So when someone asked, 'What are you doing?', Leon and I were pointing our poles southwards and replying: 'We are not able to go to Datong!'

Travelling on our own two feet, although a hard, slow mode of transport, was certainly helping us to experience out-in-the-sticks parts of China where few other foreigners would find reason to visit. And, more often than not, even in these remote places, we were still able to stay inside and avoid the cold. About once a week, we passed through a proper town in which there would be little hotels called *binguans* – guest places. *Binguans* cost about 100 RMB (£10) per night, and had clean rooms and hot showers. We tried to treat ourselves to a night in one on our days off.

But there were also more local guesthouses called *ludians*: 'road shops'. In villages and smaller towns, they were they only option. They cost half or a quarter of the price of a *binguan*, and they were the usual accommodation of choice for truckers, poor migrants – and us. *Ludian* accommodation was often just the spare rooms behind a restaurant, and typically contained a couple of beds (with a pile of blankets on each), an old TV and, if we were lucky, a coal stove.* Officially, most *ludians* were not registered to accept foreign guests, but we were rarely turned away – perhaps because most settlements we passed through were never (or seldom) visited by foreigners, so nobody knew the rules.

But in all settlements, it went without saying that Leon and I were an unusual sight, our foreign strangeness exacerbated by our

---

* In summer, in the south of China, there was a fan instead of a stove.

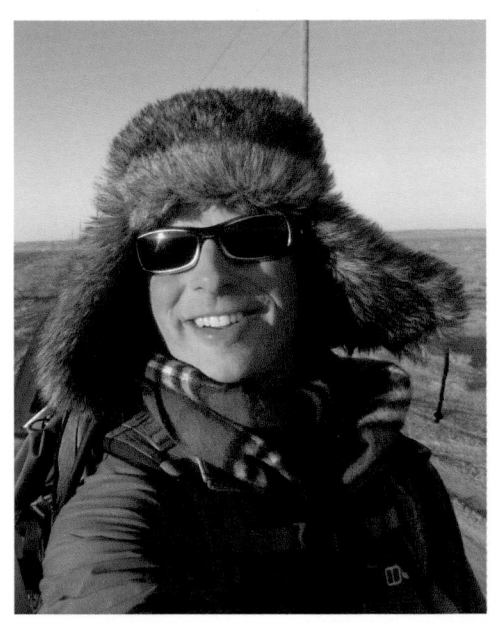

My first day
in the Gobi

Leon and Molly

The Gobi

Stretching before bed

The desert monastery of
Khamariin Khiid

Welcomed into a *ger*

Childhood
in the desert

The best way to
warm up in a Gobi
blizzard   dancing

Sauropods,
Leon, me

The biggest danger
is the traffic

Leon's hands are losing skin

A shortcut on the tracks

Mr Cheerful and friends

Leon self-filming

The friendly
faces of China

The French fry Factory. We had thought there were clouds in the sky before we saw the factory

The Yungang Grottoes

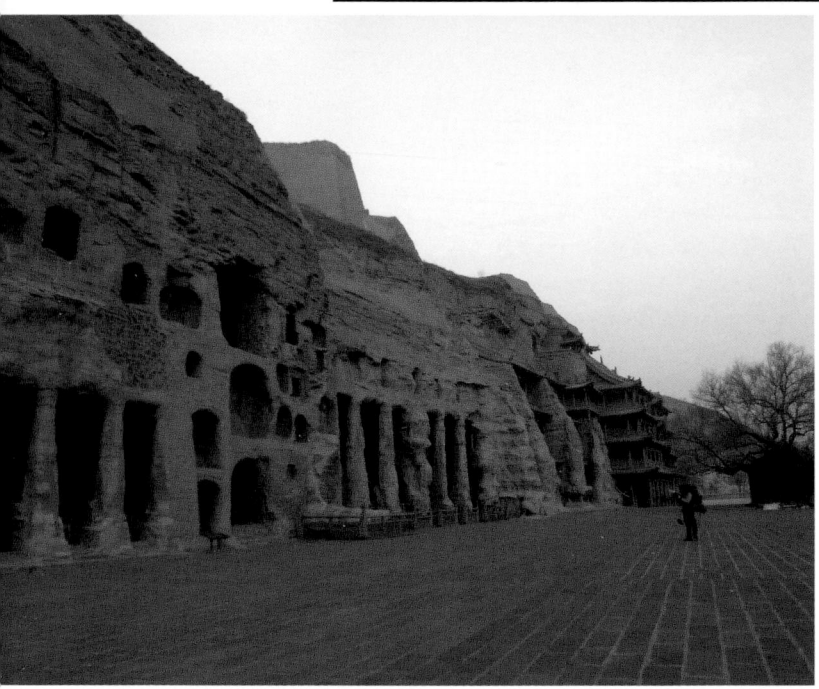

Leon and Clare's Orlandos are better than mine and Christine's

A single swig (straight from the bottle)

The Great Wall with Leon climbing into a gully

A *yaodong* village

A warm *yaodong* stable where we slept

Camping by the frozen Yellow River

Along the scree slopes

Chinese New Year's Eve with Gaoyu and his family

huge packs, strange walking poles and increasingly dishevelled beards. We were stared at by virtually everyone we passed: street-sweepers, shopkeepers, shoppers, motorcyclists, children and mothers. On one occasion a young man walking beside us was staring so hard that he walked straight into a lamppost. However, we knew that in Chinese culture staring was not rude, and while being strange-looking might have provoked suspicion in the West, here in backwater China, it often aroused generosity.*

On our first weekly day off in Inner Mongolia, in the old Qing Dynasty fortress town of Sonid Youqi, we went to an internet café. The young manager asked us for our passports – everyone who used an internet café in China was supposed to give their Chinese ID or passport number. When we explained we'd left our passports in the hotel, he pulled open a drawer of spare ID cards, and happily logged us on under someone else's name. After we finished and came up to pay, he said, 'It's free, my treat.'

That night in a restaurant, we chatted to a neighbouring table of Chinese men while we waited for our bowls of dumplings. When we came to leave and tried to pay, the owner told us that there was no bill, the men had paid for us.

But it was not always quite that pleasant. One night, staying in a truck-stop town, we entered a rough-and-tumble trucker restaurant for dinner. We then managed to forget the oldest motto in the traveller's book: ask the price of food before ordering. The lady presented us with some tasty skewers of meat, and it was only after we had finished eating that she hit us with the bill – about five times what we normally paid for dinner. We started to haggle, completely unsure if she had given us the most expensive item on the menu, or if she had raised the price just for us, or both. All the truckers sitting at

---

* I had found on previous expeditions that I was normally treated well across the world, despite my often bizarre, nomadic appearance. On my three-year bicycle ride, having ridden through twenty countries in Asia, it was only in Western Europe, on my home straight, that I was sometimes denied drinking water from petrol stations and cafés for no apparent reason beyond my grubby clothes.

other tables turned to watch the argument, and we sensed an ominous mood building. But a few minutes later, the price was slightly lowered, we paid up, and with everyone having saved face, the room was full of smiles once again.

18
Baijiu

Distance to home: 2,704 miles

5–8 DECEMBER

In our second week in China, we were starting to share the tarmac road with an increasing volume of traffic. We tucked ourselves against the verge as new cars, old cars, mopeds, tractors and trucks whizzed past. Although the driving in China was, by Western standards, fairly mad, it seemed that the Chinese drove as if they expected obstacles to appear in front of them suddenly – whether it be a donkey, a bicycle laden with large metal pipes, or a couple of foreign hikers with clinking poles. But one day we saw a dead cow lying by the roadside. Its legs stuck out with rigor mortis, and blood was frozen around the corners of its mouth. It was a stark reminder that our gravest danger on the expedition was not cold, police or robbers, but careless drivers.

Leon, who continued to take the lead with navigation, started to scan the iPhone satellite maps for possible alternative routes. One morning he led us off the main road and down a snowy path towards the railway track.

'There should be a kind of jeep track running alongside it,' he said.

He was right, and although our progress was slower on the snowy, dusty surface, there was no traffic, and we enjoyed watching the long trains rattling past us once or twice an hour. We also saw a couple of rail workers walking along the tracks themselves, one of them holding an enormous pair of pliers. The more we watched them, the more we started to think this actually looked like a good idea. The train lines passed through all the little snowy hills in cuttings, and thus it would be a much smoother route. So after we had overtaken the two rail workers, we clambered up the bank, and started marching along the tracks too. The spacing of the wooden sleepers made for an awkward stride, but overall our speed increased. After half an hour, we heard a burst of rhythmic chugging and shrill tooting – a train. Leon wanted to catch its approach on camera. We stayed nervously on the track until the iron rooster appeared from round the corner, and with a good ten seconds to spare we jumped off the track and out of the way as it rushed furiously past.

As night fell, we reached a cluster of small grey buildings beside the track. They looked like some kind of signal control complex. Having knocked on the door and received no answer, we found the door was unlocked and nudged inside. A bare corridor led us to another open door, and peering through, we saw two uniformed men – one lying asleep on a sofa, and the other staring at a wall of ancient computer screens. At first he did not notice us standing at the door.

'*Nihao, women shi yingguoren!*' (Hello, we are British people!) I said.

The man at the computer screens looked up and gasped with an open mouth. The other man woke up and let out a small shout. To calm them down we launched straight into our catechism before they had even asked any questions. We were walking (or not able to go) to Datong; we liked China; it was very beautiful, but very cold outside.

'So you work with trains?' I finished with a question.

The two men had started to recover from their shock, and they said that yes, they did. They gradually warmed to asking us more questions, and the man who had been asleep became increasingly animated. He was about fifty, with a skinhead, a chubby face, and an infectious laugh that made his lungs rasp and body shake.

Mr Cheerful, as we would call him, led us through to an office, where another man sat beside a wooden desk. A little dog leapt to its feet and ran up to us. Mr Cheerful explained what we were doing, and after they had conferred for a moment, the man at the desk, the boss, generously said we would be welcome to join them for dinner and stay the night.

We sat down in the kitchen as Mr Cheerful and a middle-aged lady started to cook. The air filled with hunger-inducing smells, and soon the table was strewn with plates of fried eggs, vegetables, noodles, rice, shrimps, and a bottle of vegetable oil. But when Mr Cheerful poured us each a glass of something from the bottle, we saw it was not vegetable oil.

'*Baijiu*,' said Mr Cheerful with a loud chuckle.

Baijiu literally means 'white alcohol', and is the drink of choice in much of China. It is usually made from sorghum or glutinous rice, very cheap, and needless to say, at 40–60 per cent alcohol level, incredibly strong. We sat around the table, the boss joined us, and the *baijiu* started to flow. Mr Cheerful's enthusiasm seemed to sum up the exuberance of the Chinese people in general. He was loud, fun and tolerant of our bad Chinese, though it was hard to follow exactly what he was saying. As the Chinese expert of the expedition I tried to translate for Leon. It was only when I subsequently watched the footage that I realised how often I had misunderstood.

'Sorry there is too much salt in the dishes,' said Mr Cheerful.

'He's asking if you want some eggs,' I said to Leon.

'*Ganbei*,' said Mr Cheerful, meaning cheers, or more literally, 'dry cup'. In other words, drink up and let's have another. But I was already on my second glass, and beginning to feel light-headed, and so I took only a sip.

Mr Cheerful broke into another drawn-out spasm of laughter, wheezing and shaking his head. He grabbed my little finger and exclaimed to us all how ladylike the British man was. I did not understand, smiled cheerfully back, and said '*xie xie*' (thank you). Next, he picked up a piece of vegetable and daintily held it up to me. I opened my mouth and he popped it in – like a mother bird feeding her chicks, or perhaps two besotted lovers. We all laughed. Before the night was over we had managed to establish that Mr Cheerful's job was to switch the lines, and organise the signals for the trains. He said there were few incidents, but that five or six horses and cows were hit by the trains each year, which always caused a mess. He lived in the city of Jining, about a week's walk away for us. When he knocked off work, he simply hitched a ride home on a passing train.

'After thirty years of hard work, I am very tired,' he said, shaking his head, and laughing sadly to himself. He was a small exhausted cog in the giant machine that kept China running smoothly.

Gradually the desert plains turned into desert hills, and signs of a more ambitious economy started to emerge. Every twenty miles we passed a petrol station. A mess of craters and bulldozers – open-cast mines – were scattered sporadically across the hillsides. Columns of electricity pylons marched across the land like tripods from *The War of the Worlds*. Factories jumbled with pipes and chimneys started to dot the valleys. One morning, we saw a big white bank of clouds rolling towards us, and rounded the corner to see that they were not clouds at all, but a colossal splurge of white fumes rising from a factory. A passer-by told us it was a French fries factory, and we noticed a pile of steaming potatoes, half a mile long, lying inside the fence. Another day we spotted some cranes putting up a new building, and a few minutes later we came to a large poster advertising what was happening: a vast new industrial zone, complete with power stations, factories and wide roads. The development was being constructed entirely from scratch, right here in the middle of nowhere.

There was also a more unlikely intrusion on the land. We had grown used to seeing only an occasional tree, making a lone, heroic stand against the Gobi. But now we also increasingly saw trees planted in ordered lines beside the road and on the hillsides. This was the beginning of the so-called 'Green Wall of China', a government attempt to thwart the advance of the Gobi. The desert was estimated to be taking over Chinese grassland at a rate of 2,000 square miles per year, and the Gobi dust storms that afflicted Beijing had also been occurring more frequently. The government believed that the problem could be curbed by a mass tree-planting campaign, though environmentalists said that the non-native species used sometimes did more harm than good as they damaged the fragile soil and ecosystem.

But whatever its flaws or merits, for us the Green Wall marked the beginning of the end of the Gobi.

19
Rivalry

Distance to home: 2,639 miles

At the end of our second week in China, we reached the town of Chahar Youyi Houqi. Menacing-looking factories lined the roadside, and we coughed in the cold polluted air as we stomped past them. Several miles of grey backstreets eventually led us to a vibrant town centre full of shops and banks, though even the hardy locals looked cold, walking fast with hands in their pockets and collars turned up high around their necks. We checked into a hotel and, after our showers, noticed large amounts of dead, frost-nipped skin peeling off our fingers. Just before we reached the town, we had celebrated our passing of the 350-mile mark of the trip, which meant we were officially over 10 per cent of the way home.

The following morning, lying in a warm bed with a day off ahead of me, I woke up early, feeling strangely claustrophobic. The reason, I realised, was that Leon was lying in a bed just two metres away. I was suddenly feeling fed up with being stuck in his company for almost twenty-four hours a day. He was still asleep, so I packed the laptop and headed out in search of a café.

The streets were sleepy, and all I could find was a little noodle restaurant. Dozens of eyes looked up at me as I walked in, and I noticed a poster of Genghis Khan on the wall. I ignored the staring, ordered a bowl of noodles and opened my diary.

'I've been getting stressed with Leon, and I suspect he with me,' I began writing.

In most senses, Leon and I had been getting on well. Many of the long hours on the road were spent in fun conversations. We debated whatever random thoughts and ideas popped into our heads, from every conceivable angle; whether it was what items of our gear we should post home, new filming ideas, or the merits and demerits of environmentalism. But irritations were continuing to mount. Sometimes they were about very specific things – such as disagreements about how to film something, or the increasingly obvious issue that Leon was a faster walker than me. But sometimes it was more a general vexation, arising out of the fact that we just spent too much time together.

The previous day a new form of annoyance had arisen. About once a week we would take a short video on our iPhone to be posted on our expedition website. On this occasion, when we recorded the message, standing side by side on an empty train line, Leon had ended the recording by making a joke about how slow I was. This was a touchy subject, and after we had finished I stomped off in a bad mood.

As I had pressed ahead, I was deluged with negativity about Leon. My thoughts spiralled out of control, and suddenly I was seeing him not as an expedition partner, but a rival. All my time pitching the TV series and appearing on camera had been making me incredibly vain, with the result that I cared a lot about how I came across on screen. And now as I saw Leon pushing himself into the limelight, I felt very jealous. Hadn't I recruited him as merely the cameraman? And yet here he was morphing himself into a co-star. On one level, I knew I was being ridiculous, pathetic and egocentric, but the thoughts were there and I couldn't shake them off.

Such a competitive and negative mindset was classic expedition stuff, and Leon and I had in fact come to label the floods of bitter thinking against each other as 'head games'.* My head game after this little iPhone video incident seemed particularly bad. I was very angry with him. It was only when Leon caught up half an hour later, and took the initiative to talk it through, that we resolved the bad feelings. He apologised for the joke and I apologised for taking

---

* A Google search reveals that sometimes 'head games' is used to refer to people giving one another confusing signals and manipulating each other's emotions in a dating relationship. That is not the sense in which Leon and I were using it!

offence. But although the rivalry head games had been stemmed yesterday, this morning they were back again.

After I had been sitting in the restaurant for a few minutes, a man came and sat down opposite me, jolting me with his knees. He proceeded to stare at me and my diary writing, before slurping his noodles and carrying on an extra-loud conversation with his friend on the other side of the room. 'I'm not in the mood for this,' I muttered, standing and walking towards the door. I glanced up at the Genghis picture. 'And why would people want a picture of a mass-murderer on their wall?'

Back on the street, I went in search of an internet café, intending to take my mind off things by reading emails. As I walked, I realised the other reason I was feeling strange and fed up was because I would be turning thirty-five the next day. I had noticed a few grey hairs in my beard that morning, and all of a sudden felt like a grumpy old man. Wasn't I too old for this adventuring stuff? Shouldn't I just grow up and get a proper job? At twenty-five, Leon was younger, stronger and quicker. An irrational sense of envy started to rise up within me.

The internet at the first café was not working. The second initially refused to let me use a computer because I did not have a Chinese ID card. They were not even friendly about it. Perhaps my bad mood was making everyone around me less friendly. I argued for a while, and was finally given a computer. Not long after, I received a text message from Leon asking where I was and saying he needed to use the laptop. With a darkening mood, I returned to the hotel and gave it to him. I spent the rest of the day in the internet café writing my weekly newspaper article which, given my state of mind, took far longer than it should have.

That evening, back at the hotel, Leon looked tired, but not as bad as me. I felt emotionally, mentally and physically exhausted – worse than if I had not had a day off at all. Because it was my birthday the next day, and we had, in any case, been moving at a good pace through China, I proposed a second day off. Leon agreed.

But the next day, my birthday, I woke up wanting to burst into tears. What was wrong with me? Was the steady, relentless exhaustion of the road getting to me already? I tried to ignore the inner turmoil, but Leon sensed I was feeling unhappy and so took me out for a birthday chicken burger brunch in a little KFC knock-off. Seeing I needed space, after the brunch he left and I sat drinking coffee and reading *There Are Other Rivers*, a book by my old adventuring friend, Al. Like me, Al was an amateur-professional adventurer, and a bit of a tortured soul. In fact, his book was all about why going on exhausting, painful adventures was actually a good thing to do with one's life. We had often debated this, and once, when he had felt like giving up in the middle of a trip, I had told him that the alternative was to work in an office all day – surely pain, fear, hunger, danger, cold and potential financial ruin were better than that? Al and I had been through many adventures together. Sometimes we had got in pretty bad moods with each other and there had been plenty of head games. Yet in the long run, our friendship had become a very solid one. I wondered if the same thing might eventually happen with Leon.

Christine called to wish me a happy birthday, and we talked and prayed about the situation for a while. She helped me see things in perspective, and cheered me on – my number one fan, as always. I realised I needed to see things from Leon's point of view, and there was nothing wrong with him trying to make the most of the trip. Leon had made his own sacrifices in order to come – borrowing money, turning down other jobs and leaving his girlfriend Clare for six months. And in fact I was very impressed at how maturely he handled my little tantrums and was often the first to initiate an apology. Of course, he often got grumpy too, but that was par for the course on expeditions. Really, I should be grateful that he was such a decent and generous person. He could easily have turned out to be a complete nightmare.

That night, I felt a lot better. I explained to Leon that I had been feeling pretty downhearted and, to cheer me up, and because it was my birthday, he gave me a double swig of whisky. Psychologically it had been a hard, dark and deeply testing forty-eight hours, but somehow I had come out the other side. It was frightening how easy it was to get into a negative tailspin of thoughts – the internal trials were sometimes even harder than the external ones. And, unbeknown to us, an even greater challenge was about to come along.

20

My right foot

Distance to home: 2,639 miles

11–14 DECEMBER

'So how did you meet Clare?' I asked. We were walking out of Chahar Youyi Houqi, where I had had my birthday, on a quiet, snowy, tree-lined track next to the railway.

'At university. We started going out about a year later, and we've been together for three years – though I was away cycling for a year and a half of that, and now I am away another six months.' Leon looked a bit sad.

'Well you can blame this trip on me,' I said.

'That's a good idea.'

We discussed the long-suffering patience of our girls for a while then, just before noon, we stumbled into our first agricultural village. Pigs lay lazily beside haystacks, birds fluttered in the trees, and men piled up wood – all this against a backdrop of frozen, ploughed fields. Signs of the end of the Gobi were coming thick and fast.

On the other side of the village, we clambered down into a dried-up riverbed, and back onto the main road. When we stopped for lunch a few minutes later, I noticed a slight discomfort in my right foot. It did not feel serious, but Dr Leon nonetheless prescribed some extra stretching and some Ibuprofen. I dutifully did as I was told. Our aim was to try and stretch at least twice a day, but in the last few days we had become lazy. Somehow I felt that, having done 10 per cent of the expedition, the risk of injury was smaller.

As the afternoon progressed, the foot pain grew steadily worse; at nightfall we reached a trucker town and checked into a *ludian*. I inspected my foot. It did not look swollen, but it felt very tender.

'Take two more Ibuprofen,' instructed Dr Leon. 'Hopefully it will be better in the morning.'

But to my horror, when I climbed out of bed the next morning, I found that I could not put any weight on it. We decided we had no choice but to continue: a truckers' junction was no place to take an injury day. I leaned hard on my poles and planted my foot on its side as I hobbled back into the world. We passed more and more villages and cultivated fields and, by late afternoon, the desert had virtually disappeared. As the sunset turned the sky purple, we crested a hill and saw our first city of the expedition, Jining, sprawling out before us. The skyline was filled with buildings, street lights and cranes, and a giant chimney towered over everything, like one of Blake's dark satanic mills. I suddenly imagined myself as an eye-witness of the industrial revolution in England two hundred years ago. But this was China and the industrial revolution was still in its prime, and it was happening on a much vaster scale.

A few hours later, sitting in a *binguan* room, I took my boots off and poked my foot. It had deteriorated significantly during the day. Dr Leon furrowed his brow, and said that the next day we should take our first injury day off, after which we both hoped it would be better.

But the next morning, it felt even worse. I had to use the support of the banister to get down the stairs, before limping along the street in search of an internet café. I sat down at a computer and fired off an email to Al, asking if he had any ideas about what it might be. That afternoon I got a reply:

'Your foot injury sounds alarmingly similar to how mine felt when I first broke my metatarsal.'

A broken metatarsal? I had never even heard of a metatarsal before, but after some Googling I discovered that it was the bone behind the toe bone – exactly where my foot was hurting. It was also the bone that David Beckham had broken shortly before the 2004 World Cup, to the distress of all England. His had been broken from a hard impact, but my pain had just begun gradually when I had been walking through the stream-bed two days earlier. I also read that a metatarsal can sometimes break as a stress fracture in response to too much walking.

'Historically, a metatarsal stress fracture has been called a march fracture because it was seen in soldiers who were marching for long periods of time,' said one authoritative-looking website.

The web pages explained that it usually took at least three months' rest to recover. In a panic, I emailed my podiatrist in Hong Kong, who replied recommending an X-ray. I sank into another deeply despondent mood. A serious injury was always at the top of my list of fears about what might undo the expedition, and suddenly it looked as if I might have one. We were barely 10 per cent of the way home; there was no way I could take three months off; and restarting the expedition was not an option.

Back at the hotel, Dr Leon was unfazed.

'Always avoid Googling symptoms,' he reprimanded, 'it is bound to make you think something is terribly wrong.'

But Dr Leon did agree to an X-ray, and thus another day off, and for the first time he also prescribed a 'things are getting bad' double swig of whisky before bed.

In the hospital reception area, people scurried in all directions, shouting, pushing and queuing up at a dozen different counters, each of which had an incomprehensible set of Chinese characters above them. Leon and I walked into the crowd.

'What do you think?' I said.

'No idea.' Even Dr Leon was at a loss.

A Chinese man walked up to us.

'Hello, can I help you?' he said in perfect English.

The man's name was Hugo. He was in his forties, smart and well spoken – it turned out he taught English at the local teacher training college. We explained our problem and he kindly showed us to the correct counter, spoke to the receptionist, and told us to pay 20 RMB (£2) for an appointment slip.

'Follow me,' Hugo said, and led us up some stairs. Along the way, we were spotted by the hospital's head of security, who joined us as a second escort.

A white corridor led us to a room full of people, and the head of security bustled us to the front where an elderly doctor in a white coat sat talking to a patient. The doctor looked up, a little surprised.

Ignoring the fact that there were at least twenty other people in the queue, the head of security told me to sit, and I removed my boot and sock, while Hugo translated. The doctor nodded, and started to press my toes in various places until I yelped. There were murmurings in the room as other patients came up with their own diagnoses for the strange foreigner. Dr Leon looked rather sheepish, and hid behind his camera.

The doctor told me to go for an X-ray, and the head of security led us through the maze to another room, where I lay under an X-ray machine, while Leon and the others joined the technician behind a screen of glass. I noticed the technician was happily puffing away, despite the no-smoking signs.

We returned to the doctor, who squinted at the X-rays against the light.

'I cannot see any broken bones,' he said. 'Your foot is strained because you have been walking too much. You need to rest for at least ten days, and it should get better.'

I felt elated that there was no broken bone, though the doctor's advice to take ten days off was going to be hard to follow. We were only a week's walk from Datong, and our Christmas break. Christine had already bought tickets to come to see me. We decided that we had to keep going, and would just have to be extra careful with my foot, and hopefully it would recover during the holiday. I emailed Al explaining the good news, but just before bed I got his reply:

'Good news on the foot. But be careful: when I first got the pain I was X-rayed and they said nothing was wrong.'

Al went on to explain that his broken metatarsal had started in exactly the same way as mine, with a gradual pain, and no indication on the X-rays. After resting it for two months, his foot had apparently recovered, so he ran the Marathon de Sables in North Africa. However, in the middle of the race, he felt a sudden crack in the same spot. After he had limped to the finish and flown home, this time the X-ray showed a fracture in the exact same place.

'I suspect what happened is that originally it was a stress fracture which more or less healed, but then I did a sudden clean break on it in the marathon,' he concluded.

Leon and I could not stop walking on the basis of Al's email, but my worries were back, and that night I did not sleep well.

21

Breaching the Wall

Distance to home: 2,549 miles

18 DECEMBER

'*Qing wen. Chang Cheng zai nar?*' (Excuse me, which way is the Long Wall?) I said.

The young man with a round face and brown jacket looked confused for a moment, and then said, 'Beijing.'

I thanked him and kept going. It was dawn in the town of Fengjie, and the sun was tearing through a polluted mist and turning the air golden. We had spent the previous two days walking here from Jining. With the help of some strong anti-inflammatory pills from our first-aid kit, and some careful limping, my foot had felt stable, though still painful. But today we had a mission to invigorate us: to breach the world's longest and most famous barricade, the Great Wall of China, or as it is called in China, the Chang Cheng, or Long Wall. Our map showed it lay just a few miles south of the town, precisely on the border between Inner Mongolia and our next province, Shanxi.*

The man I had asked was referring to the most famous segment of the Wall, but that was 300 miles to our east, a little north of Beijing. The Great Wall over there was fully bricked, and had been touched up for the millions of tourists who visited it each year. Out here, in the sticks, I knew it would be less impressive, but I had at least expected people to know it was on the outskirts of their own town.

---

* Technically, Inner Mongolia is an 'autonomous region', not a province, though in most senses this is just doublespeak for province, as there is no real autonomy.

We kept walking and met an old man with a toothy smile and a black cap.

'Chang Cheng?' I asked.

He looked confused. I repeated my question several times, varying my tones a bit, but his look of miscomprehension widened. I knew that in Chinese road atlases, the universal symbol for the Wall was ЛЛЛЛЛ so I pulled out a pen, and quickly drew the symbol on my hand.*

'Chang Cheng, Chang Cheng?' I said, showing it to him.

The old man's face lit with recognition.

'Ah, ChurChur.' He said, in his thick local accent, delighted to understand me. But although he now knew what we meant, he pointed in the opposite direction to where I thought it was. We smiled enthusiastically at each other for a moment, and then Leon and I soldiered onwards on our quest.

Since local people apparently did not know it was only a couple of miles away, I started to wonder if the Wall would be visible at ground level at all. On Google Maps, even when we zoomed in, it was not distinguishable as a Wall, but looked like a dusty road. This confirmed what I had already heard – the notion that you can see the Great Wall from space is a myth.[†] And this is not the only Great Wall myth. Another common, but false belief – this one started by a member of Britain's first diplomatic mission to China – is that the Wall is one continuous stone wall, spanning the whole of China. In reality, however, there is a network of Walls, built and rebuilt by various Chinese dynasties through the centuries. It was the Ming Dynasty, in the fifteenth and sixteenth centuries, who had built the most impressive and famous Wall, which included the stone

---

* I first came across this in Peter Hessler's modern classic about China, *Country Driving*, and we had also noticed it in our own torn-out atlas pages.
† As well as the evidence of many astronauts denying they could see the Wall from space, an article in the *Journal of Optometry* states that seeing the Great Wall from the moon would be the equivalent of being able to see a 2-cm cable from a thousand kilometres away.

sections near Beijing. However, much of their Wall, like the older Walls, was made from earth, not stone, and it was an earthen section of the Ming Wall that we were hoping to find.

A car slammed on its brakes beside us, apparently not concerned about blocking a busy lane of traffic. A smart man in his twenties jumped out and asked in English, 'Can I help you?'

We told him of our quest, and he pointed enthusiastically, encouraging us to keep going in the direction we thought we should be going. This was good news, and as we continued there was gradually more agreement: a couple of men bashing a metal pole nodded their heads and yelled that we were going the right way; a gathering of tough, gruff labourers puffed their cigarettes and in unison confirmed that we should carry on; another car stopped beside us and agreed. We were homing in. A sooty road led us out of town to a towering power station, where a group of taxi drivers at the gate looked at us expectantly.

'Chang Cheng?' we asked.

'Go straight and then turn left then turn right,' they said.

Around the corner, a gathering of cheerful street-sweepers, but still no Wall.

'It's just up there,' they said.

The area ahead of us broadened into a coal-processing zone, the breadth of several football pitches. The land was spread with wooden huts, piles of coal, bulldozers, and sooty-faced labourers – both male and female.

All of a sudden, Leon shouted: 'There it is!'

Through the haze, behind all the coal, stood the Wall. It was an earthen bank, covered partly in grass, three to four metres high, and cutting across the landscape at right angles. A hole had been cut through it for the road.

We scrambled up and let out a little cheer for reaching this monumental landmark.

Underfoot, the Wall was made of brown earth, and it ran away from us in both directions, rolling onwards forever through the flat landscape until it disappeared into a haze of hills. As well as tying east to west, it also split north from south. To the north, where we had just come from, there was a montage of power stations, electricity pylons and dirty black coal fields – it reminded me of the industrial wasteland outside Isengard in *The Lord of the Rings*. To the south, there was a spread of ploughed fields that spilled away into a blue skyline and blur of brown mountains. From our vantage point, with the south looking so tranquil and settled, and the north so grim and industrial, the old Chinese stereotype that north of the Wall was the land of the (non-Han) barbarians and south the land of the enlightened (Han), seemed very plausible. And now it was south of the Wall, and into China's historic heartland, that we had to venture.

22

The idea of China

Distance to home: 2,548 miles

18 DECEMBER

I still found it hard to grasp the idea of China, and in my formal education I had been taught only a few random factoids about the place: it had a Great Wall, it had pandas, it had lots of people, it had a one-child policy. But now, in my own ponderous and amateur way, I was trying to grasp more of what this 'China' really was.

I looked over my shoulder as the Wall receded into the haze behind us.

'So do you think that thing worked in keeping out the Mongol raiders?' I said, limping on the side of my foot.

'I suppose it would be quite hard to get a horse over it,' Leon said.

'But once you're through, you're through, like Hitler and the Maginot Line in France.'

Leon nodded.

The truth was, although historical records showed the Wall had sometimes stopped raiders from breaking in, the 'single line of defence' vulnerability was a severe one.* As masters of tactics, the Chinese were usually aware that the huge resources required to build, maintain and man the Wall was not a cost-efficient way to defend the Empire, and for much of Chinese history, therefore, Wall building was shunned.†

---

* This was well proved in 1644, when a force of Manchurian tribesmen were let through the Shanhai Gate on the northeast edge of the Empire. Once through, they swept down to Beijing and set up their own dynasty, the Qing, which lasted for more than two and a half centuries.

† Sun Tzu's fifth-century BC classic, *The Art of War,* does not talk about

But besides defence, the Wall played other useful roles. It was a giant artery along which troops and supplies could travel the breadth of the Empire. More importantly, it was a boundary marker that made visible the lines of the frontier, and laid claim to all the land that lay within it.

This was particularly symbolic in the reign of the first Emperor, Qin, who in 221 BC had conquered his rivals to create a united Chinese Empire for the first time. He had then joined and bolstered a network of existing Walls into a reasonably continuous rampart running along his northern frontier, thus defining where his Empire lay, what was the Qin's, what was China.*

Long before Emperor Qin marked out his kingdom geographically with the Wall, the foundations of Chinese civilisation had already begun to emerge.

These ideas had started in a much smaller territory in the lower reaches of the Yellow River, which even by 1000 BC knew itself by the title of Zhongguo, meaning 'Middle Kingdom'. The sense of being the centre of all civilisation was an important first foundation for China.

Another foundation of China's identity and future was the notion that a dynasty would rule by divine authority. This was known as the 'Mandate of Heaven'. When an old dynasty collapsed or was taken over, the new dynasty seizing power would be seen to have received the mandate to rule instead. Therefore changes in the ruling dynasties were possible without disturbing the foundations of the Empire. Four thousand years of Chinese history would recognise eleven major dynasties that governed by the 'Mandate of Heaven'.

---

building expensive walls, but rather about being adroit at the politics of keeping your enemies fighting each other. If possible, it was better to pay them off or make them dependent on you for trade rather than fight them head on.

* This Wall was located about a hundred miles north of the Ming Wall and, according to a historical map, we should have crossed it about a week previously. We did not, however, manage to spot it. It has apparently mostly crumbled into the dust.

The teachings of Master Kong – Confucius – made for a third, more ethical, building block of Chinese culture. From the fifth century BC, Confucianism emphasised the need for all members of society to know and accept their place: children must show respect to parents, and subjects to rulers, who in turn had to govern well. The ritual of paying due respect to one's dead ancestors was also vital.

Thus, with these (and other) conceptual foundations already in place, Emperor Qin had politically united the Chinese landmass and built the first Wall to help define the extent of the Empire.* He further deepened the sense of unity by building roads, and standardising writing, legal codes, and weights and measures. The Emperor and his state thus became the ultimate patriarch, holding the whole place together with an extraordinary bureaucracy. Emperor Qin's dynasty in fact lasted only a few decades, but the Han dynasty that followed solidified the foundations, and thus the idea of China – Zhongguo – was destined to endure.

In comparison with Europe, China has enjoyed enduring unification. In the third to fifth centuries AD, both the Roman and the Chinese Empires were going through a period of disintegration. While Rome failed to recover and Europe would never again be lastingly reunited, China was reunified under the rule of a new dynasty. By the seventh century, when Europe entered its so-called Dark Ages, the Chinese Empire was entering a golden age of art and literature. And in the centuries that followed, surrounded as it was by mountains, oceans and deserts, China remained self-sufficient and self-contained. It thus continued to see itself as the Middle Kingdom, the centre of the world and the heart of civilisation.

China's sense of superiority in the world was well founded. For seventeen of the last twenty centuries, China has had a bigger economy than Europe, and in many other ways it also often far surpassed the West – from poetry to philosophy, from science to government. The Chinese invented gunpowder, the printing press,

---

* Though Qin had actually rejected Confucianism himself, it would resurface in a major way soon after his death.

the rudder, the magnetic compass and paper money. By the 1100s, China was producing a quantity of iron that Europe would not attain until six hundred years later.

The system of imperial dynasties lasted until 1912; even to this day, China still calls itself Zhongguo. Many Chinese continue to revere the core teachings of Confucius, and the first, mythical emperors from five thousand years ago are still commemorated as the founders of the nation.

I talked to Christine about this. She was Hong Kong Chinese and definitely knew more about Chinese history than I had learned back home, but she was still amazed to grasp anew that 'we are the only ones who have survived as a civilisation.' For me, an Englishman, I found the best way I could appreciate the idea of China, and its stupendous age, cultural wealth and longevity, was to imagine a Europe in which everyone was still celebrating the achievements of Romulus, founder of Rome, still using surnames from the time of the Roman Republic, and still reading and writing in Latin.* And yet, in a sense, that was what China was like.

South of the Wall, the air temperature was still in the bitter mid 20°Cs, but my foot, although painful, was still stable enough to walk, no doubt helped by my continued consumption of strong anti-inflammatories. The physical landscape, though, was beginning to change. The scrubby agricultural fields petered out and gradually we found ourselves amid an ocean of hills. These hills were not

---

* The spoken version of the Chinese language did change, and there were, in any case, many different dialects spoken across the Empire. But the characters used for the writing remained fundamentally the same – another vital foundation (perhaps the most important one of all), which helped maintain the continuity of the Chinese civilisation and the unity of the Empire. Even today, there are still 292 dialects in China, and it is only in modern times that Mandarin has become more universally spoken. Sometimes, as Leon and I attempted to chat to local people in our poor Mandarin, but failed to understand them, they would try writing Chinese characters, assuming that even if we did not speak their language, we would at least be able to read it, which unfortunately we could not.

made from the Gobi earth, but rather loess. Loess is a soft, pale-brown soil, formed from the finest dust of the Gobi, which over millions of years had blown off and been deposited all over northern China. The resulting hills had been weathered into smooth shapes, but were also regularly lacerated by gullies and canyons. The Wall also acted as a rough environmental marker, dividing the extreme dryness of the Gobi, and the moderate dryness of northern China. And so this new landscape of arid, loess hills would be our home for the next two months.

That evening we reached the town of Xinrong, and over dinner Leon spoke on the phone to Clare. She was teaching in a secondary school near London, and was looking forward to the long Christmas holidays, but it was obvious that Leon felt sad that they would not be able to spend them together.

'So what are you going to do on our days off in Datong?' I asked him after he had got off the phone.

'Oh, I'll watch some Jason Statham movies, and eat lots of peanuts,' he said.

'Sounds fun.'

At this point, Christine rang, and we chatted for a while. I could not believe that I was going to see her in just three days' time. Leon might have overheard Christine and me talking about mince pies, by which I suppose he must have assumed Christine was bringing the good old traditional English Christmas treat with her.

But he was wrong, because 'mince pie' was actually the codename for the plan that Christine and I had been hatching: to fly Clare out to meet him for Christmas too.

23
Grottoes

19–20 DECEMBER

The next day we set off feeling exhilarated, because in the afternoon we would be reaching our first tourist destination in China – the ancient Buddhist caves of Yungang, sometimes known as the Yungang Grottoes. The grottoes were not quite in the same league as the Forbidden City or the Terracotta Warriors, but they were a UNESCO World Heritage Site, and featured in the guidebooks. Seeing tourist sites was not a core aim of the expedition, but when they fell on our route, we were glad to visit them. We wondered if we could still blend in as respectable tourists after being wild men of the desert for the previous few weeks. We decided to be on our best behaviour.

In mid-afternoon our iPhone map led us to the northern gate of the large, walled tourist park in which the grottoes were located. However, a pair of hulking wooden doors barred the entrance, and there was no one in the ticket booth. We spotted a side exit with a guard, but when we asked him where we could buy a ticket, he shook his head and pointed over the large hill behind the park. This was not mere skyward Chinese pointing; he was indicating that the main entrance to the complex was on the opposite side of the hill. It could take us two hours to walk over it, by which time it would be dark and the park would be shut.

We stood outside the closed gates and considered our options. A marshy, semi-frozen river ran beneath the park walls and we noticed a small path leading down to it and weaving its way through the swampy land. After a short debate, we concluded, in true hopeavist fashion, that the path must continue all the way to the main entrance.

We scrambled down the bank. The guard gave us a disapproving look and shouted something, but we were already on our way through the frozen mud and reeds and did not look back.

We had only been going a couple of minutes when we reached a channel of running water, one metre wide, with more solid ground on the other side. Leon was behind me. I paused for a moment, before, feeling confident that I could jump over without getting wet, planting my poles on the other side, and pushing off hard with my left foot.

In midair, I realised my mistake, and a second later I screamed as I landed with my full weight on my injured right foot.

'Aaagh, stupid, stupid idiot,' I shouted.

Dr Leon landed behind me, and looked concerned. I muttered something about needing to keep moving, and hobbled onwards. I had felt the injury was getting steadily better, but the impact had felt terrible – as if I had done some real damage. But nothing would be gained by stopping in the middle of the swamp. So I kept going, again limping on the side of my foot to prevent any more damage.

We snaked our way downstream, until we were on the left bank of the river, beneath the walls of the grotto complex, which rose vertically four metres above us. We could see the road bridge to the main entrance half a mile away, but with me limping in the swampy terrain, it would take us another hour to get there. At that moment, to our surprise, we came upon a homemade wooden ladder leaning against the wall.

Leon and I looked at each other and raised our eyebrows, and then I started carefully climbing the ladder using my uninjured foot, while Leon filmed. I felt suddenly very nervous, as if I was back at school and sneaking into some out-of-bounds area. I reached the top of the ladder and looked in. The top of the wall was level with the grounds of the park, and beyond an area of woodland I could see a couple of Chinese tourists walking around. But there were no guards in sight, so I slung my rucksack inside and rolled in myself. I squatted on the ground. A moment later Leon rolled in beside me.

'Shall we go?' whispered Leon.

'OK,' I said, adrenaline pumping.

We stood up and, looking as nonchalant as possible, Leon strolled and I limped through the trees. We followed signs towards the caves and engaged in a loud, airy conversation about how happy we were to be visiting the Yungang Grottoes. We were failing rather badly in our attempt to be conventional tourists for an afternoon, but at least we were in.

Round a corner, we found ourselves standing before a long, pale thirty-metre-high sandstone cliff face. Its surface was pockmarked with ancient eroded patterns and dozens of large caves. The cave entrances were at ground level, with additional openings set in the rock face above them. A few Chinese tourists strolled around taking photos with their mobile phones, and a uniformed guard stood expressionless in a corner.

We walked into our first cave, and immediately saw an enormous fifteen-metre-tall Buddha growing out of the rock. He sat in the lotus position and his broad, muscular chest was thrust out. One hand was raised, palm out, while the other rested calmly on his knee. His Gandharan face* was set in a ghost of a smile, beguiled and beguiling, and his eyes gazed dead ahead in a perfect Orlando. The cave walls were painted in blue and green patterns, and interspersed with worn sandstone and dozens of smaller Buddha statues.

The Yungang Grottoes are in fact home to over 51,000 Buddha statues, most of them having been carved out in the fifth and sixth centuries AD.† The message of Buddha is thought to have arrived in China several hundred years before this. It came primarily with traders from Central Asia, who crossed the western deserts on the fabled Silk Roads. At first the Buddha was looked upon as little more than a new foreign deity in the pantheon of native Daoist gods, but gradually, as scholar-monks progressed with the difficult task of translating Buddhist texts, the religion took root. By the end of the first millennium, there were thousands of monasteries

---

* The Gandhara style is a fusion of Persian, Indian and Greek influences, examples of which are still strewn across Central Asia.
† The earliest evidence for Buddhism in China comes from a mention of 'the gentle sacrifices to Buddha' in an official history written in 65 AD.

and pagodas dotting the countryside and filling the cities. And a significant proportion of the population – of high and low class – had become Buddhists. The flourishing of Buddhism in China is a case in point that, especially in the first millennium AD, China was not nearly as closed to foreign ideas as is sometimes supposed.*

Leon and I continued on through the next caves, and saw dozens more statues, but still only a fraction of the thousands that had been built. It was amazing to imagine the countless monks at work, chiselling and painting amid the rock faces, 1,500 years ago. All the other tourists around us were Chinese, and as far as we could tell, none was Buddhist. Most seemed intent on taking photos, despite the signs saying 'no photography'; although occasionally a guard told everyone to stop, as soon as he turned, the snapping resumed. Some were also keen to take photos of us, and we made friends with a group of students who gathered round with victory signs and happy smiles.

It was starting to get dark, and the guards ushered us back towards the main entrance. We walked and chatted with the students, feeling nervous that somebody at the gate might notice we had not come in that way. But as we walked past, the guards did not give us a second glance.

The next day, I hobbled into Datong alongside Leon. It was another important landmark, though my own elation was tempered by worries about whether my foot would recover in the coming week off, especially because of the previous day's swamp-jumping. We passed through grids of bland apartment blocks and shopfronts before reaching the hotel. As we went through the revolving doors, I saw Christine had already arrived. She was sitting in the lobby,

---

* The perception that China was consistently closed and xenophobic was based largely on the experience of the Jesuits who arrived in China in the 1600s, a time when China was indeed very closed. But in the broader run of history, China was actually sometimes a very open Empire – as the flourishing of the foreign religion of Buddhism in the fourth–seventh centuries AD demonstrates.

facing away from us. I could hardly believe she was really there. She turned and smiled at me.

'Hi Robbie,' she said, giving me a hug, but then immediately starting to wince.

'I'm sorry, I haven't had a shower for days.' I said.

She held her nose. 'That's OK, I brought some clean clothes for you.'

Leon was standing looking like a gooseberry. Christine said hello, and produced several large packs of chocolate for me, and two boxes of cereal for Leon.

'I brought something else for you too, Leon,' she said.

'What?'

At that moment, Clare appeared and said, 'Hello there.'

Leon nearly dropped his camera. His face changed from exhausted to shocked and then into a beaming, incredulous smile. 'Clare!' he said, 'what are you doing here?'

'I thought you might want to have some company for Christmas,' she said, giving him a big hug.

Leon's grin broadened further as Clare pulled out a bottle of whisky.

'Chocolate, cereal, whisky, and a beautiful wife, what more can a man want?' I said.

'Why does the wife come last?' said Christine, smiling.

And so 'Operation Mince Pie' had succeeded, and we had completed the second leg of the expedition. It had been a tough walk to get this far, but whatever our ailments and woes, we were 15 per cent of the way home, and now we had a week off with our girls.

Part Three

Towards the Yellow River

———

不到黄河不死心

One will not give up until the Yellow River is reached.

祸不单行

Disasters never come alone.

24
Christmas and Christine

Distance to home: 2,503 miles

My week off with Christine was glorious. Instead of rising early to walk into a frozen Chinese dawn, I slept at least ten hours a night in our warm, comfortable bed. Twice a day, I took long hot showers, and every morning for breakfast I stuffed myself with handfuls of chocolates. Christine and I spent much of our time lounging around watching DVDs in the refuge of our room, often only venturing outside to have lunch and dinner at a local restaurant.

But readjusting to being back together was not without difficulty. Without a female civilising influence, and under the harsh conditions of the road, Leon and I had been slipping into brutish habits. We blew our noses on the backs of our gloves; we burped and farted constantly; we unpacked our bags by emptying them on the floor. Christine found all this somewhat bewildering to deal with. One day, at the end of lunch in a restaurant, I wiped my mouth with a serviette and threw it on the floor. Though this is the normal custom in much of China, I looked up to see her startled face, and had to apologise quickly.

As well as seeing our degeneration into wild men, Christine was also catching a glimpse of what we had been going through.

'It's a bit cold,' I said, as we stepped out into a −20°C afternoon without really noticing it.

'My toes are going numb,' she said. 'I can't believe you guys actually camp out in this.'

Though ethnically Chinese, Christine had previously only visited Mainland China's more famous cities such as Beijing and Shanghai. Backwater Datong was therefore a new experience for her.

'Why does everyone keep staring at us?' she asked. Mixed couples were unusual around here, but I had forgotten that being stared at was not normal.

Christine and I also spent time talking about how she had coped with being alone in Hong Kong. She had been keeping very busy with running the Viva office. We hoped we might raise £80,000 for the charity from the expedition, so she was building a following through social media. She had also helped us with much of our expedition research and admin. But, despite being busy, coping with an empty home was far from easy, and the months apart still stretched ahead of us.

In fact, the expedition had been growing in length since the moment I started planning it. When I had first come up with the idea and looked at a map, I had thought it would take about four months. By the time we set off, because of the route we were taking, I already knew it would be nearer five. And now, because we were moving more slowly than I had hoped, and I had the injured foot on top of this, I thought it would probably take us a total of six and half months. Leon and I had realised that the earliest we could realistically be home was late May. I explained this to Christine, and she accepted it with resilient resignation. I felt bad, and I was now committed to not letting this new deadline slip.

After six short but wonderful days, it was time for the girls to leave. With heavy hearts, we caught a taxi back to the airport. Christine was taking home our remaining stove, a hard drive's worth of footage and some excess clothing to help reduce the weight we carried. In return she had brought us shockproof thermoses, new blank hard drives, high-quality roll mats and, for me, a new pair of walking boots as my first pair had worn out. Leon hugged Clare goodbye, and I hugged Christine goodbye, and as they disappeared I gave Christine a final smile and wave. And then she was gone, and I felt desolate.

Leon and I could not dwell on missing our other halves because, unfortunately, during the holiday, my foot had got worse, not better. I thought it must be because the muscles had stiffened up. We would therefore need to stay in Datong for longer, and hope it started to improve. We sat in a cheap restaurant and brainstormed our options.

'I think it will take at least two weeks for the foot to fully recover,' I said, 'but if we wait that long there is no way we'll finish by late May.' Leon had made a similar promise to Clare about finishing in this timeframe.

Leon thought for a minute, and said, 'How about we give it another five days, and hopefully then, even if it is not fully recovered, you will at least be able to walk again. And we will still have just about enough time to finish by the deadline.'

'It will probably start deteriorating once we set off,' I said, 'but I guess we've got no choice.'

We decided to set ourselves a short-term goal of walking to the Yellow River, about 150 miles away, after which we would reassess. If at that point the foot was still causing significant delays, we would switch to a contingency plan: 'Plan B'.

Plan B would involve buying a couple of old bicycles and riding them for a few weeks to allow my foot to get better (I assumed I would still be able to cycle). This would at least allow us to keep going, but it would undermine the purity of the trip. Unfortunately, it seemed like our only real option.

On Christmas Day, the previous week, Christine and I had gone to a local church in the city centre. It was the size of a small cathedral, and was packed with thousands of people. We had arrived in the middle of the Christmas service, which seemed to involve various members of the congregation taking to the stage to perform a hymn or dance. Everyone else chatted and cheered appreciatively. We were warmly welcomed, though we declined the invitation to give a performance ourselves.

With Christine gone, I limped back to the church on my own. It was empty, apart from a caretaker. I sat in an empty aisle and, as I have done many times before in far-flung churches across the world, leant my head against the back of the pew in front and closed my eyes.

The stresses and worries about what now awaited us flashed through my mind. I felt powerless that there was literally nothing I could do to fix my foot. We had a Plan B, yes, but I was not happy about the compromise. Using bicycles would feel like a face-saving failure. On the other hand, it was a good thing that this expedition was proving so hard that we might fail. What kind of adventure would it be if there was no chance of failure?

I prayed and wrestled through these emotions and thoughts for a while, and tried to lay down my burdens. When I left the church, I did not feel any happier, but I did feel more resolved to accept the problems. We had not failed yet. The foot was not going to be the last of our problems, and the important thing was to keep going even when things went wrong. I liked Bunyan's old story, *The Pilgrim's Progress*, about the pilgrim who sets out on his journey, but then messes up and falls down. He gets back up and keeps going. Not long after, things go wrong again, but once more he gets back up and keeps going. Onwards he goes, falling and rising time after time, and slowly getting closer to his destination. Eventually the pilgrim makes it.

Leon and I had also tried to catch up on admin on our extra days off. Since we had started, we had not had much contact with our production company, Tiberius. The day before we left Datong, I sent them a long email giving an update. Overall, I felt we had done a good job of filming so far, especially given the cold and exhausting conditions. The hard drive we had sent from the border had been delayed, though. This meant the first they would see of our footage would be when Christine gave them the back-up hard drives that week. I was confident they would be impressed with the filming we had done: our stunning desert panoramas, our raging snowstorms and our silly adventures. I looked forward to hearing their feedback.

25
Coal country

3–4 JANUARY

We set off on 3 January, with Leon marching ahead and me limping behind. The frozen air and our heavy packs were a shock after eleven days of lying around inside. I had taken more of the strong anti-inflammatories, but still my foot felt delicate. Our road followed the Shili River out of town, the same route we had come in, and the dry valley walls on both sides climbed up to barren ridge lines. But the ridge was also dotted with occasional brown beacon towers, which had once relayed messages to and from the Great Wall, a hundred miles away. Although we had already crossed the Wall as we entered Shanxi Province, in fact it looped round to the south and the west, and we hoped to intercept it again in a few days' time. Now, however, we would actually walk along it, cross-country, all the way to the Yellow River.

But there was other ground to cover first. Just after lunch, we found ourselves entering a broader section of the valley, which in fact showcased one of the things that Shanxi was famous for: coal. The valley floor brimmed with activity. Small, privately owned mines clustered along the roadside, with rusty machinery churning coal out of the ground and dumping it in piles. Dwarfing these were the much bigger, government-owned mining complexes. They were the size of towns, and packed with homogeneous, rectangular accommodation blocks and administration buildings. Towering above all this were chimneys spewing grey smoke, and huge blue and white refining cylinders.

Coal was the essential ingredient in China's industrial revolution. In 2009, China had become the number one energy consumer in the world,* and two thirds of this energy came from coal. To keep up with demand, the nation's coal production increased three-fold between 2000 and 2010, and continued to grow at 10 per cent a year, with an average of two new coal power stations opening every week. Although Inner Mongolia had recently taken pole position as the province producing most tonnes, Shanxi was the traditional coal heartland, and its output was still vast – and growing. As we walked, we sometimes caught sight of the railway that ran down the valley. A coal train rumbled past every ten minutes, pulling 200 carriages. The road was full of coal trucks, interspersed with buses transporting miners, and shiny, chauffeur-driven Audis transporting the mine bosses. They all roared past, honking their horns, and we kept ourselves tucked against the verge.

We camped behind some trees, and the next day continued through more of the same landscape. But that night, instead of camping, we decided to try our luck with staying in one of the coal-mine complexes. We walked through the entrance, and immediately found that up close, the complex town was not as dreary as we had imagined. The streets were brightly lit, clean, and lined with manicured trees and hedges; red Chinese lanterns hung from the lampposts in preparation for Chinese New Year in a few weeks' time; a broad public square was dominated by a five-metre-wide TV screen showing the news. The buildings, which included shops and restaurants, were freshly painted in a colourful mixture of oranges and greens, and many of them sported the green and white logo of the 'Datong Coal Mine Group'.

Small groups of off-duty miners wandered the pavements. Their faces were a little glazed and, unusually, they did not stare at us. We asked a couple of them about a hotel, and were eventually pointed towards a building. We walked through the main entrance and into a corridor, unsure of which door to knock on. A young man appeared on the stairwell.

'Can I help you?' he said in English, with a smile.

We explained our situation, and the man, whose name was Duan,

---

* Though it still has a far lower per capita consumption than North America and Europe.

led us through some rooms and into another block. He chatted to a caretaker lady, and we were shown to a bare but beautifully warm dormitory with four beds. We dropped our packs with relief and gratitude, and Duan said he would come back later with some friends – we could all go for dinner.

'All four of us are engineering graduates,' said Duan, as we sat down at a round table in what seemed to be the smartest restaurant in town. He had brought three friends with him, and they were all in their early twenties, wore leather jackets and spoke good English. They were happy to be able to practise their conversation skills, and Leon and I were glad that we would not be limited by our Mandarin for a change.

'We are in the technology department,' said one of the friends. 'We only go down in the mine about once a week and most of our work is to do with maintenance and machinery design. This is a very modern mine; the miners here do not use picks and shovels.'

We had caught a glimpse of this as we passed through a control room on our way to the accommodation blocks. There was a wall of TV screens showing CCTV footage of the various mine operations: conveyor belts, miners loading them and buggies driving around, all far beneath the ground.

As the food arrived, Duan and his friends told us that this mine was 300 metres deep, and produced an astonishing 20,000 tonnes of coal a day. There were many such mines in this valley.

'The coal that comes to the surface is loaded automatically onto the trains,' they explained. 'They carry it to the port of Qinhuangdao on the coast, where it is shipped to wherever it is needed.'*

---

* Until recently, one of the major problems of China's coal was its location, buried here in the arid hills of Central China. Martin Jacques, author of *When China Rules the World*, claims that a major reason that England had an industrial revolution in the 1800s, and China did not, was not because of any cultural or intellectual superiority in the West, but rather because England had much more accessible coal. Shanxi's coal was, after all, over a thousand miles from the nascent industries that were developing on the Yangtze River at the time.

I mentioned that Western media often ran stories about horrific accidents in Chinese coal mines.

'The government mines like this one are safe,' said Duan, piling a piece of chicken onto my plate. 'Most of the accidents happen in the smaller, unregistered mines.' He explained that although being a miner in this mine was tough, with fourteen-hour shifts followed by two days off, it was a decent regular wage. As far as we could tell from how well things were organised above ground, this mine did seem well run and modern – though it was hard to believe there were no accidents at all. I had spotted a shop selling life insurance at the complex entrance.

'What about non-government mines?' I asked.

'They are very dangerous, especially the illegal ones,' said Duan.

He clearly did not want to elaborate further, but I had been reading that there were still tens of thousands of illegal mines in China, despite government clampdowns. Since the reform period started three decades ago, at least 170,000 miners had died in coal-mining accidents. According to official statistics, in 2012 – the year I was walking through China – more than three miners were killed, on average, each day. But miners in these dangerous, illegal mines had little choice, because their meagre wages were still more than they could earn as farmers. The mine owners, cast as villains by the state media, reportedly lived the high life, with expensive sports cars and multiple Beijing apartments.

When Duan's friend asked about coal mining in England, I said that most of the British coal mines had been closed by Margaret Thatcher in the 1980s, resulting in furious marches and protests.

'That could never happen here,' said Duan, shaking his head, 'there are too many workers. One hundred thousand work in the mines of this valley, and with their families there are three hundred thousand people. No, they could not shut the mines here.'*

---

* The other important issue raised by Chinese coal is the damage that it is causing to the environment. In many Chinese cities, the air is unsafe to breathe for much of the year. In terms of global impact, China's increasing coal consumption is effectively wiping out the benefits of the Kyoto Treaty.

It had been a good evening and, as we walked back to our warm beds, our stomachs full of meat, fish and beer, we felt content: we were back on the road; my foot, although sore, had survived two full walking days. I was looking forward to getting into the routine again.

We got back to our room and checked the iPhone for emails. Something had come in from Tiberius, our first email from them since we had sent back the footage.

It turned out there was a major problem.

26

The fiasco

Distance to home: 2,463 miles

> Subject: Emergency!!
> Hi Rob and Leon,
> We've been going through all the footage from Cards 1–22, and there
> is a very serious problem . . .
> Most of the exterior shots, 90 per cent, are out of focus.
> Please find out what is wrong a.s.a.p.!
> Best wishes
> Kate

'What?' said Leon, sitting up in his bed, as I read him the email from the iPhone.

We pulled out the laptop in a panic and plugged in the back-up hard drive of Gobi footage. For the first minute we could not spot anything wrong, but as we scrutinised the small screen more closely, to our horror we saw what Tiberius meant. The shots in the bright sunlight were indeed slightly blurred. Not badly blurred, but bad enough to make most of it unusable for a high-definition TV show.

Leon had gone pale. 'How can this have happened?' he said. 'The cameras were mostly on autofocus.'

'I don't know.'

I was in shock too. This was a very serious situation. It meant that most of the best footage that we had shot with great effort, freezing hands and back-breaking pain in the beauty of the raw, frozen desert was probably useless. Our dreams of making an inspiring documentary suddenly seemed dead in the dust, like a pile of camel bones. In fact this was so serious that it might not be possible to make the show at all. In that case, we would be in such dire financial straits that we would probably have to abandon the trip.

We sat on our beds, looking at the blank walls and feeling numb.

'Well, what shall we do?' I said at last.

Leon looked up and said he didn't know. I thought I could almost see tears in his eyes.

'I think we should go back to Datong,' I said. 'We can get fast internet access and have a proper conversation with Tiberius. Hopefully we can figure out what has gone wrong and how to fix it.'

Leon agreed. We slept after midnight, our minds and emotions in turmoil, and hoping we would wake in the morning to discover that it was just a nightmare.

It was no nightmare. The next morning we squeezed in beside some coal miners, and a bus chugged us back down the valley to Datong. Two days' worth of walking fled past the windows in an hour, and our recently renewed sense that the expedition was getting back on track fled along with it. We checked into a hotel, and Leon shot some test footage outside, changing the settings on the camera for each clip. We uploaded the clips for Tiberius and, a short while later, they phoned us from Hong Kong.

We were nervous as the phone rang, wondering what they would say. To our relief, they did not start reprimanding us, but rather they wanted first and foremost to sort out the problem. It did not take long to establish what had gone wrong.

'The loss of focus is because of something called diffraction blur,' they said. 'You need to set the Iris Limiter, and turn the Auto-ND filter on.'

We knew vaguely the importance of an ND filter (yet it had somehow been turned off, and we had overlooked it) but the Iris Limiter was a new concept to both of us. It was good that the problem was fixed. But the damage was done, and it could not be undone.*

* In more technical terms, what happened was this: on a camera, as with the human eye, there is something called an iris, which expands and

We continued the discussion with Tiberius. Like us, of course, they were incredibly disappointed about what had happened. Suddenly their concerns about whether Leon and I were up to filming a whole TV show on our own seemed starkly well founded. 'Hopefully we can save some of the footage, but it's too early to tell how much,' they said, hinting that perhaps the series could still be made. 'You should just keep going for now, and we will send you more detailed feedback in a few days' time. You will also need to send footage back to us much more often, and we will need to have more regular phone conversations.' Leon and I would now need to do exactly as they told us. This was fair enough, but we felt daunted about coping with more pressure from them, on top of the foot injury, the severe cold, and our huge daily quota of miles to walk.

We stayed in the hotel that night, planning to catch a bus back to the coal mine the next day and keep walking. But the next morning I was awoken by the sound of my phone ringing very early, before my alarm went off. It was my father, in London. He had some sad news about my grandmother, he said. I knew what that meant. My grandmother, his mother, had died the previous day, peacefully, at her home. She was 106 years old.

After I hung up, I went into the bathroom and looked in the mirror, taking a few deep breaths, tears welling in my eyes. I had last seen her about a year previously. I remembered her stories of growing up in another world, and things long past, such as the day she came home to find out World War I had broken out. I recalled, with a smile, how, at the age of a hundred, she had read *War and*

---

contracts to control how much light comes into the lens. However, if the camera iris contracts too much, the light coming in will be diffracted, so that even if the camera is on auto-focus, the footage will be out of focus ('diffraction blur'). This is a law of science. To prevent the problem it is important to limit how small the iris can become using the Iris Limiter function. A second setting to prevent the problem is called the ND (Neutral Density) filter, which filters the light to stop the iris from contracting too much. Technically speaking, in our case, we had therefore been undone by the double mistake of the Iris Limiter having not been set, and the Auto-ND Filter having been turned off.

Peace. 'I'd been meaning to read it for ages, so thought I should get on with it,' she had said, before explaining that she had preferred the peace bits to the war bits. She had been a dear grandmother to all her fifteen grandchildren. We had been fortunate to have her around so long, and we would miss her greatly.

I went back into the bedroom and told Leon. He was very understanding, and asked if I was going to fly back for the funeral. As much as I wanted to be with my family, I knew I couldn't.

We caught a bus back to the coal mine and restarted our walk west. We were into new territory once more. Leon and I walked separately, with him walking faster and up ahead. I felt detached from the landscape, and simply ignored the coal trucks that gave us friendly honks as they roared past. My mind plodded from one downcast thought to the next. Most of all, I grieved for my grandmother and missed my family in England. But on top of this, my mind kept flooding with questions about how I was going to walk the next few hundred, let alone few thousand miles on my painful foot. I also lamented all the wasted effort we had put into the filming, and dreaded the implications for the show.

I wondered whether it had been a mistake to get involved with TV in the first place. In a sense, I had always felt a little ashamed for wanting to make a second show. It was so narcissistic and self-absorbed. On the expedition, it meant that sometimes I was thinking more about filming an experience than experiencing it. But the TV deal had helped fund the trip and also would help my freelance work, and thus justified me leaving wife and home for a big chunk of time. In other words, it was the price of being a 'professional' adventurer; though, right now, I felt neither professional nor adventurous. I just felt like a bit of an idiot carrying a very heavy rucksack down a very cold and very polluted coal valley.

If I felt bad, Leon was feeling worse. For him, this trip had been his chance to 'make his break' as an adventure cameraman. But now he had filmed the most scenically spectacular part of it largely out of focus. It would have been funny, if it had not been so serious. 'I'd offer to resign if it would help,' he had said to me on the bus ride to Datong. I was impressed by his willingness to take responsibility without making excuses, but quickly said no. He had been working in almost absurdly difficult conditions: filming his first full TV show with a camera he had never used before; sleeping in an icy tent with torn cardboard for a bed; walking over ten hours a day in blisteringly cold temperatures with a 25-kg rucksack; eating dog food or processed sausage, washed down with a laxative pill when nature required it; and putting up with grumpy old me for his companion. And for all this, although most of his costs were covered, he was taking joint liability for debts we incurred and was not getting paid a penny.

Despite these difficult conditions, Leon had not shirked from his technical responsibilities. He stayed up late watching through much of the footage when he backed it up, and was so conscientious that he spent hours polishing the lens to clean off specks of dust. However, it was part of his job description to monitor that the footage was being recorded at the required standards, and somehow he had not spotted the focus problem. On the other hand, neither had I when I had watched it with him, and so I knew the same thing would have happened to me. This was not the equivalent to leaving the lens cap on, by any measure, but it was something we definitely should have noticed. So how on earth had it happened?

There seemed to be a number of factors. Firstly, we had acquired the cameras very late, and in the rush before we left they had somehow been set up wrongly and we had not had time for sufficient test shoots; secondly, as we were usually using the autofocus, the last thing we were expecting was a focus problem (it was a meta-phorical blind spot); and finally, our laptop screen was small and we had been watching the footage on a freeware programme (which jolted the images) and so it had been hard to notice the blur.

This made good sense of what had happened. But at the same time, the more I ruminated, the more some dangerous thinking started to grow in my mind. Leon was the cameraman. Despite the mitigating factors, and although he had owned up to his mistake, offered to resign, and shown great remorse, he had still potentially jeopardised the whole expedition. My mind began to turn with resentful thoughts about Leon's ceaseless hopeavism and eagerness to be involved in non-filming aspects of the expedition – if he had concentrated fully on his camera duties, perhaps he would have spotted the problem straight away.

Sensing a gigantic head game in the making, I knew I had to get things back in perspective quickly. Leon had been very unlucky, there was no doubt about that, and the somewhat cavalier attitude that I had brought to the expedition, right from the planning stages onwards, had definitely not helped. On another level, I did not want to become a bitter person, and in the long run, nursing grudges led only to misery. Finally, if I let my head run riot with these poisonous feelings against Leon, it would be more disastrous for the longer-term prospects of the expedition than this focus fiasco in the first place. I had to nip these thoughts in the bud.

When we stopped for our next break, I explained my lurking anger to Leon. I said outright that, even though he had made an unfortunate mistake, it would from now on be water under the bridge, forgiven, and – to the best of my ability – forgotten. Leon was grateful for this, and I could see him steeling himself to increase his efforts. He had fallen down, but he had got back up. We walked onwards together, still determined to make the expedition – and the show – work.

After two days we left the coal valley and entered an open brown plain, flanked by gentle hillocks. Leon suddenly piped up.

'I've just had an idea,' he said. 'You know that when our Chinese visas run out in February, we need to somehow get them renewed.' Our current plan was to leave the country on the cheapest flight possible, spend a night in a foreign airport, and then fly back in again to get another three-month entry stamp. It was a ridiculous plan, but we felt it would work.

'Go on,' I said.

'What if,' Leon said, 'instead of flying to South Korea or wherever is cheapest, we fly back to Mongolia.'

I raised my eyebrows.

'And then we go back to Zamiin-Uud,' he said, growing more animated. 'We retrieve Molly and head back into the desert for a few days and do some filming. That way we can get some non-out-of-focus desert footage that can be slotted into the show.'

'Wouldn't that be duping the viewers?' I said.

'Not really. It's not as if we are filming something we have not already done. And we are still in the middle of the trip. It is just a very expanded version of when I ask you to walk down a street a second time because I wasn't happy with the first take.'

Leon stayed quiet to let me think about it for a minute. It was true. We needed to leave the country anyway. And Leon's crazy plan would make our lives harder, not easier. I did not think it counted as 'cheating'.

'Actually,' I said, letting out a deep breath and shaking my head, 'maybe this could work.'

Leon was delighted. He told me that he had feared the focus fiasco would hang over him for the rest of his life, but now he had a chance to redeem himself. We had already abandoned our Plan A (walking at a reasonable rate), and were waiting to see whether we would proceed with Plan B (buying the bicycles if my foot did not recover). The 'Plan A, B, C' terminology was growing stale, and we needed an altogether grander, more militaristic title for Leon's idea. We decided to call it our 'Code Z'.

27
The cave village

8–10 JANUARY

The plains led us to the town of Youyu, where we took two more days off. My foot had started to deteriorate again, and we also felt emotionally washed out by the stress of the week. We were now slipping so far behind schedule that we could hardly bear to think about it. And despite the Code Z idea, Leon was still feeling depressed about the focus fiasco. On our second day off, I went shopping and bought a huge lightweight blanket. I paid a tailor's shop to cut it in half and sew up the edges. Returning to the hotel, I gave half to Leon. This cheered us up because we were still getting very cold when we camped, and the extra layer would make things more comfortable. The night before we left, Leon spoke to his mum on the phone. She reminded him not to forget what a privilege it was to be walking across China, and that many people dream of doing things like that and never get the chance. She had a point, and it was something we needed to hear.

The next morning, our rucksacks loaded with four days' supply of noodles and processed sausages, we were ready to make a fresh start of things. We set out westwards, following a flat road lined with willow trees and stubbly yellow fields. There was almost no traffic, and according to our map the road only led to a few villages – but beyond them, in the hills, also ran the Great Wall. At lunchtime, with more and more ridges rising from the horizon, we arrived at a village enclosed in a ten-metre-high earthen wall. The narrow streets were a jumble of run-down houses, and we wandered through until we found a small restaurant where we ate a plate of egg fried rice each. While we sat eating, I realised that even though the day's first anti-inflammatory pills had worn off, I hardly felt pain in my foot. That morning, before we set off, I had dug out my ankle support, and tried wearing it in reverse, so that it was covering my foot instead of my ankle. The improvisation seemed to be working.

Through the afternoon, a land of pale brown hillocks gradually replaced the fields, and we spotted more and more beacon towers on the hilltops. As the sun went down, we crossed a frozen stream, found a beautiful patch of grass, and pitched our tents. Strangely, neither of us felt hungry. We went and sat beside the stream as a slow moon rose. Leon dug out the hip flask and, beacon towers aside, we could have been in Scotland.

I told Leon I was feeling much more optimistic about my foot.

'A single swig to celebrate being able to walk again,' said Dr Leon. Dr Leon not only used his whisky as a cure, but also as an incentive for patients to get well quickly.

'Cheers Dr Leon,' I said.

In the middle of the night I was awoken by a gurgling in my stomach. Something was not right. I lay still for a moment, hoping it was not what I feared, but seconds later I was unzipping the tent, throwing on my boots and running into the cold bushes to relieve myself. I had not taken any Mr Lax pills for weeks. This had to be something we had eaten or drunk. In the course of the night, I made three more rapid exits. In between my outings, I was slightly consoled when I heard Leon swearing and fumbling with his own tent zip and running into the bushes as well. Whatever it was, we had both got it.

The next morning, we got up feeling weak, queasy and in no mood for breakfast.

'I think it was the egg fried rice in the walled village,' I said, digging out our first-aid kit yet again. We took a Ciprofloxacin antibiotic pill each – or anti-Mr-Lax, as we called it. This would stop us needing to run into the bushes all day, and hopefully kill the stomach bug, but it would still take a while for our appetites to return.

The previous day's road now became a dirt track and led us beside a frozen stream and into a maze of green-brown canyons.

Since the end of the Gobi we had had 3G reception almost constantly, and had been growing reliant on our iPhone's ability to pinpoint our location on Google Maps. However, our increasing remoteness and the high canyon walls were cutting off our reception, and by the afternoon we did not know where we were. Although we had still barely eaten, and were running out of water, we had no choice but to keep going. We spotted a partially melted section of a stream, and I edged out onto the ice to fill our bottles, adding iodine to kill any germs. I was shivering by the time I put on my gloves, and felt unsteady as I hauled the rucksack onto my back.

We were relieved when we eventually arrived at a hillside village, but it did not consist of normal village houses. Rather, everyone lived in caves. We had heard about these villages of cave houses, or *yaodongs*. They had been popular in this part of China for centuries, and there were said to still be 30 million people living in them.* We walked up the dusty street. Each of the little dwellings was fronted with bricks, windows and semi-circular entrances, and their grass-covered roofs merged into the hillside. Most of them also had a walled courtyard out front, but as far as we could see, the place was deserted. We needed to eat something soon and so started calling out 'hello' through the gates in the hope that someone might be able to give us hot water for our instant noodles. At first only the dogs noticed us. Eventually an old man appeared, and walked slowly towards us. He frowned as he tried to understand what we were saying. Another old man appeared, and joined his friend.

I dropped my rucksack, pulled out a thermos and asked if they had some hot water. The men hesitated and talked to each other. They spoke in a local dialect, not Mandarin. I saw a little girl staring at us from around a corner, but when I smiled at her, she and her blue-ribboned pigtails quickly fled. However, within a few minutes, she was back, along with a crowd of a dozen people – the whole village had turned out to see us.

We explained we were walking to the Wall, and there was general

* Even China's new President, Xin Jinping, spent several years living in one in the 1960s.

agreement and some unusually specific Chinese pointing that we were heading the right way. I held out the thermoses again, and an old man pointed at the half-empty plastic bottles in the back of my rucksack. 'Your bottles are frozen,' he said in a thick accent. A child giggled. A lady stepped forwards, took the two thermoses and walked into a *yaodong*.

The crowd stared and discussed our rucksacks. Almost everyone was either elderly or very young. Most of the young adults, it seemed, had left the village to work in the towns and cities. The lady came back with our thermoses. We thanked her and then, feeling cold from standing around, and with my appetite starting to pick up, I asked if there happened to be a restaurant.

'No, there's not,' several people said, and then, after more discussion, and to our immense gratitude, an old man and his middle-aged son said we could come back to their house to eat. We followed them into a courtyard containing a noisy pig, an old tractor and a satellite dish resembling a giant wok.* Entering the *yaodong*, we passed through a hallway piled up with boxes and crates, and turned left into the main room. Three metres wide and six deep, the walls were lined with smoke-stained plaster. On one of the four walls there was a window. Half of the space was taken up by a *kang*, and the other half was dominated by a simple wood stove, a cheap DVD player and a large, square TV. The room seemed to function as kitchen, living room, dining room and bedroom combined.

The men told us to make ourselves comfortable, and as I sat down on the *kang* I felt relief sweep through my body. I was even more exhausted than I realised. The son started to stoke the stove and fan it with a hand-powered air pump, and the room quickly warmed. He used a huge cleaver to chop up pieces of pork and threw them plus some potatoes and generous amounts of salt into a deliciously sizzling wok. Then he set to work with flour, a rolling pin and some scissors to make noodles. The old man meanwhile put on a DVD, which showcased a middle-aged couple wearing

* The Chinese word used for satellite dishes is in fact the same word as used for wok.

gigantic 1980s sunglasses and garish grins, waving flags and singing a cheery tune. We leaned back on the beds, rosy cheeked and near delirious at the respite from the cold and the thought of hot food on the way.

When the old man said that we would be welcome to stay the night, our powers of resistance were at their weakest. It was only mid-afternoon, and stopping early would put us still further behind schedule, but we reasoned that we needed a good night's sleep to recover from the stomach bug. We asked how much it would cost, and the man said it was free. We thought we could leave him with a parting gift, and gratefully accepted. A few minutes later we were served a fine meal of deep-fried noodles, potatoes and pork.

Over the course of the rest of the evening, more and more villagers trooped in to take a look at us. All of them smoked, so combined with the belching stove, the room became thick with fumes. Again and again we were asked the usual questions, and our answers were repeated and discussed around the room. Wanting to change the subject, I pulled out a photo of Christine and me on our wedding day, which I carried in my wallet. I sometimes looked at it when I was missing her. It was passed around to various exclamations of 'very pretty'. Everyone seemed pleased that I was married to a Chinese girl.

Someone asked if we had any foreign currency. Leon had told me that on previous travels he had sometimes shown foreign currency to people he met when he ran out of things to talk about. I thought it sounded an amusingly high-risk strategy for losing banknotes, but I dug out a Hong Kong twenty-dollar bill, while Leon pulled out a US ten-dollar bill and a Mongolian one hundred-tugrik note. The notes were passed around with more murmurs of interest and conversation. The old man who owned the cave seemed especially interested in the US ten-dollar note. This was worth more than the price of a night in a *binguan* with hot showers, so we were not keen to give it to him, though I did say he could keep the Hong Kong note. The man thanked us, but kept holding onto the US dollars until, with a firm smile, we asked for it back. It was time for bed, and the old man and his son rolled out their blankets on the *kang*.

Leon and I produced our sleeping bags, and all four of us lay down to sleep.

The next morning we put on our packs, said our thank yous and stepped out of the door. As we were about to leave the courtyard, the old man came out and asked to see the ten-dollar bill again. We handed it to him. He smiled, and then, without handing it back, walked back into his house. Leon and I looked at each other and shrugged. He had taken good care of us and certainly earned it. I felt slightly ashamed that I had not let him just keep it the night before.

Leon and I soldiered out into the morning and set our sights on finding that Wall. Brown hills, brown beacon towers, brown ridges. Everything around us was brown, apart from the blue sky above and a frozen stream beside our path. Around the next hill another *yaodong* village came into view, and a man hacking ice out of the stream pointed us up a steep track. We walked up it and when we reached the top we stopped. There, once again before us, running brazenly through the empty hills, was the Great Wall.

28
The Wall, our guide

Distance to home: 2,410 miles

A line of imperial earth, three metres high and a metre wide, runs ahead and behind, up and down, veering and swerving through the contours of this twisted, rolling land. It is a line of defence to keep out the barbarians, a boundary line to mark the frontier between the land of the civilised and the wastelands of the uncouth. It is bold, confident, unfazed, enduring, magical and ancient. It is from another age, another world, from the time of uncrossed oceans and unknown continents, tyrannical emperors and horseback armies.

We walk beside it on goat-herders' paths; when these disappear, we push through brambles, or trudge through forests carpeted with snow. Occasionally we walk along the top of the Wall, our eyes minding each step – it is a three or four metre fall from either side. The walking, although hard and slow, also makes us feel liberated and joyful, for we are back in the wild beauty of China, and roaming free amid its ancient loess hills. Our worries about the filming, the foot injury and the Chinese police are falling back into perspective, and though it is still deep in the –20°Cs, we are finally toughening up. And we no longer need fear getting lost – the Wall is our guide.

Like the land, the Wall is made from loess. Every few hundred metres there is an earthen watchtower – a simple, large mound, without an entrance or room inside. Sometimes we can see ten or more such brown towers in either direction, stretching to the furthest ridges. And often there are beacon towers on the hills behind, and even another wall – a second line of defence or a wall from some other dynasty, we do not know. And made as it is from the earth, the Wall is crumbling from the centuries. When we scramble over it or along it, little pieces crumble into the dust. The hills, meanwhile, are riddled with gullies. Once the Wall would have bridged its way across these, but these sections have long since been washed away. Regularly, we have to scramble down the steep hillsides to the gully floors and launch into a long clamber and crawl back up the other side.

Often, we feel entirely alone, as if we have the Wall to ourselves, but we do encounter the occasional grizzled goat-herder and, once or twice a day, a cave village. The yaodongs *are built into the south-facing slopes to get more sun and, because we are approaching from the north, sometimes it is only when we spot a chimney at our feet that we realise we are on someone's roof. But the villagers are always friendly and happy to resupply us with hot water, and are intrigued to see Leon's camera. In one village he flips the screen round and a beautiful old lady stares at it, wondrous at being able to see a digitised image of herself, possibly for the first time.*

My diary entries, meanwhile, reflect an increasingly exhausted mind and body:

15 January: Foot feeling stable – foot support really helps.
16 January: Falling further and further behind schedule – what can we do about that? Things are turning into a bit of a blur as we are walking pretty hard, working hard filming. I'm not sure how sustainable this is?

At night, we camp amid the hillocks beneath the wall though, even with our new blankets, it is still too cold to really enjoy our sleep. One evening, at dusk, we come to an abandoned yaodong *stable, its floor lined with hay. Even though there is no glass in the window, or door in the doorway, it is still a luxurious few degrees warmer than outside. I fall into a slumber, as happy as a horse in a hay-filled stable in the cold mountains of northern Shanxi.*

One dawn, just after we have packed up camp, I climb a watchtower and stand looking along the Wall continuing through the hills. Leon and I are finding even walking beside the Wall hard work, so what kind of a gargantuan task must it have been to build it? Here, the Wall was built using the tamped earth technique – a wooden casing was constructed, and mixed earth packed inside to leave a solid earthen wall. It was built by corvée labourers; this was a form of taxation imposed on the common people whereby they not only had to pay tax in money and produce, but also by labouring for the state. The work of corvée labourers often included the hard, dangerous tasks of building elephantine public projects, like the Wall.

I imagine the mass of labourers, their quiet, hunched footsteps and groans as they dig and pack the earth. In winter, the cold would soon be deadly for those without thick clothing, good food and good shelter. In summer, forced to work in the heat all day, with insufficient water, it would have been no less dangerous.

An official history from the first century BC claims that a million people perished building the Wall for Emperor Qin. It is also said that the bodies of dead labourers were sometimes not given proper burials, but just incorporated into the rampart itself, which has resulted in the Wall sometimes being described as the world's longest cemetery. One day, some village children tell us a story about a girl called Meng Jiang Nu.

Meng Jiang Nu married the man she loved. However, no sooner had they married then he was taken away for corvée duty, building the Wall. Meng Jiang Nu was distraught, and went to look for him. But when she reached the section of the Wall where he was working, she was told he had already died. And so she wept and wept, and her tears were so many that they swept away a section of Wall.*

I now look up from the Wall to the hills, and suddenly I am imagining myself, not as a corvée labourer, but as a conscript soldier, sent to guard the frontier, keeping watch from this very tower, on some frozen dawn 600 years ago, underfed and cold. As I scan the

* We later discovered that this was a famous Chinese legend, and that there were many different versions of it, some of which included the peculiar detail that Meng Jiang Nu was hatched from a melon. Although it was impossible to establish its origins, it painted a vivid picture of the grief and death toll exacted all those centuries ago.

ridge line, the sound of horses' hooves echoes into my imagination. The raiders are coming. A moment later, a line of horses appears, bearing rugged men, outlandish, dangerous, ready to kill – though it is unusual for them to attack by day. I can almost smell the blood in the air. I freeze in terror. I cannot run; I'll be executed. And besides, behind me are my farmlands and my village. I light the beacon, a signal alerting reinforcements. But they will not get here in time. I will stand and fight, but I will not last long – I am arrow fodder for the Empire.

29

The Mother and the Sorrow

Distance to home: 2,355 miles

To speed ourselves up on our Wall walking stretch, we sometimes hiked along tracks in the valleys, the watchtowers marching along the ridge above us. As we walked, we also now got sporadic reception on our phone, so we spoke further with Tiberius. It turned out that enough footage could be saved to hopefully still make the show viable. We shared the Code Z idea with them, and they enthusiastically agreed to it. They said it would be a good way to fill in a few gaps, especially for the more epic desert panoramas. In addition, they sent us a feedback email explaining that we needed to use the tripod more to get steadier shots, and the radio mic more to get better sound. It had been hard, and sometimes unrealistic to do these things in the harsh weather, and we felt demoralised that their feedback focused on the things we needed to improve, rather than praising anything we had got right. But at the same time, although we had been working very hard, perhaps we could work harder still. At the end of the day it was not Tiberius's job to show us sympathy but to make sure we shot the necessary quality of footage. And so that was what we were going to have to do.

After five days, a twisting road led us away from the Wall, and we began to descend into a deep canyon. As we wound down through pine forests on endless switchbacks, we could see a steep cliff face on the other side, several miles away. After an hour, we still could not see the bottom. We spotted a beacon tower, and clambered up to it for a better view. And from here, finally, we caught sight of our next major landmark: the Yellow River, the Huang He.

The river's tumultuous flow was imprisoned by the cliffs, scree slopes and crags and, at the point where we sighted it, it was also unnaturally split in half by a giant dam. Upstream of the dam, the river was fifty metres higher, and its surface was frozen. Downstream, the water – a murky brown-green colour, not yellow – gushed out of the dam's base, liquid again. It swirled rapidly under a bridge and down to a bend two miles away, where it froze over once more.

The Yellow River has always been a central character in the history of China. It was sometimes referred to as 'the Mother River', which was appropriate, for the heart of Chinese civilisation had grown up in its fertile valleys downstream. But it was also known as 'China's Sorrow' on account of its frequent, terrible floods – over one and half thousand of them since China was unified two millennia ago.

Both the floods, and the river's famous yellow-brown colour, are caused by the heavy load of silt that the water picks up on its path through the loess plateau. The river carries over thirty times more sediment per cubic metre than the Nile. In the final 500 miles to the sea, as it decelerates amid the flat plains, much of the river's load is deposited on the riverbed. This causes the riverbed to rise continually and so, down through the ages, the only way to stop the river flooding had been to build huge dykes to contain it. But as the riverbed continued to rise, the river channel itself now flowed many metres above the surrounding countryside – with nothing but the dykes to hold it in. In a flood, or if the dykes burst, the river would gush out across the plains, sometimes rampaging around in different directions for years before finding a new channel in which to make a home for a while.

These floods not only killed millions through drowning, famines and epidemics, but also severely destabilised the whole Empire. The mythical Emperor Yu of the third millennium BC was the first emperor to attempt to control the river, and was attributed as saying, 'When the Yellow River is at peace, China is at peace.' This is linked to the widespread belief in China that natural disasters – whether they be earthquakes, famines, or floods – were omens from heaven indicating disfavour with the ruling dynasty, and that soon a new dynasty would be given the 'Mandate of Heaven' instead. There was actually a very literal link between such calamities and the implosion of the Empire, because huge numbers of displaced people often led to mass rebellions. Yellow River flooding had in fact been a contributing factor to the outbreak of the Boxer Rebellion at the end of the nineteenth century – often noted as a key event leading to the downfall of the Qing Dynasty, the last dynasty, in 1912.* And yet even after the death of the dynastic Empire, the Mother River, the Sorrow of China, kept on flowing.

---

* Sometimes, rulers tried to use the Yellow River as a weapon, deliberately bursting its banks to wipe out or block an advancing enemy. But the river was a Pandora's box; once unleashed, its power could not be tamed or controlled. In such an attempt by a Ming Dynasty governor in the seventeenth century, he had ended up accidentally flooding his own city, with three quarters of the population dying as a result. In 1938, Chiang Kai Shek had tried such a tactic against the Japanese, but while up to a million civilians died in the ensuing floods, there was little benefit to the war effort.

30
Hemmed in

Distance to home: 2,295 miles

We clambered down towards the river and, on the way, caught a much better view of the dam. It was an impressive sight, with its smooth wall of concrete, and series of James Bond-like control buildings and watchtowers. This was one of dozens of dams on the river. Although they had virtually put an end to the river's terrible floods, they are frequently prone to silting up, making their hydro-electric power redundant. As we continued downwards, a shopkeeper in a solitary petrol station told us there was a path beside the river that would lead us downstream.

At the bottom of the canyon, we saw that the river was flowing fast: aggressive and silent, like a fiercely disciplined army marching off for a surprise assault. It seethed with ice shards, and shelves of ice jutted several metres out from the banks on each side. In the earlier stages of planning the expedition, we had considered carrying small inflatable kayaks with us to paddle down the Yellow River. We had abandoned the idea when delays meant that we would not reach it until winter, which turned out to be the right decision. Paddling in these conditions would have been suicidal. We saw the track mentioned by the shopkeeper and, as we started walking, we found ourselves sandwiched between the silent, icy river on our right, and towering cliffs on our left. The opposite bank was also cliff-faced. All being well, we would cross over to it in two weeks' time, 300 miles downstream.

After two miles, we reached a bend where the river surface was completely frozen again, and the indignant water swirled underneath. We continued walking, hopeful that this track, although not on our map, would continue all the way to where the asphalt road met the river again, ten miles further on. It would be a good shortcut compared to the truckers' road that ran through the mountains. However, as the end of the day drew near, the track petered out into a small field. Beyond it, there was no path. It would be too dangerous to walk along the frozen river surface itself – we could see water splurging up through numerous cracks in the ice beside the bank. The only way forward would be to pick our way along a crumbly scree slope between the cliffs and the river. It looked dangerous. While I was hopeful that we could make it, Leon, in a rare display of non-hopeavism, was not sure. Perhaps all the problems with the camera had shaken his confidence.

I found the thought of walking all the way back and round, and up to the top of the canyon to join a smelly truckers' road, very unappealing. I therefore tried to persuade Leon for a few minutes, while he umm-ed and err-ed. We did not reach a conclusion, but it was getting dark anyway.

'Let's camp here and decide in the morning,' we agreed.

By morning, Leon was also keen to try the scree slope, and we began to pick our way along it. It was slow work. The ground was crumbly and, ten metres below, the frozen river chewed at the bank. The cliffs shot vertically above us for almost a hundred metres, and we were constantly alert to the sound of falling stones. I felt jittery but alive.

Stepping carefully from stone to stone, trying to stick to the more solid-looking sections, we gradually made progress forwards and upwards, until we reached the base of the cliffs, where the ground was more solid. My optimism was increasing that we could get all the way to the road, but by this point Leon was unconvinced again and kept looking further ahead. Several miles away, we could just see the river turned right and, from where we were, it looked as if the cliffs dropped straight into the water.

Suddenly Leon said, 'The Wall!'

My eyes followed where he was pointing, and saw a crumbling brown watchtower, standing on the edge of a low cliff just ahead of us. We scrambled up to it. A small section of wall ran along the ledge – not a part of the Great Wall, just a part of the river defences. But our hopes that we might be able to follow this little wall were quickly dashed, as the small cliff turned out only to be a ridge of land, sticking out into icy water. It was not long before we had to climb down into a gully and back up another ridge, and then back down yet another gully, all the time paralleling the river. We kept moving, but the further we went, the harder it became. It was now twenty-four hours since we had seen any humans. If we were to twist an ankle, it would be very difficult to get rescued. We were also starting to run out of water, and our progress was so slow it looked unlikely that we would reach the proper road before sundown.

Leon stopped walking and frowned at me.

'I think we should follow this ridge back into the hills,' he said. 'There is no way we can make it along the next seven miles of river like this.'

'I think we'll find a way through,' I said. 'I can't believe people would not have made little paths along here.' I strained my head to try and see round the next bend.

Leon pointed. 'Look up there, it's all just cliffs.'

We each contended our point of view for a few minutes, but I stood my ground and this time Leon gave in. We had now survived two major tests as a team – my foot, and the focus fiasco – and as a more robust friendship developed, we were handling disagreements more easily.

However, as we tried to descend into the next gully, we came to a much steeper slope, and I had to admit that the way forward was blocked. Three of the oldest rules in the book for hikers are: make sure you know where you are going; make sure someone else knows where you are going; don't underestimate how quickly a seemingly safe situation can turn precarious. We had managed to break all three, but we were too far along to contemplate going back now.

'Sorry,' I said, 'we'll have to try your route.'

We started climbing Leon's ridge instead, but this too led to more cliffs. We returned to the previous gully, and started clambering up the dried-out stream-bed. We had no idea if this would lead anywhere either, and the sky had now turned a menacing grey. It looked as if it might snow – a whiteout was the last thing we needed.

For an hour we scrambled over the stream-bed's smashed boulders, and eventually we found a small sheep path zigzagging up a slope. We climbed up and along, and into the mountains, and impressively, in the midst of all this, Leon still regularly stopped to set up the tripod and do some careful filming, sometimes even on the edge of narrow cliff ledges. He also insisted that I clip on the radio whenever I spoke to the camera. He was pushing our standards up.

Eventually, exhausted, we reached the summit. Far below, we could still see the frozen Yellow River, but as we looked around us, we were relieved to see a couple of scrubby terraced fields and, beyond them, a cave village. A cheerful, wrinkled farming couple met us outside their *yaodong* – the first humans we had seen in almost thirty-six hours. We were very happy to see them. They filled our thermoses while talking continuously, though their thick accents – combined with the fact that they were both chewing something and speaking simultaneously – meant we could hardly understand a word. Still talking, they led us down a path, and to our surprise we came to a brand new asphalt road. It carved across the mountain, connecting their tiny village to the outside world. Three hours later, in darkness, we arrived back on the truckers' road, thirty miles further back than we had hoped. There was a little *ludian* on the junction, and we checked in, glad to have made it back to safety.

31
Ice wine

Distance to home: 2,300 miles

Overnight, the grey clouds dumped a heavy snowfall, and the next morning the world had turned white. It was good that we were not still stuck on the Yellow River scree slopes. We spent the first three hours of the day skidding and stomping down a long hill to the town of Pianguan. It was now only two days until Chinese New Year, and the markets were buzzing with fireworks stalls, fresh poultry being sold, and live fish getting clobbered bloodily around the head. Our aborted shortcut along the river had effectively cost us another whole day. We were so tired we felt we still needed our weekly day off, though we were so badly behind schedule we could not really afford it. We sat in our hotel room assessing our progress and options. My foot was still painful and continued to slow me down because I could not push with it; I had noticed my right calf muscle had shrunk considerably. But with the help of the foot support, it was stable, and even slowly improving. The trouble was, if we were going to make our deadline of reaching Hong Kong by the end of May, we now had no choice but to start upping our distances by five to eight miles a day – an increase of about 25 per cent. And this was not just a short-term measure: we would need to keep this up all the way to Hong Kong. We reconsidered the idea of riding bicycles to make up time and let the foot recover. But it felt like a cop-out. I told Leon that I was determined to at least attempt to tackle the extra mileage on foot.

'Are you sure?' he said.

'Yes. If the foot completely starts falling apart, or I can't make the distances, we can always switch to bicycles. But that has to be a last resort.'

The next morning we set off into a frozen dawn, and the air was thick with smog. Smoke plumed from the chimney of every house and, even this early, fireworks zipped across the sky and popped. Some 1.4 billion people were waking up in anticipation of Chinese New Year's Eve. Chinese New Year is dated according to the lunar calendar and always falls between late January and late February. It is a tradition that goes back thousands of years, and in Mainland China the celebrations last for fifteen days. The most important event is New Year's Eve – the equivalent to Christmas Day – and this is an occasion when family members try their hardest to get back home to be together for the traditional evening meal. This results in the world's largest annual migration. Hundreds of millions of Chinese are on the move, and between them make over three billion trips by road, rail, ship and plane.

Over the past week, we had noticed the roads were getting steadily busier, and today was the final push. We reached a clifftop road above the Yellow River, and tucked tightly into the verge as cars and buses drove past even faster and more recklessly than normal. They were apparently paying no attention to the 'Danger Yellow River' signs – it was a fifty-metre drop off the cliff's edge. Halfway through the afternoon, with Leon somewhere ahead of me, I stopped to do some stretching. When I turned back to the road, I saw a huge cloud of dust swirling into the air 100 metres ahead of me. As I drew closer I saw several cars had stopped, and a small crowd was peering over the cliff edge. Leon was among them in his orange jacket, with the camera out. I caught up and looked down to see a car wedged in a gully ten metres below. It was facing uphill, with a smashed in bonnet. To my relief I could see the car was empty.

'What happened?' I asked Leon.

'I'd just stopped at that building to fill up my thermos, and we heard a screech outside. We came out and saw this.'

I followed Leon into the clifftop building, and saw the three survivors: two men and a seven-year-old boy. They looked shaken, and had dust all over their faces and clothes. But they were uninjured and smiling. Smiling was the expression of choice in China when someone is embarrassed or nervous, though I suppose in this case they were also genuinely happy to have just narrowly avoided an icy grave in the Yellow River.

As darkness fell, the sky above us boomed with a continuous series of fireworks; it felt as though we were entering a war zone. We reached the outskirts of Hequ, the riverside city where we would be spending our own New Year's Eve. At ground level, the street was lined with red lanterns hanging outside each house, and on each porch sat a one-metre-high pile of burning coal and a little mound of oranges.

'The fireworks are to scare away a mythical beast called a *nian*,' said Leon, who had been doing some reading on Chinese New Year. 'And the oranges are a food offering for him.'

'What happens if you don't leave the oranges?' I asked.

'The *nian* will kidnap and eat your household's youngest child.'

Through the windows, we could see families getting ready for their celebratory meals. The atmosphere around us was magical. But at the same time, after almost thirty miles, this had been our longest day yet. My feet were bruised, and I felt sorry for myself that we had to spend Chinese New Year tramping the cold, dark pavements, while the rest of China celebrated with their families. Apart from us, the decorations, and the occasional pair of young boys sneaking outside to let off a chain of firecrackers, the street was totally empty. I missed Christine.

Two miles before we reached the town centre, a black SUV drew up beside us. A man yelled out of his window in Chinese. 'What are you doing?'

We recited our catechism.

'Jump in,' he said pointing to his back seats, 'come back to my house for dinner.'

'No thanks, we're walking.'

'Oh come on, come to dinner.'

Leon and I looked at each other. Leon said, 'We could just mark our spot, and start walking from here in the morning.'

And with that our decision was made. We threw our packs in the boot, and jumped in. We had no idea what the night might hold. The man, whose name was Li, shouted into his mobile phone as we drove, explaining something along the lines of, 'You're not going to believe who I've picked up for dinner – these two bearded foreigners. They've walked here from Mongolia. Lay two extra places!'

The car pulled up in a dimly lit street, and we followed Li through a courtyard and into a simple-looking house. The first room was a small kitchen, where an old lady and two middle-aged women were busy rolling dumplings, while an old TV played loud Chinese opera. We were ushered into another room, with a round table in the middle. The walls were decorated with red patterns – the colour for good luck and prosperity. Two men and a boy walked in. The oldest man was the father of the house – another Mr Li, and the brother of the Mr Li who had picked us up. The younger man and the boy were his two sons.

'Please, let me take your coats,' said the older boy. His name was Gaoyu, and he was a twenty-year-old university student, home for the holidays. I pulled off my two coats, two hats and a scarf. Gaoyu took each item and hung them up and I dreaded to think of the smell that I might be emitting now that my protective layers were gone. At Chinese New Year, it is an age-old tradition to wear new clothes, and have a haircut, but Leon and I had turned up with bedraggled clothing, scraggly hair and bushy beards. The Li family was far too polite to show they noticed.

'I am sorry my English is not good, I have never spoken to a foreigner before,' said Gaoyu. We assured him his was the best English we had encountered for weeks. As we sat chatting we discovered Gaoyu was studying economics, was a serious Liverpool FC fan, and also played football himself. His father, who spoke no English, owned several steel mines.

Just before it was time to eat, the three men all gathered at a family shrine at the back of the room. A line of miniature 'lucky gods' sat in a row, and at the front there was an urn of ashes. The men lit a joss stick, and placed some food before the shrine – the ancient rite of venerating their ancestors.

Delicious aromas billowed into the room as the food started to arrive: fried sliced potatoes, braised bean sprouts, fried bean curd, steamed Chinese fungus and vegetables, steamed fish head, steamed fish body, fried and steamed chicken and several large bowls of dumplings. The dishes completely covered the round table in the middle of the room. I looked at Leon, and could tell that we were both thinking the same thought: tonight's dinner was going to be a lot better than the usual processed sausages.

We all took our seats at the table, and Gaoyu's father stood up and shook our hands. 'As representatives of the Chinese people, we welcome you,' he said with a huge smile.

A bottle was produced.

'Ah, *baijiu*,' said Leon and I.

'No,' said Gaoyu, showing us the label and smiling proudly, 'this is Canadian Ice Wine.' Western luxury imports were becoming all the rage.

A glass of wine was poured for everyone, including Gaoyu's little brother, and then we all took a sip and the feast began. In Chinese culture, rather than each person having a large plate of food each, everyone instead just plucks individual pieces of food from the large dishes in the middle. Chopsticks are ideal for this, as are the harmonious round tables. We ate away, gorging ourselves on the meats and vegetables. Everyone smiled at each other and looked content between mouthfuls. We found that we did not have to pluck items from the middle ourselves, because as soon as we ate something, Gaoyu placed another dainty morsel into our bowls. When I first started dating Christine, I had learnt that serving your guests – as Gaoyu was doing – was excellent manners.

Suddenly, Leon yelped.

'Ah, sorry, you must be careful because some of the dumplings have coins inside them,' said Gaoyu gently. He smiled and added, 'You are very lucky, because this means you will become rich this year.'

Leon choked a little, before producing a coin from his mouth and waving it around triumphantly. We all cheered.

'I wonder if you will get one, Rob?' said Gaoyu, waving his chopsticks at the bowl of dumplings.

I felt a little jealous, but a few minutes later, I too bit down on a hard coin in my dumpling and produced it for all to see. But soon after, Leon got another one. The evening ended with a score of 2:1 to Leon; though I was happy for him, the reality was that neither of us expected to get very rich this year.

After supper, as Gaoyu's little brother set off firecrackers in the yard, Leon and I realised we had no idea where we were going to sleep. But then Gaoyu and his father insisted on driving us to the local hotel. We arrived at a smart building and followed them through some automatic doors into a glitzy lobby. It looked way beyond our normal budget, but to top off their amazing hospitality for the night, Gaoyu's father insisted on paying for a room for us.

After our hot showers, we collapsed. It had been a long day, but China had again treated us well, and the New Year had got off to a good start.

Part Four

Into Ancient Heartlands

————

车到山前必有路

When we get to the mountain, there'll be a way through.

32
Big Nose

Distance to home: 2,200 miles

23 JANUARY—2 FEBRUARY

It is a week after Chinese New Year, and we have maintained our speed, rising each day at dawn, packing fast, walking fast, often into the frozen night. We are still in Shanxi Province, east of the Yellow River. But we have left the riverside for a while in order to follow a network of roads that runs southwards through the valleys that parallel it. Walking on these roads is not always as peaceful as when we guessed our way down shepherds' tracks by the Wall, or followed the looping Yellow River bends, but it is certainly more direct.

Sometimes our route takes us along winding ridges, surrounded by cascades of steep, brown earth that falls away into deep canyons on one side, and rises above into crumbling hillocks on the other.

Much of the soft land has been cut into terraces for growing corn, though as the winter drags on, they are carpeted only with rows of dead yellow stubs and leaves. There are still occasional beacon towers on the ridge lines, but fewer and fewer as we move beyond frontier territory and deeper into the core of China. More common are the electricity pylons running from ridge to ridge, connected by high voltage cable. The farming villages are a mix of cave, brick and concrete dwellings. Old and new China are colliding before our eyes.

We have also re-entered coal country, and the wild, tainted beauty of the more remote ridges alternates with huge mining developments. However, rather than running along a valley like they did near Datong, the mines here are up among the hills themselves. We often see giant conveyor belts pouring inexhaustible rivers of coal onto thirty-metre high piles.

157

We also occasionally glimpse less official mines. One night, walking up a mountain road with our head torches on, we pass some makeshift mines dug into roadside cliffs. The roofs are held up by homemade wooden staves. Two-man teams are still working away in them, digging out seams of coal. They stared at us as we walked past in the dark, as if we were ghosts. It looks like miserable, dangerous work. But they will get better pay for this than for farm work, so they probably have little choice.

The whole region, meanwhile, is full of coal trucks. Sometimes when we stride round a corner, we see a battalion of red trucks queuing up outside a large mine to collect their loads. These trucks also fill the valley roads, and the fields beside them are sprinkled with truckers' defecations and toilet paper. Along with pollution and jobs, the coal has brought money to this region, and many of the towns are clearly growing in prosperity. When we arrive in the towns at night we are dazzled by brand-new, neon-emblazoned hotel complexes, rising out of impressive metropolises of sculpted fountains and riverside promenades.

My diary entries continue to reflect our gradual physical deterioration:

29 January: Well yesterday was a serious slog, bashing down a main road – lots of trucks and cars and slushy snow on the shoulder, not much fun . . . Lots of hooting and sudden swerving . . . Blisters starting to develop lots on the end of my toes . . . Our bodies rather beaten . . .

2 February: A slog day – but we moved fast and slept well last night . . .

6 February: Wow, another incredible but exhausting but unpredictable day! Is this trip changing me?

Now we are walking further and for longer each day, with less time off, we notice a difference in how our bodies are coping. In the first two months of the trip, we had walked a maximum of just twenty miles a day, and apart from my right foot and a deepening tiredness, we did not have many physical complaints. But now we have upped our distances to twenty-five or thirty miles a day, our physical ailments are starting to pile up. Leon partially twists an ankle climbing a slope to do some filming; I develop a sore knee; Leon gets a sore back; I start to suffer from bruised feet every night; Leon gets stress-induced toothache so he has to take some Chinese antibiotics. When I pull my socks off in the evenings, I often see ugly white blister bubbles under my skin that I need to pop with my penknife to get the puss out, and douse with iodine to disinfect. But remarkably, however beaten up we feel at the end of a walking day, the next morning, with the help of a reasonable sleep and a few plasters, we are ready to go again.

On the other hand, our descent from civilised human beings into wild men seems intractable. We burp and fart still more. Instead of words, we speak in groans and grumbles and with increasing references to Orlando, Jase and dinosaurs. When we stop for breaks, we sit down in the dirt (though still checking that we are not about to sit on a trucker's toilet) and shovel instant noodles and processed sausages into our mouths like they are fuel. At the same time we look forward to reaching towns that have a restaurant, now a regular occurrence, where for about 10 RMB (£1) we buy bowls of dumplings or fried rice – much better nourishment than instant noodles. Our Mandarin improves slowly, but we still continually confuse shui jiao (second and third tone: dumplings) with shui jiao (fourth and fourth tone: sleep). We get bemused looks when we try to order a bowl of sleep. In fact, we would usually be happy with either – food and rest are our two great concerns.

When I look into a hotel mirror one night, I blink in surprise at the sight of a heavily bearded man looking back at me. His moustache is growing into his mouth and his hair is sticky, unwashed and moulded in strange directions from wearing a woolly hat for too long. His eyes, meanwhile, are crazed with exhaustion. The suggestion of insanity is exacerbated by the layers and layers of clothing, which make him look like the Michelin man.

Amazingly, my right foot is still stable, though in addition to wearing the foot support and taking at least two anti-inflammatories a day, it is essential to regularly and strenuously stretch my muscles.

In particular I find that stretching out my calves helps. So we stretch when we are taking a break in roadside fields, we stretch when we are in village shops buying instant noodles, we stretch when we are in restaurants having lunch. Apart from Clare and two tourists we had spotted in Datong, we have seen no Caucasians since we arrived in China. It is probably rare for local people to encounter foreigners first-hand, let alone foreigners who are constantly stretching. And yet the Chinese people are uninhibited with us. One day, during a stretch break in a warm roadside shop, the shopkeeper comes over and competes with me to touch his toes – and gets a lot closer than I do. Another time, as I lean against a tree, stretching my calves, a labourer approaches and gives my legs a good squeeze. 'Very strong,' he says, before offering me a cigarette.

On a quiet path, a goat-herder catches sight of us, and shakes his head in disbelief. He garbles questions at us in a strong accent that we cannot understand, before suddenly reaching up and grabbing Leon's cold pink nose. 'Da bizi' – Big Nose* – he shouts with a triumphant chuckle, as if pleased to confirm that we are real and not imaginary, and that we do indeed have big noses, just like he has always been told.

One night we hear a man walking towards us, and singing loudly.

'Waaa . . . yeeeee . . . hoooo . . .'

He sounds very drunk and, after he has passed us, he turns and starts walking along behind, still singing at the top of his lungs. As we reach the next town, the singing stops, and the man appears beside us, walking peacefully.

'Where are you going?' he asks. Up close he does not look drunk after all.

We explain, and then compliment him on his singing.

'Ah, singing is how I let off steam after I've had an argument with my wife!' he says. 'Tonight we had a pretty major one.'

But some people are intimidated by us. When we wave at a group of young boys playing on a frozen stream, they scream and run away. One night we stagger into a small dark town, and I approach

---

* A common derogatory slang for Caucasians in recent centuries.

a lady walking past and ask in my best Chinese if there is a ludian *nearby. I forget how I look with my beard and pack, with Leon standing beside me, even taller, and smelling worse too. I have barely said hello, when she lets out a shriek and runs headlong to the other side of the road.*

And amid our exhaustion, we keep filming, keep trying. Perhaps it is this, on top of everything else, that is making us go a little round the bend. One night, we stumble through a small town dominated by an immense, floodlit coal mine. Its massive structure has conveyor-belt corridors running over the top of the road, and it is surrounded by a high, sinister wall. From within the compound we can hear a hearty, apocalyptic Maoist male choir, belting out over a PA system.

The next morning, as we start walking Leon tells me about a dream he had had.

'We were inside that coal mine from last night, the one with the choir. But actually, we had discovered that it was not a coal mine – it was a storm trooper clone factory. We were running around, trying to find a way out of this maze of corridors, but suddenly I realised that I had forgotten to bring the camera! Can you believe it, this was one of our best adventures yet, and I was not able to film it?'

'That sounds almost as bad a disaster as the focus fiasco,' I say.

33
Chinese Li

Distance to home: 2,110 miles

3 FEBRUARY

Without realising the precise moment it happened, we left the coal region behind us, and found ourselves walking through quiet farming valleys once more. The weather was warming up a little, and the stream beside the road was starting to melt to reveal huge gluts of rubbish caught in the reeds. A few goat-herders and their flocks ambled along the hillsides, and for the first time we saw farmers out on the terraces, piling up dead vegetation from the winter.

That evening, we would reach the town of Yonghe; after a week of walking twelve to fourteen hours a day, we were looking forward to a day off. With only six miles to go, we passed through a village where a troop of teenagers poured onto the road and started taking photos of us with their mobile phones. We found that when a small crowd gathered in China, there was often an exponential effect, as passers-by joined in to see what was happening. While the teenagers snapped away, even cars were reversing back to have a look.

After a few minutes, we broke away from the crowd, walking fast. Our followers had to run to keep up. Most people started to saunter home. But no sooner had we got going again, than a black car stopped beside us.

Three young men jumped out and ran over.

'Let us give you a lift to town,' the driver shouted in friendly, husky Mandarin. He was in his late twenties and had a faint moustache.

'No thanks, we are walking.'

'We are not bad people,' said another of the men, in a high-pitched voice.

'We know, but we are walking.'

We moved off again to prove our point, and the men jumped back in their car. They quickly overtook us, stopped and jumped out again.

'It's not far, come on, let us give you a lift, we'll buy you dinner,' said the husky driver.

'We love guests,' added his high-pitched friend.

I launched into our usual response about having walked here all the way from Mongolia, but the men ignored me, amicably, grabbing our poles and throwing them in their boot. By now the crowd had caught us up.

I began to protest with a smile, but the driver shouted: 'Let's go, let's go, let's go.'

As Leon and I started chuckling, the driver subtly moved behind Leon and suddenly grabbed his rucksack. Because Leon was filming, he had to protect the camera from getting damaged, and the driver managed to slip the straps off Leon's shoulder quite easily. A moment later he was bundling the pack into his car triumphantly, with a satisfied, 'Ha ha!'

Now it was my turn, but I was ready. The driver moved towards me, and we began to hustle and tussle as if we were in a slapstick movie. The crowd grew. The children giggled. An old man puffed on his pipe and watched silently.

'We have walked here all the way from Mongolia,' I said again, 'we can't take a lift.'

'We know, we know,' said the men, 'but time is precious, and we can give you a lift back here later.'

The last thing we wanted to do was come back out here after dinner. We said we would meet them in town when we arrived in a couple of hours.

'Oh come on, it's only a few miles,' said the driver, puffing with exasperation. Leon had meanwhile managed to retrieve the rucksack and poles; when the driver saw this, with another big puff, he finally admitted defeat. He gave us his mobile number and then pointed to himself and said (in English): 'Chinese Li.' Li was the most common name in China, so who knows why he included 'Chinese', but it suited him.

An hour later, we arrived in Yonghe. The map had suggested it would be a similar size to the glitzy coal-money cities, but it was actually much smaller and had just one scruffy shopping street beside a river. We phoned Chinese Li and, a moment later, he skidded up beside us in his car, delighted. We squeezed into the back, along with several of his friends, and soon after arrived at a smart hotel-restaurant.

'We welcome you enthusiastically,' said Chinese Li as we sat down at a round table in a private room at the back of the restaurant, 'and I am going to treat you to dinner.'

After shouting some orders at the waitress, he started to open an ominously large bottle of *baijiu*.

'Just a little cup,' he said as he poured me a huge one. The whole bottle managed to fill only four cups. He opened another bottle.

'We are very hospitable,' he said, grinning and raising his drink. 'Unlike you and the eight foreign powers who invaded China.'* We all clinked glasses, and took a gulp. The sudden drink at the end of a long week made my cheeks flush.

'It's fate that has brought us together,' said Chinese Li, accidentally knocking over his cup. 'Tonight, as well as dinner, I will also treat you to a room at this hotel.' It was fortuitous that he was treating us to both dinner and a hotel room, because Leon and I were almost out of cash. We thanked him, and dishes of food started to arrive. Chinese Li put chunks of bony meat into our bowls. 'Meeeeeeer, meeeeeer,'† he cried out, growing more animated.

'OK, this must be lamb,' we said as we started eating.

We discovered that Chinese Li was a fertiliser salesman and his friend with the high-pitched voice was a goat-herder with five hundred goats. Two women soon arrived, one of whom turned out to be Chinese Li's wife – she was a mobile phone salesperson.

---

* It was only when I later watched the video footage that I realised Chinese Li was referring to the European–Japanese–American coalition's destructive encroachment in China in 1900, in order to put down the Boxer Rebellion.
† Chinese people do not go 'baaaa baaaa' but 'meeeeeer, meeeeer' in their sheep impressions. Their noise for frogs is 'gwa, gwa' rather than 'ribbit'.

'And her name is horse, neeeaaayyyy!' shouted Chinese Li, pointing to the other woman, 'and she is a policewoman.'

I'd never met a Chinese policewoman called horse before. We all clinked glasses again.

Sitting in the lovely warm room, as I ate more food and took a few more gulps of *baijiu*, I started to feel very tired, and had to work hard to stop myself from falling asleep. But Chinese Li continued to talk away rapidly, and enthusiastically. As we skipped from conversation to conversation, I was only able to pick up bits and pieces of what was being said.

'Did you see Chairman Mao's house?' asked Chinese Li.

'Yes,' we said. We had passed a roadside *yaodong* the previous day with a sign announcing that Mao had lived here during the war against the Japanese.

Suddenly Chinese Li sprang to his feet, saluted into the air and burst into song:

The East is red
The sun is rising
China produces Chairman Mao.

He sat down again. The song 'The East is Red' had virtually been the national anthem during the Cultural Revolution.

'And how is Shanxi Province?' I asked. 'It looks like it is getting very rich.'

'A lot of people here have a lot of money,' said Chinese Li, suddenly looking a bit sad, 'but even more have very little money. And the environment is not good, and the air is not clear.' He had nicely summed up China's most pressing, and potentially destabilising issues – inequality and the environment.

As the evening went on, more and more of Chinese Li's friends arrived, until the room was bursting. I was definitely ready for bed, but just when we thought it was time to call it a night, someone suggested karaoke. It was our first karaoke invitation in China, so we summoned our strength and said yes, we would absolutely love to go to karaoke.

The next morning – perhaps unsurprisingly after my appalling rendition of Michael Jackson's 'Beat It', and a bit too much *baijiu* – I had a sore throat and fluey head. The exhausting week followed by a night out with Chinese Li had hit me hard. While Leon went to get some food and withdraw some money, I sat on my bed writing a newspaper article.

Two hours later, Leon returned, with some bad news. Firstly, although there were various local co-operative banks on the high street, there were no national banks. Therefore, none of the machines accepted our foreign bank cards. We had only 220 RMB (£22) left, and Daning, the next town large enough for a bank, was two days' walk away.

Secondly, it turned out that Chinese Li had not paid for our hotel room after all. We therefore owed the hotel 340 RMB (£34). We had an additional US$35 'emergency money' which, combined with 120 of our RMB covered the hotel, leaving us just 100 RMB (£10). Having spent three quarters of this on dumplings for lunch, and a big supply of instant noodles and processed sausage to get us through the next forty-eight hours to Daning, we were left with just 26 RMB (£2.60) to our name.

34
Down and out on the Huang He

Distance to home: 2,085 miles

4–7 FEBRUARY

I am sitting in a restaurant in the International Finance Centre shopping mall in Hong Kong. A waitress comes over, and I start to order some food from the menu. The burger and chips look good. She takes the order down and starts to walk away. Suddenly I remember. I do not have any money. I panic. What should I do? This is going to be very embarrassing, but I am so hungry.

I woke up, and realised that I was not in Hong Kong. I was in my tent, in the middle of a cornfield, on the side of a Chinese hill. The previous day we had left Yonghe, made good progress through the hills, and camped ten miles short of Daning. My stomach rumbled, and the thought of more instant noodles for breakfast was not appealing.

'Are you awake, Rob?' I heard Leon call from his tent.

As we packed up, we were looking forward to reaching the town, getting some money out, and having a good, greasy restaurant meal.

Christine called a few minutes later to give me an update on the flight bookings for Code Z (our visas were nearing their expiry dates). As we chatted, I joked to her about our financial straits.

'How much have you got left?' she asked.

'Twenty-six kwai,' I said.

'What!'

'Don't worry, we're only three hours' walk from the next town.'

As we marched onwards, Leon remarked that today, the fifteenth day of the lunar New Year, was also the first full moon of the year, and last day of the Chinese New Year celebrations. 'We should look out for some good parties to film,' he said.

We felt our filming had been going well recently, but we were continuing to push ourselves hard. The pressure from Tiberius had not relented, as they regularly sent us instructions on how we needed to improve or upload more footage. This was helpful in many ways, but the one to two hours of daily filming or searching for a hotel with an internet connection made the difference between finishing the day's walk in glorious daylight with time to rejuvenate before bed, and finishing in depressing darkness with barely enough time to eat before collapsing into slumber.

Halfway down the hill, we heard the sound of drums and *suonas*. *Suonas* are Chinese reed instruments, which look like a large oboe but have a squeaking brassy sound. The band was playing traditional yet upbeat music. As we drew nearer, we saw the band members were sitting on the edge of a village, and a group of villagers were marching in a procession around some kind of tented shrine. All the villagers wore white robes, and large white cylinder-shaped hats.

'It looks like a chefs' convention,' said Leon. 'Let's go take a look.'

We wandered over, camera running.

'*Xinnian kwai le!*' (Happy New Year) I exclaimed with a smile to the white gathering, while Leon filmed.

The man at the front of the procession, about my age, looked up at me, confused and unsmiling. That was an unusual response when we said Happy New Year.

I turned to survey the scene in more detail and three facts dawned on me. Firstly, I noticed that the shrine did not have statues in it, but rather a photograph of an old man. Secondly, I recalled that Christine had told me that white was the colour of mourning in China.* And thirdly, I saw that the people looked not only confused, but also rather sad – not how you would expect people to look if they were indeed celebrating the last day of Chinese New Year.

'Leon,' I said, starting to tread backwards and away from the procession, who were now all standing and staring at us, 'I don't think this is a Chinese New Year celebration, I think it's a funeral.'

---

* It is rude to give white flowers to a Chinese person in hospital – it is like saying, 'You're going to die.'

'Ah,' said Leon, lowering his camera. We bowed solemnly and made our way back to the road. I felt bad, and hoped I had not added to the pain they were feeling that day.

We arrived in Daning at 10 a.m., eyes peeled for a cash machine. But as we approached the high street, we saw a huge crowd gathering, and we could hear the whizzing of fireworks and a cacophony of drums and other instruments. Reaching the throng, we looked over everyone's heads to see several lines of colourful floats, musicians and dancers. This was no funeral – it was a bona fide street carnival.

We walked onwards, enjoying the crackling fireworks, cheerful music and vibrant performances. Colourful dragons on sticks swirled past, held aloft by ladies in bright red costumes; a unicyclist pedalled by, juggling batons; forty women in a perfect square beat drums and cymbals as they danced; a big troop of men with *suonas* hooted out lively tunes, trying to keep in time with a group of drummers who bashed out their rhythms faster and faster. One man played two *suonas* at once, and in the middle of the song opened his mouth to reveal a lit cigarette held in his tongue. He pulled the cigarette back inside, tooted his *suona* some more, and then flicked the cigarette out again and took a puff. We all cheered.

Amid all the jovial bangs, dancing and crowds, and while Leon filmed, my stomach was rumbling. I dashed into each bank I saw and tried to withdraw some money. However, as in Yonghe, all of them were rural co-operatives, not international Chinese banks. Every one rejected our cards, so I rejoined the crowd next to Leon. A Chinese girl started speaking to us in English. She was called Faith and was home from university for the New Year holidays.

'The performers are all farmers from the villages,' she shouted above the noise, 'they have been practising for months. Most cities don't have local performances like this any more. You are lucky to be here today.' Faith said she would like to treat us to lunch, and we were immensely grateful as we sat down in the little restaurant. A huge plate of dumplings arrived, and Leon and I had to restrain ourselves from eating too quickly.

After we had thanked Faith profusely, we walked back into the street and discussed our options. From here, we would be rejoining the Yellow River, and the next town, Hukou, was another three days' walk away. Hukou did not look large on the map, but it was the site of a tourist attraction – the famed Hukou Waterfall, the biggest on the Yellow River. Because it was a long way from anywhere else interesting, Hukou was still only a small-to-medium-sized attraction, but we still hoped it would have a cash machine we could use.

On our way out of town we spent our final 26 RMB in a small shop. We bought ten packs of instant noodles and one processed sausage, leaving us with just three *mao*, the equivalent of two English pence. A road beside a small frozen stream led us back towards the Yellow River. As we walked we discussed our latest rookie error – running out of money. We had assumed that all towns of a reasonable size would have national banks but, in hindsight, this was not very clever of us.

As the cold dusk started to settle, the craggy brown cliffs above us glowed orange in the fading sun, and after two hours' night marching, we pitched our tents beside the frozen stream.

The next day, from a high, clifftop road, we caught sight of the Yellow River again. It now appeared a dirty white colour and, from our vantage point, seemed completely frozen. But as we looked harder, we saw that the pale mass was actually seething and flowing. When we reached the bottom of the canyon, we saw there was so much ice in the water that it looked like a torrent of white lava. Some ice slabs were the size of minibuses, and the canyon echoed with deep clunking and cracking sounds as they bashed into each other.

Apart from a very occasional motorbike, there was no traffic on the riverside road, and the canyon's stark beauty was breathtaking. For the next five hours, we also saw no villages, and by the afternoon we were running low on water. Deprived of nutritious food, and now liquid, and exhausted from having walked almost a marathon that day with the insanely heavy pack, my energy levels started to drop. Leon, the young man of the expedition, seemed to be doing better, and urged me to keep the pace up. 'Walking more slowly is not going to solve our problems,' he said. I nodded feebly, put on my iPod, and tried to walk faster.

Two hours before darkness, Leon spotted a *yaodong* village built into the cliffs, just above the road. He now looked as tired as me. I told him to have a rest while I scrambled up the little path with our thermoses and water bottles. Luckily, I also took a walking pole, because as I approached the door of the first house, a dog suddenly appeared, barking viciously. I shouted, waved my pole, and backed away. A boy in his late teens opened the door and I asked for some water.

'We do not have much,' he said, 'I can only fill two bottles.'

He took the thermoses and went inside. As I looked more carefully, I saw that this *yaodong* village looked even poorer than the others we had been to. Many of the houses seemed abandoned and dilapidated. From the boy's response there was clearly no running water, and although we had noticed the occasional, precarious terraced field on the cliffs beside the river, it must have been hard to eke out a living around here. The boy re-emerged and, after I had thanked him, I managed to fill our other two bottles from the next house.

When I got back to the road, Leon was lying on the verge, asleep. I gave him a kick and, after more noodles, we set off again.

On our final break of the day, at sunset, we sat on the empty road in silence, looking at the icy river, and bracing ourselves for a final hour of walking. The last part of a long day was always the hardest.

Leon suddenly perked up: 'I've just remembered something!'

'What?'

'You're not going to believe this, but for our roadside snack today I've got none other than . . . authentic instant cheesecake!'

Leon grinned and pulled the vacuum-wrapped packet out of his rucksack. Back in Mongolia, he had mentioned the legendary cheese-cake, which he had been given at the start of his bike ride across America, two years ago. He had kept it as his emergency rations throughout the ride but never needed to eat it. He had also brought it on this trip, and planned to take it on every expedition he went on for the rest of his life – and never eat it. But now, on only his second expedition, its time had come. He poured in some hot water, and we took it in turns to eat from the packet. It consisted of mushy sugar, and was beyond its expiry date, but to us it tasted like a Michelin-starred dessert. We licked our spoons until they were gleaming, and then Leon wistfully stuffed the empty cheesecake packet back in his rucksack.

35
To Hukou Waterfall

Distance to home: 2,060 miles

The next morning, the road wound upwards again to a clifftop village. The Michelin-starred cheesecake had long since been digested, and we felt weak. The sky was overcast, causing the temperature to drop into the −20°Cs. As we passed through the village, some old men filled our thermoses, and also gave us an unexpected but very welcome gift of a dozen beautiful red apples from a huge crate. We sat on a sofa in the reception of a small rural co-operative bank (which would not accept our bank cards), and ate noodles and apples.

By the afternoon, we were back by the river, approaching the Hukou Waterfall, where we hoped to get out some money. After that, we would cross a bridge onto the other side and bid it goodbye. I realised that we were into our final few hours of walking beside the famous torrent and it was, therefore, also my last chance to fulfil a little dare I had with myself. We took our next break just above a small sandy beach, beside which there was a calm patch of unfrozen water. There were a few pieces of ice floating on it, and it was protected from the main river by some large rocks.

'It's now or never, old boy,' I said to Leon, gulping down some warm water from my thermos. 'This is where you prove if you are a man or a mouse, or in your case, a girl.'

He knew about my dare, and did not look keen, but smiled back. 'It is not I who is the girl.'

Feeling suddenly cold, and nervous, we walked down a little path to the water's edge, and surveyed the ice. Leon set up the camera on the tripod and we stood in front of it.

'Go!' we shouted. We needed this, I thought, as I tore off my clothes and started to shiver. We needed this to inject some life and fun back into our world. I'd discovered before: there is nothing quite like jumping in a river to cheer you up. Furthermore, the sight of Leon and me jumping heroically into the icy water might repair our waning tough-guy status in front of the camera, especially after our recent grumbling, bad singing, blisters, and running out of money and food.

However, as we frantically got undressed, we both started to yelp like schoolgirls. I managed to strip faster than Leon, and shouted at him in a high-pitched voice to hurry up, while I stood looking cold and pathetic and the camera kept on rolling. When Leon was finally ready, together we shrieked and shuffled tentatively into the water. Suddenly Leon cried out, 'Ah, there is ice at the bottom,' and plunged his hands underwater to pull out a large, sharp shard.

'It doesn't matter, let's just do this quickly,' I squeaked. The beach was a gentle incline. I was only knee deep, and my legs were going numb. It was too full of ice to go much deeper. So instead of a swim, I just lay down where I was and submerged my head; as I did this my face hit a semi-floating piece of ice. That was enough of a swim for us and, seconds later, we dashed out of the water and, with lots of whooping and puffing, hurriedly threw our clothes back on.

It was not the finest hour in our quest to be tough guys. However, as we hit the road again, we walked fast, with huge smiles. I had a small cut from the ice on both my nose and my foot, but I felt alive like I hadn't done all week. At that moment, Christine phoned.

'Hi honey, did you manage to get some money out?' she asked.

'Err, not exactly. A nice student bought us lunch yesterday, and today some villagers gave us some apples.'

'Oh. How much money have you got left?'

'Err, three *mao*.'

'Three *mao!*'

'It's OK, honey, we just went for a swim in the river and we feel great now.'

'A swim! I thought it was frozen?'

I explained as best as I could. Perhaps we truly had become wild men, where going for a swim in an icy river was the highlight of our week, walking remote, frozen roads with empty stomachs just another day at the office, and running out of food and money just another humdrum problem to solve.

We were only a few miles from the Hukou Waterfall, but it was already late afternoon. I wondered whether we would hear the waterfall long before we saw it. It looked so breathtaking, glorious and majestic in all the photos I had seen.

'It should be in the next mile,' said Leon, a short while later, looking at the iPhone map.

We walked another mile, it started to get dark, and it looked as if the river beside us was beginning to freeze over. The road led into a car park, and Leon said, 'Right, we should be here.'

We looked around us and saw an entrance booth by the car park gate. We walked onwards, a little more slowly. Through the dimming light, we could see some giant billboard photos of the waterfall. They showed a leviathan of brown water, the lifeblood of China, crashing down into a gorge, before churning and spinning downstream. But we could see nothing on the river except a mass of ice, which seemed to protrude all the way across.

'It must be a bit further,' we mumbled to each other. 'The waterfall can't have frozen over.'

We kept walking, and emerged from the other end of the car park, where Leon abruptly stopped.

'I think we've passed it,' he said, zooming in on the iPhone map. 'What do you mean?'

'I think it was back there, beyond the frozen river. We must have walked straight past without realising.'

This was definitely not the triumphant sighting we had been hoping for. We stood looking back, but it was now almost pitch dark. We could barely even make out the frozen river.

'It's too late tonight anyway,' said Leon. 'Let's stay in the town and come back tomorrow morning.'

We kept walking, and a few minutes later saw the lights of Hukou town emerging through the darkness. There was a bridge across the river, which we would cross the following day, and also a promising-looking main street, full of tacky tourist restaurants and a hotel.

'Why don't you wait there and rest?' I said to Leon, pointing at the hotel. 'I'll go and look for a cash machine.'

Leon pulled out our last two apples, our last two items of food, handed me one, and I set off up the street. I walked past a dozen restaurants, and the people inside, all Chinese, stared at me through the glass, and I stared back at their dishes of meat and vegetables. I found two cash machines, but yet again they belonged to the rural co-operatives, and I walked back to the hotel, dejected.

Leon had just finished his final apple when I broke the news. We were now completely out of food and money. The next town was yet another three-day walk away and, even then, there was no guarantee that it would have a cash machine we could use. On the road we had brainstormed a plan of last resort: find a taxi driver, pay him to drive us to the nearest city (almost 100 miles away), withdraw some money, and drive back here. The time had come to put it into action.

The hotel receptionist called up a cabbie and, a few minutes later, in he walked. He was short, with a cheeky, boyish expression on his face. It did not take him long to figure out that Leon and I had no bargaining power whatsoever. After pretending to haggle with us for a few minutes, he magnanimously agreed to take us to the city of Xiangning and back, for the hefty sum of 450 RMB (£45). This was probably three days' wages for him, and three days' living expenses for us. But it was almost 9 p.m., and we were too tired and hungry to argue. We shook hands to prove that we were all gentlemen, and then we jumped in his car and off we went.

The high street fled past, and we whooshed up into the hills. I slumped into my seat at the front. The cabbie was eager to make sure we were comfortable and turned up the heating.

'Is it too cold?' he asked.

'No, this is fine,' I said, enjoying the hot blast.

'Music?' he asked, to my surprise putting on some acoustic jazz guitar.

'Thank you,' I smiled.

I looked behind me and saw Leon sprawled out across the back seat. 'Well, this is expensive,' I said, 'but I don't think we had any other option. I just hope this guy knows where the cash machine is, or he's not going to get paid, and we're not going to get dinner.'

'He seems pretty confident,' mumbled Leon, with his eyes still closed. 'I actually think he's a bit of a Mr Wolf from *Pulp Fiction*.'

'Yeah, he does seem that way.' I turned to the cabbie and said in English. 'We think you're a bit of a Chinese Mr Wolf, is that right?'

Mr Wolf did not understand, but grinned and put his foot down on the accelerator.

Leon seemed to have fallen asleep. I reclined my seat, pulled my woolly hat over my eyes and let out a contented groan. After months of walking at four miles an hour in the extreme cold, it was wonderful to move at such speed and in such comfort. I felt as though I was travelling first class on British Airways.

After two hours we descended a long hill, and arrived in Xiangning, where Mr Wolf pulled up beside an international Chinese bank. We nervously inserted our first card, and to our relief 3,000 RMB (£300), the maximum limit, churned into our hands. We used our other card to get out 3,000 RMB more – we did not want to make the same mistake again. We cheered and gave Mr Wolf the thumbs-up sign as we got back in the car. He gave us a grin, and roared us round the corner to a Chinese KFC rip-off to celebrate. We bought ourselves two huge portions of fries and four giant chicken burgers. Once we were back in our first-class seats, Mr Wolf flicked his cigarette out of the window, and we disappeared back into the night.

'Next time I do an expedition,' I said to Leon, taking a huge bite from my second burger, 'I want to do it by taxi or, at the very least, hitchhiking.'

'I'll second that,' said Leon with his mouth full, sprawling out further.

Mr Wolf swerved around another corner, and smiled at the pile of banknotes that we had paid him, now laid out on his dashboard.

36
Mr Wolf

Distance to home: 2,029 miles

In the cult movie *Pulp Fiction*, John Travolta and Samuel L. Jackson play two eccentric hit men who, while driving their car down a busy urban street, accidentally shoot their colleague in the head, splattering blood all over the windows. Knowing they are likely to get spotted by the police, they urgently phone up their boss, who tells them to go to a location where they will meet an apparently infamous man called 'Mr Wolf'. Mr Wolf arrives, and quickly reveals himself to be a businessman type, highly decisive and no-nonsense; a man who can keep a calm head when disaster is imminent; a man who gets you out of your predicament, whatever that predicament may be. Within minutes of arriving, he has cleaned the car, disposed of the body and, therefore, in short, fixed the problem.

As we arrived back in Hukou, Mr Wolf told us we could sleep at his friend's house. 'How much does it cost?' we asked, a little wary of how much he had already extracted from us.

'Don't worry, don't worry,' he said, waving his hand, as if to say the least he could do after the cab fare was to find us a free place to sleep. He led us up to a small, freezing box room, full of crates of apples. It was simple, but ideal for us, and we dropped our packs in relief. Mr Wolf then told us, with another grin, that it would cost 50 RMB (£5). This was good value, but we still felt he had outfoxed us. As he left, he said he would take us to see the waterfall the next morning – he knew just who to talk to. We asked how much, and although Mr Wolf responded with another cryptic wave of his hand, we still agreed to his offer: it was hard to say no to Mr Wolf.

*

The next morning, shortly after we woke, Mr Wolf appeared. While we packed, he started grabbing handfuls of apples from the crates and insisting we take them. We were not sure whose room we had just slept in, or whose apples these were, but Mr Wolf was happily in charge.

We screeched back to the riverside car park. Just as we had seen through the dying light of the previous evening, the river seemed entirely frozen, or at least an ice shelf stretched most of the way across it. But we could now also make out that the ice was spread thinly over a layer of rocks. An icy concrete path led through the rocky-icy jumble, presumably to the waterfall. But it looked precarious, and was blocked by a chain.

Mr Wolf shook his head and said, 'You cannot see the waterfall; the river is all frozen, and you're not allowed out along the path.' Suddenly, as if on cue, an old man wandered towards us. He looked like a car park attendant, and seemed to know Mr Wolf. They chatted for a moment, and with a nod and a smile the attendant lifted the chain that blocked our way.

'This man works here,' said Mr Wolf. 'He says we can go out onto the ice and have a look at the waterfall. But we have to be quick and get back before the ticket sellers arrive.'

So, following Mr Wolf, Leon and I walked cautiously out onto the concrete path. It weaved through the frozen build-up until we found ourselves walking on the ice itself. A little further on, we started to hear the sound of thundering water; all of a sudden a chasm opened up before us, and we could see a mass of river rapids swirling into it. Mr Wolf held out his arm.

'Stop here,' he said, and indicated dramatically that we were now standing on a shelf of ice overhanging the waterfall – if we were not careful, the whole thing would collapse into the gorge.

We inched a tiny bit closer and, by standing on tiptoes, could see the top of the waterfall. It was a gap measuring some fifteen metres wide, and through this squeezed millions of gallons of water, and millions of tonnes of yellow earth. It all crashed down and into oblivion. We did some filming and Mr Wolf kept pulling us back.

We concluded that if even Mr Wolf was afraid of the ice shelf collapsing, indeed there must be danger.

After a few minutes, Mr Wolf insisted our time was up. We retreated to the car park and he drove us back to town. As we prepared to say goodbye, he produced a couple of dog-eared entry tickets to the Hukou Waterfall, and announced we must pay him another 300 RMB (£30).

Mr Wolf had got us with the expensive taxi ride last night, and a place to sleep, but now he had overreached himself – the tickets were obviously old, and it was he who had no bargaining power now. We gave him 30 RMB – small change, but still more than the cost of a taxi ride to the waterfall and back. Mr Wolf held out his hand with a forlorn expression. 'Not enough,' he said.

'Sorry, Mr Wolf,' we said, smiling, and pointing out that the tickets were clearly second-hand.

He saw that the game was up but, rather than getting angry, he gave a 'you can't blame a man for trying' shrug. Then he flashed his cheeky smile again and asked if we wanted a lift to Yichuan, the next town on our route.

'No thank you, we're walking,' we explained, shaking his hand goodbye, and we all laughed. That was something I loved about China – even if you had a tussle about money with someone, once the negotiations were over, whatever the outcome, there was usually an attitude of 'no hard feelings'.

We popped into a shop to buy more supplies because it was two days' walk to Yichuan, and as we came out we saw Mr Wolf driving past in his taxi.

'Are you sure you don't want a lift?' he yelled, without stopping the car.

'No thanks Mr Wolf!' we shouted back. He gave us a toot, flipped a U-turn in front of an oncoming coal truck and revved merrily away. We would not see him again. Good luck, drive carefully, Mr Wolf.

As we crossed the bridge we took a final look at the Yellow River. It seethed underneath us in a cauldron of rapids and ice, and disappeared out of sight around the bend. It would now run down, down, down to the ancient floodplains, and ultimately out into the Yellow Sea a thousand miles away to the east. But we needed to keep going west. On the other side of the bridge, as another mass of loess cliffs rose before us, we took our first steps into our third Chinese province – Shaanxi. It was a confusingly similar name to the previous province of Shanxi, and we wondered if we would be able to pronounce it correctly.

37
Foreigners not allowed

Distance to home: 2,024 miles

Two hours after we left the Yellow River and climbed back into the loess hills, we reached a fork: to the left, a minor lane wound down into a gorge; straight on was a motorway. The motorway had a sign banning tractors, mopeds, animals, cyclists and pedestrians. A police car was parked beside the slip road, and three policemen watched us approach.

'Well, both roads lead to where we want to go,' said Leon, scanning the iPhone, 'but I'm not sure those officers would appreciate it if we took the motorway.'

We gave the policemen a friendly wave and forked left onto the smaller road. It descended steeply, while above us the motorway bridged the gully on giant concrete stilts. As we rounded the corner, we saw that as the motorway reached a mountain, it simply tunnelled straight through it.

'The motorway must be half the distance, and it doesn't have any climbs or descents,' said Leon as we puffed back out of the gorge. A truck roared past, and we leant against the barrier to get out of its way.

'And it's definitely more dangerous down here,' I said. 'There's probably a hard shoulder up there.'

The smooth motorway continued to taunt us, and we started debating whether we should try sneaking onto it for a while. We had had a few more police encounters recently – usually when a patrol car stopped to see who we were. All they did was look at our passports and let us go. Feeling hopeavistic, therefore, we convinced ourselves that if the police caught us on a 'Pedestrians not allowed' road, the worst they would do was tell us off and make us go back on the small road. And besides, it would be a fun and adventurous alternative to the country lanes for a while.

With our minds made up, we scanned the broken slopes until we spotted a sheep track that led us up to the edge of the motorway. A few minutes later we were strolling onto the beautiful smooth tarmac. It rolled ahead of us, across chasms, and through mountains, without turning, twisting or deviating, like an ideal Roman road. Immediately, our pace increased to our maximum speed of four miles per hour. As hoped, we also had a wide hard shoulder, and this turned into a slither of pavement when we reached the tunnels. The tunnels were up to half a mile long, and they bore us effortlessly through the mountains that blocked our path. There was also little traffic – probably because the toll fees were hefty. Most local traffic would prefer the free but slow road below. As we passed over a bridge we saw the little road twisting along beside the stream, and we were elated to be making double the progress we normally would in this terrain.

We had been going less than half an hour, when a police car appeared.

'Just keep walking,' I whispered at Leon. There was nowhere to hide.

We watched the highway patrol car out of the corners of our eyes. It was new and polished, and two young policemen stared at us through the windscreen, mystified. But although they slowed slightly, a moment later they accelerated away.

We relaxed again. 'I guess if they pretend they haven't seen us, we're not their problem,' said Leon.

Two days of smooth motorway cruising later, we needed to turn south. Our next landmark was the ancient capital of Xian, about 200 miles to the southwest. We climbed off the motorway embankment and continued along a smaller road, which led down a narrow valley. Fertile fields lined the roadside, and the valley slopes were filled with dense pine forests. The air was fresh and fragrant and the daytime temperature had warmed to only a few degrees below zero. Just as we were beginning to enjoy striding through this new environment, a car pulled up and a man wearing glasses leaned his head out of the window and spoke to us in English. He nodded down the road and said, 'Foreigners are not allowed on this road, or in the town at the end of this valley.'

'What do you mean?'

'Foreigners are not allowed,' he repeated. 'The police will catch you, and turn you back or arrest you.'

We tried to press him further, but he did not want to go into details and, after advising us again to go around the valley, he drove off.

Leon and I looked at each other. What did he mean?

'It's at least an extra two or three days if we go around it,' said Leon, looking at the iPhone. 'I don't think we've got any choice. I think we probably just have to go for it, and hope we don't get into trouble.'

'Or at least too much trouble,' I said. We shrugged and started to walk again.

I held my poles more tightly in my hands, and found myself scanning the tree line. Leon pointed out some red signs planted in the fields. We could not read them, but they had a distinct 'keep out' feel. Could this be one of those small, scattered localities of China that was still a 'closed zone'? From what we had read about 'closed zones', they existed because of a military, possibly nuclear, presence. After being a bit cavalier about our recent police encounters, I was suddenly nervous. If we got caught, would they be more likely to take issue with the cameras? I tried to push images of imprisonment or deportation out of my mind, and we decided to keep the main camera out of sight, and film only with the GoPro strapped to my chest.

The town at the end of the valley, Huanglong, was still twenty miles away, so that night we would have to camp. As it got dark we approached a village, which we hoped to slip through unnoticed before pitching our tents somewhere on the other side. To be more discreet, we turned off our head torches and started to carry instead of clink our poles. A lady walked out of a shack in her yard and entered her house. We thought that she had not seen us, but then a light shone against the trees beside me – she had seen us, and had come back out with a torch.

'Just keep walking,' we muttered to each other, and a moment later we were safely back in the gloom, and invisible. Fear now tainted our world.

'That lady's shack looked like a Vietnamese torture cell,' joked Leon in a whisper.

A few minutes later we heard some loud bangs coming from the village.

'Those sound more like gunshots than fireworks,' I said.

A mile beyond the village, we pitched our tents quietly in the corner of a cornfield.

After an uneasy night's sleep we were back on the road at dawn. Although the valley looked less menacing in daylight, we still walked hard and fast. At 8 a.m. we dared to stop at a little cluster of bungalows to fill our thermoses. Some wrinkled, toothy farmers grinned and gave us hot water and sweet-bean-filled buns. Thankfully they did not look as if they were going to perform a citizen's arrest on us.

Later, some dreamy snow started to fall, and by mid-afternoon, everything had turned white. We began to think we might make it to the town, after which we would just need to sneak through its outskirts and out the other side. When we had just eight miles to go, Leon was walking a hundred metres ahead of me, and the snow had almost ceased. But suddenly a police car was driving towards us, its lights flashing. It stopped beside Leon and two policemen climbed out. They handed something to him. Adrenaline started to thump through me. Leon was speaking to them, though I was still far out of earshot. He appeared to be pointing up and down the road, and telling our usual joke about walking through beautiful but cold China. However, as far as I could tell, the police were not amused. A second police car arrived, and another policeman climbed out.

I drew nearer, and they all stopped talking and turned to watch me arrive.

'Hello,' I said. No one replied and a policeman handed me a piece of paper. I looked at Leon, who looked very sombre and raised his eyebrows at me.

The paper had some big official-looking stamps on it and, printed in English, was the following:

Foreigner, you have broken the law. You are trespassing in a region of the People's Republic of China where foreigners are not permitted. You must make yourself completely obedient to whatever the police officers command of you.

My breathing became shallow. This was a potentially grave situation. Were we being arrested? Were they going to search our bags?

'Get in the car,' one of the policemen said, opening the door.

The car did a U-turn and headed towards the town – in the same direction we had been walking. It was warm inside, and I felt a strange mixture of comfort and jitters. Although the police had only spoken to us in Chinese so far, I thought they might know some English. Both Leon and I spoke a little Spanish and French, so we switched to a sort of English-Spanish-French hybrid to make sure the police would not understand.

'*Que pasa tu penses?*' (What's going on?) Leon said.

'Don't ask me,' I said, 'let's just *jugar* the *estupido* foreigner card.' (Let's just play the dumb foreigner card.)

A few minutes later we entered the town. It looked completely normal – no big missile bases to be seen, just the usual bustle of people, and shops selling clothes and televisions and fish. At the police station we were led into the office of the most senior policeman. He told us to sit on the small hard sofa, and again questioned us about what we were doing.

'We are walking through China – what a beautiful country it is!' we said several more times. One of the other policemen came in and asked for our passports and walked out with them. A part of me was still dreading that they would search our bags and take issue with the camera, but gradually, as we continued making small talk, the policemen softened. Another policeman brought in cups of tea. Everyone suddenly seemed a bit awkward.

A few minutes later a lady in her twenties came in to join the tea party. 'I am the daughter of a policeman,' she said in excellent English. 'I work as an airline hostess for Qatar Airways.' She talked with the boss for a few minutes, before turning to us and apologising that we had been arrested but, unfortunately, foreigners were not allowed in this area. We apologised in return and said we hadn't realised, which was reasonably true since we had not known how credible that one random man had been.

'There were no signposts saying it was a restricted area,' we said.

'No, there are no signs,' everyone agreed.

'We were not to know.'

'No, you were not to know.'

'Maybe you could put up some signs for the next foreigners?'

Everyone smiled politely.

The conversation continued with more questions, more explanations, more friendly apologies from both sides. Increasingly, they were happy to hear about our walk, and pleased that we were walking through huge, beautiful China, and meeting lots and lots of friendly people. The mood softened, and some smiles cracked at last, even on the chief's face.

After an hour, they told us we could soon leave, but because the closed zone continued on the other side of the town, they would give us a lift through it.

The police car drove us on through the town and dropped us in the mountains on the other side of the closed zone. As we said goodbye, the policemen took it in turns to take cheery photographs with their arms around our shoulders.

38
Spring

Distance to home: 1,894 miles

13 FEBRUARY

I felt relieved that we had made it through the closed zone without serious trouble, though it was a shame that we had been forced to 'cheat' a little by taking a ride in a police car for twenty miles. However, it certainly counted as 'legitimate cheating' because we had no choice. We wondered whether there would be any more closed zones on our route and hoped that by doing more research we could avoid them.

The road led us down onto a hazy plain – the first large area of flat land since the Gobi, and the start of a new landscape. The next day, we passed through a deep canyon. As we walked downwards, the temperature rose above zero for the first time on the trip. The river at the bottom ran smoothly, without a hint of ice, and it was getting so warm that I even removed my gloves. We stopped for some noodles and I was astonished to see a fly buzzing around my feet: our first insect of the expedition. In the afternoon we met some villagers sweeping up dross and burning it in little bonfires beside the road. All these signs led to only one conclusion: we were on the cusp of spring.

A lot had happened in the last seven days. We had seen the magnificent fifteenth day Chinese New Year celebrations in Daning, swum in the icy Yellow River, run out of money, walked down a mountain-piercing motorway, and even been arrested for walking through a closed zone. Throughout all this, our tiredness had been steadily deepening. Life felt out of control in many ways but, by pressing forwards, we were doing OK. And if the weather was going to warm up – well, surely things were going to get easier.

But we could not start to enjoy the temperate climes quite yet, for the time had come to put into action the plan – conceived in desperation – to return to the wintry wastelands of Mongolia.

39
Code Z

Distance to home: 1,819 miles

One could be forgiven for romanticising the lifestyle of an adventurer, if one's views were based solely upon TV documentaries and glossy travel books. The reality is somewhat different. Much of an expedition is full of monotony – slogging through day after day of hard, painful footsteps; endless identical conversations with strangers; growing bored of one's own company. While there are plenty of magnificent moments of extreme beauty, hospitality, adrenaline and hilarity, there are also long hours when nothing much happens at all. And when something does happen, it is often in the form of an obstacle to be bypassed, or a problem to be solved. On previous expeditions, I had to do a number of slightly ludicrous things to overcome such obstacles and problems, ranging from sneaking through military checkpoints at 3 a.m. in Tibet, to balancing a bicycle on a canoe to cross unbridged rivers in Papua New Guinea. These were all part of the adventure, and a healthy sense of the absurd was one of the most important traits necessary to prevent everything becoming too stressful.

Throw into the mix the challenge of making a TV show, however, and the challenges take on a whole new dimension.

Our 'Code Z' had two key goals. Firstly, to leave China and re-enter it, thus renewing our visa for another three months (which we needed to do at this point anyway). Secondly, to shoot, in focus, two days' worth of footage of ourselves walking around the Mongolian desert with Molly.

Implementing this plan was far from simple. We would have to fly to Beijing, successfully apply for a new Mongolian visa, fly to Erlian and cross the border back into Mongolia, retrieve Molly and head back into the desert for filming and finally cross back into China again and fly back to the place where we had stopped walking. The whole operation would take nine days – days we could ill afford – and would use up almost our entire contingency budget of £1,000. But we felt it was worth it, because it was the one way we could fix the grievous focus fiasco. At the same time, it was quite a risky plan, and there were a number of things that could go wrong: missing flights (we had four to catch within eight days), not getting the visas, trouble crossing borders, and failing to find Molly.

Our first flight was from Xian airport, and as the airport was not on our route, we planned to get as close as possible to it, mark our spot, and catch a taxi. The flight was on 16 February. However, as if to illustrate the unexpected problems that can arise, on 13 February, when we were nicely on track, Christine double-checked with the Mongolian Embassy and found out they were about to shut for Mongolian New Year. This would prevent us from getting our Mongolian visas in Beijing. We scrambled for a new plan – rebooking the flights for the following day, 14 February. We marched quickly to our next city, Pucheng, and jumped in a taxi. A few hours later we were in the air.

'The captain has switched off the seat belt sign, please enjoy your flight. Our arrival time in Beijing will be 12.05 a.m.'

I looked across at Leon who was already dozing in the seat next to me. Outside the world was black. But I knew well what was down below – the loess mountains of Shanxi. It had taken us almost two blister-filled months to walk through them. Memories of walking along the Wall, getting lost by the Yellow River, and trudging through coal valleys flooded through my head. And yet the flight to Beijing (which was over 200 miles beyond Datong) would take barely ninety minutes.

We had two days in Beijing, and were kindly hosted by Christine's old friend Enoch and her fiancé Tim. We set out early the next morning to hand in our passports at the Mongolian Embassy. This done, we wandered the streets of the capital in an elated daze. After the *yaodong* villages and remote frozen valleys, Beijing felt like a different country. Everything was bigger and greater – wider roads, more traffic, grander buildings. The grey blanket of hazy pollution was thicker. There seemed to be a Starbucks on every other street corner. It was also a welcome novelty that people no longer stared at us, for there were plenty of other Caucasians around – business people and travellers, old and young. In the evening, we went to a party with Enoch and Tim, where everyone was looking chic in the latest fashion, and Leon and I, wearing our matching 'his and hers' sponsored puffa jackets, felt slightly out of place.

We successfully picked up our Mongolian visas, and boarded a plane back to Erlian, the border town on the Chinese side. As we landed I stroked my face with my hands, and was surprised by its smoothness. In Beijing, I had shaved off my beard, because for the reshoot to work it was essential that I resembled as much as possible how I had looked when we started the walk. Leon, meanwhile, was not keen to shave. We agreed that if he appeared on camera at all, he would have to wear his balaclava – the mysterious man with no face. But the most crucial thing for continuity was that we found Molly, and to find Molly we would have to find Urult the money-changer.

As we walked out of Erlian airport in daylight, it felt different from the night three months previously when we had attempted to sleep there and had our first encounter with the Chinese police. This time we looked like conventional tourists arriving by plane; as we strolled past, I smiled at the policemen. One of them frowned in a flicker of recognition.

A taxi drove us towards the town, fifteen miles away. We noticed that although it was February, there was a lot less snow around than when we were first here, which again might look strange on camera. We would just have to do our best with the filming, making use of the banks of snow that had blown into piles.

As we drove past the route we had walked and saw all the empty desert land, it was bizarre what things had stuck in our memory.

'That's where we stopped for a noodle break,' said Leon, pointing to a lay-by.

'And, that's where you went for a Mr Lax,' I said, pointing to a rock.

Alongside walking and filming, our concerns had distilled down to life's most basic necessities.

When we reached the kissing dinosaur archway above the road, we got out, and spent an hour walking around filming, with me trying to look and speak as if I was taking my first, nervous steps into China. I had never been much of an actor – I was far too shy as a child – but now my moment of Oscar nominee glory had come. Back in Erlian, we filmed ourselves walking the streets as if we had just crossed the border – we were acting everything out backwards.

The next morning, we crossed back into Mongolia. Zamiin-Uud had not changed – it was still a grubby, frozen border town – and the sense of drab dilapidation seemed even more glaring compared to the sense of progress we had seen in Chinese towns.

Our first major task was to find Molly. We had been hoping that Urult would still be sitting in his shiny car outside the train station listening to 'Coolplay', and also that he would have kept his promise to look after Molly. But when we arrived, he and his car were nowhere to be seen. We rolled our eyes. This was the last thing we needed, having come all the way back here. Leon went shopping for food supplies, and I continued with the hunt. I eventually met a jeep driver who spoke English. He said that Urult had gone to Ulaanbaatar.

This was not good news. If Urult had left, what were the chances of finding Molly? The jeep driver suggested that I meet Sasha – Urult's older brother, the big boss in town. I was led into a building, and up to a room where Sasha sat behind a desk, Don Corleone-style, with a crony by his side. Neither of us understood a word the other was saying, apart from 'Urult'. After my attempts to describe Molly with squeaking noises and sweeping hand gestures had failed, I remembered the laptop, and flicked onto a picture of Molly. Sasha's eyes lit up. He issued a quick command to the crony, who led me into a yard and pointed underneath a parked truck. I stooped down to have a look, and there, safe and sound, sat Molly. She looked overjoyed that we had come to rescue her.

Early the next morning, we hired a jeep and a driver who drove us fifteen miles north, and dropped us in the middle of the desert. Then followed a surreal thirty hours of dragging Molly hither and thither across the plains and into the hills, again pretending we were passing through for the first time. On the afternoon of the second day, we reached the top of a hill and decided to call it a day.

It would be very hard to hitchhike back to town with Molly, so we decided to leave her on top of a hill. We did, however, make a note of the surrounding hills and tracks. An adventure friend of Leon's, Charlie Walker, was planning to walk through the Gobi in a couple of months' time. Leon would send him a kind of treasure map of how to find Molly.* We flagged down a passing car back to Zamiin-Uud, crossed back into China (acquiring our new three-month visa stamp on the way), and then caught our flights, via Beijing to Xian, and another taxi back to the city of Pucheng, where we had stopped walking nine days previously.

Sitting in the *ludian* that night, I said to Leon, 'Well I think that was a great success.'

'Yes, all things considered.' Leon looked relieved.

We had discussed at length any moral qualms about the reshoot. Were we duping viewers? Only within the bounds of being creative to make a show, we felt. Code Z was not the equivalent to, say, pretending we had done something we had not in order to make our lives easier. In fact, it had made our lives a lot harder, and we were just repeating something we had already done. We had no regrets.

Leon pulled out the whisky, took his swig and handed it to me.

I passed it back and said, 'I think you definitely deserve a double swig tonight. You've done really well with this. Code Z was a daring idea, and the darned thing actually worked.'

'Thanks,' said Leon. He tipped the flask back again, and I could see that a huge weight had fallen from his shoulders.

In addition to getting the needed footage, the Code Z palaver had also made us realise how, although we were inexperienced and

* Unfortunately, by the time Charlie got there, she was gone. Hopefully she had found a good new home with the local nomads.

cavalier when we set out, we had come a long way with our filming and teamwork. This trip was proving to be a baptism of fire (and ice) for both of us, especially for Leon, as he faced the brunt of the filming pressure. He was rising well to the challenge.

40
The Warriors

Distance to home: 1,729 miles

We now had less than a week until Christine was coming to meet us; as we resumed walking towards Xian, it felt as though we had entered a new phase of the expedition. The hints of spring from before Code Z had become more pronounced. Even at night, the temperature remained above zero. By day, although the sky was a dull, hazy grey, it was warm enough to stuff our down jackets and gloves away in our rucksacks and, instead, stroll along with bare hands, wearing a mere double layer of thermal tops. Amazingly, my foot was by now feeling quite strong, and I was almost back to walking at full speed.

The land was also changing. The flat plains were starting to brim with budding orchards and freshly ploughed vegetable fields. Clusters of farmers were hard at work, bringing life back to the world. We also passed through bigger towns in the midst of rapid expansion – whole new streets of apartments were going up, and sometimes half the buildings looked less than a year old. The narrow road, meanwhile, buzzed with agricultural traffic and buses. Whenever possible, we cut along little paths beside irrigation canals.

We seemed to have fallen smoothly back into our old routine. On our second day, at lunchtime, we sat on a muddy mound and went through the familiar procedure of pouring boiling water onto our instant noodles. On roadside breaks, instant noodles were still the easiest meal. However, on this particular day, both Leon and I had a simultaneous revelation.

'Hmm,' I said, 'these noodles aren't tasting so good today.'

Leon looked up from his bowl. 'You know what, I was just thinking the same thing.'

'In fact, I hope I never see instant noodles again in my whole life.'

'Me too. Want some peanuts?'

After three solid months of noodles, we had reached our limit. If they had been a little boring before, now they had become about as appetising as mouldy bread – OK if we were starving, but otherwise more suitable for the dustbin. We had not been able to buy takeaway meals from cheap local restaurants, because they would always freeze before we had a chance to eat them. But now, takeaways would be our strategy for instant noodle avoidance.

That night we turned our head torches on and strolled into a nice field in search of a place to camp. We were quickly startled by a night watchman's flashlight shining at us and some shouting. We backed away and walked another mile before trying again. This time we were more covert, and kept our torches off. When we reached the middle of the field we pulled out our bivvy bags for the first time. These were dark green, lightweight Gore-Tex bags, which could be used instead of a tent. We had been carrying them since Datong, in the hope that we could post our tents home and use these, but it had been too cold until now. Tonight, however, was ideal. It was warmer, and we wanted to make ourselves less visible. We climbed inside the bags and lay down next to our rucksacks. None but the most conscientious of night watchmen would be able to spot us tonight.

About eight miles from where we lay down in our bivvy bags, on one spring morning thirty-eight years previously, a few local farmers had got up and gone out to dig a well. Several metres down, a farmer, Yang Zhifa, who was at the bottom of the pit, hit something solid. It seemed to be manmade, and he thought it might be some old pottery that he could sell. But, as he dug more, he discovered it was actually a statue of some kind. The local authorities were duly informed, and archaeologists arrived to take a look and have a dig for themselves.

To their astonishment, they began to unearth one statue after another: an entire army of military figures. And, more astonishing still, these were not just any old statues. Rather, they had been built as part of the tomb complex of the most famous of all Chinese Emperors, Emperor Qin – the man who had first united China into one Empire, and who had in so many ways defined its future.

Ancient historical accounts had given fantastical descriptions of Emperor Qin's tomb – a mausoleum the size of a small mountain. It was said to have had life-size replicas of Qin's palaces, and a huge replica of the Empire – with rivers of mercury to depict the waterways. It had apparently taken thirty-eight years to build, using a slave army of 700,000. However, because it had never been discovered, much modern scholarship had thought the accounts were greatly exaggerated.

But after two thousand years of lying silent and forgotten beneath the ground, the unearthed figures – now known as the Terracotta Warriors, or Terracotta Army – changed everyone's minds. For although the statues were not even mentioned in the ancient accounts (perhaps because they were seen as a small sideshow compared to the main tomb), they proved the scale of the works, and it was not long before the tomb itself was identified, about a mile away, inside a manmade hill.

In the morning, Leon and I packed up our bivvy bags; after two hours of walking, the fields around us turned to concrete. The fields that Yang Zhifa used to farm were now covered with a vast archipelago of restaurants, car parks and shops selling life-sized replicas of the warriors. We walked through the maze and joined a throng of tourists disembarking from buses and trooping towards the entrance.

'There's the big man himself,' said Leon, turning on the camera.

Overlooking the car parks stood a large statue of Emperor Qin.

'He doesn't look like the kind of guy you'd want to have a drink with,' I said.

The statue depicted a powerful man with a hard face. The historical accounts had given him a reputation for being a callous, brutal and authoritarian leader. Millions of lives were lost to his building projects – not only this tomb complex, but also the roads, canals and the early Great Wall. He was a military leader, having destroyed other kingdoms in his quest to unite the Empire. And significantly, in contrast to emperors who came after him, he was not a fan of Confucius or his emphasis on virtuous, exemplary leadership. Rather, Qin ruled by a harsh doctrine known as legalism, with a code of punishments for all who failed to show total obedience. He also did not appreciate those who disagreed with him. Most infamously, he was alleged to have had thousands of important Confucian books burnt, and 460 Confucian scholars buried alive.

We paid our entrance fee, passed through the gate, and walked towards the first and biggest of the buildings – the size of an aircraft hangar – that housed the famous warriors. I had actually visited the site before, in the middle of my bike trip. Back then I had virtually no understanding of Chinese history; without the proper context, although they were impressive, the statues did not blow my mind. But this time I knew more about China, and what this Emperor had created. His Empire was so vast that it was taking Leon and me six months to walk down through it – largely on good roads, in a time of peace and safety. And he had united and ruled this place over 2,000 years ago.

As we walked into the building, I knew what to expect, but I was still surprised. The warriors were standing exactly as they had been last time I was here, faithfully in rows. They were still guarding their Emperor, just as they had done through the many long centuries. They seemed so human, and yet enchanted, growing out of the ground like ghoulish soldiers from a Hollywood B-movie. The guidebooks were full of interesting facts. There are thought to be over 8,000 warriors in total, though only about a quarter of these have been excavated so far. The figures were not mass produced, but rather seem to have been modelled upon a real army, for they are all entirely individual. They have different ranks, armour, facial expressions, ages and lengths of beard. But what they do have in common is that they are unarmed and their hands are empty and half clenched. Their weapons were perhaps looted shortly after they were made; or, if made from wood, have rotted away over the centuries. Their faces, meanwhile, are human and intent – a little afraid, perhaps, and yet steeled for battle and their fate as foot soldiers of the Emperor.

The Terracotta Army reflected not only the power and wealth of the first Emperor, but also his obsession with his own life, and life after death. Research has shown a remarkably consistent set of beliefs about the afterlife in ancient China: one's tomb should contain items that were needed in the next life. Qin wanted an army on standby, near to the palatial tomb in which he had been buried with sacrificed concubines and servants.

After his unexpected death (quite possibly from drinking a potion that his magicians said was the elixir of life), there was a succession crisis involving dastardly eunuchs, heirs forced to commit suicide, and then revolt and civil war. The dynasty that he had founded, and hoped would last for a thousand generations, did not outlast him by even a couple of decades. And so continued the bloody relay baton of the 'Mandate of Heaven', passed on through the centuries from one severed hand to the next. What did survive him was the idea of a coherent, united China.

Although the warriors have now been liberated from the earth, they are still servants of the State, the new Communist China, displaying the nation's former glory for millions of tourists every year. We walked through the crowds, and back out past Emperor Qin's statue at the entrance. He looked down disapprovingly on us visitors who were still alive, and I looked back up at his stern face. I had read that although he was undoubtedly harsh, like the early historical sources said, it was perhaps unfair to brand him as worse than many of the other emperors. Many of them were unimaginably brutal.*

Twenty minutes after leaving the tourist zone, we reached a large park, dominated by a giant hill. Inside this hill was the Emperor's tomb; until the discovery of the Terracotta Army, it had also been lost for 2,000 years. The task of building the mountain-tomb has been compared, in terms of scale, to the pyramids. We gazed up at

---

* Many European rulers through the ages were, of course, no better. The negativity of Qin's reputation was partly due to the fact that his main chronicler, Sima Qian, was a Confucian scholar from the Han dynasty. Naturally, to further legitimise their own rule, the Han dynasty wanted to show that Qin was a bad emperor.

it wistfully – fifty metres high, and covered in trees. However, although it has been proved that it does indeed contain the Emperor's mausoleum, archaeologists have (tantalisingly, but probably wisely) still never opened it up. They say they still lack the right technology, though of course conspiracy theories abound. I, for one, hope I live to see the day when its secrets are revealed.

41
Tunnel of Doom

Distance to home: 1,679 miles

26–28 FEBRUARY

The next day we finally arrived in Xian, the ancient capital, but now something of a concrete jungle. However, it had been hard to estimate our arrival date in advance, so we had ended up arriving forty-eight hours early for Christine and our much-needed five-day break. Rather than waste precious days waiting, Leon and I decided to keep walking and two days later we would mark our spot on the map and hitchhike back. We would have a chance to explore Xian more then, and the rest days would be all the sweeter for our extra miles.

So we walked straight out of the other side of Xian, and by lunchtime found ourselves walking across another hazy plain.

'I could get used to walking on flat ground like this,' I said. 'How long until we reach the next mountains?' We knew from the Google satellite map that south from Xian, almost until the coast, we would face line after line of rugged country.

'Probably about an hour,' said Leon, scanning the iPhone map as he walked.

Out of the haze, a vast ghostly shadow on the horizon started to form into a more solid shape – the Qinling Mountains. As we got closer, we saw that the Qinling were very different to the mountains of the north. They rose up in a more angular and vertical way, because they were made from hard limestone, rather than the soft loess that was easily moulded by rain and wind. They were also far less arid – a tangle of thick, subtropical vegetation wrapped itself around the pale cliff faces and glancing peaks, and little streams cascaded down. A winding lane led us upwards, and the mountains kept rising higher until they disappeared. It felt as though we were entering the world of ancient Chinese swordsmen and flying daggers. An enormous motorway appeared, once again boring through the cliff faces, and our road started weaving along underneath it.

The Qinling were a formidable barrier to cross; positioned as they were just south of the ancient capital, they had exerted great historical and cultural influences on China. However, for now, Leon and I were not thinking about their significance, but rather how far we could get through them in the next day and a half. Although we had reached Xian early for Christine, this did not mean we were 'ahead of schedule'. The foot injury, the focus fiasco and the nine days spent on Code Z meant that it was now inevitable that our remaining three months in China would be quite gruelling. It therefore made good sense to get as far as we could before our break. And there was one obvious way for us to do this: the Zhongnanshan Tunnel.

This tunnel was not like the short motorway tunnels we had walked through thus far. Those had usually been less than half a mile long, and we could easily see the light at both ends, even when we were in the middle. The Zhongnanshan Tunnel, at 18,040 metres (over eleven miles), was the longest road tunnel in all of China, and the second longest in the world.

That we were even considering walking through it perhaps showed that our exhaustion was making us lose all sense of reason. We were aware it would be a stupid thing to do – we had even started referring to it as the 'Tunnel of Doom' – but we did not seem able to resist the temptation.

'What about the pollution inside?' said Leon.

'It's a brand-new tunnel,' I said. 'It's only been open for a year, so the fans inside will be in top working order. Fumes won't be a problem. But what about the police?'

'Maybe we could go through it in the middle of the night,' said Leon. 'Even if there are CCTV cameras, the guards will probably be asleep. The last thing they would ever expect would be a couple of crazy foreigners walking through it at 4 a.m.'

'And it's easier to get forgiveness than permission in China,' I said. I had read that somewhere and it sounded good. It seemed to sum up our approach to the police in general.

So, with our decision made, we walked into the night, because we wanted to get as close as possible to the tunnel entrance before we slept. At 9 p.m. we came upon a group of migrant workers seated around a little bonfire. They said we could sleep in the derelict house behind them, and pointed to a bare front room, without a door. There were a couple of old doors leaning against the wall, and one of the men lay the doors on the ground and indicated, with a smile, that they would make ideal mattresses for us. We thanked him and rolled out our sleeping bags on the doors.

The alarm went off, and it took me a moment to remember why I was getting up at 3 a.m., and why there was a slight sense of dread at the back of my mind. Walking through an eleven-mile Chinese road tunnel was the last thing I felt like doing now, and it suddenly seemed like an incredibly bad idea. My hands trembled a little as we packed our sleeping bags and walked back into the darkness.

We climbed up onto the open motorway that led to the tunnel, and as we walked down the hard shoulder in single file it was completely quiet. The motorway lights shone down brightly from above, and behind them I could see the shapes of the Qinling Mountains looming in and out of the night. The double-laned tunnel entrance came into sight. It was well lit, and beside it was a small checkpoint cabin and a police car. We kept walking, and saw a guard in the cabin leaning back in his chair, watching TV. He did not notice us slip past, and a moment later we were inside the Tunnel of Doom.

It quickly lived up to the name we had given it. White lights and blackened walls shot before us, dead straight, stretching into the heart of the mountain and never coming to an end, promising no escape. There were in fact two parallel tunnels, one for each direction, and we were walking, as we always did, on the side facing the oncoming traffic. There was a decent width of pavement to walk on – at least we were safe from cars. However, I could smell fumes.

At this point, I knew we should probably just cut our losses and turn back, but now that we were here, bizarrely, we felt we had no choice.

We increased our pace, and heard the first vehicle before we saw it: a thick rumbling and booming sound, echoing off the walls. A moment later, headlights appeared and the car roared past. I tried to take only shallow breaths. We were going to have to spend at least three hours in here. I looked over my shoulder. Leon had a foreboding expression on his face and, behind him, the mouth of the tunnel gradually disappeared from view. Ten minutes in, it had vanished forever. We stopped walking and looked at each other.

'Blimey, it's hot in here,' I said.

Leon puffed and agreed. We dropped our packs, and pulled off our coats and thermal tops, until we were wearing only our T-shirts. In the Gobi, I had sometimes wondered when we would first reach 'T-shirt' weather. If this counted as weather, that time had come.

'Let's just see how it goes, I guess,' said Leon.

We kept walking, marching as fast as we could and keeping an eye on the distance markings on the tunnel wall. We had done one mile, and had ten more to go. Our surroundings did not change and followed a strict regularity of features. The blackened walls of the tunnel running ahead and behind; lay-bys every 250 metres; mysterious steel doors in the walls every 1,000 metres; CCTV cameras lining the roof. There were also regular large fans, just as we had hoped. What was worrying was that two out of every three fans were not working.

A vehicle passed every ten minutes, spewing black fumes in its wake. Not surprisingly, the air thickened the further we went. After three miles we stopped for another break, this time, nervously pushing open one of the mysterious doors. Inside, there was a little passageway, leading through to the other tube of the tunnel, going in the other direction. The air was slightly better inside, and there were a couple of brooms leaning against the wall.

'Well, if the road sweepers have to work here, maybe we will survive,' Leon said.

'If it gets bad, we can always hitch a ride out,' I said, trying to reassure myself as well as Leon, and ignoring the fact that a driver at 4 a.m. in China's longest road tunnel might not be that keen to stop for two semi-conscious foreigners. Not to mention the fact that we might not be able to tell when we were reaching dangerous levels of carbon-monoxide poisoning. It flashed through my mind how horrific it would be if Christine arrived on her flight the next day and I was not there to meet her, and then she heard the news that two foreign men had been found dead in the tunnel. I pushed the thought out of my mind – we were almost halfway anyway; it was easier to just keep on moving forward.

We kept walking. The mile markers ticked past slowly:

Eight miles left.

Just keep going . . . Just keep focused, Lilwall . . .

Seven miles left.

Keep going . . . Try to speed up . . . I wonder how Leon is?

Six . . .

Why are my palms tingling? Is that a symptom of poisoning? Could we get permanent brain damage from this? What an amazingly stupid idea.

We passed more lay-bys. Halfway through, we reached a lay-by where blackened plastic plants lined the roadside, like demonic imitations from the underworld. I touched a plant, and a thick layer of soot came off on my fingers. My right foot started to hurt again because I had not had time to do any stretching, but I did not want to stop. Leon overtook me and started to gradually move ahead.

Five miles . . .

I couldn't believe we'd been in there almost two hours, and there was still over an hour to go.

Four miles . . .

We stopped for another break in a connecting passageway, but this time the air was even worse than that in the tunnel. Leon said he was starting to feel light-headed, and I told him about my tingling palms. We looked at each other and laughed nervously, and then stopped and looked serious.

'What the hell are we doing?' said Leon.

He turned on the camera, and I talked about how I thought we should be nominated for the Darwin Award this year – the prize given out to people who are so incredibly dumb that they do the human species a favour by eliminating themselves from the gene pool by getting themselves killed in stupendously stupid ways.

Back in the tunnel, we started to run.

Three miles left . . .

Not far now . . . Maybe we can make it . . . It's 7.30 a.m. . . . It must be daylight outside now.

Two miles . . .

Leon was fifty metres ahead of me, and I continued to struggle to keep up. We were like drowning men desperate for air, imprisoned men desperate for daylight. I saw another car approaching. It had flashing lights, and a moment later my heart sank as the police pulled up beside Leon. This was not just a matter of getting told off again – it would be very disappointing if, having come this far, we could not walk all the way through.

The two young policemen sat in the car, talking. We could not blame them for being flummoxed. I do not think they had been prepared for this kind of situation in police school. One of them climbed out, slowly and cautiously, as if he were about to interact with dangerous convicts. This was clearly a situation in which we should again play the 'dumb foreigner' card.

'Hello,' I said, catching up and mustering my cheeriest Mandarin. Leon lent against the tunnel wall, and tried not to look ill.

The policeman furrowed his brow. 'What are you doing?'

'We are not able to go to Hong Kong,' I said even more cheerily. The carbon monoxide had knocked out my tonal abilities.

'What?' said the policeman, his furrows deepening.

'We started in Mongolia, and have been going for three months. China is a beautiful country!' I gestured around us at the tunnel. It did not seem quite as convincing a gesture as when we were out in the mountains and valleys. Leon tried to nod, but the way he rolled his head made him look demented.

'But you cannot walk through this tunnel,' said the policeman, starting to sound exasperated.

'Really? Why not?'

The policeman started to talk about the fumes, but realising that there was no point reasoning with the insane, he said, 'You just can't.' He turned and talked to his colleague in the police car, and then turned back to us. 'You will have to come with us.'

We protested that we only had two miles to go. The police car was going in the opposite direction to us. We would be out of the tunnel quicker if we walked. The policemen, however, were insistent. No matter how many times the argument went round, they were not going to let us go. Leon and I, for the second time in two weeks, reluctantly put our rucksacks into the back of a police car, and climbed in.

Off we drove, and suddenly the miles that had been ticking down, ticked back up: three, four, five, six, seven, eight . . . Leon said his head was still throbbing, and I noticed he looked pale.

Nine, ten, eleven, twelve . . . Our police car burst out of the tunnel and back into the world of men.

Leon wound down the window and gasped.

I laughed, nervously.

Ice beards

Through a tunnel

IRA in the desert

Insanity sets in

Instant noodles and processed sausage – our diet for breakfast, lunch and dinner

The fifteenth day of Chinese New Year

The Yellow River

A quick dip in the Yellow River

Onto a motorway

A short cut that went well

A short cut that
didn't go so well

A very steep terrace
near the Yangtze

A dip in the Yangtze

A good way to travel

Waking up to frost
on our bivvy bags

A friendly
Chinese policeman

Blisters

Ploughing

Getting hot

Beautiful China

My favourite shop name on the route

The 20 RMB note

A quick dip in
the Pearl River,
Guangzhou

Hong Kong harbour,
back with Christine
at last

Over eighty friends
joined us for the
final few miles

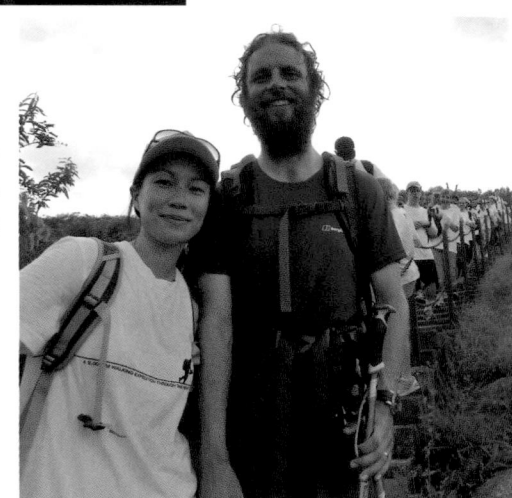

The finish line

Part Five

Into Southern China

———

一山不容二虎

Two tigers cannot share one mountain.

42
Proper sausages

Distance to home: 1,679 miles

29 FEBRUARY–3 MARCH
The police car sped down the motorway and all the way back to Xian. We were disappointed to have got this near to the end, only to then get caught. As we entered the urban area we were momentarily concerned that they were taking us to a police station for another interrogation. In fact they just wanted to drop us in the city and a long way from the tunnel – to make sure we did not just turn round and walk back through it again. This suited us well, because later that day Christine would arrive.

Xian, the provincial capital, was a gargantuan grid of roads, flyovers and apartment blocks. It was the provincial capital of Shaanxi, but for almost a thousand years it had been the capital of the entire Empire. At its peak, under the Tang Dynasty in the seventh to tenth centuries, it was the largest and most cosmopolitan city in the world. It had then fallen from favour and, because it was built mostly from wood, almost nothing from those times remained. There were, however, still some impressive city walls from the more recent Ming Dynasty, and a handful of temples and towers.

When we arrived in the city centre, instead of looking for a modest *binguan*, we headed straight for the luxury five-star Shangri-La hotel. This was way beyond our budget but, incredibly, when the hotel chain had heard that we were raising funds for a charity through our walk, they had kindly offered us free accommodation in two cities on our route.

Looking as if we had just walked 1,500 miles, we strolled into the serene lobby. We were astounded to receive a welcome fit for royalty from the staff in smart uniforms. They gave us fragrant tea in porcelain cups, took our smelly rucksacks and showed us to our magnificent rooms. A few hours later, Christine arrived. I had woken up that morning at 3 a.m., walked through a hellish tunnel, and been forced into a police car. And now I was relaxing in the tranquillity of the Shangri-La with my wife – it was the strangest day I'd had for a while, and part of me wondered whether I had passed out in the tunnel and was inhabiting a carbon monoxide-fuelled dream.

Better even than the Shangri-La's soft beds and sparkling bathrooms was the buffet breakfast. We were treated to a gigantic spread of bacon and sausages, mushrooms and melons, croissants, cereal and cappuccinos: surely just what a couple of tired, trans-China walkers needed in order to recover a semblance of togetherness of mind and body. On our first morning, Christine and I strolled into the dining room and saw Leon already there. He was eating his fourth plate and reading the paper, his large feet protruding from the white Shangri-La slippers.

'How's the headache?' I asked.

'Still there,' he replied, smiling dopily, putting another proper sausage in his mouth.

Having been married for only two and a half years, being apart for the past eight weeks had been quite hard on Christine and me. That we could talk on the phone regularly made things slightly easier; however, sometimes when we spoke, we were having very different days. When I was in a lonely, sad mood, she might be feeling elated and energetic, or vice versa, and this could lead to misunderstandings and arguments. We had to work hard to resolve these on the phone so they were not left hanging. Christine had already also managed to use the publicity platform of the trip to raise over £12,000 for Viva. This helped us to feel that the pain was worth it.

For much of our five days together in Xian, Christine and I happily stayed put in our five-star sanctuary. We just needed to spend time together – we could come back another time and be tourists. But we did occasionally go out to explore. One day, we visited the packed, narrow streets of the Muslim Quarter, where hippy backpackers and wealthy tour groups mingled with Chinese Muslims wearing skullcaps. The streets sizzled with kebabs, and the call to prayer rose up from the ancient mosque and echoed through the streets. Islam had come to the city down the Silk Roads from Central Asia during Xian's Tang Dynasty heyday. This had been a time when the Empire was very open, and Christians, Buddhists, Muslims and Confucians were all welcome to come and go.

All too quickly, after five days, and consuming (between Leon and me) fifty-six proper sausages, forty-five strips of bacon, twenty-one cappuccinos, fifteen bowls of cereal, twenty-two hot showers, forty hours of action movies and zero packets of instant noodles, it was time to say goodbye to our lives of luxury. And even more than the sausages, I was sad to leave Christine.

43
China's North–South Divide

Distance to home: 1,629 miles

We were tempted to try walking the last two miles of the Tunnel of Doom, but in the end we decided against it. Leon still had a headache and we did not think that the police would be as lenient if they caught us trying to walk through it a second time. So we caught a taxi to drive us back through the tunnel. Bursting into the open air on the other side, we then doubled back for several miles up a country lane. We resumed our walk from a point roughly parallel with where we had been caught inside the mountain five days previously.

We were now in the middle of the Qinling Mountains, and the temperature was up to 10°C. We followed the lane beside the gentle, unfrozen Qianyou River. This was a tributary that led into the much larger Han River, almost 200 miles to the south. After an hour of walking, we saw the Tunnel of Doom exit, and the motorway hurtling forth and continuing down the valley. It was raised above our little road on concrete stilts.

Like little children walking through a city of skyscrapers, we gazed up again at the soaring limestone cliffs. After months of being surrounded by brown loess hills, we had still not got used to the damp, vertical terrain. As well as the peaks above us disappearing into the clouds, lower down we saw some steep goat tracks zigzagging amid the vegetation and grey crags. I wondered what wildlife might be living in the neighbouring, inaccessible valleys – I had heard that pandas and leopards still roamed wild in the Qinling. And these mountains also marked a significant change to the route that lay ahead of us. In fact, they were sometimes cited as the dividing line between the elusive notions of 'Northern' and 'Southern' China.

Northern China, where we had just been, was a dry landscape, suited to growing millet and wheat; it was also the birthplace of the Chinese civilisation. Southern China, meanwhile, was more humid, and for much of China's early history had been less populated and less powerful in the life the nation. However, as history rumbled forwards, gradually more people migrated south, often driven by famine, invading nomads or the Yellow River pouring out sorrow. Life in the south was hard, and it took centuries of painful labour to drain the malarial swamps and build paddy fields. But gradually the entrepreneurial people, the more navigable Yangtze River and new, high-yielding varieties of rice, helped it to bloom. By the fourteenth century, the south produced a dynasty that ruled the entire Empire for nearly 300 years. It was the home of valuable and historically fateful crops such as the tea plant. In the twentieth century, it produced most of China's key leaders, including Chairman Mao and Deng Xiaoping.

On our second day in the Qinling, we stumbled upon the entrance of a C-list Chinese tourist attraction – the Zhashui caves. There were no other tourists in sight, but the two girls on the ticket desk said they could be our tour guides. We followed them through the huge entrance in the limestone cliff.

As we entered, a little path with multicoloured lights showed the way. The formations of caves, stalactites and stalagmites, protruded in every direction and, as the path weaved onwards, round corners, and up and down steep steps, we sometimes entered huge caverns, the size of churches. When we reached a point of interest, our guides would launch into a rapidly delivered rote-learned explanation, of which we barely understood a word. Gradually we worked out that the tour mostly involved pointing at what animals could be spotted in the rock formations:

'So this is a goldfish,' they said, pointing at a gnarly rock, before launching into a long, convoluted story about a man who went looking for a goldfish in these very caves (the man's image was now also borne by a rock face).

'Ah, how interesting,' nodded Leon and I, trying to see the resemblance. Leon was filming everything, and set up his tripod to get a steady zoom shot.

'That is shaped like a duck,' indicating a slightly sharper lump of rock.

'Indeed it is,' nodded Leon and I, scratching our heads.

We also came to ancient Buddhist shrines deep in the mountain, which in centuries past had been visited by members of the imperial family. The whole circuit was well over a mile long, and it was the biggest cave complex I had ever seen.

Before we left, we dug out some A4 pieces of paper from our rucksacks. These were our TV permission forms – complicated documents, written in Chinese, in which people gave permission to appear in the show. Tiberius had been asking us to get more of them signed, but we had not had much success so far, mainly because we were hesitant to show them to anyone lest the police got involved. This time, however, we asked the two tour guides if they would sign them. They both agreed and handed them back to us.

Leon, the Irishman, stopped and lifted his face to the sky with a smile. 'I've missed the rain,' he said. It was only a drizzle, but it was the first rain of the trip. Other signs of spring appeared around us too: men ploughing the fields; bulldozers digging gravel; villagers in teams building simple houses. We could also now sleep comfortably in our bivvy bags, though we did start to worry about millipedes climbing in with us.

At the same time as enjoying the spring, however, we continued to feel under pressure. First and foremost was the time pressure – of reaching Hong Kong by our late May deadline. Besides our promises to Christine and Clare, there was now another reason that we needed to make this date: the London 2012 Olympics committee had asked Leon to be a torchbearer for his home town at the start of June. In order to hit the finish date, therefore, going forward we would have to stick to a gruelling quota of twenty-five miles a day, with only one rest day a week, and two more short breaks with

Christine. However, we were still feeling tired from the cumulative exhaustion of the journey – even the days off at the Shangri-La had not served to completely refresh us. For these twin reasons of time pressure and exhaustion, Leon and I therefore decided once more to sneak onto the motorway.

At first it went fine and, as before, we made good progress. After three hours, however, the police caught us, and drove us back to where we had begun in the morning. Effectively we had to start the day again, but now walking on the slow country lane. We felt annoyed, as though we had been robbed of some miles, but the truth was we should not have been walking on the motorway! Not only did we lose time from getting caught but, more importantly, the motorway separated us from seeing and experiencing 'real China', the reason we set out on this trip in the first place. We resolved not to be tempted by motorways any more. From this point onwards, if we wanted to reduce our distances, we would have to seek out more adventurous shortcuts on shepherds' tracks.

Another ongoing pressure was from the filming side of things. Tiberius were continuing to request more sequences, shot at a very high quality. In one sense Leon and I found it hard not to resent their somewhat exacting demands, but in another it was good that they kept pushing us. We now felt quite slick in terms of setting ourselves up to film well, and enjoyed talking about potential stories to catch on camera. At the same time, the pressure was tiring us out further, and often made our lives more complicated.

On our fifth and penultimate evening in the Qinling, we reached a small town and decided that filming ourselves finding a place to stay might make a good sequence. With Leon and his camera behind me, I started our usual evening challenge.

'*Ludian zai nar?*' (Where is the guest house?) I asked each person I met in the street.

They looked surprised, asked me a few questions and did some good Chinese pointing. Gradually Leon and I homed in on a place to stay. This was typical of what happened every time we searched for a *ludian*, as was what happened next – some haggling with the hotel lady who tried to overcharge us a little. Once we had reached a reasonable price, we dropped our packs in our room, glad to have made it through another day.

Leon sat on his bed to record a video diary, and I went to the common bathroom in the corridor, musing to myself that we had done a fair job of filming the 'search for a *ludian*' sequence. I now looked forward to dinner. However, when I came out of the bathroom, I saw a troop of policemen heading for our room. I dashed over and opened the door for them, and Leon hastily put the video camera down as they entered.

The hotel manager lady was with them and everybody looked stern. She muttered a few things, and pointed at our camera, which sat guiltily on the bed beside Leon. Perhaps it had not been a wise idea to film tonight, considering we had recently had a couple of police encounters on the motorway.

After a long day, dealing with the police was the last thing we felt like doing. At first, they asked the usual questions and looked at our passports, and it seemed like another tiresome local police interrogation.

Once they had finished the usual questioning, they said, '*Zhe shi zuo shenme de?*' (What's this for?) and pointed at the video camera.

'Err, *wo xihuan FILMING*,' said Leon. '*Wo xihuan*' means 'I like'. Leon never could remember how to say filming in Mandarin. The policemen frowned.

Leon showed them some footage – the road, some villagers, the cave, nothing offensive. They also wanted to look at our GoPro sports camera, which I had unstrapped from my chest, and put on the bed. The GoPro looked like a stills camera and had no screen; as I handed it over, I pressed the record button. The policemen passed it round while, unbeknownst to them, filming themselves for us.

Just as we thought they were leaving, the policemen showed themselves to be the extra-inquisitive type, and demanded to see inside our bags. This was not good news because they contained the permission forms that would reveal we were filming for a TV show. My mind raced to find a way out of this.

'Our bags!' I huffed, lifting up my rucksack, before making a big deal of slowly emptying things out.

'Our bed!' I said, indicating that we slept on our roll mats, and making a snoring noise.

The policemen nodded.

'Our food!' I said, miming eating lots of biscuits, with a loud crunching noise, and offering them one.

The policemen smiled and said no thank you.

'Our torture ball,' massaging my leg with it, and groaning.

I handed it to the policemen, who tried it on themselves and laughed.

The main section of the bag was almost empty. I huffed and puffed some more. The policemen were now looking embarrassed.

'Our Kindle . . .'

Fortunately, before I got to the pouch containing the permission forms, the police decided that they had seen enough, and turned to leave.

As the door closed behind them, I sat down on my bed, heart still thumping.

'That was close,' said Leon.

44
Shortcuts

Distance to home: 1,419 miles

8–18 MARCH

We tumbled out of the Qinling Mountains to be greeted by the sight of the Han River. The water was blue-grey, several hundred metres wide, and full of gravel-dredging ships. But though impressive in its own right, the Han was actually only a tributary of the Yangtze, still 500 miles away. We crossed the water on a road bridge, and continued into another band of hills, now firmly on southern Chinese soil.

The first thing we noticed was that the weather was warming rapidly. The sun blazed down, the daytime temperature rose into the mid-20°Cs, and the sky filled with brigades of cumulonimbi. The colour and shape of the land had changed too. If the north was mostly brown, then the south was green. The angular mountains were shrouded in lush forests, and flattened into valleys of verdant crops – tobacco, rice and various leafy Chinese vegetables.

As well as the differences in physical geography, I had heard that the people were different too. The northerners speak in more clipped dialects, and are said to be taller, with single eyelids. The southerners speak in more lilting dialects, and are apparently shorter and darker, with double eyelids. I wondered whether I would notice any difference.

There were certainly plenty of people out and about. A cheerful salesman sold us some dough sticks from the Perspex box strapped to the back of his bicycle; a friendly drunk talked to us about his chickens; a motorbike taxi drove past, its middle-aged driver blasting trendy Chinese rap music and smiling. Most villages had a little shop with a poster of Chairman Mao on the wall. We often stopped to buy soft drinks and stock up on peanuts and biscuits. Once, while I was taking a break, a car stopped and two young men wanted a photo. I wearily stood up, and one man went round behind me to pose. Just before the snap, with no warning, he jumped on my back. I was giving him a piggy back and on the verge of collapsing as the picture was taken.

We also noticed that the doorstep life of China had begun. Families, often with a child or two on their laps, perched on plastic stools outside their doors. They watched the world go by and chatted. Two bearded foreigners clinking down the road made for a different sight, and our onlookers often called out jovial hellos. Sometimes we stopped to chat, and crowds of old and young would gather round. They pointed at our rucksacks and our beards. Once an old lady picked up my walking poles, chuckling to herself as she walked up and down the road with them.

And the conversations we had with these southerners were remarkably similar to those we had in the north:

Me: *Hello! Please could you tell me how far it is to the next town?*

Then, simultaneously, the whole group would ask:

Do you speak Mandarin?

Are you walking? Why are you walking?

Which country are you from?

A few more people joined in and all happily disagreed on how far away the next town was.

The children meanwhile stared shyly at us with bright little faces. When we said hello, they broke into wide smiles, and peeked at us from behind the adults. 'What is your name?'* a young mother encouraged her little boy to ask in English. He pulled from her grasp and ran away. Children seemed very visible and loved in these rural communities, and we rarely saw them crying.

In one village, I bought a cheap big straw sunhat to shade my head. A four-year-old girl with rosy cheeks and pigtails ran up and

---

* This was usually the sum total of the English language that most villagers spoke.

pointed her finger at us. '*Qiguai*,' (Strange) she said, before running off giggling. I looked across at Leon. He had no sunhat but was wearing a headband that made him look like a 1980s tennis player.

'She has a point,' we agreed.

One lunchtime, we stopped to eat in a little junction town. There were dozens of market stalls, and hundreds of people milled around in the sun. Many of the stalls sold vegetables, but there were also more unusual ones – a portable dental practice selling false teeth; a lady selling fried gooey snacks, but behind her stall she also ran a small, smart shoe shop. Against the shop front, a welder was at work on a metal door, sparks flying, and we noticed that his eye guard consisted of a pair of sunglasses with a big square of cardboard taped around the edges.

At a roadside restaurant we tucked into our bowls of fried noodles. A man on another table called across, asking to see some foreign money. Christine had given us more US dollars, so I showed him a ten-dollar bill.

'*Wo keyi kan yi kan?*' (Can I have a little look?) he asked. We handed him the note.

'*Duo shao qian?*' (How much?) he asked. He was flicking through a pile of banknotes, and seemed to be a buyer.

'Sixty *kwai*,' we said, giving him the approximate market rate.

The man hesitated. A crowd was now gathering. Another man chirped up and said he would buy the ten dollars. We agreed and the money exchanged hands. The first man looked disappointed, and asked if we had any more. We did, and so more money swiftly exchanged hands. The noodle chef, who, in between flipping noodles, had been watching over everybody's heads, now also barged in and also bought ten dollars. We thought we had rounded up the rate and made a slight profit, but when we checked later on, we realised we had made a slight loss. Perhaps doing shady money deals in China was not our forte.

To our fresh, amateur eyes, there were few differences in the people in the south. We did notice more women driving cars here, but there could have been many reasons for that. I once asked a small friendly crowd if they were northern or southern Chinese, and they looked at me, slightly confused, before tentatively saying southern. The concept did not seem important to them. And thus my layman's conclusion was that these southerners were not really different to the northerners. Above all, they were still just the friendly, exuberant, irrepressible, unpredictable Mainland Chinese!

The heat, though pleasant, brought a different type of exhaustion to the cold. The early hours of the morning were especially beautiful. But, as the day warmed up, we started to sweat, and soon got blisters from our damp socks and rashes from our rucksacks. It sapped our strength. The tiredness felt as if it was sinking deep into our bones and our minds. Yet, each day, we got up and did it again, walking twenty-five miles, one step at a time. Through the green hills, through the deep shady gorges. Past the farmers and villages and rivers and trees. There were many new roads being built through the mountains of southern China – tunnels blasting out of hillsides, and bridges spanning gullies. In quick succession we spotted two exceedingly dangerous-looking jobs: a man welding the outside of a high bridge without a harness, and a truck reversing to the edge of a cliff to tip its load over – with the back wheels stopping just a foot from the crumbly cliff edge.

Keen to implement our plan to find adventurous shortcuts, Leon scanned the iPhone. After spotting a good opportunity to cut a corner through some hills, we turned right at the next tobacco field and followed a track past a series of farmhouses and beehives. The path led upwards for an hour, then fizzled out. We scrambled through a bamboo forest to the summit. Unsure of where we were, we used a compass and descended through some terraced paddy fields, and after two hours stumbled back onto the road. We had saved ourselves perhaps five miles, and it had been a fun little adventure. Thus encouraged, and our hopeavism brimming, we kept a lookout for more shortcuts in the following days.

Two days later we set our sights on a longer one. Armed with a double takeaway each from a cheap restaurant, we followed the Google satellite maps onto a small path leading into the mountains. The limitation with using satellite maps, however, was that they did not show contours. It was impossible to tell how high or steep the slopes were. As we climbed, the path became gradually steeper, and less worn. And yet we were still hopeful that, despite the height we were gaining, and the prevalence of precipices rising all around us, we would still be able to get through.

'This is clearly a human track,' we told ourselves, as we ascended higher and higher.

'Other people have come here too,' we announced, whenever we saw an old beer bottle or biscuit wrapper.

'No one would climb up here, unless there was a way down the other side,' we said as darkness arrived.

We were still not even at the top, and the mountain was a lot bigger than we had thought. We camped on a little island in the middle of the stream and determined to keep going the next day. But when morning came, as we continued, the path grew smaller still, and we were soon being forced to scramble up steep rocks and waterfalls – dangerous work with our heavy packs. It was forecast to rain the next day and, if this stream flooded, it would be extremely difficult to get back down.

'That's got to be a human-made path,' I said to Leon, when we spotted another little track through the undergrowth.

'But it could be made by animals,' he said, growing more sceptical.

Eventually we made it to the top, but we had lost all human trails. We could see only the prospect of cliffs on the other side. The rain would come in the evening, and we could not risk being stuck up here and so, reluctantly, we turned back. We had climbed for more than a day to try and save a day, but had ended up where we started, a day and a half behind our already hard-pressed schedule.

We reached the road where we had started, and as I stomped down the tarmac my thoughts started to spiral. I was annoyed at Leon, and no doubt he was annoyed at me. But the fact was it had been a joint decision, and so the fault lay with both of us, though it felt easier to blame someone else. I was hot and tired. I felt frustrated that we had got ourselves into this position of being pressed for time. At moments like this, the expedition seemed a far cry from the epic walk I had envisioned.

But that was the stark reality of going on adventures. There were good days and bad days, and if we went exploring we were bound to get lost sometimes. On a long expedition there were certainly going to be plenty of long, painful days. We had to take the good with the bad. Push through the bad times, and the good times would come again. We walked past a field where in the blazing sun an aged farmer ploughed the soil with his hoe. He was not complaining and his life was far harder than mine.

'Come on, pull yourself together, Lilwall,' I muttered to myself. I increased my pace, and tried to catch up with speedy Leon who, as usual, was starting to move further and further ahead of me.

45
The Yangtze

Distance to home: 1,169 miles

19—24 MARCH

To claw back time in the schedule, for the next four days we had to temporarily abandon the shortcuts through the hills and instead hit the tarmac for twelve or fourteen hours a day. We crossed a jigsaw intersection of strangely shaped provincial boundaries – briefly through Hubei Province, into Chongqing Province, back into Hubei, and back into Chongqing. The road meandered up and down monumental valleys, forcing us to trace the indented contours along their sides for miles on end. The mountains rose in orchestras of vegetation and rock, with clouds of mist dancing around the cliff faces. We also came to see how impenetrable the slopes were on this side of the watershed, and this justified our decision to turn back when we did on the aborted shortcut. We might never have got down and, if it had rained, we could have been trapped up there for days.

But despite the treacherous terrain, there were some new-looking villages hanging off the valley sides. An old man worked the ground on an implausibly steep sloping terrace. At the bottom of the slope there was a sharp 100-metre drop down a sheer cliff. I did not think that I would dare to walk along a gradient like that, let alone tend the vegetables on it.

It started to rain, and a series of little paths led us through a maze of tangerine groves, until, through the wet haze, we caught our first glimpse of the Yangtze. It was as if the colours of the dark earthy bank had dripped into the serene, green-grey water. Downstream, two vertical cliffs hemmed the waters into a narrow channel – the start of the famous Three Gorges. We walked beside the river for a while and reached the riverside town of Fengjie. We were due a day off, and decided that – instead of sitting around resting our feet – we would catch a local ferry downstream to see the first of the gorges. We would hop off the ferry in the evening and hitchhike back to Fengjie and resume our walk from the same spot the next day.

The boat chugged away from the shore, and Leon set up the tripod on the deck. I said a few words to the camera. Even though it was our day off, we had to keep filming when the opportunity arose. Leon took some shots of the bridge as we dawdled underneath it. There was other boat traffic too: large cargo ships, almost the size one would normally expect on the sea; and red hydrofoils, speeding past, heading for Chongqing 500 miles upstream.

Our fellow passengers were mostly made up of farmers and schoolchildren, who sat below deck playing cards and chatting. But there were also a few businessmen who joined us outside, and took photos of both us and the river. We motored slowly towards the towering cliffs, and suddenly we were between them. The rocks rose sheer and confident, but actually they were a shadow of their former selves, because the river level had risen 170 metres in the past twenty years. For of course, a hundred miles downstream the infamous and record-breaking Three Gorges dam had been built – the biggest dam in the world, the height of a sixty-storey skyscraper. It had caused this entire middle section of the Yangtze Valley to fill up.

Our ferry emerged from the gorge and started to zigzag from side to side of the channel, visiting the numerous villages scattered along the steep slopes. We picked up more farmers and cows and dropped off schoolchildren, donkeys and bags of tangerines. The animals stood on the bow of the boat, and we saw that one cow had a terrible festering wound on its leg. A few minutes later, another cow slipped and almost fell into the passenger cabin.

All along the banks, a few metres above the waterline, we noticed signs on which was written '175'. This was a marker indicating how many metres above the original river level the water had risen. The signs had actually been put up when the dam was first being built, two decades ago, in order that everyone would know how high they needed to move. Of course, back then, the '175' markers were high in the hills. When the American journalist Peter Hessler was a Peace Corps teacher in the Yangtze Valley in the late 1990s, he used to go jogging in the hills, and after a long ascent would stumble upon the signs. With the river running through the valley far below, it had seemed implausible that the water could ever reach that high. But here it was, and anything below it had been submerged.

A population of well over a million people had had to be relocated. 'Forsake the small home to support the big home,' the former inhabitants were told, before being given small amounts of compensation and being forced to move. I peered over the side of the boat and imagined the countless villages, towns and cities that were down there. It occurred to Leon and me that perhaps the farmers we had seen eking out a living on the absurdly steep slopes over the past few days had actually been relocated there from their previous homes beside the old Yangtze.*

The ferry dropped us off at the town of Wushan, the original version of which was now underwater. A motorbike taxi took us to the start of the motorway, from where we hoped to hitchhike back to Fengjie. It would soon be dark and the motorbike taxi driver stayed with us to see if we got a lift.

'It's too late, and no one hitchhikes from here,' he said. 'Why don't I give you a ride to a nice hotel, and you can catch a bus tomorrow.'

We needed to start walking again early the next morning, so we told him we would take our chances. But as we stood there flapping

---

* The big benefits of the dam were that it reduced flood risks, and generated huge amounts of electricity (the equivalent of ten nuclear power stations). But aside from evicting many people from their homes, it was also controversial in many other ways. Its cost had spiralled to four times the original estimate of £5 billion; the flood waters had buried many archaeological treasures; it damaged the environment – including contributing to the probable extinction of the Yangtze dolphin. More dramatically, some scientists questioned whether such huge dams increased the chances of earthquakes, and there were even (unofficial) concerns that one day the dam would collapse.

our hands at passing vehicles,* Mr Motorbike Taxi watched us with a smirk.

A succession of SUVs passed, but did not stop for us.

'I told you,' said Mr Motorbike Taxi.

We smiled. A farmer's truck loaded with pigs drove past.

'Why don't you go with the pigs,' he said. 'Plenty of room in there.'

We grimaced. A security van from the bank passed.

'Or how about this one. I'm sure they'll let you in with their money.'

It was almost dark and we began to wonder whether he might have a point. Eventually, a car did stop. We were happy to prove Mr Motorbike Taxi wrong, and half an hour later we arrived back in Fengjie. Our little boat ride had been a fun break, but it meant that we had not had a proper rest from the previous week of hard walking.

The next morning, before we set off, we had one final piece of business to transact with the Yangtze. The sun was rising above the valley walls, and I felt nervous as Leon and I poised on the edge of the water. A crowd of workmen gathered on the road above to watch. I braced myself and jumped, and as I plunged deep into the cold, ancient waters, I felt, at least for a few seconds, all the tiredness, the aches and the stresses of the road wash away.

---

* This is the standard hitchhiking gesture in China. Peter Hessler refers to it as 'petting the dog'.

46
Meaningless penance

Distance to home: 1,069 miles

I awake at 6 a.m. to the sound of my alarm going off and open my eyes to see that I am inside a bivvy bag. I push my face towards the small drawstring hole, and inhale the fresh morning air. As I sit up I groan from my aching back and legs, but can't help smiling at the limestone cliffs and forested hillsides that surround us. My campsite is in the middle of a terraced potato field, and everything is covered in a thin layer of frost – despite the warming daytime temperatures, it is still only March, and we are high in the mountains.

We get up fast and start packing. After four months, everything has its place in our rucksacks. In go sleeping bag, laptop, filming wires, hard drives, personal things, food and bivvy bag. We will walk in the same clothes we slept in. While packing, I pour a cup of instant coffee and now, with everything stowed away, I down the dregs and slot the thermos into a side pouch. We swing the heavy packs onto our backs and wander back onto the road.

Although our eyes are still half closed, and our clothes are damp, the morning, as always, is magical. I wonder what China has in store for us today. As if on cue, at that moment, long, loud yells echo from a small mountain beside the road. We keep walking and see a line of people on the hillside doing a blend of Tai Chi and aerobics, occasionally stopping to have an enormous shout. We follow a little path towards them; when we reach their bit of the cliff, they welcome us to join in. Even after I have taken my pack off, I can hardly balance on one foot, but I can at least add my voice to the final hearty shout as the morning's session ends.

Onwards we go, and time blurs from one day into the next. As we walk, like a couple of retired spinsters with nothing else to do all day, Leon and I yabber at each other. Sometimes we talk about practical matters, or trivia. But other times we talk about more meaningful things: personal heroes; who will be remembered a thousand years from now; famous people we have met – Leon's granddad used to be the Provost of Aberdeen so he has met Gorbachev and the Queen, I haven't really met anyone except the parents of The Edge from U2 at a Rotary Club event. We attempt to memorise Tennyson's Ulysses, testing each other on alternate lines, until we think we have it down well enough to wow all ears at a dinner party.

And, unsurprisingly, with no one to talk to except each other, we continue our steady descent into exhausted insanity, so much so that we sometimes make strange meaningless comments.

'From this point, that road is either going down or going up,' I say as we walk down a flat bit of road.

'That truck's come from somewhere,' says Leon, as a truck comes round the corner.

'This warmth will be nice until it's not nice,' I say as the sun rises.

We have also been inadvertently developing more and more of our own language for things – Orlandos, Jases, the Tunnel of Doom, needing to go for a Mr Lax. A word we have recently started using a lot is 'bashing' – as a replacement for walking. When we have to walk down a long tarmac road we call it tarmac-bashing; around lots of spurs, spur-bashing; up lots of switchbacks, switchback-bashing. But however much we talk about bashing things, the truth is, it is us who are getting bashed. Our feet are bashed by the enormous features of Chinese geography, our heads are bashed by the hot sun, our shoulders are bashed by the heavy rucksacks, and on top of all this we are just feeling generally very bashed by the ongoing filming pressure.

My diary entries are increasingly illegible:

14 March: 73 days to go, I am sick of this, want to cry and
go home.
Showing little initiative filming.
19 March: [the *ludian* owners] think we are mad . . . hopping
around like we are insane . . . groaning . . . refuse to wash . . .
don't eat much
we are losing it
20 March: ridiculously tired
gross chicken
21 March: amazing – we feel regenerated the next morning
– the human body!
Expect thunderstorm
Is life a competition I wonder? If so, who is the winner? The
most flourishing? The person who dies with the largest bank
balance?
Bodies getting beaten down, sore feet
tired, ChinesePod
horrible chicken
25 March: Leon burps like toad
26 March: Finding suppressed emotions bursting out. Sometimes
anger. I prayed a lot.

Our exhaustion is also making us less enthusiastic about meeting
people, and we are beginning to get seriously tired of reciting our
catechism. It seems easier to talk to each other, though even that is
getting ridiculous and boring. But how can we get ourselves out of
this state? We are too behind schedule to take any more time off,
too tired to muster new enthusiasm. We still have two months to
go, and that is a long time to be slogging through a blur of sweat
and pain.

What's more, although we are now working well as a team, and
have developed a solid friendship, we are also getting snappy with
each other. Small annoyances are intensifying, escalating; whether
it is Leon getting more impatient with my slowness after a break,
or a misunderstanding about the filming, or something as silly as
my grievance over how, while I think I always listen to the music

Leon recommends and puts on my iPod, he never seems to listen to mine!

It is not that we dislike or do not respect each other, but that we have simply spent too much time together – we are feeling claustrophobic with each other's company. However, we are still bound together by filming needs – and the fact that we only have one iPhone to navigate with, and always have to sleep in the same small ludian rooms, or share the same farmer's field at night, just makes it all the harder. With the twin problems of exhaustion and claustrophobia, we wonder what we can do to avoid the rest of this expedition becoming a meaningless penance.

47
The radical solution

Distance to home: 1,044 miles

27–30 MARCH

Leon and I glared at each other.

I finally said, 'Well, you go on the road, and I'll go along the stream then.'

Leon shrugged and picked up his poles. 'Fine, I'll see you in the next town.'

For the past few minutes we had been squabbling about which route to take. I wanted to try a potential shortcut along a stream, while Leon wanted to play safe and go back to the road. We were both tired, and wanted our own way, and for the first time we decided not to agree, and instead go separate ways. Our routes intersected again after two hours.

A couple of days later, the same thing happened. This time, I wanted to take another shortcut, walking through a forest up the side of a mountain, while Leon wanted to follow the road up the switchbacks. My hopeavist tendencies were continuing to nudge ahead of Leon's. However, this time, my shortcut ended up taking longer, and Leon waited for me for half an hour at the top. Then, as we set off again, I realised that I had lost the camera's furry microphone cover. I had to climb back down into the bushes to find it, leaving Leon to wait another hour. He was fuming by the time I got back, and stormed off in a mood. Thankfully a few minutes later he stopped and we both apologised.

Out of these small incidents, a new idea began to grow that would soon have far-reaching consequences for the expedition. We decided that we needed to split up – not just for an hour or two, or even a day or two, but for several weeks. It would be just what we needed to spice things up, a total break from our routine, a breath of fresh air.

Over the past four months we had become dependent on each other – I was doing most of the speaking to the locals and presenting to the camera, while Leon was doing the majority of the map reading and filming. If we split up, we would both be forced to handle all these tasks on our own. More important, it would make this into an exciting challenge again. Together we had survived a winter in the Gobi, the steep cliffs of the Yellow River, and getting lost on jungle-clad mountains. But now, things seemed too easy. Perhaps it was strange that we wanted to make our lives harder again, but we did.

Naturally, our plan needed an appropriate name. We brainstormed for a while, and in the end came up with one that fitted the bill: 'Operation Lone Wolves'. The main reason we had set out walking together in the first place was for the filming, so our biggest new challenge was that we would have to film ourselves. We would ask Christine to bring back the spare camera when we met her in the city of Enshi the following week, and we could make the split after that. We informed Tiberius, who recognised that we needed the break from each other, and agreed to it. They just asked us to make sure that we filmed any angry words about each other before we split. We told them that the spectacular punch-up they seemed to be hoping for was not on offer, but we would have a good whinge to the camera about each other when the opportune moments arose.

We stumbled down a hillside and arrived in Enshi, a small city nestled amid vast mountains. Leon and I were virtually dead men walking, but we had made it to another pit stop. With a renewed sense of excitement about what was ahead, I dumped my pack in a *binguan*, and jumped in a taxi to pick up my wife from the airport.

It was one of the benefits of the modern age that Christine had been able to come out on cheap flights to see me several times during the walk. That, and affordable international calls, certainly made things easier. But by the time I reached Enshi, apart from her brief visits to Datong and Xian, we had been apart for four months, and we still had two to go. Time was dragging.

In many senses, the trip was harder on Christine than on me. While I was out having adventures, with more than enough things to keep me preoccupied, Christine was at home, with an empty flat. She had been making the most of it – having friends and family to stay, investing in people. And she had thrown herself into running Viva's Hong Kong office.

But sometimes it had been hard for her not to worry, especially when I was out of phone reception for a few days. In the Gobi, when she had been unable to get through for more than a week, her imagination had got the better of her.

'I was thinking that if something did happen,' she said, 'then the voicemail message would remain the same forever and I would never speak to you again.'

I felt guilty that I was causing her worry. But I was also incredibly proud of how well she had coped and pushed through the tough times. 'Walking Home From Mongolia' was a test for her too.

And so, in Enshi, with two long months still ahead, we reminded ourselves that the time would pass and then I would be home once more. And once I was home, the adventure of 'normal' life for us would restart. Hopefully, having got through the test of the walk, we would together be stronger in facing the other tests of marriage and of life that would, no doubt, come our way.

48
Heigh-ho

Distance to home: 934 miles

The day Leon and I parted ways, the sky broke open with our first Chinese thunderstorm. It was five days after we had left Enshi, and we had just entered Hunan Province. Thunder boomed up and down the valley, and lightning flashed, but as I walked alone through the downpour, I could not help but feel a strange sense of liberation. Leon was up ahead somewhere, yes, but now he would not be waiting for me to catch up, or standing with his tripod and preparing to film me. In fact, we hoped we would not see each other for another three and a half weeks, until we reached the city of Guilin. My mind felt clearer, and my surroundings seemed to have come alive: the mountains, bold and imposing; the valley, lush and inviting; the rain, cool and glorious.

But although I had always felt reasonably content in my own company, I also now felt more vulnerable, and strangely nervous. Not that this was a bad thing. The extra adrenaline made me feel like I was on an adventure again. I had a new spring in my step, despite the fact that my pack was actually heavier. In order to be self-sufficient, we now carried a camera and a tripod each. Some items we had been forced to split. I had kept the laptop to write articles and the basic phone, while Leon had kept the iPhone. For navigation I would have to rely on the pages torn out from the road atlas, supplemented by my best attempts to interpret Chinese pointing.

The rain eased off as I began a long climb, and I scrambled on little tracks between the switchbacks. I could now take shortcuts to my heart's content, without the risk of annoying Leon if they did not pan out. My foot was almost completely better too, and I felt fit as I walked. At the top of the hill, I set up the tripod and camera on a ledge, and climbed back down. I walked backwards and forwards in front of it a few times, and then climbed back up and packed it all back up again. The whole thing took half an hour. My appreciation of Leon's hard work increased dramatically.

As I descended, the hillsides burst into colour, with blossoms of pink, white and yellow. It was getting dark by the time I reached the valley floor. Now that I was on my own, I had been moving, and taking breaks, at a slightly more leisurely pace, and this meant that I would probably have to walk for an extra hour in the evening to cover the necessary distance. Tonight, I had my sights set on a town about five miles ahead, where I hoped to find a *ludian*. My phone beeped – a text message from Leon.

'I have reached the town. I am staying at a *ludian* on the left just as you enter. Try and find a different one.'

The potential of accidentally bumping into each other was one of the flaws in Operation Lone Wolves. This was because for the first few days at least, it was impossible to find alternative routes that did not massively increase how far we had to walk. We would therefore warn each other when there was a chance our paths might cross, and so hopefully avoid each other, even if sometimes we stayed in the very same settlement.

I marched on into the night, and after an hour saw a few buildings – the town. I kept walking, expecting it to grow into a high street. But two miles later, I saw the lights receding behind me, far across some fields. Without Leon and his iPhone, I had missed the turn-off. My Chinese road atlas map showed only simple little lines for roads, and dots for settlements. It was far too inaccurate for knowing which turn-off to take.

I tramped onwards, alone in the Chinese darkness. I was now surrounded by empty fields, and passed only the occasional farmhouse. The moon was hidden behind thick clouds. I adjusted my heavy rucksack on my shoulders, and resigned myself to bivvying in a field – not a glamorous start to my solo walk. However, having expected to reach the town, I had now run out of water. I hated going to bed thirsty, so I started looking for a farmhouse that was still awake where I could hopefully fill my bottles.

I spotted a large white-tiled bungalow with a light on in the porch. There was a bulldozer parked beside it, and three people stood outside finishing dinner. They had not seen me approaching through the dark, and I hesitated about whether to approach them. Had I been with Leon, this would have been no big deal, but I suddenly felt butterflies in my stomach.

'Stop being a wimp,' I whispered to myself. I needed some water, and what was the worst that could happen?

So I walked out of the gloom and gave my usual cheery hello and recited my catechism. I was a *Yingguoren* (a British man), I loved China, I said. I held out my water bottle and asked if they might fill it up. It was strange to hear the sound of my own voice.

At first, the three faces looked up at me, wide-eyed, as if I was an apparition. One of the men, who was topless with an impressive belly, burst into a grin.

'*Yingguoren!*' he said loudly. '*Yingguoren!*'

Everyone laughed, and suddenly I was given a stool to sit on and offered a cigarette. A motherly looking lady went inside and re-emerged with a flask of tea, and a bowl of bony meat and steaming rice. Tremendously grateful for this unexpected hot meal, I started eating and, meanwhile, more people appeared from out of the house.

'*Yingguoren!*' everyone exclaimed, staring, bewildered, at my dishevelled clothes and rucksack. It felt as if the people were looking at me slightly differently to when I was with Leon. Did it make them more protective of me (because there was only one of me), or more suspicious (because strange people tend to travel alone)? I did not know, but I decided there was no harm in asking for a place to sleep.

'Can I dumpling here?' I asked, getting my tones wrong again.

Everyone looked at me as if I were deranged. I repeated myself a few times until they understood. There were some slightly awkward looks, and another man, who seemed to be the boss, appeared. I had initially assumed this was a farmhouse, but now more and more people were appearing from inside it, and I concluded it was some kind of workers' accommodation.

The boss looked at me suspiciously. I said I would be quite happy to sleep on the concrete slab on the porch. 'It's very comfortable and dry here,' I enthused. It would certainly be better than a muddy field.

His eyes narrowed, but the crowd all shouted at him, and a moment later he uttered a reluctant yes. Everyone disappeared back inside and I started to lay out my roll mat and sleeping bag. But before I had lain down, the motherly looking lady reappeared. She seemed to be the night guard, and she beckoned me inside and said I could sleep on the floor. I gratefully dragged my things into the empty front room, and collapsed. I was sleeping in a random house in China with dozens of mysterious people living in it, but I was warm, safe and dry, and that was good enough for me.

At 5.45 a.m. I awoke to the sound of loud conversations, laughing and some heavy rain outside. Opening my eyes, I saw an army of Chinese peasants traipsing through my room, staring, chatting and lighting cigarettes.

Sitting up, I clicked the camera onto the tripod, turned it on and then lay down in my sleeping bag. I pretended to be asleep for ten seconds, before feigning waking up, rubbing my eyes and explaining where I was to the camera. Self-filming was going to require a lot of motivation. I got up properly, and followed the workers through into the kitchen. I realised that it was not raining outside at all, but rather the noise was coming from a line of sizzling woks loaded with food. I was ushered into the queue, given a big bowl of fried noodles, and then I followed the crowd outside.

About fifty people stood eating, smoking and staring at me. They beckoned me over, and I stood among them, wolfing down the greasy, delicious noodles.

'What is your work?' I said.

Everyone replied at once, but I did not understand the replies. They started trying to act out some kind of digging motion, but I was still at a loss. Eventually they said, 'Come and see.'

A few minutes later, everyone dumped their bowls in a communal washing-up tub and filed around the back of the house. They then all grabbed a shovel or pickaxe and, together, like a troop of merry dwarves, we set out marching briskly into a pine forest. There were young boys in their mid-teens, and middle-aged ladies in their forties, there were old men who looked tough and sombre, young women who looked frail yet cheerful. The lyrics of heigh-ho, heigh-ho started to drift through my head as we walked.

We arrived in a section of the forest with lots of holes in the ground. Without any orders being given, everyone split into teams of two or three, and got to work. They approached the trees, which were all about three metres tall but, rather than starting to chop them down, they began digging away at their bases. Once they had dug underneath them, they pulled the trees out of the ground, and bound their roots in huge balls of rope. They worked hard, and fast, and almost without speaking. Although I tried asking why they were doing this, I could still not figure it out. Were they transferring the trees because a road was about to built here? Or were the trees to be sold? I did not want to be in their way, and I needed to get going, so I waved goodbye to my hard-working new friends, and hit the road, alone again.

49
Tea

6—8 APRIL

The waitress slapped a small china cup on the table, and poured some hot tea into it. Virtually every restaurant in China offered free tea. I took a sip. It was my fourth day since the initial split, and I had spent the morning walking up a valley lined with neat rows of tea bushes. Standing among them were two ladies with weathered faces and jet-black hair. They had looked up at me only briefly before returning to their intense work – plucking the little tea buds and placing them in wicker baskets. Tea, of course, originally came from China, and had been the beverage of choice here for thousands of years. Yet ultimately, tea had been a mixed blessing to the Empire, for it had played a significant role in bringing China's multimillennia-long dynastic era to a tragic close.

In contrast, for most of history, tea was virtually unknown in Great Britain. But as the British East India Company began to trade more and more with China in the 1700s, they were delighted to discover a budding market in London for the exotic dry leaves. By the 1800s, tea was transported back by the shipload, and the British were completely addicted – consuming pots of the stuff for break-fast, on 'tea breaks', and at 'tea time'.

China, at this point, still knew itself as the centre of civilisation, completely self-sufficient, just as it had been for thousands of years. And what was more, under the Qing Dynasty of the seventeenth to nineteenth centuries, China was a very closed Empire, and certainly not interested in building strong mutual trade links with the strange-looking Europeans who were increasingly starting to arrive. These distant nations would be permitted the honour of being vassal states, but all trade was restricted to the port of Canton (now Guangzhou), where foreigners were sequestered to a single island and even forbidden from learning Chinese (anyone who tried to teach them could be imprisoned or executed).

The British were humiliated, yet had no choice but to buy the precious tea under these strict terms. And what made matters harder for them was that they could not find anything that they could offer to the Middle Kingdom in return. This meant that they were paying for all the tea with British silver, resulting in an enormous profit for China and a gaping trade deficit for Britain.

Gradually, however, the British realised that there was something they could sell to the Chinese people: opium. This substance was derived from the poppy plant and grew well in the new colony of India. Once the foreigners started selling it, it did not take long for drug addiction to sweep across the Chinese nation. The drug profits were then used to buy tea, which in turn was sold to thirsty Britain. For the British, this arrangement was, of course, extraordinarily profitable and ideal. For the Chinese, however, it was a disaster. It not only cost the Empire its former tea profits, but, with the proliferation of drug addicts, also wrought havoc across society. The Chinese outlawed opium, and protested to the British, but were unable to stem the trade.*

Eventually, in 1839, a highly motivated and industrious Chinese court official came down hard on the foreign drug traders. He blockaded them in Canton, until a huge stock of opium was handed over, which he then destroyed. The British were furious, and things quickly escalated into what became known as the First Opium War. At this stage in history, the British gun ships and tactics were far superior to China's, and they quickly beat the Chinese into submission and forced upon them the first of the infamous 'unequal treaties'.

This treaty forced the Chinese to cede to the British an island off the south coast, as well as grant them access to five 'treaty ports'

* At its height, levies from the tea trade amounted to almost 10 per cent of the British government's entire revenue.

for freer trade.* This successful outcome (for the British) also unfortunately set a terrible precedent for the other foreigners – and soon the Americans, the Japanese and other European nations also vied for treaties of their own. And so both the opium and tea trades prospered, and the foreign powers began to meddle more and more in the affairs of the Middle Kingdom.

At the same time as (and in large part because of) this foreign meddling, internal unrest now rattled the Chinese Empire. And then, as the twentieth century dawned, Japan, in particular, began to show more colonial ambitions towards its ancient rival. Having taken over Korea, the Japanese moved aggressively into China's northeast, and from there set their sights on bigger goals still. In the decades that followed, the ancient imperial system collapsed, and the Middle Kingdom tumbled into an era characterised by feuding warlords, invasion by the Japanese and, eventually, civil war.

As Sarah Rose notes in her book about China and England's tea trade: 'No one can reasonably lay the blame for this [the fall of the Empire] on tea alone, but neither can one ignore the role that foreign desire for this quintessentially Chinese commodity played in opening China up to the West, and in the country's subsequent fall from Imperial self-sufficiency.'

I had been sitting in a daze as I drank my cup of tea. Two portions of egg fried rice arrived. One of them was in a polystyrene box – a takeaway for dinner that night in case I got lost. At this village, the road heading south had run out. I was about to attempt to find a shortcut over a mountain, and down to a reservoir on the other

---

* However, reaping their vast, immoral profits from the opium and tea trade was not enough for the East India Company – they also wanted to possess the secret of tea. In the 1840s, they sent an expert botanical spy to China, Robert Fortune, who disguised himself as a Chinese official, and covertly visited the mysterious inland tea plantations, which the Chinese had hitherto managed to keep secret. Once there, he stole both the secrets of tea manufacture, and samples of the plants themselves, and thus the precious 'botanical gold' was transported to India and beyond for cultivation, and China forever lost its monopoly. The story of Robert Fortune is told in detail in Sarah Rose's book *For All the Tea in China*.

side. The thought of taking shortcuts on my own made me nervous, because I would be much more vulnerable than before. This time, however, I had a new strategy: I would gather local knowledge and find a guide.

A crowd of ten-year-old boys had started to gather around me. I chatted to them while I ate, answering my catechism, and letting them ask questions. I asked them whether there was a path over the mountain.

'Yes, there is,' everybody said, including an old lady who was watching us and smiling. This was a good start.

'Could you show me the way?' The boys had a couple of skate-boards, and looked as if they were up for an adventure.

'We can,' everybody said.

'Good!' I said.

'Good!' everybody said, and we all laughed.

So we set off, me and my carefree little band of guides. One of the children skidded ahead on his skateboard, while another, the most confident, sang me a cheerful song, which I did not understand. In return I sang him 'For he is an Englishman' by Gilbert and Sullivan, which he clearly did not understand either, but we both complimented each other on our respective vocal skills.

A mud road led us to the start of a small path, at which point the boys gave me some instructions, which I vaguely understood. They then said they had to go back to the village.

'OK, thank you very much,' I said, waving a little downheartedly as they walked away. This was not going exactly according to plan, but at least I had made it to the start of the correct path. I climbed up through some terraced fields until I came to a village where everybody was out on their terraces, sowing and planting vegetables. They pointed me onwards, and I found a stone-slabbed track which, over the next two hours, led me to the summit. At the top, I saw a small Buddhist temple which, from the various offerings on display, looked as though it was still visited regularly.

'So far so good,' I said out loud to myself. 'Now to find my way back down.'

The stone slabs continued downwards for a few minutes, until I reached a large spread of wide paddy fields, filled with several inches of water.

'This looks promising,' I mumbled, as I balanced my way along a series of earthen banks leading me through them.

However, I was still high up the side of the mountain. At the edge of the fields, I reached an abrupt cliff edge. Looking out, I saw that on this side of the mountain everything was much steeper, and I was now in the midst of thick, precipitous jungle, from which sprang huge moons of limestone rock. This seemed to be the trend with Chinese mountains – one side was reasonably easy to climb up, but the other side was very hard to climb down.

I spent the next hour walking up and down the paddy fields looking for a path going down. I did find one promising track, but after a few minutes it became steeper and steeper. I had to turn round and walk back up. It would be dark in a few hours and I was starting to feel anxious. If I twisted an ankle up here, there was no Leon to go and get help.

Thankfully, after another half an hour, I found a more promising route, which had been hidden by some bushes. This led me down, down, down, until two hours later, at dusk, I arrived back on a tarmac road.

I felt very relieved, and very tired. I did not know exactly where I was. But I knew this road ran parallel with a long reservoir, which lay somewhere in the gloom below me. Somehow, the following day, I would need to find a path around the water, or a ferry across it. But first I had to find a place to sleep. There was no traffic on the road, and as I started walking along it I thought I would probably have to bivvy.

A moment later, a motorbike dragging a farm trailer appeared. It was being driven by a young man in his late teens, and he stopped beside me.

'I live a few miles further up the road,' he said. 'Why don't you come and stay?'

This was perfect. I said thank you very much and that I would be along in about an hour.

Darkness arrived, as did the pain in my feet from a hard day of getting lost in the hills. Half an hour later, Christine called. While we chatted, I sat down on the roadside and removed my boots to rub my feet. At that moment, I saw some headlights, and the man on the motorbike appeared again.

'You are getting near,' he said.

'Great,' I said.

But then the man started to talk about money. I had not thought he was going to charge me to stay, and I could not really understand. Christine was still on the other end of the phone, and in my exhaustion, I asked her if she could talk to him. I handed him the phone. They talked briefly, and he handed the phone back to me.

'Rob, are you safe?' Christine asked. An ominous question.

'Yes, I think so. Why?'

'Well, the guy is asking for 300 RMB (£30) to sleep on the floor. He does not sound very friendly.'

I made a show of picking up my poles, and got to my feet, trying to make myself look like a tough gruff crazy Englishman. 'It's fine honey, I'll just tell him I'm not interested, and sleep in a field,' I said, trying not to alarm her, before I said goodbye.

I stood shining my head torch in the young man's eyes while we negotiated.

'You will have to pay 300 RMB,' he repeated. He did seem rather aggressive suddenly.

'That's too much, I can pay 100 RMB at most.' A generous amount to sleep on someone's floor.

'No, 300 RMB.' Perhaps he did not realise I could just camp.

'Sorry, no thank you, goodbye.' I started walking off, feeling annoyed, disheartened, and a little jittery. I braced myself as the man drove his motorbike back past me, but he disappeared into the night without looking back. I let out a sigh. He had, of course, been well within his rights to ask me to pay, but it was an exorbitant amount, and he should have told me when he first gave the invitation. For a moment I felt vulnerable – out here on my own on some unknown Chinese road in the dark. Although rural China usually seemed a safe place, especially when I was with Leon, I had heard stories of cyclists getting robbed. I would be a fool to think I was immune from that.

It was 10 p.m., I had been walking for almost fifteen hours, and it was time to hide and camp. I spotted an orange grove, set out my bivvy bag underneath it and climbed inside. I used the camera tripod to drape my mosquito net over my head, and closed my eyes.

I wondered how Leon was doing? Staying in some luxurious *ludian*, no doubt. We had exchanged a few text messages. It sounded as if he too was invigorated by the renewed sense of adventure from being alone. But although we had been on separate tracks for the past few days, we were now about to converge in the city of Yuanling, where we would both be taking a day off. We hoped that we would not bump into each other.

50
KFC

Distance to home: 774 miles

kfc all clear

I read Leon's text message and left my hotel room. On our days off, Leon and I had both fallen into the bad habit of eating at Kentucky Fried Chicken, China's Western fast-food joint of choice. And now, as we were both in the same city, and there was only one KFC, we had to coordinate our movements carefully, or we would end up eating together. In order to experience the adventure of walking through China alone, we were doing our best to maintain our solitude.

The next day, I let Leon leave the city two hours before me, to give him a head start. We were stuck on the same route for the next few days, but with his increased walking speed, we hoped he would stay ahead. It was raining heavily as I set off at 9 a.m., and mid-morning my phone rang. It was Leon.

'Hi Rob, I've been hauled into the local police station about ten miles beyond the town.'

'Why? Is this a closed zone?'

'No, I think they just want to find out what we're up to. A patrol car has already seen you, and they've told me to wait here until you arrive.'

And so, an hour later, I strolled through the entrance of the police station. Leon was sitting on a hard seat, bedraggled and bored, surrounded by a few policemen. It was good to see him again. We went through the usual routines with the police for half an hour, after which they let us go.

As our common road was about to lead us into a compulsory shortcut through some big mountains, we decided it would be safer to stick together for the next couple of days.

'What I've been wondering,' I said, resuming our latest movie debate, 'is why Al Pacino is so rarely in a decent movie these days?'

'That's a very good question,' said Leon, 'I've been wondering the same thing about Robert De Niro.'

The following day, the road deteriorated into a muddy track, and the mountains around us became thickly forested. The villages were mostly built from wood, and the people all seemed to work in the logging industry. We saw wood mills beside the road, and trucks loaded with logs rumbled past regularly.

By the afternoon, there were no longer any bridges to cross the rippling streams. We had to remove our boots and socks to wade through, following the villagers in their flip-flops. The mountains loomed bigger and bigger and we knew the road would run out soon. Because the forest was dense, Leon agreed that we should search for a guide.

At one of the final houses before the road disappeared, we stopped and asked a young man if he knew anyone who could show us the way through the mountains. The man frowned at us, and stroked his chin. He seemed to be weighing us up, or rather, in the tradition of Mr Wolf the cabbie, he seemed to have understood that we were in a weak bargaining position.

He started at 300 RMB (£30), and we haggled for a while. He eventually agreed that for 200 RMB (£20) he would feed us and let us stay the night in his wooden hut and the next day someone would guide us through the mountains.

'Who?' we said.

'Him,' said Mr Wolf II, pointing to a little old man who had appeared. 'He is my father.'

The old man barely reached up to my armpits, and was wrinkled and slightly hunched. We wondered if he was fit enough for a long, mountainous trek, but we did not seem to have any choice. We shook hands with Mr Wolf II.

At that moment another small old man walked past. He was carrying a large log – so large that it could really be called a tree. He broke into a wide smile when he saw us, and put down his tree. He walked over with twinkling eyes, shaking his head. He looked as if he could not believe we were there.

'Where are you from?' he asked, smiling and with an air of wonder in his voice.

'We are *Yingguoren*,' we said in Mandarin.

'*Yingguroren!*' he replied, amazed. 'British people are foreigners!'

It seemed he had never seen a foreigner before, buried as he was in these mountains, carrying trees around on his back all day. He shook our soft hands with his leathery hand.

'Can I try and lift your tree?' asked Leon.

'Of course,' said the man. He was two feet shorter than Leon.

Leon bent over, and tried to lift up the tree, but was barely able to get it off the ground. We renamed the man 'Mr Steel' for his strength.

Mr Steel also looked at our map, and was astonished by our reading ability.

'You cannot read Chinese characters, but you can read English letters!' he exclaimed.

The next morning it was raining hard, and Mr Wolf II's father led us into the mountains. We soon renamed him 'Mr Iron' because, although he was not as tough as Mr Steel, he was still very hardy. He wore Wellington boots and a mackintosh, and plodded before us at a steady pace. We followed a series of winding paths. Sometimes the path had been washed away by landslides and we had to scramble along collapsing slopes. Other times we waded up streams, or passed through abandoned logging camps. We would never have made it through without Mr Iron. After five hours, we crested a final mountain, and he pointed us down a path into a new, much less forested valley, with a proper road running down the middle of it.

The next day Leon and I split up again, now hoping that we really would not see each other until Guilin, about two weeks away. But although we were separate again, we both had an immediate obstacle to overcome: another closed zone. This time we knew about it, because a few backpackers who had got in trouble there had mentioned it on online forums. And it seemed that this was no small closed zone, but a colossal one, perhaps a hundred miles long and wide. Rumour had it that it was the site of a monumental bunker, complete with nuclear missiles, and thousands of miles of underground tunnels.

However, all this information was quite vague and it was difficult to establish exactly where the closed zone began and ended. The task fell to hardworking, Mandarin-speaking Christine to call up all the county police stations, asking them one by one if their county was 'open' or 'closed'. Sometimes the police did not even know the answer for their own county, let alone for their neighbours'. After making many calls, she emailed Leon and me the results of her research, and we marked them on our respective maps.

As Leon and I were both determined to avoid any more lifts in police cars, we had two options for the way forward. One was to take the most direct road south, which would cut across a corner of the closed zone. The other was to follow a tiny road that veered just outside the boundaries of the zone, and would be an extra day's walk. Over the phone, Leon and I tossed a coin to decide who did which. Leon won, and chose his preferred route of sneaking through the small ten-mile section of closed zone in the middle of the night. I would go around on the longer route, using my speciality of getting lost in the mountains for a day or two, and then stumbling out on the other side.

51
Mao

Distance to home: 685 miles

14–20 APRIL

My shortcut, for once, worked well, and after two days in the hills I arrived back on a road, heading for the city of Dongkou. Ten miles out, I saw a crowd of villagers gathered in front of a display of some kind. A young man with a microphone was exhorting them about something very, very loudly. From a distance, it looked like one of the old 1960s Cultural Revolution Rallies – for the youthful and zealous Red Guards. But, as I got closer, I saw that the small crowd were not youthful, but middle-aged, and they were not zealous, but appeared somewhat weary and unenthused.

I joined the back of the crowd, and attempted to ask a man what was going on, but the microphone was so loud that it was impossible for us to hear each other. I nudged forwards, and saw a huge plastic banner covered with photos of Chairman Mao. The man with the microphone spotted me and grinned happily. He continued his exhortations with even more volume, passion and rapidity, because now there was a foreigner in his audience. I could not make out much of what he was saying, apart from the fact that he was clearly talking about how wonderful Chairman Mao was.

I squinted at the banner. It depicted the Chairman doing various amazing things: a charismatic leader on the Long March in the 1930s; a heroic soldier fighting the Japanese in the 1940s; a marvellous leader declaring the People's Republic in 1949; a strong old man swimming the Yangtze in the 1960s. He had firmly reunified the country after the civil war; he had made China a nuclear power; he had helped spread the wondrous benefits of socialism.

I pulled out my camera and, standing as far back from Mr

Microphone as I could, I asked a few bored-looking villagers what they thought of Mao.

'*Hao bu hao?*' (Was he good?) I asked. It was a dumb question, but we were in a public setting, and my Mandarin was not up to in-depth investigative journalism.

'Hao,' (Good) they mumbled, but with a telling lack of enthusiasm.

'*Mao cong Hunan lai*,' (Mao comes from Hunan) I said. We were still in the Chairman's own Province.

'*Dui*,' (Correct) they said, nodding, but with blank faces.

I was getting a headache from the noise. I said goodbye, and continued along the road. I wondered what the villagers really thought of Mao. Were they proud of the fact that he was from their province? About 300 miles east of here, just over 100 years ago, little Mao Zedong had been born. His village was so remote that when the Empress Dowager had died in 1908, Mao did not find out until he left the village two years later. He grew up during a time of great change in China, and by the time he reached adulthood, the Emperor had abdicated, the country was starting to fracture, and the Japanese were well established in the northeast. As a young man, he had drifted between jobs, and it had been when he was in Beijing in the 1920s, working as a librarian, that he had been recruited by the fledgling, Soviet-backed Chinese Communist Party (CCP, or 'the Party'). He was at first given only minor responsibilities, and even though he did not seem a particularly outstanding leader at the time, what he lacked in charisma he made up for in guile. Over the next two decades, he manoeuvred himself through the Party leadership, until by the end of the Long March* in 1936, he was its undisputed leader. And, most importantly, he was recognised as such by the CCP's then ardent sponsor, Joseph Stalin.

Meanwhile, in the 1930s, China had descended into full-scale war

---

* The downtrodden CCP's escape from near annihilation, via a circuitous and perilous journey around southern and central China. It stills holds a legendary status in the history of the CCP.

with the Japanese. After Japan's defeat in 1945, civil war broke out between the two main powers in China, the Communists and the Nationalists. At first, it was expected that the Nationalists would win, but with Soviet backing, and against the odds, it was Mao's Communists who prevailed. The Nationalists fled to Taiwan where they declared themselves to be the real government of China, but in exile – a situation that endures to this day.

By the time of this remarkable victory, Mao was already fifty-six years old. His real impact on China, however, had scarcely begun. Although he had managed to unite a badly fractured country, the scale of his mismanagement from this point onwards was almost unprecedented in world history. In his 'Great Leap Forward' campaign of 1959–62, he attempted to increase the nation's food production. To achieve this, among other things, he instigated a 'death to all sparrows' policy, because sparrows ate certain crops. Villagers had to dutifully make a racket all day and night to stop the birds from landing anywhere, thus causing them to fall dead from the sky. But with the top of the food chain knocked out, the result was a plague of insects that decimated crops and contributed to a mass famine that killed tens of millions of people.*

Even more infamous was his unleashing of the Cultural Revolution in the 1960s, a ploy to eliminate his political enemies. Youths became 'Red Guards' and, whipped up into hysteria, rampaged across the nation, beating up their teachers, and destroying whatever they could find that belonged to 'old China'. Millions died, uncountable historical treasures were destroyed, and as the movement veered out of control, China almost imploded.

The horrors had lasted into the 1970s, and I found it strange to imagine that they had occurred so recently. All those villagers I had just met would have been about the right age to have been Red Guards. I wondered what they made of me – a foreign devil, whom

---

* Mao was a great enthusiast for intervening in nature generally. Journalist Jonathan Watts summed up the Chairman's attitude as 'Think big, move fast, worry about the consequences later.'

they had been taught to hate when they were young?* I did not know. I had not wanted to ask.

And what had they really made of the Mao propaganda being blasted out by the enthusiastic young man? As I had walked through China over the past five months, I had on an almost daily basis spotted posters of Mao pinned up, in pride of place, in homes and shops. The portraits usually depicted the Chairman with a slightly smug half-smile, his big forehead taking centre stage, framed by his strange tufts of hair. I felt angry about what Mao had done, and that his reputation was still being guarded.

But I took some comfort from the knowledge that he was gone forever. Even into the 1990s, China was a famously drab country of morose people, extreme poverty and grey clothing. But, for all China's ongoing human rights issues, at least those darkest of times were over. There had been so little joy in those times. But today, China buzzed with life and optimism.

---

* During his travels through China in the 1980s, Colin Thubron had stumbled across an old pile of English-language textbooks in a school. They were left over from the times of the Cultural Revolution, and included English pages in which children were taught how to interrogate foreign POWs.

52
Solitude

Distance to home: 585 miles

It was now late April. The temperature was pushing up to the mid-30°Cs, and the humidity was intensifying. By the end of each day my shirt was drenched in sweat, and all I needed from my *ludian* was a bucket of cold water to pour on myself. I pressed onwards, through valley after valley, over mountain after mountain. The valleys were filled with pristine paddy fields, gleaming in the sun, often with grizzled old men walking behind an ox and plough. The trio of man-ox-plough moved back and forth together, churning the smooth mud into slushy beds for the rice. Sometimes there were mechanical ploughs too – a sign that, slowly, the benefits of China's prosperity were reaching these rural communities. The mountains, meanwhile, were covered in thick bamboo forests, and I saw teams of men at work chopping them down and loading the thick poles onto trucks.

In the heat, I wore my wide-brimmed hat, and sweat dripped off my nose and stung my eyes. My left knee had been getting steadily sore from the long days. I strapped it up with a knee support, which helped – though in the sweaty conditions, blisters started to develop underneath. In less than two weeks I would reach Guilin, where Leon and I would meet up, and where Christine would be visiting me a final time. Home was still almost 600 miles' walk away. I hoped my body would hold out.

My hot, tired brain, meanwhile, was often on autopilot. I would wave and say '*nihao*' hundreds of times a day to the various people who called out to me. One day, as I walked past a house with a fiercely barking dog, I only noticed a few seconds later that I had just said a friendly '*nihao*' to the dog as well. The beard I had shorn for Code Z had regrown and, along with my big hat, made me even more of an object to be stared at than ever.

One day, as I walked through a valley of paddy fields, a moped sped past. The young man driving it, and the middle-aged lady on the back, stared at me, as usual. A moment later, I heard a sudden bang and turned to see them veering across the road. They hurtled off the verge and landed in a paddy field with a splash. I dashed across to see if they were OK. Fortunately, they were, but it looked as if the bike engine was waterlogged. The lady started shouting at the man and pointing at the road – the reason they had lost control was because they had driven into a rock in the middle of the road. And it dawned on me that they had hit the rock because they were too busy staring at me.

As I approached the end of Hunan Province, I set out on my final shortcut. This one led me past a reservoir and up some shepherds' tracks into the hills. That night, I camped on a crest of grassy meadows, at least ten miles from the nearest village, and surrounded completely by nature. I was precisely on top of the watershed that separated Hunan from Guangxi – our penultimate province. Clouds were rolling across the horizon, turning pink in the sunset, and I realised this was probably my most peaceful campsite of the trip. We had sometimes been very remote in the Gobi, and in Shanxi, but I had always had Leon with me. Now, I was completely alone. Not a single person on earth knew I was here.

It had been good to walk for several weeks without Leon. To face the tests of the road on my own. To be stretched, pushed out of my comfort zone. To encounter China by myself. The challenge had invigorated me in just the way I needed. At the same time, I was looking forward to seeing Leon again. My time alone had helped me appreciate how much we had been through as a team. I had learnt a lot from him – about filming, about perseverance, about out-of-the-box thinking. About the medical science of hopeavism and about the secret of Jason Statham's acting-career success. I had also learnt about teamwork – the need to appreciate each other's strengths, the danger of head games, the importance of apologising, and the essential role of forgiveness.

An expedition is like a furnace. Often teams go into one as friends, but before they are even halfway, they have ended up as lifelong enemies. In Leon's and my case, seemingly by providence, we had been thrown into the expedition hardly knowing each other. We were ill-prepared, out of our depth, and there was much that could have gone wrong. And indeed, much did go wrong, and we had certainly had our fair share of ups and downs. But through the trials and tests we shared and endured, a deepening friendship had developed. While I had greatly relished the solitude of the past few weeks, I was now looking forward to catching up with Leon in Guilin and hearing what he had been up to. I hoped he would make it to our meeting point, and I suspected, as usual, he would get there before me.

Part Six

The Home Straight

铁杵磨成针

Perseverance can reduce an iron rod to a sewing needle.

53
Two haggard wild men

Distance to home: 465 miles

28 APRIL–16 MAY

I arrived in Guilin city, and walked up through the gates of Yushan Park. Leon was standing at the top of some steps, next to a flower-bed. I raised a weary hand to wave. He saw me and raised the video camera, filming as always. I walked over and saw it was the same old Leon, though his clothes were dirtier, his beard had turned slightly ginger and his face looked sunburnt. Before we split up he had said to me, 'This expedition has made me age at an unnatural speed.' The ageing process was evidently continuing apace.

We exchanged an awkward manly hug.

'Good to see you survived,' I said. 'How was life in China without me as your fearless guide to help you along?'

'It was great!' he said. 'How was life without a tough-guy camera-man to stop you getting lost?'

'It's more fun getting lost on my own, without you complaining all the time.'

Leon pulled out the hip flask. 'Whisky?'

'Thought you'd never ask.'

We sat on the grass and had a celebratory 'we're both still in one piece' swig. Leon told me that he had made it through the closed zone in the middle of the night, and had also enjoyed being forced to speak more Mandarin.

'The most crazy thing, though, was when I was attacked by a flying squirrel,' he said.

'A squirrel!' I raised my eyebrows.

'No, not a squirrel, a flying squirrel. I saw it up on a rock face above the road. I thought it was just a normal squirrel and I started filming. Suddenly it jumped off and flew straight at my head. I had to duck to avoid being hit.'

'Wow, Leon, you're moving up in the world of intrepid TV adventurers.'

It was good to see him, like catching up with an old friend.

Our destination in Guilin was none other than the Shangri-La. The hotel had again generously invited us to stay, and the thought of constant air con, clean rooms and the enormous buffet breakfasts had often been on my mind throughout the past few sweltering weeks. After I had taken a much-needed shower, I jumped in a cab to the airport to pick up my dear Christine. This would be our final break before I got home, and the pressure of the previous months seemed to be lifting. With just four more weeks to go, we could start dreaming about living a normal life again, without our time together being limited to a few days every month or two. The four weeks would be busy for Christine – she was organising a sponsored walk for Viva whereby friends and supporters could join Leon and me for the final few miles of our long walk home. We were all excited that the end was almost in sight.

The break passed quickly but, in some ways, we were all eager to get the final stage underway. Christine flew home, and Leon and I set out walking through a mostly flat landscape of paddy fields, sprinkled with hundreds of limestone karsts. The tall bolts of limestone were draped in greenery and sprouted from the lush land like giant, camouflaged soldiers.

After three days we approached the final tourist zone of our journey: the town of Yangshuo. It was set beside a tranquil stretch of the Li River, and I had actually visited it about seven years previously. I remembered it as being full of Western tour groups and backpackers. However, this time, as we walked into the town centre, I noticed not only many new hotels and restaurants, but also that the Westerners were now far outnumbered by large Chinese tour groups.

All the way from the north of China, I had regularly seen aspects of the country's ongoing economic boom: the factories and mines;

the entire streets of new apartment blocks; the roads filling with shiny cars.* Now, here I was seeing another fruit of the swelling middle-class: tourism.†

In addition to this mass tourism that we were now witnessing, Leon and I had also occasionally encountered more independent and adventurous Chinese tourists, including some young people on long-distance cycle tours. I was glad to see that the Chinese were starting to appreciate their own country, beyond the tourist spots. I wondered whether the day might come when a proper national hiking trail would be marked out through the Middle Kingdom, going from east to west, or north to south. Perhaps a route a little like the one we had just walked, but with more trails through the mountains, and less scope for getting lost.

That night, we boarded a boat with thirty other tourists, and chugged out onto the Li River – we had signed up to see some traditional cormorant fishing. Our vessel drew up beside a wooden skiff, on which stood a grizzled, wiry man wearing a traditional Chinese straw hat. It quickly became evident that his job was not so much as a fisherman, as a man who showed us tourists how he fished. He had half a dozen cormorants on his bow, and at his command they jumped off and dived down into the water. The idea was that when a cormorant seized the fish in its ample beak, the string tied around its neck prevented it from swallowing. It had been trained, therefore, to jump back onto the skiff instead and drop its catch on the deck for the fisherman. We only spotted a couple of tiny fish being caught in this way and, after half an hour, the fisherman drew up on the land. He fed the industrious birds with his own supply of fish (bought from the market), and we all applauded.

We marched back into the countryside, knowing that we would have no more days off until we reached the industrial mega-city of

---

* In 2000 there were four million cars in China. By 2010 this had gone up twenty-fold to over eighty million, with growth expected to continue for a long time to come.
† In recent years, the Mainland Chinese, with all their new wealth, have also become the biggest single source of global tourist income.

Guangzhou on the Pearl River Estuary, about 300 miles away. So for the next two weeks we moved forward like pre-programmed robots. One foot in front of the other, left, right, left, right. Each day followed a similar pattern. We woke, we gulped down instant coffee, we walked, we ate, we collapsed. After six months, this was our way of life, our day job, our night job, our meaning and purpose. We were two haggard wild men on the loose in southern China.

The weather was now up in the mid-30°Cs, and we walked in shorts and T-shirts. We each had a pair of running shorts from a sponsor, which reminded us of the kind of shorts that middle-aged German men wear when on holiday, so we renamed them our 'Germans'. As the sun beat down my mind filled with memories of all that we had been through: the cold, harsh emptiness of the Gobi; the bleak loess mountains of Shanxi; the unstable scree slopes of the frozen Yellow River. All that seemed unreal to me now. Back then, in the cold, I had thought that I would never complain when the weather grew warmer. And now here I was in the searing, waterlogged air, dazzled by views of valley floors carpeted in thick green crops; grey karsts rising out of the land; ageing farmers, hard at work with their oxen for all hours of the day.

Back together, Leon and I enjoyed being able to relaunch our rambling conversations. When our morale dipped, we recited Tennyson's *Ulysses*, which we had memorised in Shaanxi, or got to work on a Jason Statham script we had come up with. In our exhaustion, though, sometimes our moods became irritable. Some things that had been a part of our routine for months started to seem tedious. One night, we reached a *ludian*, and Leon took the lead with haggling for a better price. His conversation with the *ludian* lady was going playfully, but slowly; as I stood watching, suddenly I lost my patience and rudely demanded a lower price. Leon shot me a look, so I shut up. I later apologised and tried to be especially polite to the *ludian* owner.

On the other hand, things that had once been a source of stress were now barely noticeable. Being questioned by the police, for example. They still stopped us occasionally and asked what we were doing. Now, when we explained we were walking to Hong Kong, they were not quite as disbelieving as before – for Hong Kong was only one province away. After a few minutes chatting, and perhaps a glance at our passports, they sent us on our way. Spread out in filing cabinets across the Middle Kingdom there were now records of us staying in random Gobi *ludians*, getting caught in a closed zone, walking through the nation's longest tunnel, strolling down motorways, filming *ludian* owners, and (on numerous occasions) simply being a bit odd and insisting on walking through China. Judging by how vast the country was, and how minor and random all our transgressions, it seemed unlikely that the paper trail we had left behind us was going to land us on a list of 'China's most wanted'. Perhaps we should never have been worried about the police finding out about the TV show in the first place.

Leon pulled the rain cover over the camera as an electric storm flashed across the sky and rain thumped down on the paddy fields. We were crossing into our final province – Guangdong. Foreigners used to call it Canton, and from this came the English name for the local dialect – Cantonese. I soon noticed shopkeepers talking in the singsong tones, and I felt as though I was entering more familiar ground. For Cantonese was spoken in Hong Kong, and it was Christine's mother tongue. Rather than counting down in months or weeks, we were starting to count down in days. My pace quickened, with the incredible thought that I really would be home soon.

54
Guests of honour

Distance to home: 165 miles

'That's five McDonald's and eight KFCs,' I said.

'No, four McDonald's and nine KFCs,' said Leon.

'Really?'

We had just spent the previous day and a half walking fifty miles through the industrial suburbs of Guangzhou city. We were finally nearing its heart, and in the space of a couple of hours we had seen more McDonald's and KFCs than we had done in the last six months. The streets were becoming more and more glitzy, with fashion shops, luxury brands and smart office blocks. Through the smog we glimpsed our first skyscrapers.

Guangzhou is the capital of Guangdong Province and one of the biggest cities in China, and in the world. It was part of a vast conurbation known as the Pearl River Delta, which stretched around the coastline for over 100 miles. A quarter of all China's goods were made in or passed through this prosperous and booming region. In fact, it had been near here that post-Mao China had first reopened itself to the world.

In 1978, two years after Mao had died, his successor, Deng Xiaoping, had declared a new approach to China's economy: 'Communism with Chinese characteristics'. He had released farmers from collectivisation, allowing them to sell their excess crops and thus having more incentive to work. He also authorised entrepreneurship, liberating the latent and extraordinary Chinese talent for doing business. Most notably, Deng had begun to implement an 'open doors policy', whereby foreign investment was permitted. And so China's huge, industrious and cheap labour force was unleashed.

The results were staggering. From this point forwards, China's growth continued at an average of over 10 per cent per year for more than thirty years. Six hundred million people had been lifted out of poverty. Hundreds of millions moved from the countryside to work in the burgeoning coastal factory cities, turning them into some of the fastest-growing settlements in world history. This meant that now, far more than any perceived north–south divide, China had a stark coastal–inland divide.*

As we drew closer to the coast and the Pearl River Delta, we looked at the map, and were daunted by the size of the urban area. It was so much larger than any city we had been through so far. We also noticed the extensive transport networks sprouting from it, like a spider's legs. To try and redistribute some of the nation's wealth, the government had been investing more and more in transport links, and encouraging the industries requiring cheap intensive labour to move inland. This made sense of the multitude of newly built road and rail links we had seen during our walk.†

We arrived at the Pearl River near to the city centre – the very stretch of water on which the British had traded their tea and opium in the 1800s. We were now heading for the American International School; we had been invited to give a talk about our experiences to its pupils. We arrived, soaking wet from a thunderstorm, but were warmly greeted by posters stuck all along the front of the school saying: 'Welcome Rob and Leon, keep walking!'

An audience of several hundred young children of many nationalities was gathered in the hall. The pupils sat cross-legged and wide-eyed as we showed photos and recounted our adventures. We

* A similar rich coast–poor interior divide also emerged in the nineteenth century, when the coastal areas opened up to foreign trade
† In 2000 there were 10,000 miles of roads in China. By 2009 this had increased to over 40,000 miles. By 2020, it is predicted there will be 60,000 miles – the same as in the USA. China's infrastructure development received a huge boost when, in 2008, the Chinese government injected four trillion RMB (£400 billion) into the economy. Transport projects were mentioned as one of the key beneficiaries of these funds.

described how we had dragged Molly across the Gobi, walked along the Great Wall, and got lost in the mountains. We also did an onstage demo of our now polished filming routine, whereby I pulled the camera out of Leon's rucksack and he pulled the tripod out of mine and we were ready to shoot in seconds. Next, we emptied our rucksacks to show them all the gear we were carrying. Lastly, we called for a volunteer to get inside it, and a six-year-old girl came up and bravely climbed in. As I walked around the stage, she felt unimaginably light compared to our normal load. Everyone giggled.

At the end of the talk, several dozen little hands shot up.

'What was your favourite place?' asked one girl.

'The Gobi,' said Leon.

'The Wall,' said I.

'Where did you go to the toilet?' asked a boy. More giggling.

'Behind rocks and trees,' we explained.

'Why did you do it?' said a more serious-looking child.

'To have an adventure and to explore China,' we said.

They were all good questions, and this last one in particular gave me pause for thought. Why *had* we done it? It was easy to give this short, simple answer, but sometimes when I had asked myself that question along the way, it had not seemed enough. When I could not sleep because of the cold, or I could not walk properly because of my foot, or the filming pressures were drowning our enthusiasm, or when I felt like punching Leon, or when he felt like punching me, I occasionally wondered whether the whole trip was just fuelled by vanity and ambition, or maybe just stupidity. Yet, as we now stepped back and told the story, I saw how much we had learnt, how far we had come. And, actually, the things that had gone wrong, or caused us grief along the way, were part of the adventure, the test, and were part of what had made it all worthwhile.

The American International School was not our only appointment in Guangzhou; through our little talk, the American Chamber of Commerce (AmCham) had heard about us. It happened to be their annual summer ball that weekend, so they invited us to come along as their 'guests of honour'.

The ball sounded like an elaborate affair, with tickets costing roughly the same amount of money that we would spend in a whole month of walking. Suspecting that our expedition clothes might be inappropriate for the occasion, Leon and I went shopping. We each bought ourselves the smartest shoes, trousers, shirt and tie we could afford for a total of £50. However, I ended up buying trousers to fit my usual waistline, having forgotten that I had lost some weight on the walk.

Despite our incongruent beards, we felt quite respectable as we walked into the lavish hotel in our new clothes. A jazz band was playing, hundreds of guests were milling around in black tie, and non-*baijiu* alcohol was flowing freely. Everyone was shown to their seats and, just before the entrées were served, Leon and I, the inadvertent 'guests of honour', were called up to say a couple of words. We walked slowly to the front. We had not been expecting this, and I suddenly felt like a hedgehog caught in the headlights. Before us, the banqueting room was filled with a distinguished crowd, including a number of ambassadors and consular-generals, several Chinese billionaires, and one of Barak Obama's brothers.

'This is a bit of a change to living in a Chinese field,' I said, holding the microphone in one hand, and holding up my trousers with the other.

'And the food here is certainly better than instant noodles,' declared Leon.

There was a moment of awkward silence from the room. I realised that perhaps when they invited us to be the guests of honour, the AmCham folks might have assumed we were some sort of all-American heroes. And yet, here we were, a couple of tramp-like Brits with ill-fitting trousers. But then the kind Americans and their guests all laughed and applauded politely, and Leon and I returned to our seats, relieved, and ready for a well-earned feast.

Seeing the opulence around us, it was hard not to feel strangely disconnected from the China outside the ballroom. Our walk into this immense, prosperous city over the past two days had also displayed a very different side of the nation to what we had experienced in the interior. Was this the future of China, I wondered?

In his bestseller *When China Rules the World*, Martin Jacques argues that China is all set to move beyond being a mere economic superpower. Rather, it will soon have a far-reaching cultural and political impact on the world. China's cultural power is in fact already visible – one just needs to look at how few Western restaurants there are in China compared to the vast number of Chinese restaurants in the West.

I got talking to a clean-shaven economics advisor from one of the foreign consulates. He was probably less than ten years older than me, but clearly much more intelligent. Nonetheless, I felt I might be able to impress him with my knowledge of Jacques' arguments, so I asked what he thought about the theories. To me, a layman, they seemed quite persuasive.

'Ah, it's horseshit if you ask me!' he said.

'Oh!' I said, trying not to sound too surprised. 'What are your views?'

The economist explained that in his view all the 'China's going to rule the world' theories were based on an assumption that China's strong economic growth would continue as it had been doing for the past thirty years. That, he said, was not necessarily going to happen. And besides, China faced a great number of challenges.

I had heard about some of the challenges, and had even seen some first-hand on the walk: an increasingly severe environmental crisis; growing social inequality; the subversive potential of the internet*; the enormous, precarious property bubble; rabid nationalism; the terrible 'test'-based education system; a corrupt credit system in which many loans were granted more on the basis of political connections than business merit. Perhaps the biggest problem was that a generation of spectacular growth had fuelled the Chinese people's expectations. If the economy faltered now,

---

* Chinese internet users are five times more likely to have blogs than Americans. The Chinese government is increasingly struggling to keep the expression of views under control. There are a purported 30,000 cyber-police making up the the 'Great Firewall of China'.

there would be widespread social unrest, and the authoritarian system might not be able to handle it.

But then I remembered a point made by Jacques in response: the Chinese government has just successfully overseen the biggest economic transformation in history – for 1.3 billion people. If it can do that, surely it is capable of coping with these other new challenges too.

There seemed to be so many competing views. Perhaps it was futile to try and predict the future, especially for China. Just look at the past century. Who would have guessed that Marx's radical ideology would take over the ancient Middle Kingdom? Who would have predicted that Mao could do so much harm in the last twenty years of his life? Who would have said that after almost imploding in the 1970s, China would go on to become the world's second biggest economy in just three short decades?

The Chinese people we had encountered on our walk were, without a doubt, among the most vibrant and industrious people I had ever seen. And China's size alone makes it sure to be one of the great nations of the future. But more precisely what that future holds, I would have to leave to the experts.

My conversation with the economics advisor moved onto a new subject.

'I'm about to change postings,' he told me, 'and in the interim I'm going to drive around my own country for a month.'

'Well, in that case,' I said, feeling more confident in my own area of expertise, 'you should definitely grow a beard.'

He thought for a moment and then nodded. 'You know, I've never grown a beard before, so I might just do that.'

55
Countdown

Distance to home: 80 miles

20–24 MAY
'Your Mandarin's not bad now, Rob,' said Leon, as he finished filming me chatting to a passer-by.

'Thanks.' We picked up our poles and started clinking forwards again. 'Your filming skills aren't bad either.'

'I was thinking, with your knowledge of Chinese history and language, and my filming experience, we're just about ready to go on a walking expedition across China, filming a TV show as we go.'

'That's a great idea. I reckon it would take about six months. When are you free in the coming year?'

We continued talking as we walked along a promenade that followed the Pearl River out of the city. However, Leon was being quieter than normal, and actually looked quite pale. A few days earlier, as we had entered the city, he had mentioned that he was feeling unwell. We had put it down to exhaustion. But the late night out at the AmCham Ball seemed to have made matters worse. Now he said he could feel a fever coming on. He was, however, determined to keep going, because eighty friends and supporters would be joining us for the final few miles, in just five days' time, and we could not be late for them.

We came to some steps leading down into the murky Pearl waters.

'We've done the Yellow and the Yangtze, do you want to complete the hat trick?' I said.* Leon, feeling unwell, did not, so I quickly

*Although small compared to the Yellow and Yangtze giants, the Pearl was the third great river of China. Other significant rivers such as the

274

stripped off and jumped in wearing my Germans, much to the surprise of a bunch of Chinese fishermen lining the bank. The water was beautifully cool, but it smelt bad, and I could see a lot of rubbish floating around, so I swam around for less than a minute before rejoining Leon on the promenade.

We soon left Guangzhou behind us, but this was not the end of the buildings, for industrial compounds and factories continued to crowd the roadsides. The thick, smoggy air was full of dust, and the grime stuck to our sweaty arms and faces. Industry would, in fact, envelop us all the way down to the border with Hong Kong.

As the early evening arrived, the streets filled with tens of thousands of young men and women, out for dinner after a hard day's work in their factories. They often walked in groups, chatting to each other or on their mobile phones. Some contacts from the AmCham ball had invited us to visit two factories on our way through. We were glad to have the chance to catch a glimpse into the lives of China's famous young workforce, who had changed the world.

The first factory we visited made medical accessories, such as swabs and face masks, for export to hospitals in the USA. As we were led onto the factory floor, we saw hundreds of women hard at work. Each job was highly specialised, whether cutting, or measuring, or attaching one item to another. The labourers worked incredibly fast, and barely looked up as we passed. They were paid per item they made – time was money.

Then, the day before we reached the border, we visited the factory of Dahon folding bicycles – a company that held a two-thirds market share of the folding bicycles industry. Luckily for us, Dr Hon, the mastermind behind these bikes, was also at the factory. He was having a busy day, so we were told we had only a few minutes to interview him in his office. I hoped that after my countless hours of appearing on camera, my TV-documentary interviewing skills were up to it.

Mekong, the Amur, and the Brahmaputra pass through only parts of China.

We entered the room. Dr Hon sat behind his desk, looking intelligent and dignified. I became conscious of my sweaty, unkempt appearance. We shook hands, and I sat down opposite him. I thought I should attempt to build a little rapport before I moved on to my more serious questions. I explained our long walk and how I was now almost home.

'In fact, my wife is from Hong Kong,' I said, pointing over my shoulder in the rough direction of Hong Kong.

Dr Hon frowned.

'That is your wife?' he said.

I looked over my shoulder and saw a bearded, dizzy-looking Leon holding the video camera.

'Err, no, that's not quite what I meant.'

We all laughed, and Dr Hon's remark was probably the most memorable moment of the interview.

Back outside, the sales manager, Dennis, let us take a couple of their latest bikes for a lap of the car park.

'Next trip, Leon,' I shouted, enjoying the incredible smooth spinning, 'we have got to go on folding bikes, these are amazing!'

As we hit the road, back on our weary feet again, I reflected on how different this walking trip had been from my three-year bicycle adventure. Although I had been through considerably more dangerous places when I had cycled home from Siberia, this trip had actually felt like the harder one. This was partly because I was now married and partly because of all the filming pressure. But perhaps, most of all, it was because walking was so much physically harder than riding a bike.

By pedal power, I had been able to easily cover four times the distance each day and, crucially, all the weight was carried not on my body, but on the bicycle racks. When cycling, though I often felt tired, I was never in serious pain. When I fell behind schedule, it was easy to ride a few extra hours a day to catch up without dire physical consequences.

All that said, I did not regret choosing to walk instead of cycle through China. As well as being able to sometimes go entirely off road, the walking had allowed me to encounter China at ground level, just as I had hoped.

We were now less than twenty-four hours from the China–Hong Kong border. For most of history, Hong Kong had been part of the ancient Chinese Empire, but then, in the nineteenth century, almost by accident, the tiny piece of territory had become the dominion of another Empire.

In 1841, during the build-up to the First Opium War, the British were evicted from the Portuguese trading settlement of Macao. They took their ships and set sail, heading east, looking for a suitable place to set up a new base. They came to a somewhat unpromising, mountainous island, about a mile off Mainland China. Upon landing, they were still unimpressed. There were only a couple of dozen local villages on it, and the rocky terrain was largely uncultivable. The space between the island and the mainland did, however, form a well-protected, deep-water harbour – a significant factor because the region was notorious for typhoons. And so the British stayed. In Cantonese, the name of the island meant 'fragrant harbour'. The British called it by its Cantonese name: Hong Kong.

As a result of the British victory in the First Opium War, the Chinese were forced to cede the island and a tiny area of mainland (Kowloon) to the British as a permanent possession. The colony then expanded when, in 1898, the British obtained a ninety-nine-year lease on a further piece of land, stretching twenty miles into the mainland, known as the New Territories.

History rumbled on, and during World War II, and the subsequent Chinese civil war, the territory flooded with refugees.* In the years that followed, the concentrated labour force, combined with Hong Kong's strategic location, allowed the colony to bloom. However, the end of the ninety-nine-year lease from China was approaching.

* Hong Kong was also occupied by the Japanese for several years during World War II.

In 1984 Margaret Thatcher agreed that, in 1997, Britain would hand back not only the New Territories but all of Hong Kong. The Iron Lady was a strong negotiator, and was able to include an agreement that although Hong Kong would come under the ultimate sovereignty of Beijing, it would keep its laws, its freedom of speech and its currency.*

And thus the unique notion of 'one country, two systems' was born. To most people's surprise, this arrangement has so far worked reasonably well.

On 24 May, bang on time, we arrived in the border city of Shenzhen, itself a major conurbation of over ten million people, and full of skyscrapers and crowded streets. However, Leon's health had been gradually deteriorating. 'I've never felt this bad in my whole life,' he mumbled. 'This is even worse than when I had malaria in Cambodia.'

Although he was still coherent, and keen to film everything he could, both Dr Leon and I were beginning to grow concerned. Dr Leon had originally diagnosed heat stroke, but this no longer seemed to fit. Perhaps it could be malaria (which was rare in China), or dengue fever (also mosquito-borne and far less rare). As I noticed Dr Leon starting to worry, I remembered that a sense of humour was what had got us this far. So I told him it was most likely 'girl's disease', which only afflicted girls like Leon. This was just what Dr Leon needed to hear. He turned to me and told me not to be so sure. In fact, in his expert opinion it was far more likely to be 'hero's fever.'

As we walked through Shenzhen's crowded streets, I took over the filming and navigating. Dr Leon leant hard on his poles and concentrated on not falling over. We spent our final 20 RMB on ice cream and water and, just before dark, we were stunned to see signs pointing to Hong Kong.

The signs led us to an immigration building, where we were stamped quickly out of China. We then joined the queue to enter

* For fifty years after the handover.

Hong Kong. Most people in the line were business people or commuters. I reached the front. The immigration official narrowed her eyes at my thick beard and sunburnt face, unsure whether I could be the same person as in my passport photo. I smiled back at her. I was not afraid of Hong Kong border officials. This was my home.

56
Journey's end

Distance to home: 40 miles

25–26 MAY

I open my eyes and it takes me a moment to remember that I am no longer in Mainland China. I am in Christine's uncle's flat, in the town of Sheung Shui, just across the border.*

I have only one and half day's walk through Hong Kong territory to get home. I rise, dress and pack for the penultimate time. In the living room, Leon is up and looks worse than ever.

'How are you feeling? How's the girl's disease?' I ask.

'Still pretty bad,' he says, 'but I'll make it. It'll take a lot more than hero's fever to stop me now.'

We haul on the packs with a groan. Our packs have served us well, but boy, we will be happy to get rid of them and walk like free men again. Today we must walk twenty-five miles to the Hong Kong harbour waterfront. I have told Christine I will meet her there at sunset.

We head out into Sheung Shui town, in search of the road south. We find ourselves in a different world: cars drive on the left; they do not jump the traffic lights; the pedestrian crossings make funny clicking noises; the street signs are in English as well as Chinese. The people are different too. They are still almost all Chinese, but they do not shout or smoke so much. They still watch us, but they are not staring. When we look back at them, they quickly look away. Hong Kong is a different way of being China.

We follow the main road into the open countryside. Although

---

* The previous evening, after crossing the border, we had been forced to take the metro through two miles of no man's land.

famous for its cityscape, much of Hong Kong, especially the New Territories, is green and wild, the land rugged and steep. We pass through another town and start climbing a hiking trail into the hills. On the other side of the next mountain is the start of the main Kowloon urban area, through which we must pass to reach the water.

It is hot again, 31°C. Leon continues to wilt, and says his fever is worsening. But he staggers on. Remarkably, even as we climb, he still summons the strength to film. He continues to insist on using the tripod and wireless mic to get the highest quality possible. From start to finish, this expedition has been a professional rite of passage for him, with plenty of drama and moments of despair. He has passed the test: no one can dispute that any more.

'Seeing as both your big bicycle trip, and now your big walking trip are finishing at my house,' I say, as we walk, 'maybe you should write two books and call them "Cycling to Rob's House", and "Walking to Rob's House". It would be a great brand.'

Leon is unfazed. 'What about: "If you think Rob is some kind of tough guy, then look at Leon – Parts 1 and 2"?' he says.

I smile. I will miss bantering with Leon.

After two hours we reach the summit, and meet some local mountain bikers. They smile and point us down the right track. We continue down, and see some monkeys dancing through the trees above us. I had known there were monkeys in Hong Kong and yet I had never seen them before. There are so many places to explore, even this close to home. Maybe I don't need to fly 3,000 miles with a one-way plane ticket the next time I want an adventure.

We wind around the edge of a reservoir, and along a clifftop path. Through a gap in the hills we catch a glimpse of something we have long awaited: the ocean. It is grey-blue, immense and tranquil. Super-freighters lumber back and forth, carrying raw materials into China, or manufactured products out of it.

It has been a long walk from the Gobi to reach this point. Most people in Mongolia have never seen the sea. Most people from Hong Kong have never seen the desert. The sea is quite a similar environment to the desert in some ways – monochrome, sterile, dangerous for humans, and yet somehow peaceful and enticing.

'I've missed the sea,' says Leon. He stands and smiles, in a daze. He grew up on the wild north coast of Ireland.

Around another corner, the mountains part again and we see the earth erupting into a mass of steel and concrete, ten thousand apartment blocks breaking through, standing to attention. In the distance, we can see Hong Kong Island. Dozens of skyscrapers are montaged against the mountain. Helicopters flit through the sky beneath like tiny insects.

'This is it,' we say. A long hill winds us down through a spaghetti junction of motorways, and an hour later we reach Nathan Road. This will lead us all the way to the harbour.

It is now 5 o'clock on Friday afternoon. Hong Kong is always in a hurry, and we are about to walk down its busiest road, at peak time, wearing enormous rucksacks. We are instantly swept up in a deluge of frantic shoppers, dating couples, stressed-out employees, laughing teenagers and gruff tradesmen. The shop fronts are brightly lit with displays of delectable foods, sleek outfits and futuristic electronics. Sizzling street restaurants cram into the alleyways beneath bulky tower blocks. The further we go, the thicker the crowd becomes. It is every man and every woman for themselves. People do not even notice us, for this is a city that has seen it all.

At 6.30 p.m. the sun is setting, and we are only halfway down Nathan Road. Three more miles to go. That will take us at least an hour, maybe two in these streets. I send Christine a text apologising. I can't believe she is only a few miles away now.

A mile before the water we meet some of the Tiberius team, who have come to help film the end. It is good to see them. At times, it has been a strained relationship during our months on the road. Now, a smile and a handshake remind us they are on our side.

As we continue down the road, trying not to bash anyone, or be bashed, we cannot help but notice it is a beautiful night. Gentle clouds drift across the sky, illuminated by the city lights. The air is unusually clear. Finally, we approach the Star Ferry Clock Tower, which started ticking back in 1921. We climb some steps onto the viewing platform, which overlooks the waterfront. It is crowded with tourists taking photos. Hong Kong's epic skyline towers all around us, and the water is rippling with the reflection of a million lights.

I wander forwards, followed by Leon and the Tiberius team filming. I am supposed to meet Christine on this platform, but how will I find her? I panic.

Then I see her. Sitting, waiting, looking beautiful, tender. What has she been through to get to this point? The waiting and the worrying. I must never take her for granted.

I walk towards her, and she sees me and my unwieldly rucksack through the crowd.

'Hi honey,' I say.

'Oh no, cameras!' she says, seeing Leon and the Tiberius team behind me.

And then, finally, she is in my arms again.

*

The next morning, I wake up with Christine in a hotel on the waterfront. I am still not home. That is today's task.

My old friend Tobi has offered us a lift on his junk across to the island where I live. Christine catches a fast ferry ahead of us to help all the sponsored walkers to gather.

Leon and I sit out on the deck as the junk churns its way across the sea. The water is thick with cargo ships. The sky is grey. Leon looks ill, but steeled to make it to the end.

The junk draws into the small pier at Discovery Bay, where the sponsored walk will begin. I see a crowd gathered, all in white T-shirts proclaiming: 'Walking Home From Mongolia in support of Viva'. I stand on the edge of the boat and wave. There is a cheer from the shore, and a hundred arms wave back.

'Do you want to swim ashore?' I say to Leon.

'Sorry, I feel too rough, you go for it.'

'OK, well done Leon, we're almost there.'

I leave my rucksack on the deck, jump and am suddenly underwater. I rise to the surface and start to swim, though also realising that I have jumped too soon. I am still over a hundred metres from the shore. It will take me five minutes to reach land. The crowd cheers again and laughs.

I laugh too and start to paddle slowly. This will be my last moment of solitude before the end. I look up and make out familiar, smiling faces on the shore. I think of the multitude of faces I have met on my path to get here:

Sahana the throat grabber,

Uruult the money-changer,

Mr Cheerful the train signaller,

Gaoyu the hospitable student,

Chinese Li the Mao singer,

Mr Wolf the taxi driver,

Mr Steel the tree carrier.

Faces I will most probably never see again. They had all looked after me well.

I reach the shore finally, and grab a piece of rope trailing down to the rocks. As I climb, the rope snaps and I fall back into the sea.

More laughing and cheering from the friends above. I scramble up the rocks instead, and I am on dry land again, dripping wet, being hugged and greeted. Leon arrives off the junk.

For the final walk, our happy group of home-bound walkers form a procession stretching along the waterfront, the children running ahead at the front. People ask me how it was. It is difficult to answer. So much has happened. So much learnt. So much to be thankful for.

'What's next?' someone asks.

It's a good question. I wonder how it will be settling into 'home' again.

We pass along the clifftops and reach a viewing point. From here, I can see down to my own village. With Christine at my side, we descend a long staircase and reach the end of the waterfront. Leon joins us.

We stroll onto the beach, and drop our packs for the last time.

'Ready for a swim now?' I say.

'Ready,' says Leon.

We sprint down across the sand, into the water and dive in. A moment later, half the sponsored walkers are running in too.

We have made it.

We will all have a celebratory dinner together that night on the waterfront. Before that, I need a shower. Christine and I slip away from the crowds and walk down the little village paths hand in hand.

Soon after, we turn a familiar corner and there is our flat. I turn the key.

We are home again – together. At long last. Home.

Epilogue

A few days after our return, Leon flew back to the UK, arriving just in time to carry the Olympic torch through his hometown in Northern Ireland. He wore the compulsory white baggy torchbearer uniform. We joked that in the photos, with his ragged beard and sickly demeanour, he looked as though he had just escaped from some kind of madhouse. In the weeks that followed he continued to feel unwell, but after the Hospital for Tropical Diseases had tested him negative for malaria, dengue fever and brain problems, they concluded that it was simply a virus that his exhausted body would take a month or two to fight off. Thankfully, he was soon back to normal.

A few months later I was back in London to see my family, and Leon came round to my parents' house. He had forgotten to bring the whisky, but he had brought his Germans, so we went for a run. It was surreal moving at such speed along a flat, murky English canal, after walking for six months through the deserts and mountains of China.

'Would you prefer to run fifty miles a day without a pack, or walk twenty-five miles a day with one?' I asked as we ran.

'Run, definitely,' said Leon. I agreed. We started talking about potential running expeditions. It was easy to dream up exciting trips from the comfort of home.

Leon was in fact about to embark on a new expedition. My old friend Al had recruited him to walk across the Empty Quarter on the Arabian Peninsular. They designed and built a trailer considerably bigger than Molly, and loaded it up with the two essentials for desert survival: water and instant noodles. They set off from Oman, and six weeks later arrived in Dubai, dusty but smiling.*

* Leon's latest adventures and shenanigans can be discovered at www.leonmccarron.com

In the middle of walking through China, when everything seemed to be going wrong, Leon and I had sometimes joked that we were filming 'the worst TV show ever made'. Indeed, we had made some serious mistakes that had nearly undone us. In part, this was due to our overly cavalier attitude when we set off, inexperienced as we were in the ways of the TV world. But if we had not been so cavalier, perhaps we would never have set off in the first place.

Back in Hong Kong, Tiberius waded through the 240 hours of footage that we had shot, going the extra mile to produce a TV programme that did an impressive job of capturing the wildness, the people and, at times, the hilarity of the journey. Some episodes paid a lot of attention to our more clownish moments, which I found rather embarrassing. But I decided that being able to laugh at my own bumbling silliness was probably no bad thing. The magic of television also made my Mandarin abilities look quite good!* The show premiered on the National Geographic Adventure Channel across Australia and Asia during the final stages of writing this book. A photo of Leon dancing in the Gobi whiteout made the front page of the TV section in the *South China Morning Post*.

Back in my settled life, I started working for Viva again, and writing this book. I went running in the Hong Kong hills to keep up my fitness. The metatarsal on my right foot continued to ache, especially when I forgot to stretch my calves. Perhaps I really had walked across China on a fractured foot, though I suspect it has now healed too much for anything to show up on X-ray.

I have also wondered if I have another big expedition in me. It is a question I am often asked. What's next? Will I again fling myself far from home, and set off on a long journey to try and get back again? After his Arabia trek, Leon emailed me about a new idea

* Less than one minute of 'Code Z' footage was used in the final show – mainly to depict a few wide montage shots of walking through the desert. But we were still glad to have gone on that little side trip to help ensure the show was made in the first place, and to give Tiberius more to work with.

– a world record he wants to break, no less. We have scheduled a call to discuss this more next month.

Then, the other day, as I sat writing, I thought I heard a soft whisper:

'I've got adventures enough for you here, Rob.'

Indeed there are adventures here. The adventure of working for a charity that I passionately believe in, and find it a great privilege to be a part of. The adventure of deepening my friendship and marriage with Christine.

Sometimes, on the walk, I pondered on the Tennyson poem that Leon and I had been memorising – about Ulysses, who spent so long on his Odyssey, trying to get home to Ithaca. And I knew Joseph Campbell's theory about the hero's journey: that in many of the world's greatest stories, a somewhat reluctant protagonist finds himself or herself dispatched far from home, having to go through all sorts of ordeals to get back again. Like Dorothy trying to get back from Oz, Frodo and Sam wanting to get home to the Shire, Luke Skywalker trying to figure out his destiny.*

And all this made me wonder what 'home' actually meant. For many people, 'home' is where they grew up. I once asked a group of teenagers what they thought, and one of them replied, 'It's where my stuff is.' During the walk, I had many temporary homes: on desert plains, in *ludians*, as a guest in other people's homes. And, of course, before me constantly was the ultimate goal of my flat – the place where I lived. But was that really my home?

And then recently, I listened to a group of wise people debating what 'human flourishing' was supposed to look like. One of their conclusions was that human flourishing is what happens when we know ourselves to be unconditionally loved. And it seems to me that the place where we are unconditionally loved, and hence can flourish, is home.

I am blessed to have grown up in such a home.

---

* Or more recently, the character of Tony Mendez in the film *Argo*, who goes to Iran to bring his fellow Americans home, and ends up rediscovering his own home in the process.

I belong to a faith, at the heart of which is the claim that I am completely loved and which also calls me to live courageously as a pilgrim. On this pilgrimage of life there will be times when I fall down. But instead of giving up or becoming bitter, I must get up and keep walking and reject the view that life is all about winning. Rather, I must keep a soft heart which, despite the tests and trials, is learning to love.

And I am blessed to have found Christine, someone who is committed to loving me. We are pilgrims together. Yet all the time, when I am with her, I am home.

> Fount of mercy, call back the one who flees from you.
> Draw towards you the one who attempts to escape.
> Lift up the one who has fallen.
> Support the one who is standing.
> Guide the one who is on a journey.

THOMAS AQUINAS

Acknowledgements

There are many people to thank, both from the expedition itself, and from the writing of the book.

First, the expedition.

Thank you to the countless hospitable people of Mongolia and China, who looked after us and helped us on our way as we walked. Some of you are mentioned; most of you are not. I hope my attempts to depict your exuberance and kindness do you justice. A special thanks to Gaoyu and the Li family for hosting us on that cold Chinese New Year's Eve in Hequ. Also, Enoch and Tim for putting us up on our way through Beijing during Code Z.

Thank you to those new friends we made in Ulaanbaatar who showed us round before we caught the train to Sainshand. Especially Uuree Sangi, Trish Neufeld, Kyle Gunther, Sharon Goldhawk and Marti Lambert.

Thank you to Ripley Davenport for giving us Molly Brown.

Thank you to the brilliant sponsors of the expedition who helped to make the whole thing possible*:

Berghaus – for saving the day by stepping in at the last minute, and providing all the warm clothing and accessories;

Kobold – for an excellent expedition watch;

Osprey Packs – for the rucksacks;

Mountain Hardwear – for the warm sleeping bags;

Hilleberg – for the sturdy tents and bivoanoraks;

ECCO Shoes Oxford – for the three pairs of comfortable Yak skin boots each;

Aquapac – for helpful waterproof bags;

* For a specific kit list, please see the expedition website www.walking-homefrommongolia.com

Casio – for stepping into the breach at the last minute with point and shoot stills cameras;

ChinesePod.com – for the brilliant podcast lessons which were such a fun way to learn Mandarin on the road;

Karina Moreton from Panoramic Journeys – for so helpfully sorting us accommodation and giving us a tour of Ulaanbaatar;

Sports Performance, in particular Doug Horne and Aaron Smith – for providing physio and podiatry sessions, and expert advice during the expedition. If I need physio or podiatry in Hong Kong, I know who to go to.

Giovanni Tomaselli for helping to source GoPro cameras at the last minute.

Tobi Doeringer for generous support and giving us a junk ride on the final day. Ward Platt, Sun Young Moon, Mark Francis and Stephen Hunter for the TV opportunity. Luxson for the innovative Punkt app.

Kalun Lau for designing the 'Walking Home From Mongolia' 'brand', Mark Nam for rescuing us with a great website after ours crashed, Josh Boyle for bringing heavy gear out for us from the US, Ashu Kher for the indispensable iPhone, and Chris Niem for donating an iPod shuffle to Leon. Dr Aric Hui for medical advice during the trip – definitely more credible than Dr Leon!

Friends who have sent messages of encouragement and prayed for us while we walked. Christine's good friend, Sarah, for watching *Ugly Betty* and playing Scrabble with her during those winter months. The eighty-plus friends and supporters who came on the last few miles and helped us raise the grand total of over £63,000 for Viva's work with children at risk.

Thank you to the Tiberius Team – Cohen Leung, Kate Kun, Nicholas Shay, Philip Yang and Elain Yu for your dedicated and extraordinary hard work. And thank you to Charmaine and Duncan Jepson for pushing this forward and, at the end of the day, pulling it off. We certainly had our ups and downs, but I am glad we made it through. Thank you for persevering, and making such a fine and entertaining show from the footage.

Jeanette Wang (*South China Morning Post*), Esther Au Yong and

Olivia Lim (Silverkris online), and Jill Alphonso (my paper) for commissioning articles to be written during the expedition.

Todd Miller, Colin Brown and Steven Ballantye for invaluable advice.

Al Humphreys – for great advice and regular reminders not to take ourselves too seriously. And for brutal feedback on the early drafts of the book.

Clare Symons – for letting your crazy other half come on a walk for six months.

Thank you to Leon McCarron for coming on the mad old trip in the first place, and for putting up with my foibles, irritability and annoyances. I think you got a lot more than you bargained for, but you did well!

Second, the book.

A number of friends took time out of busy schedules to read and give extremely helpful comments on parts of or all of the manuscript. Thank you to: Sarah Cheng, Andrew Gardener, Pam Golafshar, LaDonna Hall, Ian Huen, Alastair Humphreys, Queenie Lau, Leon McCarron, Kate McGeown, Anneli Matheson, Mary Ann Mhina, Will Ng, Jacinta Read, John Snelgrove, Martin Thomas, Nury Vittachi, and my sister Rosanna Brodie.

Gus Seebaran, for inviting me to the Creative Writers' forum in Oxford all those years ago.

Everyone at Viva. For prayers, encouragement, and being such great people to work with. Thanks especially to Martin Thomas for patience and support as I took time off work to get this finished, and to Justine Demmer and Chris Niem for your understanding that I was busy writing.

Tim Steward, for your generous and brilliant work on the atmospheric sketches which start each section of the book.

My parents-in-law, TW and Mazi Susie, for your encouragement and prayers, and for feeding me delicious meals, ice cream and chocolate when I was writing the book in your flat.

Joanna Davey, my editor at Hodder. For commissioning the book, patience after uncountable missed deadlines, brilliant work with honing the text, and some good, bold decisions on what we needed to cut.

Acknowledgements

My parents, for your feedback on the book, and even more for your amazing patience with – and generous encouragement of – your unconventional son.

And most of all, to my darling fellow-pilgrim Christine. We discovered a hidden gift during this book – you have an amazing talent for seeing through my forest of words, and grasping the story that I am trying to tell. Thank you for the countless times you read through the manuscript, and your many brilliant suggestions. And thank you for loving me so well.

Sources

The following books were the background reading to the expedition and the book.

Jung Chang, *Wild Swans*, HarperPress, 2012

Jung Chang and Jon Halliday, *Mao, The Unknown Story*, Vintage, 2007

Leslie T. Chang, *Factory Girls*, Picador, 2010

Frank Ching, *Ancestors*, Rider, 2009

Frank Dakota, *Mao's Great Famine*, Bloomsbury Paperbacks, 2011

Jonathan Fenby, *The Penguin History of Modern China*, Penguin, 2009

George Friedman, *The Next 100 Years*, Anchor Books, 2010

Valerie Hansen, *The Open Empire*, W. W. Norton & Co., 2000

Peter Hessler, *River Town*, John Murray, 2002

Peter Hessler, *Oracle Bones*, John Murray, 2007

Peter Hessler, *Country Driving*, Harper Perennial, 2011

Martin Jacques, *When China Rules the World*, Penguin Books, 2012

John Keay, *China: A History*, HarperPress, 2009

Michael Khon, *Lama of the Gobi*, Blacksmith Books, 2009

Henry Kissinger, *On China*, Penguin, 2012

Chai Ling, *A Heart For Freedom*, Tyndale House, 2011

John Man, *Gobi: Tracking the Desert*, Wiedenfeld & Nicholson, 1998

John Man, *Genghis Khan*, Bantam, 2005

John Man, *The Terracotta Army*, Bantam, 2008

John Man, *The Great Wall*, Bantam, 2009

Rana Mitter, *Modern China: A Very Short Introduction*, OUP, 2008

Bill Purves, *China on the Lam*, Asia 2000 Limited, 2002

J. M. Roberts, *The New Penguin History of the World*, Penguin, 2007

Sarah Rose, *For All the Tea in China*, Arrow Books, 2010

Sources

Colin Thubron, *Behind the Wall*, Atlantic Monthly Press, 1988
Jonathan Watts, *When a Billion Chinese Jump*, Faber and Faber, 2011
Jack Weatherford, *Genghis Khan and the Making of the Modern World*, Broadway Books, 2005

Specific sources quoted

Chapter 2:   *Genetics study about Genghis' offspring:*
                John Man, *Genghis Khan*, Bantam, 2005. p. 15.

Chapter 10:   *Wisdom on choosing an expedition partner:*
                http://www.bbc.co.uk/news/magazine-21878839.

Chapter 14:   *Like discovering a new room:*
                Colin Thubron, *Behind the Wall*, Atlantic Monthly
                Press, 1988, p. 1.

Chapter 15:   *For a modified version of Dr Brown's talk:*
                http://bit.ly/15eetsM.

Chapter 18:   *More on the controversy surrounding the Green Wall
                of China:*
                http://www.theepochtimes.com/n2/china-news/
                desertification-in-china-20291.html.

Chapter 21:   *On seeing the Great Wall from space:*
                http://www.journalofoptometry.org/en/is-it-really-
                possible-to/articulo/13188744/.

Chapter 25:   *For more information and statistics relating to number
                of coal mines and coal consumption in China, see:*
                Watts, Jonathan, *When a Billion Chinese Jump*,
                Faber and Faber, 2011. Chapter 10; and http://www.
                worldcoal.org/resourcesfrequently-asked-questions/.

Chapter 45:   *For the cost of building the dam, and its social impact:*
                Watts, Jonathan, *When a Billion Chinese Jump*,
                Faber and Faber, 2011, p. 64.

Chapter 45:   *Mao's attitude to intervening in nature:*
                ibid. p. 70.

Chapter 49:   *For the role of tea in the eventual fall of the dynastic
                rule in China:*

Rose, Sarah, *For All the Tea in China*, Arrow Books, 2010, p. 255.

Chapter 53:   *For more on Chinese tourists spending abroad:*
http://www.bbc.co.uk/news/world-asia-china-22573572.

Chapter 53:   *For number of cars in China:*
http://www.guardian.co.uk/world/2012/dec/14/china-worlds-biggest-new-car-market.

Chapter 54:   *For miles of road in China:*
ibid.

Chapter 54:   *On Chinese internet users are five times as likely to have blogs as Americans:*
http://www.businessinsider.com/15-facts-about-china-that-will-blow-your-mind-2010-2?op=1#ixzz2Vnkmk5tO.

Chapter 54:   *Statistics relating to China's boom:*
http://www.worldbank.org/en/country/china/overview.

Chapter 54:   *On Pearl River District and moving jobs inland:*
http://www.asiabusinesscouncil.org/docs/PRDBriefing.pdf.

A note about the charity
I raised funds for: Viva

I think Viva is an amazing charity. Their work has helped motivate me to cycle around the world and walk across countries. It's because Viva is all about life – about inspiring lasting change in children's lives through the power of collective action. They know that the best possible way of bringing that lasting change to tens of thousands of vulnerable children across our world is by walking and working together.

As Archbishop Desmond Tutu said about Viva's strategic work:
'Just imagine what the impact would be if everyone demonstrated a little genuine compassion for our suffering children . . . sadly much of the work for children is not sufficiently supported and takes place in isolation, disconnected and uncoordinated. Viva points toward how much more we can do together. I urge you to get involved and make a difference.'

The next time you run a marathon, climb a mountain, or take on some other challenge, why not consider helping vulnerable children at the same time. Find out how you can get involved in this and other ways at www.viva.org.

About *Cycling Home From Siberia*

Cycling Home From Siberia

Before he walked home from Mongolia, Rob Lilwall spent three years cycling home (to London) from Siberia. He rode through twenty-eight countries, including Papua New Guinea, Afghanistan and Iran. Along the way he was robbed at gunpoint, chased by thugs with machetes, and camped at −40°C. It was in the middle of this journey that, quite unexpectedly, he met Christine.

Lilwall's critically acclaimed first book tells the story of his first major expedition.

'I'm not sure Rob Lilwall knows it, but he has penned a two-wheeled classic. I wanted to rise up singing and strap on my bicycle clips.' *The Guardian*

'Lilwall's story is a remarkable one . . . enhanced by the fact that he has a writer's skill for conveying a sense of place.' *The Sunday Telegraph*

'This book is a rite-of-passage adventure full of thrills, excitement and endurance tests . . . If you're a cyclist – and even if you're not – go for this book.' *The Irish Times*

Walking Home From Mongolia **TV Series**

To watch the series that Rob and Leon made, order the DVD from: www.roblilwall.com

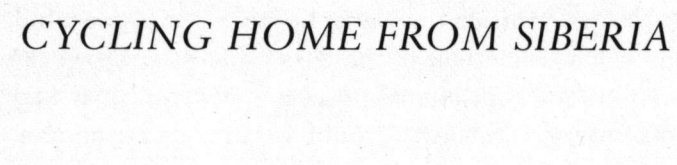

CYCLING HOME FROM SIBERIA

I
Over Mordor

Siberia . . . impends through the darkness as the ultimate
unearthly abroad. The place from which you will not return
COLIN THUBRON

We had been flying east all night and I awoke to notice that it was
already daylight outside the plane. Looking out of the window onto
the empty landscape below, the dark shades of brown and green
reassured me that, although it was mid-September, it had not yet
started snowing in Siberia. I could see no sign of human life and
the view rolled away in an otherworldly blend of mountains, streams
and forests to an endless horizon. I shook my head and it brought
to mind Tolkien's gloom-filled Mordor.

My neighbour woke up and smiled at me sleepily.

'Good morning, Robert!' he said, pronouncing my name in a
slow, Russian accent.

Sergei was a Muscovite salesman of my age who was flying to
the outer limits of civilisation in order to sell safety clothing to the
local mining industries. We had met the night before when we
boarded the plane in Moscow. His English was almost as poor as
my Russian, but with the help of a dictionary I had managed to
explain to him that I was flying to the far-eastern Siberian city of
Magadan with only a one-way ticket because it was my intention
to return home to England by bicycle.

'But, Robert,' he had reasoned with me, 'there is no road from
Magadan; you cannot ride a bicycle.'

I explained that I had reason to believe that there was a road,
though not many people used it these days.

'Alone?' he asked, pointing at me.

'No, I will be riding with a friend.'

'One?'

'Yes, just one friend,' I nodded, hoping that my friend, Al, would arrive, as planned, in three days' time.

Sergei still looked unconvinced and pointed outside:

'*Holodna, Zeema?*'

Holodna was a word that I would grow accustomed to hearing over the next few months. It meant simply 'cold'. *Zeema* meant 'winter'. I had to agree with Sergei that, although the weather did not look too bad right now, the infamous weather of Siberia would not stay away for much longer. The road that we would have to follow, the only road that existed, would take us past the coldest inhabited place in the world.

I tried to bolster my case by explaining to Sergei with hand gestures towards my arms and legs that I had lots of very warm clothes, though I left out the fact that, because the trip was self-funded and without sponsorship, I was on a tight budget. Most of my clothes and equipment had been bought at slashed prices on eBay. In reality, I was not at all sure if they would be up to the job. This was especially the case for my enormous Royal Mail over-trousers which I had bought for £10. They were several sizes too big and probably more suitable for the mid-morning drizzle of London than the long, hard winter of Siberia.

Of even greater concern was the tent. It had been given to us by a kind lady who had taken an interest in the expedition after seeing our website, though we had never actually met her. We had not yet tried putting it up, but it was free, so it seemed like the ideal option at the time. Furthermore, we would have neither a satellite phone nor a global positioning system (GPS) and, in fact, no back-up whatsoever. I also did not admit to Sergei that the coldest temperature I had experienced prior to this was during a camping weekend in Scotland, nor that my main fitness training had been in the form of badminton matches against a colleague after work. Because I was not entirely sure why we were setting off at the start of winter (other than it was when we were ready to start), I just told Sergei that the winter would be an exciting and beautiful time of year to see Siberia.

'How long?' he gestured a bicycling motion.

'One year,' I said confidently. In fact, though I did not know it at the time, the ride would take several times longer than this and for the vast majority of it I would be on my own.

We dropped below the cloud level and, as the land rose to meet us, the broad, dark shapes converged as distinct mountains. They were shrouded in sparse, green forest. I felt a twinge of claustrophobia as we landed on the runway.

Inside the small, grey, terminal building the young lady at the immigration counter stamped me through, but did not return my smile. I collected my bicycle and bags and loaded them onto a 1970s-style bus outside. The gruff driver revved the engine, lit a cigarette and drove out onto the road. I was excited that I would soon be arriving in the city from where I would begin riding, but I was also daunted. Magadan did not have a good reputation with the Russians. Half a century beforehand they had nicknamed it 'The Gateway to Hell'.

An invitation from the publisher

Join us at www.hodder.co.uk, or follow us
on Twitter @hodderbooks to be a part of
our community of people who love the very
best in books and reading.

Whether you want to discover more about a book
or an author, watch trailers and interviews, have the
chance to win early limited editions, or simply browse
our expert readers' selection of the very best books,
we think you'll find what you're looking for.

And if you don't, that's the place to tell us what's missing.

We love what we do, and we'd love you to be a part of it.

www.hodder.co.uk

@hodderbooks

HodderBooks

HodderBooks